The Earthscan Reader in Rural–Urban Linkages

The Earthscan Reader in Rural–Urban Linkages

Edited by

Cecilia Tacoli

London • Sterling, VA

First published by Earthscan in the UK and USA in 2006

Copyright © 2006, International Institute for Environment and Development

ISBN: 978-1-84407-316-0   paperback
        1-84407-316-5   paperback
        978-1-84407-315-3   hardback
        1-84407-315-7   hardback

Typesetting by Composition and Design Services
Printed and bound in the UK by Cromwell Press, Trowbridge
Cover design by Andrew Corbett

For a full list of publications please contact:

Earthscan
8–12 Camden High Street
London, NW1 0JH, UK
Tel: +44 (0)20 7387 8558
Fax: +44 (0)20 7387 8998
Email: earthinfo@earthscan.co.uk
Web: www.earthscan.co.uk

22883 Quicksilver Drive, Sterling, VA 20166-2012, USA

Earthscan publishes in association with the International Institute for Environment
and Development

A catalogue record for this book is available from the British Library

Library of Congress Cataloging-in-Publication Data has been applied for

The paper used for the text of this book is FSC certified.
FSC (The Forest Stewardship Council) is an international network
to promote responsible management of the world's forests.

Printed on totally chlorine-free paper

Contents

Part 1 Introduction

Part 2 Rural–Urban Linkages and Livelihood Transformations

Part 3 Policies that Address, Ignore or Misunderstand Rural–Urban Linkages

Part 4 Mobility and Migration Between Rural and Urban Areas

Part 5 Beyond the City Boundaries: Peri-Urban Areas and Environmental Issues

List of Figures, Tables and Boxes

Figures

Tables

Boxes

About the Authors

Mahmoud Bah holds a Masters in philosophy and sociology from the Ecole Normale Supérieure of Bamako, Mali. He has evaluated projects financed by the African Development Foundation, was a cabinet chief at the Ministry of Public Affairs and Employment, a technical consultant at the Ministry of the Environment and the Ministry of Youth and Sports, and a national expert on cooperatives and rural credit for the United Nations Development Project (UNDP)/Food and Agriculture Organization (FAO) project Replication and Dissemination of Selected Crops from 1988–1992 in Mali. He can be contacted c/o Groupe de Recherche Action pour le Développement (GRAD), BP 5075, Bamako, Mali; tel: 223 2218873; email: grad.mali@malinet.ml.

Jonathan Baker is professor of development studies at Agder University College, Norway. He was born in London and has a PhD from the London School of Economics. Between 1989 and 1996 he was senior research fellow and leader of the Urban Development in Rural Context in Africa research programme at the Nordic Africa Institute, Uppsala, Sweden. His major research interests are concerned with the role of small towns for rural development and the importance of rural–urban linkages in socio-economic transformation. He has extensive research and fieldwork experience from Africa, especially Tanzania and Ethiopia. He can be contacted at Agder University College, Service Box 422, 4604 Kristiansand, Norway; email: jonathan.baker@hia.no.

Ian Bradbury (see Richard Kirkby) email: i.k.bradbury@liverpool.ac.uk.

Salmana Cissé holds a PhD in Sociology from the Université Paris VII and is a researcher at the Rural Economics Institute in Mali (IER). He is also national coordinator of Sustainable Agriculture and Natural Resource Management Collaborative Research Support Programme (SANREM CRSP) activities in collaboration with University Tech Blackburgh in the US. He has published variously on natural resource management, and was team leader for Systems of Rural Production in the Fifth Region (1987–1993), and coordinator for the Consolidation of Rural Associations/Mopti project (1993–1996). He can be contacted c/o GRAD, BP 5075, Bamako, Mali; tel: 223 2218873; e-mail: grad.mali@malinet.ml.

José Cortés has a first degree in veterinary medicine at the Universidad Nacional Autónoma de México (UNAM), an MSc in animal reproduction at Universidad Autónoma de México (UAM) and a doctorate in animal production at UNAM. He has research experience in urban agriculture.

Priya Deshingkar is a research fellow at the Overseas Development Institute. She is a social scientist and has worked on rural livelihoods and poverty reduction for the last 20 years. Her recent work has examined the policy implications of circular labour migration in Asia and Africa. She has co-authored a book on *Policy Windows and Livelihoods Futures* with John Farrington and colleagues (2006, Oxford University Press). Email: pdeshingkar@odi.org.uk.

Gouro Diallo holds a Masters in Philosophy from the Ecole Normale Supérieure of Bamako, Mali. He specializes in the management of development projects and in participatory methods. He is a consultant in social sciences and coordinator for the GRAD/IIED Rural–Urban programme in Mali. He can be contacted c/o GRAD, BP 5075, Bamako, Mali, tel: 223 218873; e-mail: grad.mali@malinet.ml.

Bitrina Diyamett is senior scientific officer at the Tanzania Commission for Science and Technology (COSTECH), responsible for a programme on the Interface Between Science and Society, and also a national coordinator for African Technology Policy Studies Network (ATPS), Tanzania Chapter. She is currently on study leave to complete a PhD at the University of Dar es Salaam. She can be contacted at: PO Box 4302, Dar es Salaam, Tanzania; tel: 255 22 700752; mobile: 255 741 247094; email: bitrind@yahoo.com.

Mike Douglass is professor of urban and regional planning and the director of the Globalization Research Center at the University of Hawai'i. He received his doctorate in Urban Planning from the University of California at Los Angeles (UCLA). He has lived and worked for many years in Asian countries where he engages in research and planning with international development institutions as well as national and local governments on spatial dimensions of local and national development and globalization. He has taught at UCLA, Stanford University, the Institute of Social Studies in The Hague and the University of East Anglia. Current research includes the urban transition and mega-urban regions in Asia; civil society and civic space; poverty and the environment; and the globalization of migration and householding. He can be contacted at: Globalization Research Center, University of Hawai'i, 1859 East West Road, TP 1 Room 115, Honolulu, HI 96822; tel (808) 956 4609; fax (808) 956 9431; email: global@hawaii.edu; website: www.hawaii.edu/global.

Shen Guanbao (See Richard Kirkby)

Haydea Izazola obtained a degree in economics from UNAM, and a Master's degree in demography and a PhD in social sciences from El Colegio de México. She is a member of the Leadership for Environment and Development (LEAD) Programme-Mexico and, since 1991, has coordinated the Mexican Society of Demography (SOMEDE) Working Group on Population and Environment. She is a lecturer in population and environment for different Masters programmes in Mexico, and is a researcher at El Colegio Mexiquense where she conducts research on the migration responses of middle-class women to environmental deterioration in Mexico City. She can be contacted at: El Colegio Mexiquense Apartado Postal 48-D, Toluca, Mexico, C.P. 50110; fax: (72) 180358; email: hizazola@correo.xoc.uam.mx.

Philip Kelly is associate professor of geography at York University. He has conducted research on labour processes, industrialization and urbanization in Southeast Asia, and more recently has been examining the transnational dimensions of Filipino immigration to Canada. He is the author of *Landscapes of Globalization: Human Geographies of Economic Change in the Philippines* (2000, Routledge).
He can be contacted at: Department of Geography, York University, 4700 Keele Street, Toronto, Ontario, Canada, M3J 1P3; tel: 1 416 736 2100 ext. 22499; fax: 1 416 736 5988; email: pfkelly@yorku.ca; website: www.yorku.ca/pfkelly.

Richard Kirkby and **Ian Bradbury** (University of Liverpool) and **Shen Guanbao** (Shanghai and Fudan Universities) carried out a multidisciplinary investigation of the environmental issues associated with rural industrialization in China during the late 1990s. Although their chosen study sites varied considerably in social and economic status and in the pace of change, similar developmental processes were evident in each. In an introductory chapter to a book resulting from this investigation the authors contextualize their study and stress the key role of the small town in China's recent extraordinary development. Contact: i.k.bradbury@liverpool.ac.uk.

Fred W. Kruger is full professor of geography at the University of Erlangen-Nuremberg, Germany. He is member of the board of directors and currently head of the Institute of Geography. His research and teaching interests focus on urban studies and development geography. Major research fields in the urban studies arena cover urban planning, inner city development, urban cultures and the social production of urban public spaces. In development geography, he specializes in theoretical approaches and the empirical, actor-oriented analysis of poverty (especially in cities), vulnerability, coping, livelihood security and concepts of risk. His research focuses on southern Africa. He can be contacted at: Institute of Geography, University of Erlangen-Nuremberg, Kochstrasse 4, 91054 Erlangen, Germany; email: fkrueger@geographie.uni-erlangen.de; website: www. geographie.uni-erlangen.de/fkrueger.

Fred Lerise is a senior lecturer in the Department of Urban and Regional Planning at the University College of Lands and Architectural Studies, Dar es Salaam. He was trained as an urban and rural settlements planner and later specialized in rural land use planning practice. He is also a co-director of a local private consulting firm by the name of Consulting Environment and City Planners Limited (CECPltd) in Dar es Salaam. He can be contacted at: PO Box 35176, Dar es Salaam, Tanzania; tel: 255 744 826 899; email: lerise@uccmail.co.tz.

H. (Tito) Losada holds a first degree in veterinary medicine at the Universidad Nacional Autónoma de México and a Masters degree in Agricultural Science from the Instituto de Ciencia Animal (ICA) at the University of Havana, specializing in animal nutrition in the humid tropics of Mexico. In addition he holds a PhD from the GRI at Reading University, UK on the topic of urban agriculture in Mexico City. e-mail: hrlc@xanum. uam.mx.

Catherine Marquette obtained a Masters degree in demography from the London School of Economics and a PhD in sociology from Fordham University, New York. She is a researcher at the Centro Centroamericano de Población (CCP). She can be contacted at: Universidad de Costa Rica, San José 2060, Costa Rica, San José 2060, Costa Rica; email: cmarquette@ccp.ucr.ac.cr.

Carolina Martínez obtained her MD from the Universidad Nacional Autónoma de México, a Masters degree in social medicine from UAM-Xochimilco and a PhD in social sciences from El Colegio de México. Since 1980 she has been professor and researcher with tenure at the Faculty of Health Care at UAM-Xochimilco. At present she conducts qualitative research on mental health and environment in Mexico City. She can be contacted at: Universidad Autónoma Metropolitana (Xochimilco), Calz. del Hueso 1100, Col. Villa Quietud; México, D.F.; email: msoc1298@correo.xoc.uam.mx; website: www.xoc.uam.mx.

H. Martínez holds a Bachelor's degree in veterinary medicine from UAM. He studies rural anthropology at Instituto Nacional de Antropología e Historia (INAH) and is a lecturer on urban agriculture at the Metropolitan Autonomous University.

Gordon McGranahan is Director of the Human Settlements Group at the International Institute for Development (IIED). Trained as an economist, he spent the 1990s at the Stockholm Environment Institute, where he directed the Urban Environment Programme and coordinated an international study of local environment and health problems in low and middle income cities. He has published widely on urban environmental issues, and was the lead author of *The Citizens at Risk: From Urban Sanitation to Sustainable Cities* (2001, Earthscan) and co-editor of *Air Pollution and Health in Rapidly Developing Countries* (2003, Earthscan). More recently, he was coordinating lead author of the chapter on 'Urban Systems in the contribution of the Conditions and Trends Working Group for the Millennium Ecosystem Assessment'. He can be contacted at: IIED, 3 Endsleigh Street, London WC1H 0DD; tel: +44 (0)20 7388 2117; fax: +44 (0)20 7388 2826; email: gordon.mcgranahan@iied.org; website: www.iied.org.

David Okali is chair of the non-governmental organization Nigerian Environmental Study/Action Team (NEST), based in Ibadan, Nigeria. He can be contacted at: NEST, 1 Oluokun Street, Bodija, UIPO Box 22025, Ibadan, Oyo State, Nigeria; tel/fax: 234 2 751 7172; email: dokali@yahoo.com.

Enoch Okpara is a retired professor of geography and was deputy vice-chancellor of Imo State University, Owerri, Nigeria. He is a member of the board of directors of NEST. Professor Okpara can be contacted at NEST, 1 Oluokun Street, Bodija, UIPO Box 22025, Ibadan, Oyo State, Nigeria; email: n-cogep-d@usa.net.

Janice Olawoye is Dean of the Faculty of Agriculture, University of Ibadan. She was also a member of the board of directors of NEST when the paper was written. Professor Olawoye can be contacted at: NEST, 1 Oluokun Street, Bodija, UIPO Box 22025, Ibadan, Oyo State, Nigeria; also at the University of Ibadan, Nigeria.

R. Pealing has a BSc and an MSc in landscape and urban design from London University. Her experience is mainly in landscape assessment of urban agriculture.

William Rees received his PhD in population ecology from the University of Toronto. He has taught at the University of British Columbia's School of Community and Regional Planning since 1970 and served as Director of the School from 1994 to 1999. As an applied human ecologist, Professor Rees researches the policy implications of global environmental trends and the necessary ecological conditions for sustainable socio-economic development. Much of this work falls in the domain of ecological economics, where he is best known for inventing the 'ecological footprint' concept. In 1997, William Rees was awarded a UBC Killam Senior Research Prize. He can be contacted at: University of British Columbia, School of Community and Regional Planning, Vancouver, BC, Canada, V6T 1Z2; email: wrees@interchange.ubc.ca.

Jonathan Rigg is based in the Department of Geography at Durham University. His research focuses on rural change and associated livelihood transformations in Southeast Asia, with a particular focus on the countries of Thailand and Laos. He is the author of *Southeast Asia: The Human Landscape of Modernisation and Development* (2003, Routledge) and, most recently, *Living with Transition in Laos* (2005, Routledge). He is currently part of a Danida-funded project examining evolving rural–urban relations and interactions in Asia and Africa. He can be contacted at: Department of Geography, Durham University, South Road, Durham DH1 3LE, UK; email: j.d.rigg@durham. ac.uk.

J. Rivera has a Bachelor's degree in Animal Production from UAM and a PhD in sustainable agriculture from Wye College at the University of London, UK. He is a lecturer and researcher at the Metropolitan Autonomous University in Mexico City with particular experience in urban agriculture and agro-ecology. E-mail: rmjg@xanum.uam. mx.

David Satterthwaite is a senior fellow at IIED and also on the teaching staff of the London School of Economics and of University College London. He has been editor of the international journal *Environment and Urbanization* since its inception in 1989. He has written or edited various books published by Earthscan, London, including *Squatter Citizen* (1989 with Jorge E. Hardoy), *The Earthscan Reader on Sustainable Cities* (1999), *Environmental Problems in an Urbanizing World* (with Jorge E. Hardoy and Diana Mitlin, 2001) and *Empowering Squatter Citizen: Local Government, Civil Society and Urban Poverty Reduction* (with Diana Mitlin, 2004). In 2004, he was made an honorary professor at the University of Hull and also awarded the Volvo Environment Prize. He can be contacted at: IIED, 3 Endsleigh Street, London WC1H 0DD; tel: +44 (0)20 7388 2117; fax: +44 (0)20 7388 2826; email: david.satterthwaite@iied.org.

Cecilia Tacoli is a senior researcher with the Human Settlements Group at IIED, where in 1996 she set up the Institute's programme of collaborative work on rural–urban linkages. Research and advocacy with partners in Africa, India and Southeast Asia focus on the links between rural and urban development, with special attention to: the role of small towns in the development of their surrounding rural regions; migration and mobility and how they interact with gender and generation; livelihood diversification and changing urban and rural labour markets; socio-economic and environmental transformations in the peri-urban interface. She can be contacted at: IIED, 3 Endsleigh Street, London WC1H 0DD; tel: +44 (0)20 7388 2117; fax: +44 (0)20 7388 2826; email: cecilia.tacoli@iied.org.

Mary Tiffen studied history at Cambridge University, and began researching the economic development of Gombe Emirate 1900–1968 while teaching at Ahmadu Bello University, Nigeria. This became her PhD thesis at the London School of Economics. While her husband was working for the British Council she had a variety of consultancy posts in the Middle East and Africa. She worked for the Overseas Development Institute in London 1983–1994. Initially she was in charge of its Irrigation Management Network, before becoming Chair of its Agricultural Administration Unit. At the request of the World Bank she undertook with Michael Mortimore and a team of scholars at the University of Nairobi a study of change in Machakos District, Kenya, intended to differentiate between long run forces of change and climatic variation, and the impact of particular projects (Tiffen et al, 1994). Subsequently, she and Michael Mortimore established the Drylands Research Partnership, undertaking studies in Senegal, Nigeria, Kenya and Niger to look at long term change in economies under different policies – see www.drylandsresearch.org.uk. She now regards herself as retired, but can be contacted at mary@tiffen16.demon.co.uk. She lives in Crewkerne, Somerset, UK.

Jorge Vieyra has a BSc in Biology from UAM. He is currently undertaking a PhD on the use of animals in urban agriculture under the supervision of H. Losada, J. Cortés and C. Arriaga.

R. Zavala has a BSc in animal production from UAM, an MSc in sustainable agriculture from Wye College at the University of London, UK and a PhD in development studies from East Anglia University, UK He is a rural developer and researcher on sustainable development agriculture with experience in landscape assessment and rural sustainable development projects.

Chapter Sources

Part 1 Introduction

1 Satterthwaite, D. (2006) *Outside the Large Cities: The Demographic Importance of Small Urban Centres and Large Villages in Africa, Asia and Latin America*, IIED Working Paper, IIED, London

Part 2 Rural–Urban Linkages and Livelihood Transformations

2 Baker, J. (1995) 'Survival and accumulation strategies at the rural–urban interface in north-west Tanzania', *Environment and Urbanization*, vol 7, no 1, April
3 Bah, M., Cissé, S., Diyamett, B., Diallo, G., Lerise, F., Okali, D., Okpara, E., Olawoye, J. and Tacoli, C. (2003) 'Changing rural–urban linkages in Mali, Nigeria and Tanzania', *Environment and Urbanization*, vol 15, no 1, April, pp13–24
4 Rigg, J. (2003) 'Evolving rural–urban relations and livelihoods', in Chia Lin Sien (ed) *Southeast Asia Transformed: A Geography of Change*, Institute of Southeast Asian Studies, Pasir Panjang, Singapore

Part 3 Policies that Address, Ignore or Misunderstand Rural–Urban Linkages

5 Tiffen, M. (2003) 'Transitions in Sub-Saharan Africa: Agriculture, urbanization and income growth', *World Development*, vol 31, no 8, pp1343–1366
6 Douglass, M. (1998) 'A regional network strategy for reciprocal rural–urban linkages: An agenda for policy research with reference to Indonesia', *Third World Planning Review*, vol 20, no 1
7 Satterthwaite, D. and Tacoli, C. (2003) *The Urban Part Of Rural Development: The Role of Small and Intermediate Urban Centres in Rural and Regional Development and Poverty Reduction*, Rural–Urban Working Paper 9, IIED, London
8 Kirkby, R., Bradbury, I. and Shen, G. (2000) *Small Town China: Governance, Economy, Environment and Lifestyle in Three Zhen*, Ashgate, Aldershot

Part 4 Mobility and Migration Between Urban and Rural Areas

9 Izazola, H., Martínez, C. and Marquette, C. (1998) 'Environmental perceptions, social class and demographic change in Mexico City: A comparative approach', *Environment and Urbanization*, vol 10, no 1, April, pp107–118

10 Sharma, R., Samra, J. S., Scott, C. A. and Wani, S. P. (eds) (2005) 'Improved livelihoods in improved watersheds: Can migration be mitigated?' in *Watershed Management Challenges: Improved Productivity, Resources and Livelihoods*, International Water Management Institute, New Delhi, pp144–156

11 Krüger, F. (1998) 'Taking advantage of rural assets as a coping strategy for the urban poor: The case of rural–urban interrelations in Botswana', *Environment and Urbanization*, vol 10, no 1, April

Part 5 Beyond the City Boundaries: Peri-Urban Areas and Environmental Issues

12 Losada, H., Martínez, H., Vieyra, J., Pealing, R., Rivera, J., Zavala, R. and Cortés, J. (1998) 'Urban agriculture in the metropolitan zone of Mexico City: Changes over time in urban, suburban and peri-urban areas' *Environment and Urbanization*, vol 10, no 2, October

13 Kelly, P. F. (1998) 'The politics of urban–rural relations: Land use conversion in the Philippines', *Environment and Urbanization*, vol 10, no 1, April, pp35–54

14 Rees, W. E. (1992) 'Ecological footprints and appropriated carrying capacity: what urban economics leaves out', *Environment and Urbanization*, vol 4, no 2, October

15 McGranahan, G. (2005) 'An overview of urban environmental burdens at three scales: Intra-urban, urban-regional, and global', *International Review for Environmental Strategies*, vol 5, no 2

Acknowledgements

Many friends and colleagues have helped in preparing this book. The case studies we have been conducting with partners in Africa, Asia and Southeast Asia in the past ten years have allowed us to discuss many of the ideas included in this book, and to find out the most useful. Special thanks are due to Fred Lerise at the University College of Lands and Architectural Studies in Dar es Salaam, Tanzania; to Bitrina Diyamett also in Dar es Salaam; to Gouro Diallo at the Groupe Recherche Action pour le Developpement in Bamako, Mali; to David Okali at the Nigerian Environmental Study/Action Group in Ibadan, Nigeria; to John Devavaram at the Society for People's Education and Economic Change in Tamil Nadu, India; and to Hoang Xuan Thanh and Dang Nguyen Anh in Hanoi. The stimulating discussions that have followed presentations to donor and international agencies' staff, as well as to academic audiences, have greatly helped in sharpening the focus of this book. Thanks are due to the participants throughout the years. And I am grateful to my colleagues at IIED, David Satterthwaite – who started IIED's work on small towns with Jorge Hardoy in the 1980s and to whom I owe an intellectual debt – Gordon McGranahan, Diana Mitlin, Stephanie Ray and Jane Bicknell, for their unfailing support and good humour.

Thanks are also due to the authors of the papers, who have agreed to the re-publication of their work, and to the publishers who granted permission for the republication. Special thanks to the Liverpool University Press, publisher of *Third World Planning Review* (now *International Development Planning Review*), the International Water Management Institute, and to the Institute for Global Environmental Strategies, publisher of the *International Review for Environmental Strategies*, for allowing this without charge, thus helping to keep the price of this reader down.

The international and donor agencies that support IIED's work on rural–urban linkages also have to be thanked for their long-term interest in this topic. The Swedish International Development Cooperation (Sida) has long supported this work, and so have the Danish Ministry of Foreign Affairs (Danida) and the UK Department for International Development (DfID).

Thanks are also due to staff at Earthscan, especially Rob West, Mike Fell and Camille Adamson for their patience and help in shaping the Reader.

List of Acronyms and Abbreviations

ATPS	African Technology Policy Studies Network
CARL	Comprehensive Agrarian Reform Law
CCP	Centro Centroamericano de Población
CECPltd	Consulting Environment and City Planners Limited
CISED	Centre for Interdisciplinary Studies in Environment and Development
COSTECH	Tanzania Commission for Science and Technology
CPR	common property resource
CRIDA	Central Research Institute of Dryland Agriculture
Danida	Danish Ministry of Foreign Affairs
DAR	Department of Agrarian Reform
DDP	desert development program
DFID	Department for International Development, UK
DPAP	drought prone area program
DTI	Department of Trade and Industry
ESCAP	Economic and Social Commission for Asia and the Pacific
FAO	Food and Agriculture Organization
FCFA	CFA Franc
FD	Federal District
GDP	gross domestic product
GRAD	Groupe Recherche Action pour le Développement
GRDP	gross regional domestic product
ICA	Instituto de Ciencia Animal
IDT	Presidential Decree for rural poverty alleviation
IER	Rural Economics Institute in Mali
IIED	International Institute for Environment and Development
INAH	Instituto Nacional de Antropología e Historia
IRD	integrated rural development
IWDP	Integrated Wasteland Development Programme
IWMI	International Water Management Institute
JRY	Jawahar Rozgar Yojana
LEAD	Livestock, Environment and Development Initiative
LGA	local government authority
LGC	Local Government Code
MIEC	Metropolitan Index for Environmental Contamination
MORD	Ministry of Rural Development

MZMC	Metropolitan Zone of Mexico City
NDC	National Development Corporation
NEST	Nigerian Environmental Study/Action Team
NGO	non-governmental organization
NWDPRA	National Watershed Development Projects for Rainfed Areas
PIA	project implementing agency
PPA	Participatory Poverty Assessment
TSh	Tanzanian shillings
TVE	town and village enterprises
SANREM CRSP	Sustainable Agriculture and Natural Resource Management Collaborative Research Support Programme
Sida	Swedish Agency for Development and Cooperation
SOPPECOM	Society for Promoting Participatory Ecosystem Management
SSA	sub-Saharan Africa
UAM	Universidad Autónoma de México
UCLA	University of California at Los Angeles
UFRD	urban functions in rural development approach
UNAM	Universidad Nacional Autónoma de México
UNDP	United Nations Development Project
USAID	United States Agency for International Development
WSD	watershed management

Part 1

Introduction

Editor's Introduction

Cecilia Tacoli

Why an interest in rural–urban linkages?

For the majority of policies that address directly (or more often indirectly) poverty reduction and economic growth, people and their activities are classed as either 'rural' or 'urban'. The administrative specialization and segregation between the 'rural/agricultural/ natural resources' sector and the 'urban/manufacturing and services/infrastructure' sector does not seem to allow policy makers and officials to fully recognize the significance of the linkages between 'rural' and 'urban' locations, people and activities. These linkages are important not only for their contribution to livelihoods and local economies, but also as engines of economic, social and cultural transformation.

But there is at the same time an increased interest, especially among government officials, policy makers at the local level and international agencies staff, in better understanding the opportunities and the constraints that rural–urban linkages offer. This is due primarily to recent changes in thinking about 'development' and in broader policy priorities. For example, at the micro-level, there have been profound transformations in the understanding of how people make a living, and of the non-income dimensions of poverty. From this perspective, rural–urban linkages are a useful lens for understanding the complexities of people's livelihoods and their strategies, which often include some form of mobility and the diversification of income sources and occupations.

At the macro-level, the emphasis on market-based economic growth that has prevailed since the 1980s has led to the realization that, for rural producers, urban-based markets are important as they concentrate demand, and act as links to regional and international markets. At the same time, incomes from farming have decreased in many regions, especially for small-scale producers who increasingly engage in non-farm activities in rural settlements and local small towns. Occupational diversification within households is closely linked with the increase, in virtually all nations, of mobility and migration, especially circular movement, which involves traditional migrant groups, such as young men, but also groups previously unlikely to migrate such as young unmarried women.

With the implementation of decentralization programmes in many nations since the 1990s, small and intermediate urban centres are again attracting interest for their role in the provision of services and goods to their surrounding rural regions, and as potential engines of regional economic growth. And finally, rapid urban expansion in many nations goes hand in hand with the growth of peri-urban areas that combine 'urban' and 'rural' characteristics, and present new challenges to urban growth management.

As this short list suggests, rural–urban linkages can be seen as critical elements of most policy issues and priorities – certainly of most policies that directly or indirectly try to promote poverty reduction and economic growth. Policies that address environmental issues also need to take into account rural–urban linkages, as the chapters in Part 5 of this Reader describe. The risk of this pervasiveness is that rural–urban linkages are not clearly defined, and therefore remain as elusive as ever to policy support.

The rest of this Introduction is organized along the same lines as the different parts of this book. However, these parts are not entirely separate categories and, indeed, several chapters address far more than their part's focus. It would be impossible for a Reader to cover the vast literature that in one way or the other relates to rural–urban linkages. The papers included in this collection share a special attention to the impact of rural–urban linkages on different aspects of sustainable development. The combination of conceptual and empirical work will hopefully contribute to a better understanding of the nature and role of rural–urban linkages, and of how they can best be supported.

Defining rural–urban linkages – and what is 'urban' and what is 'rural'

The interactions between urban centres and their surrounding – as well as more distant – rural regions include 'spatial' linkages such as flows of people and goods, money and information, and other social transactions that are central to socio-economic and cultural change. They also include linkages between different sectors: for example, many urban enterprises rely on demand from rural consumers, and access to urban markets is critical for many agricultural producers. And there is a general underestimation in official census and employment data of the number of rural residents that engage in 'urban' activities (manufacturing and services), and perhaps even more so of the number of urban residents that engage in agricultural production, either for household consumption or for sale, or for both.

The latter raises the question of what is rural and what is urban. In general terms, most nations define what is 'urban' – rural is effectively a residual category. But even definitions of 'urban' are not straightforward, and make comparisons between nations as well as, in some cases, comparisons within one nation over time, problematic. Most governments define urban centres in one of four ways: through population size thresholds; through population size thresholds combined with some other criteria (population density, or the proportion of the population employed in non-farm activities); through administrative or political status; and through lists of settlements named as 'urban' in the national census. A first problem is that population size thresholds can vary widely between nations. For example, while many European and Latin American nations use a threshold of 2500 inhabitants, many other nations – among them the most populous in the world – apply a threshold of 20,000 inhabitants.

There are related differences in the ways in which the boundaries of urban centres are set. In some nations, urban boundaries correspond to the built-up area, and as the urban centre expands populations clearly associated with the settlement find themselves outside the urban boundaries. In other nations, or even other urban centres in the same country, boundaries are set to include large areas into which urban development is expected to expand or over which urban centres are expected to govern, with the result that largely agricultural populations living in low density areas may find themselves within the urban boundaries. Very large urban centres often have different boundaries for the city proper, the metropolitan area and the urban agglomeration, and total population can vary by several million inhabitants depending on which boundaries are employed.

Recently, many experts have argued that planners are being misled by the continued reliance on a somewhat artificial distinction between urban and rural (Montgomery, Stren et al, 2003; Hugo and Champion, 2004). However, while the often neglected sectoral and spatial interdependencies between urban centres and countryside are critical, there are also crucial differences between urban and rural contexts which, in turn, affect the determinants and characteristics of the vulnerability and poverty of their populations, and which require more careful understanding and consideration. But it is also important to recognize the great diversity between and within urban contexts, especially larger cities, and between rural areas. Hence, to understand poverty and the best means to address it, including ways to stimulate local economic growth, it is necessary to understand the diversity of local contexts, be they urban or rural. The difference between rural and urban contexts is one useful way to emphasize these important and often significant variations, but it is essential to keep in mind the diversity between different urban areas and different rural areas, and the many links between rural and urban areas and people that make the dividing line between rural and urban contexts imprecise.

The chapter by David Satterthwaite in this collection (Chapter 1) offers a detailed analysis of recent census data, with special attention to small urban centres. The latter are given insufficient attention in analyses of urban change, although a high proportion of the world's urban population live in such settlements. They also often play an essential role in the provision of services to their own populations and that of the surrounding rural regions, as well as acting as important market centres for agricultural production. But the variations in the ways in which national censuses classify their urban centres, as well as the huge diversity in the economic bases of small urban centres, suggest that generalizations should be treated with great caution.

Rural–urban linkages and livelihood transformations

Perhaps the best understanding of the importance of rural–urban linkages and of their significance for economic, social and cultural change in low-income nations comes from detailed analyses of the livelihood strategies of poor and non-poor groups. These show how most individuals and households straddle the rural–urban divide through increased income diversification and mobility, sometimes involving long-term migration. An important distinction that emerges from this work is that between strategies that lead to the accumulation of assets, and strategies that only ensure the survival of those who undertake them.

The chapters in Part 2 include a detailed case study of northern Tanzania by Jonathan Baker (Chapter 2), a summary of case studies in Mali, Nigeria and Tanzania by Mahmoud Bah et al (Chapter 3) and an overview of the Southeast Asia region by Jonathan Rigg (Chapter 4). Despite the differences in geographical focus and approach, they all show a marked increase among most rural households of the time devoted to, and the income share derived from non-farm activities.

National employment data tend to underestimate the significance of income diversification as they usually only record people's primary activity. This neglects the fact that individuals are more likely to engage in multiple activities, often with variations over time. These can be seasonal (and therefore dependent on changes in the labour demand for different activities, especially agriculture) or related to individuals' life courses (such as, especially for women, different demands on their time from childcare and caring for older and ill relatives). National data also usually omit informal sector activities, including home-based work and petty trade, which can be important income-generating activities for low-income groups. Available studies, usually based on relatively small and location-specific household or enterprise surveys, suggest that the proportion of rural households' incomes derived from non-farm sources, including migrants' remittances, is between 30 and 50 per cent in sub-Saharan Africa, reaching as much as 80–90 per cent in some regions, such as southern Africa (Ellis, 1998). This proportion is estimated to be around 60 per cent in South Asia, and roughly 40 per cent in Latin America (Reardon et al, 2001). On the other hand, farming, either for household consumption or as an income-generating opportunity, is widespread among low-income urban residents and, increasingly, as an investment for wealthier urban groups in peri-urban (emerging extended metropolitan) areas, as the paper by Bah et al describes (Chapter 2).

The increase in livelihood diversification can be triggered by increased demand for manufactured goods and services by a wealthier rural population. This, in turn, can be a major stimulus for the growth of local towns. At the same time, limited access to land, credit, labour and markets for agricultural produce can push small farmers into non-farm occupations to make ends meet. Emerging employment opportunities and affordable transport links ensuring higher levels of mobility also facilitate income diversification. These may include domestic trade liberalization, as in Tanzania in the mid-1980s where it spurred the growth of small-scale trade; the establishment of manufacturing plants in peri-urban areas; and demand for services by urban-based residents and enterprises (for example, domestic services and services in restaurants and bars, especially for women), and, increasingly, by international tourist resorts.

The three chapters also have in common an emphasis on how gender and generational relations shape transformations in rural–urban linkages. Within households, women and younger generations have limited access and control over family assets. This can be particulary significant in family farming, where young people are expected to contribute labour but have little say on how the farm is run. In addition, in many nations women do not gain or retain property of land in traditional tenure systems. In Chapter 2, Baker describes the striking differences in the number of women-headed households in the small town of Biharamulo in northwest Tanzania (29.4 per cent) compared with that in the surrounding villages (7.1 per cent), which suggests that urban labour markets offer far more work opportunities for women than the rural areas, especially for women who may lose their rights to land following the death of – or separation from – their husbands.

For younger generations throughout the world, increased flows of information, new employment opportunities and the erosion of traditional generational relations, together with declining incomes from farming, have resulted in the steady increase of mobility. Until recently, migration in sub-Saharan Africa was predominantly undertaken by men, but the proportion of women moving on their own (that is, not accompanying their fathers or husbands) is growing fast. Chapter 3 by Bah et al describes how the increase in employment opportunities in urban services and international tourism attracts growing numbers of young unmarried women who are no longer prepared to work on their family's farms with little prospect of inheriting any of the land. As a sign of profound social transformations, women's independent migration is now socially acceptable even in remote rural areas, provided they contribute financially to their parental household. The increased dependence of many African rural households on migrant members' remittances signals further profound changes in rural economies. These trends are per- haps even stronger in Southeast Asia, as described by Jonathan Rigg in Chapter 4.

The chapters in this collection are part of a growing empirical literature on how livelihoods in the rural areas of most low- and middle-income nations are changing. These transformations depend on specific contexts, and on the different constraints on farming and opportunities in non-farm activities. As mentioned earlier, generalizations on rural–urban linkages and their relations with livelihoods are, at best, unhelpful, as they show a wide diversity not only between but also within nations and regions. It seems that the only comment that can be made to capture the general trends in these transformations (which are not only economic, but also social and cultural) is that, while households remain central social institutions, they are far from being the homog- enous, relatively stable units of production and consumption as assumed by much rural development theory and practice. They are probably best defined instead as multi-activ- ity and multi-local units, in which members engage in a variety of income-generation in a number of different locations. This has important implications for policy.

How policies address – or ignore – rural–urban linkages

While the interest in livelihood transformations in response to changing rural–urban linkages is relatively recent, the interest in the relations between agriculture, manu- facturing and services is a traditional concern of development economics. In the 1950s and 1960s, the prevalent view was that modernization would depend on a shift of labour to higher productivity sectors; that is, from agriculture to manufacturing and services. This was to be funded by governments through high levels of taxation of agriculture. However, it soon became clear that job creation in manufacturing was much lower than expected and could not absorb the fast-growing urban populations. As policies failed to induce rapid industrialization, the emphasis moved again to the agricultural sector and, through structural adjustment programmes, to export crop production. The dualistic approach of modernization theories, where the traditional, often subsistence agri- cultural (and by extension, rural) sector needs to give way to supposedly more efficient agri-business production systems and to modern, urban-based industrial and services sectors, has pervaded economists' and donors' views for several decades.

Mary Tiffen's chapter in this collection (Part 3, Chapter 5) suggests that the current emphasis on export-oriented crop production as the key to economic growth is not supported by evidence. She draws on her work of over 40 years in sub-Saharan Africa's drylands, where some 30 per cent of the population live and which provide a difficult environment for agriculture. Much of the current pessimism on the continent's economy – negative growth rates in income per capita and falling agricultural output per capita – is based on population and national income data which, in most cases, are far from reliable. Tiffen uses a wealth of longitudinal, qualitative and quantitative data from four districts to describe change between 1960 and 2000. She shows how the growth of local urban markets and increased demand has stimulated small-scale farmers to respond by a 'multitude of small investments linked to technologies and products', often funded by family members engaged in non-farm activities. This reflects recent data on West Africa showing that urban centres are the largest and fastest growing markets for food producers, and that over 80 per cent of the total agricultural production is consumed within the region (Club du Sahel, 2000).

Reliance on export crops, in which large commercial farms tend to specialize, does not seem to be the route out of poverty for many African nations (and other low-income nations) given declining terms of trade, global over-production and tariff escalation on processed produce. On the other hand, demand for more diverse foodstuff, including high-value fruit, vegetable, meat and dairy produce, will continue to grow along with population growth and urbanization, and is likely to provide more stable markets for farmers who are able to respond to consumer demand (Toulmin and Gueye, 2003). This puts into a different perspective the debate on the future of small family farms in Africa and other low-income regions, but also underlines the need for consistent support to small-scale farmers in the form of technical assistance, credit, access to inputs and marketing, as well as access to non-farm income sources.

Planners have also had an on-going interest in managing population distribution and economic development through spatial strategies. In the 1960s, in line with the modernization development paradigm, 'growth poles' policies aimed to stimulate industrial development in designated centres through public investment, with little, if any, explicit interest in rural development. The expected trickle-down effect generally failed to materialize, and in many cases only benefited already privileged social groups, regions and large conurbations. In the 1970s, the notion of 'urban bias' (Lipton, 1977) highlighted the profound divide between urban planners and rural planners. This was reflected in the different views on the role of small towns in regional and rural development. In the negative view, echoing the urban bias argument, small towns are seen as the bases used by colonial powers, national elites, multinationals and other external agents for the extraction of raw materials and the exploitation of the rural poor. In the positive view, small towns are the centres through which innovation and modernization would trickle down to the rural populations. In this highly ideological debate, little evidence was offered to support either argument. An exception to this was a series of case studies in Latin America, Asia and Africa, which showed that, above all, the universal generalizations and prescriptions that formed the basis of most spatial planning models, are not valid (Hardoy and Satterthwaite, 1986).

Chapter 7 by David Satterthwaite and Cecilia Tacoli expands on this previous work and draws on recent empirical literature to examine whether planners' assumptions on the roles of small towns in regional rural development are supported by evidence. Perhaps unsurprisingly, we conclude that small urban centres can indeed play a considerable potential role in regional and rural economic growth. However, their capacity to trigger development that is balanced across different regions and across different groups is much influenced by regional characteristics, including the natural resource base, population density and infrastructure, by land ownership patterns and by socio-economic and cultural transformations at the local, national and international levels.

Chapter 6 by Mike Douglass provides a detailed critical review of past spatial planning strategies. Drawing on empirical work in Indonesia, the paper proposes an alternative paradigm for regional development planning that recognizes the significance of both rural and urban dimensions, and the variations in the form and nature of rural–urban linkages. On this basis, it recommends that policies be based on clusters of settlements of various sizes, rather than on a dyadic urban centre–rural area relationship. This certainly reflects the reality of how people make a living across rural–urban areas and activities in most parts of the world, and the complex, web-like structure of economic and social relations between different locations. The paper also makes the important point that, in many cases, local towns have a limited role within their region as they are bypassed by links to larger urban centres; hence, improved infrastructure such as roads and transport networks may not necessarily benefit them. Such lessons from empirical studies are often set aside when national governments and donor agencies become nervous of funding long-term processes that support development 'software' (for example, supporting the capacity of local governments and local civil society groups through shared learning processes) and favour more visible investment in 'hardware' such as infrastructure. This is not to say that infrastructure spending should be avoided; what should be avoided is basing it on assumptions and generalizations rather than on a careful understanding of the local context.

A key issue in any regional development strategy is that of the role of local government. Given the variations in rural–urban linkages, it makes sense that local policy makers and officials are in the best position to formulate and implement policies that support local economic development and poverty reduction for both rural and urban populations within their administrative area. But local governments in low-income nations, especially those in small urban centres and their surrounding districts, often have limited revenue and poor capacity to carry out their jobs effectively. In some nations, decentralization policies are addressing these issues, but especially in poor regions this is likely to be a long process. In other nations, however, strong local decision making has been in place for decades, as in the case of China.

Chapter 8 by Richard Kirkby, Ian Bradbury and Guanbao Shen describes China's urban policies since 1978 with special attention to small towns. An understanding of Chinese urbanization strategies is important not only because this nation has one of the world's largest populations and one of the fastest growing economies, which have inevitable repercussions on its urbanization levels and forms. It is also important because China is one of the few nations that has developed policies that directly address the interactions between urban centres and their surrounding regions, for example, by extending municipal boundaries well beyond built-up areas to include vast tracts of surrounding rural areas. Administrative boundaries, often a major cause of the neglect of rural–urban linkages in many other nations, are based on a wider understanding of the economic and social links between city and countryside.

In China, rural industries, known as town and village enterprises (TVEs) expanded rapidly in the post-reform period, when increases in agricultural procurement prices increased farmers' incomes and their demand for goods and services. At the same time, the household responsibility system allowed farmers to move from agricultural to non-agricultural employment. Between 1978 and 2000, the rural labour force grew by 2.6 per cent annually, but workers in the rural non-farm sector increased by 27 per cent per year, most of them employed in TVEs based in small towns (Fleisher and Yang, 2004).

As the Chinese economy grows and opens up to world markets, however, new challenges emerge, which also bring lessons for other contexts. Economic liberalization has exacerbated differences between remote centres in sparsely populated regions and well-connected towns in expanding peri-urban regions, making generalizations about small towns misleading. Stagnating purchasing power in their surrounding rural areas and internal and external competition have negatively affected many TVEs. Finally, stricter environmental regulations introduced in the 1990s have affected many TVEs: in 1997, the national government ordered the closure of tens of thousands of TVEs engaged in highly polluting activities such as tanning, paper making and dyeing textiles (Webster and Muller, 2002). Increasingly, survival for the most successful TVEs has meant relocating to county and township industrial estates that provide pollution control facilities, and organizing into clusters of specialized production. How China's policy makers strive to balance economic growth and environmental protection will be extremely significant for the rest of the world, and provide important lessons for the many low-income nations where non-agricultural employment and production are concentrated in small-scale, geographically dispersed enterprises with limited capital.

Population mobility and migration between (and within) rural and urban areas

Migration and mobility are extensive topics, on which there is a huge amount of conceptual and empirical material. This Reader has no pretence to do justice to such a vast literature. But while the section in the collection dedicated to migration and mobility (Part 4) is relatively short, both issues are interwoven with all the others. Hence, mobility (in the form of commuting between rural settlements and urban centres) and migration for varying periods of time and to a range of destinations are important elements of livelihood strategies, as described by the chapters in Part 1.

Policies that address economic growth and local economic development also have elements of population movement, although often this is implicit. For example, the modernization paradigm prevailing in the 1950s and 1960s held a positive view of rural–urban migration, as this reflected the labour shift from farming to manufacturing and industries. Later, however, migration (especially to larger cities) started to be seen as problematic and a cause of growing urban poverty (in most instances, a convenient way to push into the background the shortcomings of economic policies and the incompetence of municipal governments). Policies that attempt to restrict internal migration (such as the household registration systems in China, Vietnam, Mongolia and other countries, and the more restrictive apartheid system in South Africa prior to 1991) inevitably rely on authoritarian methods, and in most cases fail to reach their aim, creating instead additional insecurity and hardship for migrants with limited, if any, access to housing, education and health services and who are often forced to work in exploitative and dangerous conditions. Finding ways to attract rural migrants to local towns rather than the larger cities has long been an objective of regional development planning, as described in Chapter 7 (Satterthwaite and Tacoli).

It is also important to keep in mind that urbanization (the proportion of the national population of a given country living in centres classed as urban) is primarily a consequence of rural–urban migration. Fertility rates in urban centres are usually lower than in rural areas for a variety of reasons: urban women tend to be better educated (perhaps the most important factor of lower fertility); bringing up children tends to be more expensive, as urban residents pay higher prices for housing, transport, food, water and sanitation services and so on; and while children can help on the family farm, their economic role in an urban economy is much more limited. So any decreases in the proportion of rural residents (who tend to have higher rates of natural growth) and increases in that of urban residents are because people move from a rural to an urban area. Changes in urbanization levels can also be linked to the reclassification of some settlements, from 'rural' to 'urban', but this usually happens because these centres have reached a minimum population size threshold – in other words, they have grown in size because of migration from rural areas.

But population movement is far more complex than just a purely economically motivated demographic shift from rural to urban areas. Chapter 9 by Haydea Izazola, Carolina Martínez and Catherine Marquette describes how different groups move to different destinations and for different reasons in and out of Mexico City. Young professional families tend to move out of the city for what can be described as a combination of 'push' factors (the deteriorating environment of Mexico City, seen as a problem particularly by families with young children) and 'pull' factors (the relocation of enterprises, and the demand for skilled workers, in intermediate urban centres). But low-income migrants from rural areas still hold Mexico City as their preferred destination where they hope to make a better life for themselves and their families. Deteriorating environmental conditions are eclipsed by concerns with land and home ownership, and with the opportunities to combine waged employment with some subsistence agriculture. These differences, and especially the growing importance of environmental perceptions, are important for a better understanding of urban change, and of the longer-term trends in the social fabric of cities.

In Chapter 10, Priya Deshingkar addresses one traditional aim of many rural development programmes, that of reducing rural–urban migration. This draws on a pervasive negative view of population movement, which is often held to signify a 'failure' of rural livelihoods, based on the assumption that people and locations are either 'rural' or 'urban'. Therefore, improving agricultural production should reduce or reverse migration – if this does not happen, then programmes must have failed. With specific reference to India's Watershed Development Programmes (which have a budget of US$1000 million) Deshingkar describes how migration in project areas should be expected to continue to increase. This is in part because of the failure of the projects, often due to factors beyond their reach such as population growth and world markets; but also because of the actual success of the projects, which gives local residents the financial and educational resources to migrate to better destinations.

The contribution of migrant remittances to rural economies and to household livelihoods is well documented in the growing literature on this topic. Chapter 3 describes how in the study areas, between 50 and 80 per cent of households have at least one migrant member. Migrant remittances contribute to households' expenditure on food, consumer goods, health and education services, and also, crucially, are reinvested in local productive activities. For example, in Vietnam's Red River Delta, seasonal migration to work in the urban construction sector is an essential source of cash, which in turn is invested in the intensification of agricultural production in migrants' home villages (Hoang et al, 2005). For many migrants, both poor and wealthier groups, maintaining and increasing assets in both home (rural) areas and in destination (urban) areas is a crucial livelihood strategy.

Chapter 11 in Part 4, by Fred Krüger, describes the lives of migrants in low-income areas of Gaborone, Botswana's capital city. For these migrants, retaining strong links with their home areas is not only desirable, but a necessity in the face of declining urban incomes and employment opportunities, and growing costs of living in the city. Decades after moving away from their villages, migrants still retain strong linkages and invest in rural assets, especially livestock and land. In some cases, looking after these assets means engaging in monthly or seasonal movement between the urban and the rural homes. But because policies do not recognize that assets can be distributed in different locations, urban residents are not entitled to compensation for cattle or harvest losses by government drought relief measures, which focus exclusively on rural residents.

Beyond the city boundaries: Peri-urban areas and environmental issues

Part 5 includes chapters on peri-urban areas and on the rural–urban dimensions of environmental issues. As in the case of migration, there is a significant and growing literature on this topic, and the Reader does not aim to provide a definitive account, but rather to point to some of the key emerging issues.

Chapter 12 by Horacio Losada et al, and Chapter 13 by Philip Kelly describe the changes in agricultural production in the areas surrounding Mexico City and Manila. Areas within the sphere of influence of large metropolitan areas, especially dynamic cities with high economic and population growth rates, usually undergo rapid transformations in the use of natural resources, especially land and water, reflecting changes in the occupational base and population density. It should be noted, however, that the peri-urban interface of metropolitan areas is far from homogenous. Differences in residents' occupation and wealth can be significant: some areas, especially those upstream of any river flowing through the urban area, often have high concentrations of high- and middle-income residential developments that in many instances encroach on high-value agricultural land. In contrast, downstream locations where streams and rivers tend to accumulate urban waste as they pass through the city, almost universally host low-income housing and heavy industries (Van den Berg et al, 2003). Some peri-urban farmers, such as those around Mexico City, have successfully adapted their production systems, often drawing on traditional methods to compensate for the environmental deterioration brought about by urban expansion. In the Philippines, however, the conversion of rice land into residential, industrial and recreational use benefits large landowners at the expense of small and tenant farmers.

Proximity to large and expanding urban centres greatly affects the residents of peri-urban areas. Responding to increased demand from urban consumers, many farmers, especially wealthier ones, are able to specialize in the intensive production of vegetables and livestock. But potential conflict over land and water use, environmental deterioration and encroachment over farmland are frequently issues that are not adequately addressed, in view of their impact on poor and vulnerable groups. Local governments, where they still have 'rural' status, often lack the revenue, capacity and political clout to negotiate with urban authorities and national governments. As Kelly notes, it is important to understand how different priorities underpin power struggles and political dimensions, which in turn affect rural–urban relations. While this is a crucial aspect of rural–urban linkages, it is often more visibly played out in the peri-urban interface.

Many of the environmental pressures that originate in urban centres have major impacts on their surrounding regions, and the ability of rural areas to respond to these pressures (such as pollution and resource use) is critical to the long-term sustainability of urban centres. With urban growth, and with the increase in affluence of urban residents, these relations tend to change. In Chapter 14, William Rees describes how wealthier cities' ecological footprints have become wider and encompass more distant 'elsewheres'. The paper was first published in 1992, and remains an important reminder that it is increasingly necessary to understand rural–urban linkages beyond the local/regional level, to include the global dimension.

Chapter 15 by Gordon McGranahan provides a framework for the understanding of urban environmental burdens based on specific attention to the scale of burdens. Scale is important because it affects the nature of the burdens. Within urban centres, local environmental quality (water, sanitation, solid waste management…) affects the lives of residents, especially the poorest ones; in surrounding regions, the relations between urban development and rural natural resources and ecosystems are key issues; and globally, the emphasis is on the impact of urban-based consumption and production on distant resources ('elsewheres'). While McGranahan's chapter is concerned with a wider range of issues that goes beyond rural–urban linkages, it emphasizes the importance of understanding scale and space in order to understand the appropriate roles and responsibilities of different levels of government. This is a common thread in the majority of the chapters in this Reader, and a critical factor for any policy that aims to build on the positive impacts of rural–urban linkages, as well as to minimize their negative impacts.

References

Club du Sahel (2000) 'Urbanization, rural–urban linkages and policy implications for rural and agricultural development: case study from West Africa', SAH/DLR (2000)1, Club du Sahel, Paris

Ellis, F. (1998) 'Livelihood diversification and sustainable livelihoods', in Carney, D. (ed) *Sustainable Rural Livelihoods: What Contribution Can We Make?* DFID, London

Fleisher, B. M. and Yang, D. T. (2004) 'Problems of China's rural labour markets and rural–urban migration', Presented at the International Symposium on China's Rural Economy after WTO, Chinese Economists Society and Zhejiang University, Hangzhou, China, 25–27 June

Hardoy, J. E. and Satterthwaite, D. (eds) (1986) *Small and Intermediate Urban Centres: Their Role in National and Regional Development in the Third World*, Hodder and Stoughton, London and Westview

Hoang, X. T., Dang, A. N. and Tacoli, C. (2005) 'Livelihood diversification and rural–urban linkages in Vietnam's Red River Delta', Rural–Urban Working Paper 11, IIED, London

Hugo, G., Champion, A. et al (2003) 'Toward a new conceptualization of settlements for democracy', *Population and Development Review*, vol 29, no 2, pp277–297

Lipton, M. (1977) *Why Poor People Stay Poor: Urban Bias in World Development*, Temple Smith, London

Montgomery, M. R., Stren, R. et al (eds) *Cities Transformed: Demographic Change and its Implications in the Developing World*, National Academy Press, Washington, DC

Reardon, T., Berdegué, J. and Escobar, G. (2001) 'Rural non-farm employment and incomes in Latin America: Overview and policy implications', *World Development*, vol 29, no 3, pp395–409

Toulmin, C. and Gueye, B. (2003) 'Transformations in West African agriculture and the role of family farms', Drylands Issue Paper 123, IIED, London

Van den Berg, L. M., van Wijk, M. S. and van Hoi, P. (2003) 'The transformation of agriculture and rural life downstream of Hanoi', *Environment and Urbanization*, vol 15, no 1, pp35–52

Webster, D. and Muller, L. (2002) *Challenges of Peri-urbanization in the Lower Yangtze Region: The Case of the Hangzhou-Ningbo Corridor*, Asia/Pacific Research Center, Stanford University, Stanford

Chapter 1

Small Urban Centres and Large Villages: The Habitat for Much of the World's Low-Income Population[1]

David Satterthwaite

Introduction

The world's urban population today is around 3 billion people[2] – the same size as the world's total population in 1960. During the 20th century, it increased more than ten-fold, and around 50 per cent of the world's population now lives in urban centres, compared to less than 15 per cent in 1900.[3] The urban population of Africa, Asia, and Latin America and the Caribbean is now nearly three times the size of the urban population of the rest of the world. United Nations (UN) projections suggest that urban populations are growing so much faster than rural populations, that 85 per cent of the growth in the world's population between 2000 and 2010 will be in urban areas, and nearly all this growth will be in Africa, Asia and Latin America.[4]

Although concerns regarding this rapid urbanization tend to focus on large cities, half the world's urban population (and a quarter of its total population) live in urban centres with less than half a million inhabitants. The increasing number of 'mega-cities' with 10 million or more inhabitants may seem to be a cause for concern but there are relatively few of them; in 2000, there were 18 of them, they concentrated less than 5 per cent of the world's population and they were heavily concentrated in the world's largest economies.[5]

This chapter has a particular interest in exploring the proportion of national and of urban populations that live in small urban centres, drawing on the most recent census data available from each nation. It also has an interest in the proportion of national populations that live in 'large villages' that have urban characteristics but which national governments choose to continue classifying as 'rural' – because these also house a considerable proportion of the world's rural (and total) population.

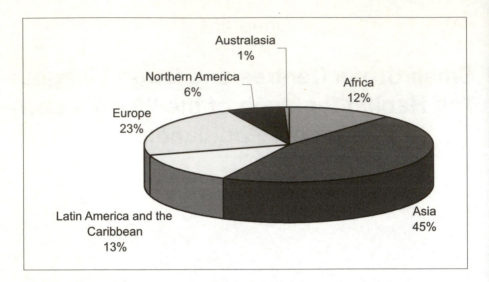

Source: United Nations (2004) *World Urbanization Prospects: The 2003 Revision*, Population Division, Department for Economic and Social Affairs, ESA/P/WP.190, New York

Figure 1.1 *The regional distribution of the population living in urban centres with less than half a million inhabitants in 2000*

How many people live in small urban centres?

If small urban centres were taken to mean all settlements defined by governments as 'urban' with less than half a million inhabitants, then by 2000, around 1.5 billion people lived in small urban centres, including more than a billion in low- and middle-income nations.[6]

Taking 'small urban centres' to be those settlements defined as urban by their government with less than half a million inhabitants is an inadequate definition – for reasons discussed in more detail below. But there are statistics covering all the world's regions and nations for this and these will be presented and discussed, before moving to a more detailed discussion of what constitutes a small urban centre and the proportion of people that live in them.

In regard to their role within national populations, in 2000, a quarter of the world's population lived in urban centres with less than half a million inhabitants. Nearly half of this small urban centre population lived in Asia, nearly a quarter lived in Europe – see Figure 1.1. Although Africa is seen by most people as a predominantly rural continent (even if two-fifths of its population now lives in urban areas), it is worth noting that it had twice as many people living in urban centres with less than half a million inhabitants as Northern America. There are also good reasons for suggesting that the scale of Asia's 'small urban centre' population is underestimated by these figures – as discussed in more detail later. Table 1.1 is also a reminder of how small a proportion of the population in all regions live in very large cities, including the 'mega-cities' with 10 million plus inhabitants. However, care is needed in interpreting these statistics since, as the

Table 1.1 *Population distribution between different size categories of urban centres and rural areas in 2000*

Nations and regions	Proportion of the total population in:				
	Rural areas	Urban areas with fewer than 500,000 inhabitants	Urban areas with 500,000–4.999 million	Urban areas with 5–9.999 million	'Mega-cities' with 10 million plus inhabitants
Africa	62.9	22.3	12.4	1.1	1.3
Asia	62.9	18.4	12.4	2.5	3.9
Europe	27.3	46.1	20.5	4.7	1.4
Latin America and the Caribbean	24.5	37.1	23.4	3.7	11.3
Northern America	20.9	29.8	35.6	4.3	9.4
Oceania	27.3	31.7	41.0		
World	52.9	24.5	15.7	2.7	4.1

Notes: These statistics need to be interpreted with caution. Obviously, the proportion of the population in 'rural areas' and 'urban centres with fewer than 500,000 inhabitants is influenced by how urban areas are defined. And obviously, the proportion of the population in larger cities is influenced by how these cities' boundaries are defined.
Source: Derived from statistics in United Nations (2004) *World Urbanization Prospects: The 2003 Revision*, Population Division, Department for Economic and Social Affairs, ESA/P/WP.190, New York

note below the table explains, differences in how nations define urban centres and urban boundaries limit the accuracy of these cross-regional comparisons – and the cross-national comparisons made later in this chapter.

Some nations had half or more of their national populations in urban centres with less than half a million inhabitants in their most recent census – for instance Venezuela, Chile and Brazil – and many more have more than a third – for instance Argentina, Peru, Colombia, Guatemala, Iran, Malaysia and Turkey. Some relatively small population nations also have a large proportion of their national population in urban centres with less than half a million inhabitants because they are relatively urbanized and have no urban centre of more than half a million inhabitants – for instance Central African Republic in its 1988 census and Botswana in its 2001 census.

Seeking a more precise definition of small urban centre

The statistics in Table 1.1 demonstrate that a sizeable proportion of the world's population live in urban centres with less than half a million inhabitants. But this does not fully capture the proportion in 'small urban centres'. To ascertain how many people live in small urban centres requires a more precise definition as to what is a small urban centre – both in terms of a lower threshold (at what point does a rural settlement or village

RURAL	AMBIGUOUS	URBAN
Unambiguously rural settlements with most of the inhabitants deriving a living from farming and/or forestry	'Large villages', 'small towns' and 'small urban centres'. Depends on each nation's definition of 'urban' what proportion of these are classified as rural or urban	Unambiguously urban centres with much of the economically active population deriving their living from manufacturing or services
Population of rural settlements range from farmsteads to a few hundred inhabitants	Population range typically from a few hundred to 20,000 inhabitants	In virtually all nations, these include settlements with 20,000+ inhabitants;[7] in most they include many settlements with much less than 20,000 inhabitants

Increasing population size
Increasing importance of non-agricultural economic activities

Figure 1.2 *The continuum of settlements from rural to urban*

become a small urban centre?) and the upper threshold (when is an urban centre too big to be called small?). Neither threshold is easily defined. And to set some specific population size that is applied to all nations – for instance, an urban centre stops being 'small' when its population exceeds 500,000 – would exclude some urban centres that are 'small' within their national context, especially in large population nations such as India and China and in the larger population, relatively urbanized nations in Latin America. Figure 1.2 highlights the ambiguity – and this ambiguity has importance because 20–40 per cent of the population in many nations lives in settlements that could be considered rural or urban – or as large villages or small urban centres.

Where any government chooses to draw the line between 'rural' and 'urban' has great significance for the proportion of their population in 'rural' and 'urban' areas. One of the dominant debates in development for 40 years has been over the relative priority that should be given to 'rural' and 'urban' development. Within this debate, both rural and urban proponents try to establish how much 'poverty' there is in rural and urban areas, to bolster their claims for more attention to 'rural' or 'urban'. This debate rarely acknowledges that a large proportion of the population lives in settlements that could be termed small urban centres (and thus urban) or large villages (and thus rural). Many 'predominantly rural' nations would become less rural or even predominantly urban if their 'large villages' were reclassified as 'small urban centres'. For example:

- In Mauritius, in the 2000 census, around a quarter of the population lived in settlements with between 5000 and 20,000 inhabitants and these settlements included various capitals of their district but these were not classified as urban areas.[8] If they had been classified as urban centres, Mauritius's population would have been more than two-thirds urban in 2000, rather than less than half urban.
- Egypt is still seen as predominantly rural yet in its 1996 census, nearly a fifth of its population lived in settlements with between 10,000 and 20,000 inhabitants, most of which have strong urban characteristics – and if these had been reclassified as

urban, Egypt would have had nearly two thirds of its population in urban areas in 1996.[9]

- In India, in the 1991 census, there were 13,376 villages with populations of 5000 or more and if the 113 million inhabitants that lived in these were classified as urban, the level of urbanization would have risen from 25.7 to 39.1 per cent.[10] If those who lived in 'rural' areas but worked in urban areas were classified as urban, this would also raise the proportion of India's population living in urban areas by a few percentage points (see Box 1.2 for more details).[11]

- In Pakistan, the 1998 census showed that 90 per cent of the rural population lived in settlements with more than 1000 inhabitants, including many in settlements with more than 5000 inhabitants. There were more than 3500 'rural' settlements that had more than 5000 inhabitants. If these had been classified as urban centres, it would have increased the number of urban centres from 501 to over 4000 and around half the nation's population would have been living in urban areas – instead of the official figure of 32.5 per cent.[12]

- México can be said to be 74.4 per cent urban or 67.3 per cent urban in 2000, depending on whether urban centres are all settlements with 2500 or more inhabitants or all settlements with 15,000 or more inhabitants.[13]

However, there are also cases of nations whose urban population may be over-stated. For instance, in Ethiopia, in 1994, nearly half the urban population lived in some 881 urban centres with less than 20,000 inhabitants and these centres included many with less than 2000 inhabitants.[14] It could be argued that some of these were better classified as 'rural'.

The lower threshold, to establish at what point a growing rural settlement should be classified as urban, is not easily defined. Within most nations, there are many settlements with concentrations of shops and services and some manufacturing (indicative of urban economies) with 1000–2000 inhabitants while within many low-income nations, there are other larger settlements with several thousand inhabitants that have few shops and services and with most of the population engaged in farming (indicative of a rural settlement).

This difficulty in establishing a clear typology of settlements also illustrates the difficulties in drawing a distinction between 'rural' and 'urban' since the line between the two can be based on settlement size or administrative importance or economic structure. Even when settlement size is chosen as the sole or main criterion for distinguishing rural from urban settlements, there are the ambiguities as to where settlement boundaries should be drawn. There are also forms of 'urban' settlement for which boundaries are not easily drawn – for instance, where 'urban' activities are clustered each side of a road for considerable distances. There is also the inertia in government systems which often means that settlements' official boundaries are much smaller than their built-up area, as they have not been adjusted to reflect population growth and growth in the built-up area. There are also many urban centres whose boundaries encompass large tracts of rural land and significant numbers of farmers.[15]

The smallest urban centres and large villages

In most nations, many of the settlements with less than 20,000 inhabitants (for instance all those with more than 2500 or more than 5000 inhabitants) are considered urban centres; in a few, all settlements with less than 20,000 inhabitants are regarded as rural. For nations that have urban definitions that include all settlements with more than 2000 or 2500 inhabitants as urban, up to a quarter of their national population can live in urban centres with less than 20,000 inhabitants. Table 1.2 shows the proportion of national populations living in urban centres with under 20,000 inhabitants, although this needs to be interpreted with caution, in that, for each nation, this proportion is heavily influenced by how urban centres are defined. The nations with the highest proportion of their national populations in urban centres with less than 20,000 inhabitants tend to be relatively urbanized nations that also have urban definitions that include most settlements with a few thousand inhabitants as 'urban'. For instance, Guatemala with more than a quarter of its national population in urban centres under 20,000 inhabitants in 2002 has an urban definition that encompasses most settlements with 2000 plus inhabitants,[16] while for Cuba it includes all settlements with 2000 plus inhabitants, and some others with urban characteristics;[17] Venezuela classifies places of 2500 inhabitants or more as urban centres, while for Costa Rica, urban areas are administrative centres of cantons, including adjacent areas with clear urban characteristics such as streets, urban services and electricity.[18]

Many censuses do not publish figures for the populations of all the smaller urban centres or give details of their numbers and the population they concentrate. In regard to some that do:

- Mozambique had 68 towns (*vilas*) each with less than 20,000 inhabitants in the 1997 census.
- Indonesia had over 1000 urban centres with less than 30,000 inhabitants in 1990.
- Mexico had 234 urban centres with between 15,000 and 50,000 inhabitants in 2000 (with a total population of around 6 million) and around 7 million in hundreds of urban centres with between 2500 and 15,000 inhabitants.[19]
- Ghana had 298 urban centres with 5–20,000 inhabitants in 2000 and a total population of 2.7 million.[20]
- In 1991, 19.4 per cent of Bangladesh's urban population lived in settlements with fewer than 25,000 inhabitants, including 6.3 per cent living in centres with fewer than 10,000 inhabitants.[21]

Settlements with under 20,000 inhabitants can have strong and obvious urban characteristics – for instance economies and employment structures dominated by industry and or services and/or large, diverse concentrations of retail stores. They can include some settlements considered as cities – usually urban centres that had importance historically but that have not been successful in recent decades. They also include millions of settlements where much of the population works in agriculture, forestry or fishing.

One way to get more clarity in regard to whether a settlement is rural or urban is to define urban centres based not only on population thresholds but also on the extent of its non-agricultural economic activities or the proportion of the economically active

Table 1.2 *Proportion of the national population in urban centres with under 20,000 inhabitants*

Nation (and date of census used)	Proportion of the national population in urban centres with under 20,000 inhabitants
Costa Rica (2000)	27.5
Guatemala (2002)	25.8
Cuba (2002)	21.4
Venezuela (2001)	19.4
Brazil (2001)	15.0
Colombia (2003)	14.8
Peru (1993)	14.7
Ghana (2000)	14.7
Chile (2002)	14.3
Paraguay (2002)	12.3
Argentina (2001)	11.4
Dominican Republic (2000)	11.3
Mexico (2000)	9.6
Namibia (1991)	9.0
Morocco (2004)	8.9
Mauritania (2000)	8.1
Tanzania (2002)	8.0
Bolivia (2001)	7.4
Botswana (2001)	7.3
Thailand (2000)	7.2
Central African Rep. (1988)	7.2
Indonesia (1990)	6.9
Malaysia (2000)	6.9
Ethiopia (1994)	6.0
South Africa (1996)	5.9

Note: Note that the figures for any nation in this table depend heavily on how urban centres are defined. For the nations with low proportions (and the many nations with much lower proportions than these that are not included in this table – see Table 1.4), changing their urban definition could increase the proportion considerably).

population working in non-agricultural activities. But this is problematic because many very small settlements have most of their workforce working in non-agricultural activities (for instance, small mining centres, tourist centres or small river ports) while some much larger settlements can have much of their workforce still working in agriculture. In addition, many rural and urban households have both 'rural' and 'urban' components to their livelihoods so it is difficult to classify them as 'rural' or 'urban'.[22] For instance, is a rural household that derives most of its income from family members who commute daily to an urban centre 'rural' or 'urban'? Is an urban household that draws most of its income from farming 'rural' or 'urban'? And an urban centre may have most of its work-force in activities that are classified as non-agricultural yet a high proportion are based on processing local crops or providing goods and services to local farmers and local rural populations.[23]

For any settlement, being classified as 'urban' often brings some potential advantages if it means that there is a local government there with capacity to contribute to the provision of basic services including water and sanitation (being designated as an urban centre can mean more scope for local revenue generation too) – but it may also bring changes that local elites fear, which explains why they may oppose their settlement being classified as 'urban'.

Box 1.1 *Are these large villages or small urban centres?*

BENIN: Béroubouay with 5000 inhabitants and So-Zounko, a lakeside settlement of 8750 inhabitants dependent on fishing and trade are considered villages.[24]

PAKISTAN: In 1998, a very considerable proportion of the rural population lived in over 1000 settlements with more than 5000 inhabitants which in most nations would have been classified as urban centres – including many that were considered urban in the 1972 census. In the 1981 and 1998 censuses, such settlements were not considered as urban centres unless they had a municipal government. This changed the status of 1483 settlements with more than 5000 inhabitants which, in the 1972 census, had been classed as urban centres.[25]

KERALA: Most of the population of the state of Kerala in India (which has more than 32 million inhabitants) live in 'villages' with populations exceeding 10,000;[26] in most nations, these would be classified as urban centres.

In China, several hundred million people live in small urban centres as defined by this paper – but it is difficult to get precise statistics. Official sources give different figures for the total urban population, in large part because of different definitions for what consti-tutes the 'urban' population – see Box 1.2. For instance, statistics from the China's Ministry of Construction stated that by the end of 2002, there were 660 cities and 20,600 administrative towns in China with a total population of 502 million.[27] Another report by the Ministry of Construction suggested an urban population of 338 million at the end of 2003[28] – although this may be the figure for the population in 'cities' and so does not count the population in administrative towns. China's 'small urban centre' population would include many of its 'cities' as well as its administrative towns; it was reported that in 2005, more than half of the 660 cities on the mainland had populations of between 200,000 and half a million people.[29]

This issue of the lower threshold used to determine when a settlement becomes urban can be politically charged in that both governments and international agencies make decisions about resource allocations between rural and urban areas depending on the proportion of the population that live in them. They also have 'rural' and 'urban' programmes which may only be applicable in areas designated as 'rural' or 'urban' so the

Box 1.2 *How urban are China and India?*

In China, the criteria for urban designation have changed dramatically in response to changing urbanization policies and economic development strategies. It has been estimated, for example, that the urbanization level in China in 1999 would have been 24 per cent according to the pre-1982 urban definition, 73 per cent according to the 1982 definition and 31 per cent according to the 1990 definition.[30] Much of the difference between these relate to how the residents of small urban centres and peri-urban areas are counted. Two different classification systems have been used, one registering a segment of the population as urban and the other designating a selection of places as urban. Until the late 1970s, there was a reasonable degree of consistency between the two; people in urban places had urban registration. From the 1980s onwards, there was an extremely rapid growth in the number and area of (urban) designated towns and cities. After new criteria for town designation were issued in 1984, the number of designated towns jumped from 2781 at the beginning of 1984 to 6211 by the end of the year and continuously increased to over 20,000 by the end of 2000.[31] Urbanization policies encouraged townships to apply for town designation, and for the spatial extent of designated towns and cities to expand.[32] Especially for migrants, however, the conversion of rural to urban residence (hukou) continued to be tightly restricted. Thus on the one hand many designated towns and cities extended over large and often agricultural areas with low population densities, and on the other hand many people with rural (agricultural) registration lived in high density areas and worked in non-agricultural employment.

The 2001 census in India suggested that 27.8 per cent of the population were urban – i.e. that nearly three-quarters of the population lived in rural areas. But much of the rural population live in settlements which would be classified as 'urban' if India chose to adopt the urban definitions used in most European nations – and most of the rural population would live in urban areas if India adopted the urban definition used in Sweden or Peru. In Sweden, all settlements with built-up areas with at least 200 inhabitants and with houses at most 200m from each other are considered urban while in Peru, urban centres are populated settlements with 100 or more dwellings grouped contiguously, and administrative centres of districts.[33]

If India became reclassified as a predominantly urban nation, it would change the perspective of both the government and international agencies. The idea that India is a predominantly rural nation could also be questioned by the fact that by 2001, 76 per cent of value added within India's gross domestic product (GDP) came from industry and services, most of which is located in urban areas. This is not to suggest that India's urban definition is 'wrong' – and to apply Sweden's urban definition in India would clearly be very misleading in terms of how urban India's population would become and how this would make tens of thousands of settlements that were underpinned by agriculture 'urban'. But it does highlight how a large part of the population in India and in most other nations live in settlements that can be considered urban or rural.

In 1991, there were 13,376 villages in India with populations of 5000 or more and if these 113 million inhabitants were classified as urban, the level of urbanization in 1991 would have risen from 25.7 to 39.1 per cent.[34] In 1987/88, 4 per cent of urban workforce were rural-based commuters (National Sample Survey data) and this proportion has probably increased since then.[35]

> The populations of many settlements in India that have urban characteristics prefer to retain their rural status, partly because of concerns about paying higher taxes.[36]

possibilities of getting government funding may depend on a settlement being reclassified as 'urban' or on avoiding such a reclassification, long after the settlement has developed a strong non-agricultural economic and employment base. There are also some anomalies – for instance 'small town' programmes that are for rural areas or implemented within rural programmes and even statements claiming that small towns are not urban areas.

But a concentration of people and non-agricultural economic activities implies a need for water and usually for waste water management – regardless of whether this concentration is in a settlement classified as a village, town or urban centre. There will be economies of scale and proximity in most of these settlements, which can lower unit costs for better provision for water and sanitation. There may be important synergies between demand from households and from enterprises (including many household enterprises). This link between economic activities and domestic needs may also span rural–urban definitions, as demand for water for livestock and crops can help fund improved provision for water that serves these needs and also serves domestic needs. In many such settlements, there may also be sufficient demand for electricity, and also economies of scale and proximity, which make its provision economically feasible – and this brings obvious advantages with regard to power for water pumping.

As the interest in small urban centres or other categories of settlements such as secondary cities or intermediate cities has begun to grow, so too have certain myths about them become common. Box 1.3 outlines these.

The proportion of people living in small urban centres

Small urban centres probably house far more people than the cities with more than a million cities in Africa, Asia and Latin America, but it is difficult to get accurate measures of the proportion of people in them because many are still classified within the rural population, as described above. Census reports rarely give details as to the proportion of the population living in different settlement categories according to their population size. Table 1.3 shows the proportion of national populations living in different size categories. This table drew only on census data – and was constructed from data tables that had figures for the populations of urban centres. Only nations for which such data tables were available could be included so it is an incomplete list. As noted earlier, the figures for each nation for the proportion of the national population in urban centres with less than 20,000 inhabitants will be strongly influenced by how urban centres are defined. For the other urban categories, the figures can be compared between nations.[38]

Table 1.3 shows how high a proportion of national populations can live in urban centres with less than 50,000 inhabitants – for instance around 45 per cent in Costa Rica, around 30 per cent for Guatemala, around a quarter of the population in

Box 1.3 *Common myths about small urban centres*

Myth 1: That small urban centres are growing faster than large cities. An analysis of population growth rates for all urban centres for the most recent inter-census period for 70 nations (and for many other nations for other inter-census periods) showed that there is great diversity among small urban centres within each nation with regard to their population growth rates; also great diversity in the extent of in-migration and out-migration. It is not possible to generalize about demographic trends in small urban centres. A review of population growth rates between cen-suses for all urban centres in a nation usually shows great diversity – including a group of small urban centres that grew very rapidly and a group that grew very slowly (and often some that did not grow or even some that had declining popula-tions). Certainly, some small urban centres will have grown faster than the largest cities, but this can be misleading in that, adding 1 million people to a city of 10 mil-lion in a decade appears as a slower population growth rate than adding 600 people to an urban centre of 5,000 inhabitants in that same decade. Analysing why there are such large differentials in the population growth rates of different urban centres, and what underpinned the rapid growth of those that grew rapidly, is much more useful for policy purposes than any attempt to find relationships between the size of settlements and their population growth rates. The potential of small urban centres to grow and develop more prosperous economic bases depends not so much on their current size but, rather, on their location, on the competence and capacity of their government, on their links with other urban centres, and on the scale and nature of economic change in their region and nation. Generally, there is also con-siderable diversity between large cities in terms of their growth rates, although many of the largest cities experienced considerable slow-downs in their population growth rates during the 1980s and/or the 1990s, and proved to be much smaller in 2000 than had been anticipated).[37]

Myth 2: That there are valid generalizations about small urban centres' economic base or employment structure. Again, there is generally too much diversity in regard to the economic or employment base of small urban centres to allow generaliza-tions, although agriculture-related goods and services and local government serv-ices and employees are generally important for the employment base of most small urban centres.

Myth 3: That governments can push new investments to small urban centres to control the growth of large cities. The record of governments in successfully doing this is very poor; they often push investment into unsuitable locations, or the choice of location in which public investment is concentrated is determined by political reasons not economic potential. More dispersed patterns of urban development (in which some small urban centres become increasingly important and grow to become large urban centres) are likely to develop, without economic losses, if national economies grow and through effective decentralization (especially increas-ing the competence, capacity and accountability of local governments in small urban centres).

Table 1.3 *The division of national populations between rural areas and urban centres of different sizes*

Nation and date of census	Proportion of the population in urban centres with							
	Rural areas	Under 20,000	20,000–49,999	50,000–199,999	200,000–499,999	0.5–1.99 million	2–4.99 million	5 million+
Africa								
Benin (1992)	77.0	3.0	6.3	5.8		7.9		
Botswana (2001)	47.6	7.3	18.4	10.0	16.8			
Burkina Faso (1996)	83.0	2.7	3.2	1.2	3.0	6.9		
Central African Rep. (1988)	64.2	7.2	10.3		18.3	17.4		
Cameroon (2001)	57.1	0.9	4.0	12.9	7.5	17.4		
Cote D'Ivoire (1988)	61.0	3.0	7.8	7.2	3.1	17.9		
Egypt (1996)	57.4	1.6	3.0	8.4	7.4	1.5	9.4	11.4
Ethiopia (1994)	86.3	6.0	1.8	2.0			4.0	
Ghana (2000)	56.2	14.7	6.5	6.9	1.1	15.0		
Guinea (1996)	69.0	3.5	4.3	8.0		15.3		
Kenya (1999)	80.6	1.6	2.3	3.9	1.9	2.3	7.5	
Mali (1987)	83.6	1.4	2.0	4.5	8.6			
Mauritania (2000)	50.6	8.1	16.2	2.9	0.0	22.3		
Mauritius (2000)		57.3 ————	————	42.7				
Malawi (1998)	86.4	1.5	1.0	1.5	4.4	5.1		
Morocco (2004)	42.0	8.9	5.9	10.7	4.6	17.9	10.0	
Mozambique (1997)	71.5	3.6	2.3	9.2	7.3	6.1		
Namibia (1991)	73.2	11.6	4.7	10.4				
Niger (2001)	84.6	2.2	2.0	5.0		6.3		
Nigeria (1991)	64	6.1	6.1	9.0	4.7	7.9	2.4	5.8

Rwanda (2002)	83.2	0.1	2.6	6.6		7.4		17.9
Senegal (2002)	60.3	3.2	2.6	11.6	2.4	19.4		
South Africa (1996)	46.3	5.9	2.0	6.9	3.7	5.1	12.1	
Tanzania (2002)	77.0	7.4	1.4	4.2	3.3		6.8	
Uganda (2002)	87.7	1.6	2.8	2.7		4.9		
Zambia (2000)	63.0	6.6	2.8	9.2	7.5	11.0		
Zimbabwe (1992)	69.4	3.3	2.9	4.4	2.6	17.4		
Asia								
Bangladesh (1991)	79.9	4.2	3.1	2.6	1.0	1.3	1.9	6.1
Cambodia (1998)	84.3		3.4	3.1		9.4		
India (2001)	72.2	— 6.0 —		5.6	3.0	5.3	2.0	5.8
Indonesia (1990)	69.4	6.9	1.4	6.6	4.2	4.5	2.5	4.6
Iran (1996)	38.7	— 12.1 —		14.3	9.3	14.3		11.3
Jordan (1994)	24.4	1.0	2.8	16.0	9.2	46.6		
Korea, Rep. Of (2000)	n.a.	n.a.	2.6	9.1	11.2	20.1	18.5	21.4
Kyrgyzstan (1999)	65.4	4.5	6.2	4.0	4.3	15.6		
Malaysia (2000)	38.2	6.9	7.3	16.8	17.4	13.5		
Philippines (2000)	52.0	— 9.8 —		13.0	9.2	3.2		12.9
Saudi Arabia (2004)	— 24.3 —		5.8	10.3	13.8	15.3	30.4	
Sri Lanka (2001)	84.4	2.2	2.9	4.8	1.1	3.4		0
Thailand (2000)	69.0	7.2	5.3	6.3	1.8			10.5
Turkey (2000)	35.3	5.5	8.6	12.9	7.7	9.1	8.0	13.0
Yemen	76.5	7.7	2.6	2.5	4.2	6.5		

Table 1.3 The division of national populations between rural areas and urban centres of different sizes

Nation and date of census	Rural areas	Proportion of the population in urban centres with						
		Under 20,000	20,000–49,999	50,000–199,999	200,000–499,999	0.5–1.99 million	2–4.99 million	5 million+
Latin America								
Argentina (2001)	11.6	11.4	7.7	11.1	10.3	14.8		33.2
Bolivia (2001)	37.6	7.4	2.3	9.0	2.4	41.3		
Brazil (2000)	19.1	15.0	9.3	17.3	12.6	13.5	4.0	9.2
Chile (2002)	13.2	14.3	6.9	17.4	18.5	0	29.6	
Colombia (2003)	23.6	14.8	4.6	6.9	9.8	11.6	12.0	16.7
Costa Rica (2000)	41.0	27.5	17.2	2.9	11.5			
Cuba (2002)	24.1	21.4	10.4	11.8	12.6		19.7	
Dominican Rep. (2002)	36.4	11.3	5.8	18.5		28.0		
Ecuador (2001)	39.0	7.3	6.8	15.0	4.0	27.8		
Guatemala (2002)	53.9	25.8	4.8	4.7	2.5	8.4		
Honduras (2001)	55.2	13.0	6.5	6.8	6.7	11.8		
Mexico (2000)	25.3	9.6	4.9	5.6	8.7	20.9	7.0	18.4
Paraguay (2002)	43.3	12.3	3.0	3.6	6.5	31.4		
Peru (1993)	29.9	14.7	5.1	8.6	7.9	5.1		28.7
Venezuela (2001)	13.0	19.4	5.0	23.5	12.8	26.4		

Notes: Getting data for any nation for a table such as this depends on being able to get population figures for a complete list of all urban centres. Inter-country comparisons of the proportion of the population in rural areas and in urban centres with fewer than 20,000 inhabitants are not valid because of the differences between nations in how urban populations are defined. Inter-country comparisons of the proportion of the population in large cities only have limited validity because of the differences in the ways that governments set boundaries for large cities. Three points need noting:

1 The size of 'large cities', and thus the proportion of the population in 'large cities', is much influenced by the way in which governments define large cities' boundaries. For many large cities, their total population is overstated because the city boundaries encompass large areas that are rural and also villages and small urban centres that are at some distance from the city's built-up area. This helps explain why significant proportions of the workforce in many large Chinese or Bangladeshi cities work in agriculture. By contrast, the total population of some large cities is greatly understated, as boundaries have not expanded to reflect the large numbers of people and enterprises that have spilled over the official boundaries.[39] For nations with large cities, it is possible to create two different tables showing the population distribution in different size urban centres: one based on the population of cities, the other based on the population of metropolitan areas or urban agglomerations (where the population of the metropolitan areas or the largest urban agglomerations are made up of many different cities). Where there were data on both, the population in metropolitan areas and urban agglomerations was used – for instance for Mexico, South Africa and Bangladesh. For Brazil, only population figures for cities and municipalities were found for the 2000 census, not figures for metropolitan areas and urban agglomerations – so the cities or municipalities around major cities that are within the major cities' metropolitan areas are counted as independent cities. This will have considerably elevated the population in some small urban centre categories and considerably decreased the population in the large city categories. For Sri Lanka, the population figure used for Colombo was for the city, not for the metropolitan agglomeration.

2 The distribution of population between rural areas and urban centres with fewer than 20,000 inhabitants is much influenced by the census definition for what constitutes an urban area. Thus, in Peru, where the urban definition includes small settlements (populated settlements with 100 or more dwellings grouped contiguously, and administrative centres of districts), the proportion in 'urban centres with fewer than 20,000 inhabitants' is high, and the proportion in rural areas low. In some nations, complete lists of all urban centres were not available so part or all of the population in 'urban centres with less than 20,000 inhabitants' was derived from subtracting the population of all urban centres with 20,000 plus inhabitants from the rural population. For most nations where this was done, some verification for the validity of the figure could be obtained from the national definition of 'urban'.

3 Some censuses understate total urban populations because of the difficulties in defining urban centres or applying the definition to census data. For instance, the statistics on Sri Lanka suggest that 14.6 per cent of Sri Lanka's population was urban in 2001, but the government census office suggests that this will increase to around 30 per cent, when a more refined analysis is applied to what proportion of the population live in urban areas.

For Indonesia, the figure for the proportion of the population in urban centres of 20–49,999 inhabitants is only for the population in urban centres with 30–49,999 inhabitants while the population in urban centres 'under 20,000' is for urban centres 'under 30,000'. For South Africa, the figure for the proportion of the population in the 20,000–49,999 inhabitant category is for urban centres with 25,000–49,999 inhabitants, which means that the proportion of the population in this category is understated and the proportion in urban centres with fewer than 20,000 inhabitants is overstated. *Source:* These figures are derived from census data – from lists of urban centres and their populations (for virtually all nations listed here, the data come from www.citypopulation.de/) and from figures for national urban and rural populations, drawn mostly from websites of government statistical offices; for a complete list of all sources used, see Satterthwaite, 2006.

Botswana, Mauritania, Brazil and Venezuela and around a fifth of the population in Ghana, Chile, Peru, Colombia and Egypt.[40] For most of the other nations shown in Table 1.3 it was less, but for many nations, this is because the urban criteria their governments use do not classify most (or any) settlement with between 2000 and 5000 inhabitants as urban.[41]

Several nations have more people in urban centres with less than 50,000 inhabitants than in urban centres with more than 200,000 inhabitants – for instance Costa Rica (2000), Guatemala (2002), Benin (1992), Botswana (2001), Ghana (2000), Ethiopia (1994), Mauritania (2000) and Thailand (2000). Namibia (1991) is also in this list, but because its largest urban centre had less than 200,000 in 1991.

Many nations have more than 10 per cent or more of their national populations in urban centres with between 50,000 and 199,999 inhabitants – see Table 1.4. Obviously, for some small population nations, this is because they have no urban centre that is larger than 199,999 inhabitants – as in Mauritius. Most of the other nations in Table 1.4 with the highest proportion of their national populations in this size category of urban are relatively urbanized nations – and it shows the importance of what might be termed 'intermediate sized' urban centres within their nation. Table 1.4 also shows how numerous these can be – for instance more than 750 urban centres in this size category in China in 1990[42] with more than 600 in India in 2001, more than 300 in Brazil in 2000, 147 in Indonesia in 1991 and 100 in Turkey in 2000; urban centres of this size category also contain significant proportions of the population in most high-income nations.[43] It is also worth noting the number of nations in Table 1.4 with 5–10 per cent of their national populations in this size category of urban centre which are predominantly rural nations – for instance Mozambique, Nigeria, Benin and Niger.

Bangladesh had a low proportion of its national population in urban centres with 50–199 thousand inhabitants in the 1991 census – but still had 34 such centres which had a total population of close to 3 million inhabitants.

One final comment in regard to the statistics in Table 1.3 is the importance of urban centres with between 200,000 and 499,999 inhabitants in the national populations of many relatively large population, relatively urbanized nations. Table 1.5 provides some examples – for instance Chile, Malaysia, Saudi Arabia, Venezuela, South Korea and Argentina.[44] There is also a group of low-income nations within this table which are less urbanized but with several urban centres in this size category that are important regional centres, including some that may have increasing economic and demographic importance, if their economies grow – for instance Cameroon and Tanzania.

Large population nations can have many urban centres in this size category – for instance in China with 125 in 1990 and India with 100 in 2001 (even if these concentrate only a few per cent of their national populations), Brazil with 70, Mexico with 26, Indonesia with 25 and the Philippines with 24. A few small population nations also have a relatively high proportion of their population in urban centres in this size-class because their largest city falls into this category – as in Botswana in 2001, the Central African Republic in 1988 and Mali in 1987.

Table 1.4 *Number of urban centres with 50,000–199,999 inhabitants and the proportion of the national population they contain*

Nation (and date of census used)	Proportion of the national population in urban centres with 50,000–199,999 inhabitants	Number of urban centres with 50,000–199,999 inhabitants
Mauritius (2000)	42.7	4
Venezuela (2001)	23.5	55
Chile (2002)	17.4	26
Brazil (2000)	17.3	312
Malaysia (2000)	16.8	36
Jordan (1994)	16.0	6
Iran (1996)	14.3	92
Philippines (2000)	13.0	88
Cameroon (2001)	12.9	21
Turkey (2000)	12.9	100
Cuba (2002)	11.8	13
Senegal (2002)	11.6	10
Argentina (2001)	11.1	45
Morocco (2004)	10.7	36
Saudi Arabia	10.3	24
Botswana (2001)	10.0	2
Mozambique (1997)	9.2	16
Korea, Rep. Of (2000)	9.1	47
Nigeria (1991)	9.0	84
Peru (1993)	8.6	19
Egypt (1996)	8.4	63
Guinea (1996)	8.0	6
Cote D'Ivoire (1988)	7.2	9
South Africa (1996)	6.9	n.a.
Colombia (2003)	6.9	36
Ghana (2000)	6.9	14
Indonesia (1990)	6.6	147
Thailand (2000)	6.3	41
Benin (1992)	5.8	4
Mexico (2000)	5.6	62
India (2001)	5.6	633

Table 1.5 *Number of urban centres with 200,000–499,999 inhabitants and the proportion of the national population they contain*

Nation (and date of census used)	Proportion of the national population in urban centres with 200,000–499,999 inhabitants	Number of urban centres with 200,000–499,999 inhabitants
Chile (2002)	18.5	10
Central African Rep. (1988)	18.3	1
Malaysia (2000)	17.4	13
Botswana (2001)	16.8	1
Saudi Arabia (2004)	13.8	11
Venezuela (2001)	12.8	10
Brazil (2000)	12.6	70
Cuba (2002)	12.6	5
Costa Rica (2000)	11.9	1
Korea, Rep. Of (2000)	11.2	18
Argentina (2001)	10.3	11
Colombia (2003)	9.8	13
Iran (1996)	9.3	18
Philippines (2000)	9.2	24
Jordan (1994)	9.2	1
Mexico (2000)	8.7	26
Mali (1987)	8.6	1
Peru (1993)	7.9	6
Turkey (2000)	7.7	18
Cameroon (2001)	7.5	4
Egypt (1996)	7.4	14
Mozambique (1997)	7.3	3
Zimbabwe (1992)	6.9	1
Paraguay (2002)	6.5	
Nigeria (1991)	4.7	13
Morocco (2004)	4.6	4
Malawi (1998)	4.4	1
Indonesia (1990)	4.2	25
Yemen (1994)	4.2	2
South Africa (1996)	3.7	
Tanzania (2002)	3.3	5
China (1990)	3.3	125
Cote D'Ivoire (1988)	3.1	1
India (2001)	3.0	100

Small urban centres and the rural–urban continuum

Two conclusions can be drawn from the above. First, that small urban centres have a high proportion of the urban population in most nations and a high proportion of the national population in most relatively urbanized nations. Second, the pattern of small urban centres and their relation to rural settlements and other urban centres defies simple categorization or description. The spatial distribution of any nation's urban population is best understood as the 'geography' of its non-agricultural economy and government system.[45] Or, to put it another way, it is the map of where people whose main income source is not from agriculture make a living.[46] In general, as nations' per capita incomes increase, so too does the concentration of their population in urban centres, because most new investment and income-earning opportunities are concentrated there.[47] Most low-income nations and all middle-income nations have less than half of their gross domestic product (GDP) in agriculture, and all nations with growing economies have decreasing proportions of their GDP derived from agriculture and decreasing proportions of their labour force in agriculture. These figures on the proportion of GDP or of the labour force in industry and services can be misleading in that a considerable part of the growth in industry in most low-income nations may be from forward and backward linkages with agriculture – for instance, the production and sale of agricultural machinery, fertilizers and other agricultural inputs, cold stores, and packaging and processing industries.[48] In addition, a considerable part of the growth in urban services can be to meet demand from agricultural producers and rural populations.[49]

As noted earlier, it is difficult to generalize about the economic bases of small urban centres. In most nations, many will be 'market towns', concentrating markets and services for local agricultural producers and retail and service outlets for their populations and the surrounding populations (including entertainment and financial services). Many are 'administrative towns', in that a significant proportion of their population directly or indirectly derive their income from the concentration of government functions there – including the staff who work for the local district government and those who work for government-funded services (health care, hospitals, schools, post, police, courts...). Obviously, many small urban centres have both market functions and concentrate government employees. Among the many other economic underpinnings of small urban centres are mining enterprises, tourism, border posts, river ports (or 'land ports' in the sense of being key nodes linking local settlements to larger markets), education centres (for instance, one or more secondary schools or a higher education institution), hotels/boarding houses, agricultural processing, retirement centres (sometimes with foreign retirees being an important economic underpinning for the urban centre), centres for the armed services, etc. Most urban centres will also have a proportion of their population working in agriculture. Economic trends in small urban centres will also vary – usually from among the most dynamic to among the least dynamic. Many urban centres close to large and prosperous cities may develop stronger economic bases as they attract new enterprises whose output largely serves demands in the large city or external demands organized by enterprises located in the large city. They may also develop into dormitory towns, or at the least have their economy strengthened by having a proportion of their workforce commuting to the larger city.

With regard to comparing small urban centres' economic and employment bases between different size categories, empirical studies have found no easily defined or clear dividing line although, in general, the larger the urban centre's population, the smaller the proportion of the economically active population working in agriculture and the greater its importance within the government's administrative hierarchy. In nations with effective decentralization, including democratic reforms, many municipal governments in small urban centres have become more successful in supporting economic growth and in improving infrastructure provision.

Dividing a nation's population into 'rural' and 'urban' and assuming that these have particular characteristics in terms of the settlements they live in and the sector in which they earn a living misses the extent to which (poor and non-poor) rural households rely on urban income sources (through remittances from family members, commuting, or producing for urban markets) while many urban households in low-income nations rely on rural resources and reciprocal relationships with rural households.[50] It even gets to the point where rural specialists will talk at length about rural industrialization and 'off-farm' and 'non-farm' employment without mentioning 'urban', although much of the so-called 'rural industrialization' and much of the non-farm employment is actually in

RURAL	Rural–urban interface	URBAN
Livelihoods drawn from crop cultivation, livestock, forestry or fishing (i.e. key for livelihood is access to natural capital)		**Livelihoods** drawn from labour markets within non-agricultural production or making/selling goods or services
Access to land for housing and building materials not generally a problem		**Access to land for housing** very difficult; housing and land markets highly commercialized
More distant from government as regulator and provider of services		**More vulnerable to 'bad' governance**
Access to infrastructure and services limited (largely because of distance, low density and limited capacity to pay?)		**Access to infrastructure and services** difficult for low-income groups because of high prices, illegal nature of their homes (for many) and poor governance
Less opportunities for earning cash, more for self-provisioning; greater reliance on favourable weather conditions		**Greater reliance on cash** for access to food, water, sanitation, employment, garbage disposal...
Access to natural capital as the key asset and basis for livelihood		**Greater reliance on house as an economic resource** (space for production, access to income-earning opportunities; asset and income earner for owners – including *de facto* owners)
Urban characteristics in rural locations (e.g. prosperous tourist areas, mining areas, areas with high value crops and many local multiplier links, rural areas with diverse non-agricultural production and strong links to cities...)		Rural characteristics in urban locations (urban agriculture, 'village' enclaves, access to land for housing through non-monetary traditional forms...)

Source: Satterthwaite, D. and Tacoli, C. (2003) *The Urban Part of Rural Development: The Role of Small and Intermediate Urban Centres in Rural and Regional Development and Poverty Reduction*, Rural–urban working papers series, no 9, IIED, London

Figure 1.3 *The rural–urban continuum*

small urban centres.[51] Meanwhile, urban specialists almost never recognize the importance of prosperous agriculture and a prosperous agricultural population for urban development.

There is a need to forget the rural–urban divide and see all settlements as being within a continuum with regard to both their population size and the extent of their non-agricultural economic base. Figure 1.3 illustrates this. Here, key 'rural characteristics' are listed on the left and key 'urban characteristics' on the right.

But the characteristics listed under each column are two ends of a continuum. As noted already, many rural settlements have households that rely on non-agricultural jobs, and non-agricultural employment opportunities may be very important for reducing rural poverty. In many nations, landless labourers are among the poorest of the rural poor, and they too require better income-earning opportunities, just like the urban poor. Meanwhile, most urban areas exhibit some rural characteristics – for instance, the importance of urban agriculture for many low-income urban households. And, in addition, in the middle of this continuum between 'rural characteristics' and 'urban characteristics', is a 'rural–urban' interface in which rural and urban characteristics are mixed, and most small urban centres in low- and middle-income nations will have such a mix.

Notes

1   This paper is available at IIED's website (www.iied.org) and contains a full list of all references consulted. This was prepared as a background paper for the United Nations Human Settlements Programme (UN Habitat) for the second report on *Water and Sanitation in the World's Cities* which focused on small urban centres – and is published by Earthscan.

2   Unless otherwise stated, the statistics for global and regional populations are drawn from United Nations (2004), *World Urbanization Prospects: The 2003 Revision*, Population Division, Department for Economic and Social Affairs, ESA/P/WP.190, New York.

3   Graumann, J. V. (1977) 'Orders of magnitude of the world's urban and rural population in history', *United Nations Population Bulletin 8*, United Nations, New York, pp16–33.

4   United Nations (2004) op cit.

5   Satterthwaite, D. (2005) *The Scale of Urban Change Worldwide 1950–2000 and its Underpinnings*, Human Settlements Discussion Paper, IIED, London.

6   United Nations (2004) op cit.

7   One exception to this: the figure for the proportion of the population living in urban areas in South Korea is sometimes based on the proportion living in places with 50,000 or more inhabitants.

8   www.clgf.org.uk/2005updates/Mauritius.pdf; www.citypopulation.de/.

9   Bayat, A. and Denis, E. (2000) 'Who is afraid of Ashwaiyyat: Urban change and politics in Egypt', *Environment and Urbanization*, vol 12, no 2, pp185–199.

10 Visaria, P. (1997), 'Urbanization in India; An overview', in Jones, G. and Visaria, P. (eds) *Urbanization in Large Developing Countries*, Clarendon Press, Oxford, pp266–288.

11 Dyson, T. and Visaria, P. (2005) 'Migration and urbanization; retrospect and prospects', in Dyson, T., Cassen, R. and Visaria, L. (eds) *Twenty-First Century India: Population, Economy, Human Development and the Environment*, Oxford University Press, Oxford, pp108–129.

12 Hasan, A. and Raza, M. (2002) *Urban Change in Pakistan*, Urban Change Working Paper 6, IIED, London.

13 Garza, G. (2002) *Urbanization of Mexico during the Twentieth Century*, Urban Change Working Paper 7, IIED, London.

14 For a discussion of this, see Golini, A., Said, M., Casacchia, O., Reynaud, C., Basso, S., Cassata, L. and Crisci, M. (2001) 'Migration and urbanization in Ethiopia, with special reference to Addis Ababa, Central Statistical Authority, Addis Ababa and Institute for Population Research, National Research Council (Irp-Cnr), Rome, Addis Ababa and Rome; accessed at www.irpps.cnr.it/etiopia/sito/progetto3.htm.

15 Satterthwaite (2005) op cit.

16 In the 2002 census, urban areas were defined as cities, towns and settlements (pueblos) (capitals of departments and municipalities) and some other populated places that were in the category colonia or condiminium and that had more than 2000 inhabitants – www.ine.gob.gt/content/consul_2/pob/censo2002.pdf.

17 For Cuba, urban centres are places with 2000 inhabitants or more, and places with fewer inhabitants but having paved streets, street lighting, piped water, sewage, a medical centre and educational facilities (United Nations, 2004, op cit).

18 United Nations (2004) op cit.

19 Garza (2002) op cit.

20 Owusu, G. (2005) 'Small towns in Ghana: Justifications for their promotion under Ghana's decentralisation programme', *African Studies Quarterly*, vol 8, no 2, pp48–68.

21 Afsar, R. (2002) *Urban change in Bangladesh*, Urban Change Working Paper 1, IIED, London.

22 Tacoli, C. (1998) 'Rural–urban interactions; a guide to the literature', *Environment and Urbanization*, vol 10, no 1, pp147–166; Tacoli, C. (1998), *Bridging the Divide: Rural–Urban Interactions and Livelihood Strategies*, Gatekeeper Series no 77, IIED Sustainable Agriculture and Rural Livelihoods Programme, London.

23 See many empirical studies summarized and discussed in Hardoy, J. E. and Satterthwaite, D. (eds) (1986) *Small and Intermediate Urban Centres: Their role in National and Regional Development in the Third World*, Hodder and Stoughton, London and Westview – especially Chapters 2–7.

24 Etienne, J. (1998) 'Formes de la demande et modes de gestion des services d'eau potable en Afrique subsaharienne: spécificité des "milieux semi-urbains"', PhD thesis, ENPC, Paris.

25 Hasan A. and Raza, M. (2002) *Urban change in Pakistan*, Urban Change Working Paper 6, IIED, London.

26 Visaria, P. (1997) 'Urbanization in India: An overview', in Jones, G. and Visaria, P. (eds) *Urbanization in Large Developing Countries*, Clarendon Press, Oxford, pp266–288.

27 http://english.people.com.cn/200405/19/eng20040519_143708.html.

28 http://houston.china-consulate.org/eng/nv/t140010.htm.

29 Zheng Xinli, deputy director of the Policy Research Office of the Central Commit-tee of the Communist Party of China, http://english.people.com.cn/200512/17/eng20051217_228778.html.

30 Liu, Shenghe, Xiubin Li, and Ming Zhang (2003) 'Scenario analysis on urbaniza-tion and rural–urban migration in China', International Institute for Applied Sys-tems Analysis, Vienna.

31 Chan, Kam Wing and Ying Hu (2003) 'Urbanization in China in the 1990s: New definition, different series, and revised trends', *The China Review*, vol 3, no 2, pp49–71; Liu et al (2003) op cit.

32 Ma, L. J. C. (2004) 'Economic reforms, urban spatial restructuring, and planning in China', *Progress in Planning*, vol 61, no 3, pp237–260; Ma, L. J. C. (forthcom-ing) 'Urban administrative restructuring, changing scale relations and local eco-nomic development in China', *Political Geography*, in press, corrected proof.

33 For summaries of how each nation defines urban centres, see United Nations (2004) op cit.

34 Visaria (1997) op cit.

35 Dyson, T. and Visaria, P. (2005) 'Migration and urbanization: Retrospect and pros-pects', in Dyson, T., Cassen, R. and Visaria, L. (eds) *Twenty-First Century India: Population, Economy, Human Development and the Environment*, Oxford University Press, Oxford, pp108–129.

36 Dyson and Visaria (2005) op cit.

37 Satterthwaite (2005) op cit.

38 However, there are at least two possible sources of error for cross-country compari-sons in these size categories. The first is the differences between nations in the ways that the boundaries of urban centres are defined – for instance, in some nations, defined 'too small' in relation to urban expansion, in other nations defined 'too large' as they include significant numbers of rural populations. The second is whether the populations of local government units within or close to major cities have been incorporated into the population of these large cities as metropolitan areas or urban agglomerations or reported as distinct urban centres in their own right. See the notes to Table 1.3 for more details.

39 For more details, see Satterthwaite (2005) op cit.

40 This is the case in Egypt, if settlements with 10,000–20,000 inhabitants are consid-ered urban.

41 The list of nations is restricted by the availability of census data that provide a list of all urban centres and their populations. The reader should also note the 'words of caution' listed at the end of Table 1.3.

42 1990 was the latest year for which a complete set of population statistics for urban cen-tres in China with 50,000 plus inhabitants was found; see www.citypopulations.de.

43 In 1999, France had 84 urban centres in this size class with 12.7 per cent of the national population; in 2001, England had 86 urban centres in this size class, with 14.4 per cent of the national population. For both of these nations, lists of urban agglomerations were used, not cities.

44 This size category of urban centres is also important in high-income nations; in England, in 2001, there were 20 urban centres in this size category with 10.7 per

cent of the population; in France in 1999, there were also 20 urban centres in this size category with 9.9 per cent of the population.

45 See Satterthwaite (2005) op cit. This often also reflects in part the nation's or region's agricultural economy, as the areas with the most prosperous agriculture often have among the most dynamic urban centres, which are markets and service centres for farmers and rural households.

46 There are exceptions – for instance, urban growth in places where retired people choose to live or in tourist resorts but, even here, the growth is largely due to the growth in enterprises there to meet the demand for goods and services generated by retired people and/or tourists. Advanced telecommunication systems and the internet also allow some spatial disconnect, as a proportion of those who work for city-based enterprises can work from locations outside the city (including working from homes that are outside the city); these may be growing in importance, but are unlikely to be significant in low- and middle-income nations. Many urban centres also have farmers and agricultural workers among their populations.

47 See tables at the back of *World Development Reports*, published by the World Bank.

48 In many nations, a significant proportion of the total value of agricultural production is within urban areas (from urban agriculture), but it may also be due in part to city boundaries encompassing large areas of agricultural land so the produce grown in what are clearly agricultural areas (with no urban characteristics) is counted as urban.

49 Satterthwaite, D. and Tacoli, C. (2003) *The Urban Part of Rural Development: The Role of Small and Intermediate Urban Centres in Rural and Regional Development and Poverty Reduction*, Rural–urban working papers series, no 9, IIED, London; for a detailed case study of this, see Manzanal, M. and Vapnarsky, C. (1986) 'The development of the Upper Valley of Rio Negro and its periphery within the Comahue Region, Argentina', in Hardoy, J. E. and Satterthwaite, D. (eds) *Small and Intermediate Urban Centres: Their role in Regional and National Development in the Third World*, Hodder and Stoughton, London and Westview, pp18–79.

50 See vol 10, no 1 (1998) and vol 15, no 1 (2003) of *Environment and Urbanization*, both of which were on rural–urban linkages. See also Tacoli, C. (1998) 'Bridging the divide: Rural–urban interactions and livelihood strategies', *Gatekeeper Series, no 77*, IIED, London.

51 See Satterthwaite and Tacoli (2003) op cit.

Part 2

Rural–Urban Linkages and Livelihood Transformations

Chapter 2

Survival and Accumulation Strategies at the Rural–Urban Interface in North-West Tanzania

Jonathan Baker

Introduction

Small towns as potential catalysts for rural development in Africa have not received the attention they deserve. Most development research has traditionally focused on the large and primate cities in Africa. In addition, much foreign aid has been directed to rural development in the narrowest sense, meaning agriculture, and this implies that rural change is an autonomous process that can be divorced from the urban component.[1]

This view of a dichotomous relationship between the rural and urban economies must be rejected as the two are interdependent and complementary. For example, the role of small towns may have a positive influence on rural development and agricultural productivity through the provision of a range of goods (agricultural inputs, consumer goods, and so on), urban cash flows and other forms of flows, and services (agricultural extension, welfare services, and the diffusion of innovation). In turn, rural hinterlands provide resources (such as food, payment for public services through taxation, labour, and demand for urban goods and services) that enable small towns to expand their economic and social functions.

Much rural income is not derived directly from agriculture but takes the form of off-farm and non-farm income generated by farm households, often in small rural towns. In some cases, probably as much as one-third of rural income in sub-Saharan Africa is derived from non-farm sources. It appears that in the African context, it is those rural households which are most adept at utilizing small town opportunities and exploiting urban niches, in addition to using agricultural land resources, that are most successful in ensuring household survival and pursuing accumulation strategies. By contrast, and at the risk of oversimplification, the least successful households are those which do not pursue such strategies or are, in other words, non-diversified. Much more research

Note: Reprinted from *Environment and Urbanization*, vol 7, no 1, Baker, J., 'Survival and accumulation strategies at the rural–urban interface in north-west Tanzania', copyright © (1995), with permission from IIED, London.

attention and policy consideration should be directed at this important and fascinating area of development. One writer has even suggested that '... few discussions of development can avoid referring implicitly or explicitly to rural–urban linkages. They lie at the heart of economic development and the structural transformation of the economy'.[2] This chapter provides an empirical contribution to this discussion. The main focus of the chapter is an investigation of the town of Biharamulo and four surrounding villages in Kagera Region in north-western Tanzania.[3] The objectives of the chapter are as follows: first, to understand the nature of village economies from a household perspective; second, to investigate the kinds of links village households have with the town of Biharamulo; third, to investigate the degree of economic differentiation between households within the villages. Finally, an attempt is made to analyse the types of urban and rural households that have adopted successful survival and accumulation strategies, and those which might be poor or, at least, vulnerable to poverty.

The setting and contexts

The town of Biharamulo

Biharamulo is the headquarter town for Biharamulo District, which is one of the six districts comprising Kagera Region. In 1993, the town had a population of about 20,000; the total population of the district is estimated at about 230,000. The growth of Biharamulo town has been strongly influenced by in-migration: in 1992, the urban growth rate was 5.0 per cent a year, of which 2.6 was attributable to natural increase and 2.4 per cent to in-migration. Consequently, the ethnic complexity of the town is very varied largely as a result of in-migration of people from different regions within Tanzania, as well as from neighbouring countries. Fifteen different ethnic groups are represented in the town, although the Subi (from within the district) and the Haya (from around Bukoba) account for nearly 20 per cent each of the total town population. Another 20 per cent are migrants from Rwanda, Uganda and Zaire. A surprisingly high number of households are headed by females. Of a total 1020 households in the town, 300 (29.4 per cent) are female headed. This compares with only 7.1 per cent of village households which are headed by women. What this indicates is that the town offers greater possibilities of employment for females, particularly in the informal service sector, although some independent women are also engaged in the urban formal economy, particularly in teaching and in district government. The town is centrally located within its district and is connected by major roads to Bukoba in the north, Burundi and Rwanda to the west and Mwanza (Tanzania's second largest city) to the east (Figure 2.1). A World Bank funded road upgrading scheme is currently underway, and connections with the main Mwanza highway have been greatly improved. As the district headquarters for Biharamulo District, the town is the seat of the District Commissioner and is an important administrative and control centre for the district. Consequently, a good deal of urban formal employment is in activities related to local government. In addition, a brigade of the Tanzanian army is garrisoned on the outskirts of the town, and this creates significant demands for town services and goods. Biharamulo also fulfils important

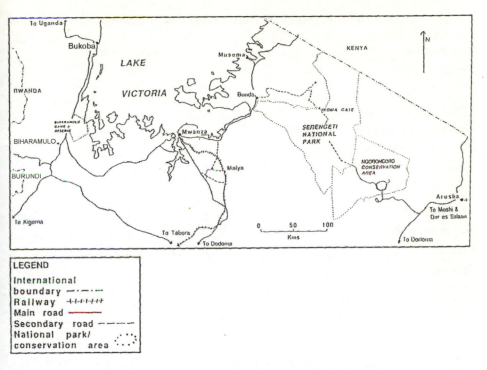

Figure 2.1 *The location of the town of Biharamulo*

market, service and transport functions. There are daily bus services to Bukoba and thrice-weekly bus connections to Mwanza, Ngara and Kigoma. The most common commercial links for the town are with Mwanza and Bukoba, although trade with neighbouring countries, particularly Burundi, is important for some imported consumer goods such as beer and cloth. Moreover, many trucks on their way to Bukoba, Burundi and Rwanda pass through the town and it has developed into an overnight stop, which has stimulated the development of a significant bar, prostitution and lodging sector. As will be demonstrated below, the town of Biharamulo offers a range of economic possibilities and niches for surrounding village populations.

As Table 2.1 illustrates, Biharamulo is overwhelmingly a service centre, and most business is concentrated in retailing or providing lodging, food and beverage services. Many businesses have a small turnover although exceptions are the petrol station, grain mills and butcher shops where daily turnover is high. There is little manufacturing activity, and what exists is concentrated in the small-scale micro-enterprise sector producing, for example, simple agricultural implements, household items such as furniture, and metal lamps and charcoal stoves using recycled materials. The town has a very good district hospital (run by the Ministry of Health in conjunction with a Catholic mission from The Netherlands), a number of primary schools and a secondary school. There is a newly built post and telecommunications office and a bank.

A sample of households in four villages surrounding Biharamulo was surveyed and social and economic profiles were drawn up. The villages are non-nucleated settlements

Table 2.1 *An inventory of economic activities in Biharamulo*

Type of activity	Biharamulo
General stores	80
Petrol station	1
Vehicle repair garages	2
Hotels and guest houses	9
Restaurants/snackbars/cafés	7
Bars	n/a
Grain mills	3
Carpentry workshops	6
Bicycle repairers	3
Butchers	4
Bakeries	n/a
Others	64
Total	179

with households widely dispersed. Three of the villages, Nyamahanga, Bisibo and Katoke, are located approximately 7km from the town, while Rusabya is 10km away. Walking, it will take 2–4 hours to reach Biharamulo, depending on the route taken, and on any goods carried. With the exception of Bisibo, all towns are located close to dry-weather roads. A few householders (particularly those who worked in Biharamulo) had bicycles and mopeds, which greatly eased the aggravation of distance.

All villages have their own elected councils which consist of not less than 15 and not more than 25 members, of whom 25 per cent must be women. The village executive officer is a paid employee of the District Council and is always the Secretary of the village council. Each village has a primary school, although facilities are poor. Bisibo and Rusabya lack village dispensaries, which obliges people requiring drugs and treatment to

Table 2.2 *Population profiles of the four survey villages*

Village Population (1993)	No of households	Population (1993)		
		Male	Female	Total
Nyamahanga	413	1047	1083	2130 (5.2)[a]
Katoke	361	1192	1086	2278 (6.3)[a]
Bisibo	543	977	1184	2161 (4.0)[a]
Rusabaya	476	1222	1473	2659 (5.6)[a]
Total	1793	4438	4826	9228

Note: [a] Represents mean household size.

visit Biharamulo or, alternatively, to depend on mobile medical teams which make regular visits. In Nyamahanga, the Finnish Pentecostal Mission runs, as part of its operations, a dispensary which serves the needs of the local village population, while in Katoke, a Catholic seminary provides similar services. The villages are largely ethnically homogeneous; 90 per cent of household members are of Subi ethnicity, the dominant group of the district. Although there has been some in-migration to the villages from other parts of Kagera Region, the overwhelming majority of the population were either born in the villages or moved to them from other rural areas in Biharamulo District. Of the 84 households surveyed, 57 heads of households and 47 spouses were born in their villages, 19 householders and 26 spouses were born in other rural areas of the district. Only five householders and two spouses were born elsewhere in Kagera Region, and two householders and three spouses came from other regions in Tanzania. One householder was born in Uganda but had migrated to the village of Nyamahanga 35 years ago. Unlike the more densely populated districts in the north of Kagera Region (particularly in rural Bukoba), land scarcity was not considered a problem generally by householders, and few cited lack of land as a problem. What was surprising, however, bearing in mind Tanzania's earlier experiment with rural socialism, was the very unequal distribution of agricultural land as is demonstrated by the data in Table 2.3. Eighty-two village households (97.6 per cent) owned land. The two households without access to land were both female headed. One worked as a barmaid cum prostitute in a village bar, while the other was a village community development worker who rented a house in the village.

The average amount of farmland per household was 7.4 acres in Rusabya, 3.4 in Nyamahanga, 3.1 in Katoke and 2.7 in Bisibo. These average figures mask, however, substantial variations as shown in Table 2.3, with the smallest landholding being 0.5 of an acre and the largest 100 acres. Of the 84 village households surveyed, 6 were headed by women; 5 were divorced and 1 was a widow. Four female headed households had access to land but had below average sized plots, ranging from 1 to 2 acres.

The most usual way of acquiring land was through inheritance, most commonly from the father's family. Fifty-eight householders (69.0 per cent) had obtained land in this way. In some cases, where insufficient family land was available through inherit-

Table 2.3 *The distribution of village household land (acres per household)*

Size in acres	No of households	% of total
No land	2	2.4
<1	2	2.4
1–2	17	20.2
2–3	22	26.2
3–4	18	21.4
4–5	7	8.3
5–10	14	16.7
>10	2	2.4
Total	84	100.0

ance, land could be acquired by applying to village councils for a plot. Ten householders (11.9 per cent) had obtained land in this manner on payment of a small fee (which varied between 1000 and 5000 TSh) and a tin of local banana beer *(rubisi)*! It was stated by informants that the amount of land allocated depended on the size of the applicant's household. Five households (5.9 per cent) from other parts of the district had been allocated land by village councils as a result of villagization in 1974, while eight immigrant households (9.5 per cent) had purchased land privately from other villagers. Land was purchased from households who had surplus land, or from those with money problems. In the villages, no surveyed households had been forced to sell land, and it is consequently impossible to say whether this was a common phenomenon. The price of land varied between the villages; in Rusabya an acre of land could be purchased for about 50,000 TSh, while in Nyamahanga, which is much drier and soil quality is poorer, the same amount would cost 20,000 TSh.

What most concerned villagers was the unreliability of rainfall, the cost and/or the unavailability of fertilizers and, in some cases, particularly in the village of Rusabya, the damage caused by wild pigs. The latter was something of a mixed blessing, however, as pig meat did provide a supplement to household protein requirements.

In terms of agricultural production, well over 90 per cent of households produced maize and beans, followed by bananas and cassava. All crops were grown for household consumption and marketing. It was stated that cassava was grown by all households as it could withstand a range of climatic extremes and acted as a kind of insurance crop when others failed. Bananas are a very valuable and versatile crop in the village, district and regional economies. Three kinds of bananas were grown: sweet bananas for eating *(bunana)*, plantains for cooking *(ebitoke)*, and beer bananas *(embele)*.

The cash crop is coffee but this was grown by only 20 per cent of households. All of it is marketed through village coffee cooperative societies. Smith,[4] in his study of Muleba District, adjacent to Biharamulo District in the north, reports that smallholder farmers are 'exiting' from coffee production in favour of the cultivation of beer bananas for a number of reasons. These include, inter alia, the longer time required to mature and harvest coffee trees, and the resistance of banana trees to insect attack, in contrast to coffee. Banana trees produce year round and consequently provide a steady flow of cash on a regular basis. In comparison, coffee is harvested once a year and is a tedious and labour-intensive procedure. Whether a similar process of 'exiting' from coffee to beer banana production is taking place in the survey villages is impossible to judge. However, what is clear is that a significant number of village households are dependent on bananas and banana alcohol as an income source.

The production, consumption and marketing of local beer (from beer bananas and millet) and spirits (distilled from banana beer) form an integral part of the economic, cultural and social life in the survey villages and Biharamulo and, indeed, throughout Kagera Region.[5] The most common kind of beer produced was from bananas *(rubisi)*. Millet and sorghum beer *(pombe)* were less common as few households (only eight) cultivated either grain. However, some households reported buying millet or sorghum to produce beer. The production of beer for commercial purposes is relatively easy and is, without doubt, profitable as the following examples illustrate. For a non-millet producing household, 20kg of millet grain can be purchased for 1000 TSh. Apart from the input of millet, production of *pombe* requires only water and labour to prepare a mash prior to fermentation. The final product can be sold for 1600 TSh, a mark-up of more than 60 per cent. As most households grow bananas, the production of *rubisi* beer is presumably even more profitable; 20 litres of beer sells for 900 TSh. However, the most lucrative alcohol of all is derived from the distillation of *rubisi* beer for the production of *gongo*, a highly potent and illegal spirit.

Twenty litres of *rubisi* beer with a retail value of 900 TSh would, after distilling once, produce 10 litres of *gongo* with a retail value of 300–400 TSh per litre, or 3000–4000 TSh for 10 litres. Premium grade *gongo*, which is distilled twice, sells for at least 500 TSh a litre although the liquid loss is considerably greater than with only one distillation. Even households which do not cultivate beer bananas do produce *gongo*. One respondent stated that he purchased 60 litres of *rubisi* beer a month for 2700 TSh. After distilling twice he obtained 20 litres of high-quality spirit which he sold for 500 TSh a litre or 10,000 TSh in total, resulting in a profit of 7300 TSh, assuming firewood is gathered and labour and transport costs are not included.

The equipment used to distil alcohol is fairly rudimentary and can be constructed from local materials: large ceramic pots and connecting bamboo pipes, and a continuous fire to maintain the distillation process. Because *gongo* production is illegal, distillation takes place well away from farmsteads and the eyes of the police although presumably with the knowledge of the village councils. Revealingly, an important reason given by respondents as to the advantages of living in their village was precisely the fact that the police rarely 'snooped around', in contrast to Biharamulo town.

All or most village households produce some local beer, whether from millet and sorghum or bananas. Many informants stated that they consumed alcohol daily, often in village groups, and that this was often arranged on a 10-cell basis. However, the increasing commercialization of alcohol consumption has meant the opening up of a very important income-generating avenue for many households.

A few households had adopted specialized agricultural production techniques and had created marketing niches in Biharamulo. In Rusabya, one householder who had been educated as an agricultural extension officer had used his training and skills to cultivate tomatoes, onions, carrots, cabbage, paw-paws and passion fruit specifically for the urban market. Two farmers were producing and marketing milk commercially; one based in Nyamahanga supplied the orphanage at the Finnish Pentecostal Mission with milk on a daily basis, while another in Katoke village regularly supplied milk to the two best hotels in Biharamulo.

While agriculture is a vital element in the village economies, the majority (83 per cent) of households depended upon a variety of income-generating activities as survival and accumulation strategies. In many cases, non-farm and off-farm activities (such as the production of alcohol and craftwork for marketing locally and in Biharamulo, as well as employment and asset ownership in town) were essential components in the household economies of these villages.

The nature of rural–urban interaction in the study area

Data were collected on aspects of interaction of village householders with the town of Biharamulo. Table 2.4 indicates the main advantages and disadvantages of village life as perceived by villagers.

What is perhaps more surprising was the number of village householders who preferred living in the village than in the town. In response to the question 'Would you like to live in Biharamulo, rather than in this village?' only four (4.7 per cent) out of 84 household heads replied in the affirmative. Of these four, three were carpenters who felt a Biharamulo location would benefit the marketing of their furniture. The remaining householder preferred Biharamulo because of the lack of welfare services in his village. However, for the overwhelming majority of village householders, urban life was not attractive as it was too expensive, whereas rural living was considered much cheaper and people could also easily produce their food needs. A few respondents thought that town life was hard compared to that of the village, while one respondent expressed the view that village life was easy!

Whereas most villagers preferred rural life, the majority of householders did, however, have frequent contacts with Biharamulo and more than 90 per cent visited the town more than once a month, with 57 per cent visiting at least once a week. What this suggests is that rural people, at least in the context of the study area, exploit the benefits of both the rural and urban sectors without having the major disadvantages associated with living in the latter, for example, the higher living costs. The reasons for interacting with the town were many and varied. The main reasons are summarized in Table 2.5.

Table 2.4 *Village household perceptions of the advantages and disadvantages of living in their villages*

ADVANTAGES:

- Land availability always possible to produce some food
- Free firewood
- Free housing
- Lack of crime, no robbery
- No interference from the police – no hassle, no bribe payments

DISADVANTAGES:

- Lack of good infrastructure: dispensaries, poor quality of primary schools, poor village roads
- High incidence of disease, particularly malaria
- Lack of good drinking water
- Lack of shops
- Lack of modern recreation facilities, e.g. cinemas

Table 2.5 *The nature of interaction of rural dwellers with the town of Biharamulo*

- Employment in town: a few people commute to the town on a daily basis for work. Some work for the District Council on a permanent basis, while others are temporarily engaged as labourers on construction sites, and on road maintenance and construction projects
- Ownership of income-generating assets in town: a few villagers own or rent shops and kiosks, while others own houses which they rent out
- Marketing of rural produce at the town market and through shops: includes crops, livestock produce (eggs, chickens, goats), *pombe*, and *gongo* (illegal). Selling in town is often preferred to selling in local village markets because better prices are obtained in town, although transport costs, time and market fees have to be considered. Purchasing of food and other household commodities in town: food (for example, rice), sugar, salt on a weekly basis; paraffin on a weekly basis; clothing, shoes, agricultural implements purchased infrequently, often yearly
- To visit health facilities and chemist shops: Biharamulo Hospital is considered by villagers to be far superior to village health facilities. As the villages of Bisibo and Rusabya lack dispensaries, many villagers are obliged to visit Biharamulo to obtain medicines and treatment
- Socialization: the social aspects of coming to town should not be understated, and this is often combined with a visit to the market and shops, or after work. Men (both rural and urban) are frequent visitors to the many bars
- Educational facilities: all four villages have primary schools although village children proceeding to secondary level are obliged to attend a school in Biharamulo
- Access to bus and truck transport to Bukoba, Mwanza, Arusha and Dar es Salaam

Urban and rural economic differentiation

Biharamulo town and the four villages exhibited striking economic differentiation. Much conventional wisdom informs us that rural populations are often less economically differentiated than town dwellers and that urban populations have a generally superior economic status to that of their rural counterparts. However, data from the urban and village surveys show that both sets of populations are highly differentiated in terms of reported incomes, household expenditure, size of landholding, as well as having access to opportunities for exploiting urban and rural resources. Table 2.6 provides data on urban and rural household incomes.

Deriving accurate income figures and reconstructing household budgets is complicated and extremely time-consuming. The figures presented here are, however, considered to be of the right magnitude although to quantify the value of barter trade, 'free goods' such as firewood and meat from game animals, as well as remittances into households from the outside, may understate the level of household income and consumption. In Biharamulo, the richest household had an income of 103,750 TSh per month, while the poorest received only 950 TSh per month, showing that the richest household had 109 times more income than the poorest! The rich household had a well diversified income-generating structure which included farmland, a wholesale shop, and employment in Biharamulo hospital. By contrast, the poor household comprised only an

Table 2.6 *Household income per month in the town of Biharamulo and the four survey villages*

No of households in income class (TSh)	Biharamulo	Nyamahanga	Katoke	Bisibo	Rusabya
Less than 10,000	6	6	7	3	6
10,000–19,999	4	11	10	15	10
20,000–29,999	5	2	2	2	3
30,000–49,999	7	1	1	–	3
50,000–69,000	2	–	–	–	–
70,000–100,000	–	–	–	–	–
More than 100,000	1	–	–	–	1[a]
Total	25	20	20	20	23
Mean household income per month	29,253	14,551	14,101	13,780	16,653

Note: [a] The income for this household (of TSh 300,000) has been omitted from the calculation of village mean income.

elderly widower, with no other household support, and a small house garden which provided insufficient income for a livelihood; consequently, this man was obliged to work as a casual labourer in town to supplement his meagre income from farming. In the four villages, income differentials, although not as striking as the example above, were nevertheless considerable. In Nyamahanga, the household with the lowest income earned 4400 TSh per month, while the richest earned 45,521 TSh: a 10.3 times differential between the richest and poorest. In Katoke, the poorest earned 5700 TSh, the richest 31,300 TSh, a differential of 5.5 times; in Bisibo, the poorest earned 5600 TSh, the richest 20,800 TSh, a differential of 3.7 times; and in Rusabya, the poorest earned 6516 TSh, the richest up to 300,000 TSh; a differential of 46 times. In the latter village, the richest household was headed by a herbalist, who owned 100 acres of productive farmland. This household was the richest of all households surveyed in both the four villages and in Biharamulo. As an illustration of its wealth, it is worth noting that the income of this household was approximately 80 per cent of the combined incomes of the 22 other households in the Rusabya survey!

The question which needs addressing, and which is a central issue in this paper, is why does such differentiation exist? As Evans reveals in his excellent survey of the literature, much has to do with resource endowments of individual households but also with the way that households are successful with income diversification strategies. The data collected for this study show that the most successful households are those which are characterized by multi-activity and risk-spreading. In the context of the study area, this is achieved by urban and rural households alike exploiting rural and urban opportunities simultaneously. The least successful and poorer households are generally those which are non-diversified and/or which do not attempt to maximize the utilization of rural–urban resources. Table 2.7 presents the main income sources for urban and rural households.

Table 2.7 *Sources of household income (by main categories) in Biharamulo and the four survey villages*

	Biharamulo			Four villages		
	N	%	Mean income[b]	N	%	Mean income[b]
Crop production and agricultural labour	1	4.0	950	7	8.5	7148
Crop production only[a]	4	16.0	13,340	14	17.0	10,115
Crop and alcohol production	1	4.0	10,710	32	39.0	14,588
Crop production and non-farm income	14	56.0	36,132	26	31.7	19,392
No crop production, all non-farm income	5	20.0	32,096	3	3.7	17,022
Totals	25	100.0	29,253	82	100.0	14,817

Note: [a] Includes livestock, if any.
[b] Income in TSh per month. Data on the richest household have been excluded from the calculation of this table.

Table 2.7 reveals the central importance of agriculture to residents of both Biharamulo and the four surrounding villages. In Biharamulo, 80 per cent of surveyed households derived all or part of their income from farm produce. In total, income from farm sales represented 70 per cent of all urban household income. Two households had farms in the vicinity of Biharamulo, seven had home gardens (which because of urban land planning regulations could not exceed three-quarters of an acre) and 11 had both a home garden and a farm outside the town. No data were collected on the size of farms owned by urban dwellers.

In the villages, only three households did not produce marketable crops; two were women (referred to earlier) and one a soldier who had recently been transferred to the Biharamulo garrison from Iringa Region and who had purchased agricultural land in Rusabya village. Livestock and livestock produce made insignificant contributions to total farm sales, although eggs and chickens were marketed. There were, however, two farmers with dairy cattle who produced milk commercially (see above).

Poverty and wealth: The contexts

Farm income plus labour sales

Households with little land supplemented household income by selling labour and these households form an extremely vulnerable category. The poorest category of households were those which made a living from sales of farm produce, supplemented by sales of labour to neighbouring farms. As a group, these households have little land (an average of 1.7 acres), tend to have elderly household heads (the oldest was 80), either have no education or only primary standard, and additionally may be divorced or widowed. The latter characteristic means that divorced women and widowed men (the usual pattern) have little or no support in doing the important labour tasks traditionally reserved for the other sex. While most of the labour tasks undertaken by these households relate to agricultural work (digging with a hoe is a common activity), some said that they collected firewood for other households. The payment for agricultural work is a meagre 100 TSh per day and, of course, demand for agricultural labour is highly seasonal. This category of households may be considered as survivors rather than having any kind of well thought-out survival strategy. One respondent, a man of 55, probably epitomized the apparent hopelessness of this category when he stated 'I am waiting for death'.

Farming-only households: A high-risk category

Only 14 village households and four in Biharamulo relied entirely on crop sales as the single source of household income. Crops marketed included beans, maize, bananas, sweet potatoes and, very infrequently, groundnuts and tomatoes. There was an insignificant amount of specialization regarding crops grown and little attempt to grow high-value produce such as horticultural crops. There were two farming households which were exceptions to this lack of specialization – one in Nyamahanga and the other in Biharamulo, with a farm outside the town. The Nyamahanga farmer was referred to earlier in this paper. He sold milk to the Nyamahanga Mission orphanage and, in addition, tomatoes and onions to the district prison in Nyamahanga, and in Biharamulo. His monthly income of 17,900 TSh was, by far, the highest of any village farming-only household. The Biharamulo farmer grew bananas and coffee (the only coffee cultivator of any rural or urban farming-only household) and was in the process of purchasing an additional 10 acres of land for timber production (for construction and fuelwood) to supply the Biharamulo market. This farmer was obviously very business oriented and this was reflected in a household monthly income of just under 26,000 TSh.

It is clear that farming-only households generally are characterized by conservatism and an absence of dynamism which might suggest that they have adopted a risk-aversion strategy. However, on closer inspection, this argument is not tenable for the simple reason that relying on only crop income can prove risky and even disastrous in the event of a poor harvest, making them highly susceptible to the vagaries of rainfed agriculture.

According to district council agricultural officers and elderly respondents, there has been drought in the district every 10 years since at least 1944. During the period of fieldwork in November 1993, villagers were very worried about the lack of precipitation in what was the main rainy season, and their fears were subsequently realized when the rains did, in fact, fail. Farming-only households are consequently a vulnerable and high-risk group, likely to face problems of temporary poverty.

Households combining alcohol with crop production: A more secure category

Households producing and marketing a combination of crops and locally produced alcohol comprised 39 per cent of all village households. One crop/alcohol household was surveyed in Biharamulo (representing 4 per cent of the urban sample). No *gongo* was apparently produced in the town. However, many more village households produced alcohol commercially (exclusively those with non-farm income sources) but income from alcohol as a percentage of total household income was smaller than the above figure indicates. In total, 43 households (52 per cent) produced some alcohol commercially, with 26 producing *pombe* and *rubisi*, 13 producing primarily *gongo*, and four producing both kinds of beverages. All villages, except Nyamahanga, produced both beer and *gongo*. In Nyamahanga, only three households produced beer, none *gongo*. The explanation for the low commercial production figure for Nyamahanga may certainly be related to the evangelizing influence of the Finnish Pentecostal Mission.

For the 14 crop/alcohol producing households, alcohol sales made significant contributions to total income; for example, in one household *gongo* sales accounted for 78 per cent of total income, while in another, beer accounted for 46 per cent. The production of beer and spirit was defined by a sexual division of labour. All beer production was undertaken by women, all *gongo* production by men. There were three main commercial outlets for selling alcohol: from individual households, in village bars, and bars in Biharamulo. No data were collected on the relative importance of these three outlets. Alcohol retailed in Biharamulo fetched a higher price than in the villages. Twenty litres of *rubisi* beer sold for 900 TSh in town bars, while in the villages the same quantity only sold for 600 TSh. Thus, the incentive to sell in town was considerable. It was also reported that some village *gongo*, because of its value and transportability, was marketed away from Biharamulo, even as far as Bukoba town, although this related to sales of premium quality spirit. Because of the illicit nature of *gongo*, care was needed in its disposal. Some producers reported bringing it to Biharamulo, where it was sold in particular bars early in the morning or late at night to avoid detection by the police. Larger-scale producers also sold *gongo* directly to middlemen with pick-up trucks who purchased 25-litre jerrycan amounts at the farm. However, it is difficult to understand how such a trade was kept secret from the police but most likely it was tolerated in return for bribes.

The commercialization of locally produced alcohol has meant that it has become an important source of income for some village households. Unlike crop-only households, which are vulnerable, households combining crop and alcohol sales are more secure and are assured of a fairly constant flow of cash to meet necessary household expenditures and to ensure survival. In the absence of longitudinal data, it is impossible to determine whether this kind of household uses income for purposes of accumulation, such as purchasing more land or investing in off-farm activities. For female headed households, however, it does provide an opportunity to supplement income and enhance the security of the household, as can be illustrated by the fact that five of the six female headed households derived a part of their income from beer production.

Rural–urban straddler households as successful accumulators

The most economically successful and secure group of households are those which combine crop production and marketing with a variety of non-farm and off-farm income-generating activities. Non-farm production refers to activities which are carried out on the farm but which are not related to crop production, for example, furniture and brick-making for marketing in both urban and rural markets. Off-farm production refers to activities carried out away from the farm, and includes village school teachers, village medical personnel, road construction and maintenance workers, administrative, clerical and army personnel working in Biharamulo, and ownership of urban assets such as a shop or rooms for renting. Through processes of risk aversion, income diversification and multi-activity, straddler households are successful accumulators who generate wealth which is used, inter alia, for purchasing more land, acquiring more urban assets or improving the value of existing assets (for example, through the expansion of shop premises or increasing the range of goods stocked), and sending children to private schools or for private tuition.

The upshot of these kinds of investments is to increase the wealth-creating foundation of the household, as well as to enhance its security. It is difficult to determine whether any of the above sources of accumulation are given priority. However, in situations of increasing land scarcity, where the acquisition of extra land is problematic (as, for example, in rural areas of Bukoba in northern Kagera), investments would need to be made for improving the productivity of the existing land and/or shifting to more lucrative crops, in acquiring urban assets or emphasizing the education of children. Investing in the education of children is obviously a long-term and relatively expensive strategy. Moreover, given the great uncertainties surrounding formal sector employment opportunities for school leavers in Tanzania and elsewhere in Africa, it is possible that parents will increasingly see no advantage in making such an unprofitable kind of investment.

Conclusions

This paper has attempted to highlight aspects of rural–urban interaction between the district headquarter town of Biharamulo and four surrounding villages in Kagera Region, north-western Tanzania. While agriculture is the mainstay and dynamo of the district economy, it was shown that for many village households non-farm and off-farm economic activities, in addition to agricultural land, are central components in household security and accumulation strategies. Moreover, for urban dwellers, access to agricultural land, in addition to urban employment, is an important element in household diversification strategies.

The discussion was contextualized within a framework which attempted to identify those households which would most likely be poor or, at least, vulnerable to poverty. Poor and vulnerable-to-poverty households were identified as those being economically non-diversified. These were of two types. First, those with small areas of land, who were obliged to sell their labour to other farmers. Second, crop-only households with no off-farm or non-farm income-generating sources, where a poor harvest could have severe implications for the economic viability of the household.

By contrast, more secure rural and urban households adopted a range of diversification strategies involving risk-spreading by having one foot based in rural activities and one based in urban activities.

The results of this research raise two issues for further investigation. First, would the interaction of village households with a town be less frequent and less beneficial (for example, fewer off- and non-farm income sources) if the villages had been located further away? Second, how important are remittances to poor households in ensuring survival, and to richer households in sustaining accumulation?

Notes

1   Baker, J. and Claeson, C.-F. (1990) 'Introduction' in Baker, J. (ed) *Small Town Africa: Studies in Rural-Urban Interaction*, Scandinavian Institute of African Studies, Uppsala, Sweden.
2   Evans, H. E. (1990) *Rural-Urban Linkages and Structural Transformation*, Discussion Paper (Report INU 71), Infrastructure and Urban Development Department, World Bank, Washington, DC.
3   The data for Biharamulo were collected between January and March 1993 as part of a study of three north Tanzanian towns for the Swedish International Development Authority (Sida). See Baker, J. and Mwaiselage, A. A. (1993) 'Three-town study in Tanzania', report prepared for the Infrastructure Division, Sida, March. The data for the village surveys were collected during November 1993. Interview schedules were administered to a structured sample of 25 households in Biharamulo. In each village, 20 households were selected for investigation although in one village (Rusabya) 24 households were interviewed. In addition, data were obtained from district council and village council authorities, as well as from more informal interviews with rural and urban entrepreneurs. In March 1993, the official exchange rate was US$1:330 Tanzanian Shillings (TSh), while in November 1993, it was US$1:440 TSh.
4   Smith, C. D. (1987) 'Smallholder farming in Kagera Region, Tanzania: Constraints to coffee production', *Labour, Capital and Society*, vol 20, no 2, November.
5   For a discussion of brewing activities in the northern part of Kagera Region, see reference 4; also, Smith, C. D. and Stevens, L. (1988) 'Farming and income-generation in the female-headed smallholder household: The case of a Haya village in Tanzania', *Canadian Journal of African Studies*, vol 22, no 3.

Chapter 3

Changing Rural–Urban Linkages in Mali, Nigeria and Tanzania

Mahmoud Bah, Salmana Cissé, Bitrina Diyamett,
Gouro Diallo, Fred Lerise, David Okali, Enoch Okpara,
Janice Olawoye and Cecilia Tacoli

Introduction

In the past two decades, economic crisis and reform have affected both rural and urban African populations. Small farmers' production has been negatively affected by the cost of agricultural inputs and consumer goods rising faster than the prices of agricultural produce. This cost–price squeeze has created a high-risk environment which makes it difficult for small farmers to compete on domestic and international markets. Urban incomes have fallen following retrenchments of public sector workers and restrictions on wage levels, which have affected both formal sector workers and the informal sector activities which depend largely on their demand.

Increases in food prices and service charges, cuts in public expenditure – especially health and education – and in infrastructure expenditure have been felt particularly by low-income groups. This has resulted in changes in livelihood strategies along two main lines: a widespread increase in mobility accompanied by strong social and economic links with home areas, which depend on migrants' remittances but also provide them with safety nets and social identity; and high levels of multi-activity, with most households and individuals combining farming with non-farm activities and, especially among younger generations in rural and peri-urban areas, a trend towards moving out of farming altogether in the long term.

This chapter considers the nature and scope of rural–urban linkages and how they are affected by variations in socio-economic, political, cultural, historical and geographical contexts, both between and within nations. It draws on case studies in central and northern Mali, south-eastern Nigeria and southern and northern Tanzania (Box 3.1

Note: Reprinted from *Environment and Urbanization*, vol 15, no 1, Bah, M., Cissé, S., Diyamett, B., Diallo, G., Lerise, F., Okali, D., Okpara, E., Olawoye, J. and Tacoli, C., 'Changing rural–urban linkages in Mali, Nigeria and Tanzania', April, pp13–24, copyright © (2003) with permission from IIED, London.

Box 3.1 *The case studies*

The case study locations were:

- the town of Himo, in northern Tanzania, and two rural settlements in its proximity;
- the town of Lindi in southern Tanzania, again with two villages in the surrounding region;
- two peri-urban settlements around Bamako, Mali's capital city, and two similar settlements around Mopti, an important Malian secondary urban centre; and
- the intermediate urban centre of Aba, in south-eastern Nigeria, and five smaller centres in its region ranging from medium-sized villages to small towns.

All the case studies used a combination of tools to explore how different groups of households and individuals rely on rural–urban linkages for their livelihoods, and the differences between them.

Qualitative and participatory tools, including mapping, wealth ranking, seasonality and Venn diagrams were used in the first phase of each case study to map out the nature and scale of rural–urban interactions in the different locations. In the Tanzanian case study, the team also used intra-household matrices and mobility/migration matrices. After a first round of general meetings, some tools were used with homogenous focus groups based on the combination of gender, age and wealth.

Interviews with key informants were also conducted to gather additional information. The second phase of the case studies consisted of commodity chain analyses for selected products and, in Mali and Tanzania, a small questionnaire survey. Review workshops were held throughout the duration of the projects to validate findings and develop key questions for the following phase of fieldwork.

Detailed reports for each case study are available as working papers in the *Rural–Urban Interactions and Livelihood Strategies Series*, IIED, London, as follows:

- Diyamett, B., Diyamett, M., James, J. and Mabala, R. (2001) 'The case of Himo and its region, northern Tanzania', Working Paper 1.
- Kibadu, A., Lerise, F., Mbutolwe, E. and Mushi, N. (2001) 'The case of Lindi and its region, southern Tanzania', Working Paper 2.
- Diyamett, B., Diyamett, M., James, J., Kibadu, A., Lerise, F., Mabala, R., Mbutolwe, E. and Mushi, N. (2001) 'Exploring rural–urban interactions in Tanzania: A critical review of the methods and tools used', Working Paper 3.
- Okali, D., Okpara, E. and Olawoye, J. (2001) 'The case of Aba and its region, south-eastern Nigeria', Working Paper 4.
- Groupe Recherche/Actions pour le Développement (2001) 'Potentialités et conflits dans les zones péri-urbaines: Le cas de Bamako au Mali', Working Paper 5.
- Groupe Recherche/Actions pour le Développement (2001) 'Potentialités et conflits dans les zones péri-urbaines: Le cas de Mopti au Mali', Working Paper 6.
- Tacoli, C. (2002) 'Changing rural–urban interactions in sub-Saharan Africa and their impact on livelihoods: A summary', Working Paper 7.

All the working papers and related briefing papers can be downloaded from www.iied.org/pubs/search.php?s=RUWP&x=Y

includes a list of these studies). It is not intended as an overall account of rural–urban interactions in sub-Saharan Africa, but rather as a discussion of the main factors that underlie current transformations in rural–urban linkages in these five relatively different contexts. The case studies focus on the ways in which rural–urban linkages underpin and affect livelihoods in the study locations. This involves attention to the changes in the live-lihood strategies of different groups, and to the reasons underlying these changes. These, in turn, may vary depending on location, household wealth and status, and individuals' gender, age and ethnicity. These characteristics are likely to affect access to assets such as: land and water; education, skills and health; credit, transport and markets. Social assets are especially important, since they often mediate access to material assets. In the context of rural–urban linkages, they include migrant networks and social relations between rural producers and urban-based traders. It is also important to understand intra-household dynamics and the relations between genders and between generations, since these often reveal a great deal about processes of social and cultural transformation.

Farming systems and urban expansion

For much of Africa's rural population, farming is still the primary activity. Changes in the scale and nature of rural–urban linkages and their relevance to the livelihoods of different groups are thus largely related to transformations in the agricultural sector. Farming is affected by access to natural resources, especially land and water, financial capital and information on market prices and fluctuations. Access is also mediated by a combination of factors, ranging from national policies (e.g. land tenure systems and agricultural policies), village-level characteristics (such as population density and natural resource features), differences between households (e.g. wealthier and vulnerable, migrant and indigenous) and within households (on the basis of gender and genera-tional status).

Access to land and water

Mali, Nigeria and Tanzania have complex and evolving land tenure systems. The main characteristic is the co-existence of different types of rights. The state is the overall trus-tee of all land within the national boundaries and has absolute authority over its alloca-tion. At the local level, there is often a mixture of customary and statutory rights. In broad terms, customary rights (land management and allocation by traditional authori-ties such as village chiefs and village councils) are more likely to apply to rural areas, whereas statutory rights (formalized land titling and registration) are more likely to dominate in urban centres. However, formal and informal market transactions are increasingly important under both systems,[1] especially in peri-urban areas where the two systems often overlap. Under customary tenure, non-landowners can access land through a variety of secondary rights arrangements, ranging from sharecropping to tenancy to borrowing of land. These arrangements are especially important for low-income farmers and for migrants, who are often excluded from land allocation under customary tenure, but are increasingly under strain as land becomes scarcer and its value increases.

Box 3.2 *The constraints and benefits of urban proximity: Peri-urban farming in Mali*

In northern Mali, urban residents have introduced modern farming equipment such as tractors and mills, which the villagers could not afford to purchase and which are no longer provided by agricultural extension services. Demand for waged agricultural labour by urban farmers with no time or family labour has also increased employment opportunities for small farmers, although this can be at the expense of their own farm work. Hence, while there are certain benefits in urban residents' entry into peri-urban farming, there is also a strong tendency for small farmers with limited access to credit and labour to move entirely out of farming their own land and become waged labourers, or migrate.

By contrast, in the village of Baguinéda in central Mali, secondary rights are still widely practised. This allows small-scale farmers to hire migrant labour in exchange for temporary rights to cultivate their own plots. The system is highly structured, with specific days of the week allocated to work as labourers and others to work on the borrowed land. Two aspects are central to the functioning of the system: first, land tenure in the village is almost exclusively customary and controlled by the village council, allowing for secondary rights allocation. Second, the strong demand from the nearby capital, Bamako, for horticultural produce in which the village specializes makes cultivation of even a small plot relatively profitable, and therefore attractive for migrants.

Especially in peri-urban areas, small farmers' access to land is subject to a number of pressures. Even in areas under customary tenure, outright purchase rather than allocation is increasingly frequent and, in many cases, buyers are urban residents who invest in commercial farming and land speculation. This is the case in the case study areas in southern Tanzania and in Mali, where middle- and higher-income urban residents tend to displace undercapitalized small farmers. Severely restricted access to credit following liberalization in Tanzania,[2] and credit recovery problems and mismanagement of parastatal institutions in Mali and Nigeria, increases small farmers' vulnerability and often their willingness to move out of farming (Box 3.2).

Access to markets and the role of traders

Poor physical infrastructure has far-reaching consequences for producer prices and, in the long run, affects production and activity patterns. Small producers and poor farmers are often much more affected than large farmers by this (Box 3.3) and may be forced to abandon farming their own land and turn to waged agricultural employment and migration.

Where physical access to markets is not a problem, access to information can be equally important (Box 3.4).

But as state extension services become increasingly underfunded and officers rarely visit the rural areas, informal networks spanning rural and urban settlements have become the most effective information channels used by producers. However, these generally benefit larger farmers who have good city connections, and disadvantage poor farmers with few such connections.

Box 3.3 *The impact of poor infrastructure on farming*

In Tanzania, collection, transport and sale of previously controlled cash crops has been liberalized since the mid-1980s. Cashew nuts from the southern region are primarily grown for export, and a small number of private companies control their purchase, collection and transport to the main shipping port of Mtwara. Road infrastructure in the area is extremely poor, making transport costs prohibitive. Although private companies are only allowed to buy the nuts from farmers' cooperatives in designated locations, in practice these are out of reach for small farmers, who can hardly afford transport costs. Smallholders tend to sell directly to traders, an arrangement which puts buyers in a strong bargaining position and weakens producers' ability to negotiate prices. It also makes it difficult for local government to maintain effective control of the quantities traded and collect taxes from traders, despite this being a major source of revenue.

In southeastern Nigeria, road and transport infrastructure is generally good, but some remote settlements, such as Ndi Ebe, can be cut off at certain times of the year, when soil erosion combined with heavy rains can wipe away feeder roads. Only larger-scale farmers have the means to hire tractors to transport produce to markets. Small farmers who cannot afford this expense often prefer to seek employment as wage labourers on large commercial farms or abandon their farms altogether and migrate to urban centres or to other rural settlements.

Box 3.4 *How lack of market information affects producers in northern Tanzania*

In the past few years, farmers in the plains around the town of Himo have increasingly invested in the production of tomatoes. Most farmers grow their crop after the rainy season, when production costs are lower; however, this results in a glut in both the local and national markets, and prices can be as much as 10 times lower than during the rainy season, when production costs are higher but demand outstrips supply. The few farmers who grow tomatoes during the rainy season rely on a network of social relations, from local traders to relatives and petty traders based in a number of urban centres in Tanzania. The information they gather on prices allows them to negotiate with local traders.

Farmers' limited access to formal credit means that traders have an increasingly important role in this respect. However, with the exception of export crops, trade in agricultural produce is not usually controlled by large, well-capitalized traders. Especially for horticultural produce, the marketing system in much of sub-Saharan Africa is dominated by small-scale traders, even in the case of wholesale dealers. They provide a vital link to urban markets for small and diversified production flows that cannot be handled efficiently by large-scale trading organizations.[3] In West Africa, traders are often women who tend to establish personal relations with both producers and retailers. In this way, financial exchanges are embedded in wider social relations, which provide the basic rules of trust needed for commercial transactions. The major problem confronting most of these traders is limited financial liquidity, which makes them and, as a result, those who

---

Box 3.5 *The role of traders in central Mali*

In central Mali, traders are an important source of credit for horticultural producers. However, despite strong demand from the nearby capital, Bamako, this informal credit system is prone to a number of risks. The most important one, linked to the highly perishable nature of the produce, is loss due to the almost complete lack of processing and storage facilities. Since wholesale traders often also sell to retailers on credit, they tend to absorb losses at both the transport and retail levels. This, in turn, affects their financial liquidity and their capacity to offer credit to producers. This vicious circle results in sharp decreases in horticultural production around Bamako, despite strong urban demand and increasing producer prices.

---

depend on them for credit, vulnerable to market losses which, in turn, are compounded by poor infrastructure (Box 3.5).

Occupational diversification and mobility

Non-farm income is increasingly important in the livelihoods of African rural households. Survey data on the proportion of income derived from non-agricultural sources give an average range of 30–40 per cent, excluding Southern Africa where it can be as high as 80–90 per cent,[4] to more recent findings of 60–80 per cent.[5] Occupational diversification is defined here broadly as non-agricultural income-generating activities undertaken by rural residents, and farming by urban residents.

There is a dynamic dimension to diversification, which is increasing in all the case study locations. This is reflected by higher levels of multi-activity among younger generations than among their parents.

The increase in non-farm rural employment can sometimes be triggered by agricultural growth and increasing demand for manufactured goods and services by wealthier populations. However, the case studies show a bleaker picture where, with the possible exception of Baguinéda in central Mali, the small-scale farming sector is negatively affected by severely limited access to credit, markets for agricultural produce show serious shortcomings and land shortages are a growing concern. Especially for younger people in the rural areas, farming is an increasingly unattractive option. At the same time, emerging opportunities facilitate income diversification. For example, domestic trade liberalization in Tanzania since 1984 has increased opportunities for small-scale trade; manufacturing industries have developed in peri-urban areas of south-eastern Nigeria; and there is urban growth and the related demand for service workers in northern Mali.

The nature, scale and scope of non-farm employment opportunities are heavily influenced by the local context. Population density, sectoral and spatial patterns of industrialization, access to affordable transport and demand for services by wealthier, and often urban-based, groups determine the nature and scale of opportunities. At the same time, their increase can result in potential conflict between farmers and enterprises over the use of natural resources (Box 3.6)

Box 3.6 *Occupational diversification in south-eastern Nigeria*

In densely populated south-eastern Nigeria, commuting to the regional urban centres of Aba and Port Harcourt is encouraged by the efficient and cheap state-
subsidized transport system. Low-income rural women commute to work as cleaners
and gardeners, men as construction workers and in the oil industry. Peri-urban settlements have attracted small and medium-sized industries such as paper mills, creating opportunities for local salaried employment but also polluting the local river
with industrial effluents and therefore increasing constraints on farming. As out-
migrants invest in building homes for retirement, new opportunities in the construction sector have emerged in some rural settlements, displacing agriculture as the
main activity and reducing the availability of farmland around the villages. At the
same time, traditional rural non-farm activities such as cloth weaving are declining
due to competition from cheaper imports, lack of investment in technological innovation, lack of inter-sectoral linkages, for example, with yarn production, and inadequate infrastructure such as electricity supply, which affects most rural settlements.

The case studies also show that farming is an important activity for urban residents. In
Tanzania's southern town of Lindi, farming is the main occupation for over half its inhabitants and is a second occupation for another quarter. In the northern, more dynamic town
of Himo, farming is the main occupation for only 13.5 per cent of its inhabitants, but a
second occupation for another 40 per cent. In both urban and rural settlements, it is
mainly low-income groups who engage primarily in farming, often on a subsistence or
mixed (subsistence and cash crops) basis, or as wage labourers. Wealthier households and
individuals usually concentrate on commercial production, often in peri-urban areas that
benefit from proximity to urban markets. The Malian case studies show a similar trend.

This suggests that, especially in peri-urban areas but not only there, the small-farm
sector is undergoing major transformations, including a switch from mixed (subsistence
and cash crops) to predominantly commercial orientation, and from small-scale family
farms to larger farms relying on wage labour. This has important repercussions for small
peri-urban farmers with limited skills and education, who often have little alternative
but to engage in low-income occupations such as seasonal agricultural wage labour,
petty trade or portering in urban markets.

Within households, gender and generational differences in access to and control
over resources can be an important reason for some groups diversifying their income-
generating activities. Family farming is usually under the control of the household's
older man, and younger generations may prefer the greater independence of non-farm
activities. This is especially important for young women, who often are not even entitled
to inherit the family land. An important consequence of these transformations is that
the family as the traditional unit of production and consumption is replaced by more
individual priorities and behaviours. In northern Tanzania, young people will no longer
provide unpaid family labour on the farm. As a result, in the village of Lotima, for example, 46 per cent of households rely on wage labourers whose primary task is to take the
cattle out to pasture, traditionally the sons' responsibility.

Traditional divisions of labour along gender lines also mean that there are differences in the ways in which women and men perceive new opportunities and constraints

linked to urban expansion. In the peri-urban settlement of Dialakorodji, in central Mali, men complain of the loss of agricultural land to residential use and see no benefit in the proximity of the city of Bamako now that, under economic reform, many large employers such as peri-urban and urban factories have closed down or down-sized their operations. Women, however, for whom access to land is traditionally limited and who have a long tradition of independent small-scale trade, see great opportunities in the ever-expanding urban demand for horticultural products and in their strategic location between rural producers and urban consumers.

By disaggregating income diversification patterns along gender and generational lines, a picture emerges of radical change in the structure and internal relations of rural households in the three countries. Migration trends also show high levels of transformation. This has important implications for policy formulation and implementation, as much analysis and practice, especially in sub-Saharan Africa, still relies on the view of rural households as homogenous, relatively stable units of production and consumption. The case studies show that, in many instances, this is no longer true.

Migration, remittances and social networks across space

Historically, migration has been a key factor in shaping Africa's settlement patterns and livelihoods. It is also a central interaction between urban and rural settlements, and between rural settlements, in the three countries. In the case study locations, between 50 and 80 per cent of households have at least one migrant member. This proportion is not affected by household wealth because, while economic motivations are the main reason for moving, they overlap with the desire to widen one's experience and, for younger generations, to escape from obligations and control from elders. In south-eastern Nigeria, migration is considered essential to achieving economic and social success, and young men who do not migrate or commute to town are often labelled as idle and may become the object of ridicule. At the same time, demands on young people's time for community works are perceived by the young men themselves as conflicting with their own pursuit of 'making money'. However, while rural-to-rural movement is widely practised by the poorest groups, often on a seasonal basis, large and small urban centres are important destinations for all migrants.

Although young men remain the bulk of migrants, the independent movement of young unmarried women has greatly increased in recent years. This is linked to employment opportunities as domestic workers in urban centres or in new international tourist resorts. Women's migration is also increasingly socially acceptable, provided they contribute to their parental household's finances through remittances.

Another noticeable trend is the increase in movement to distant destinations, often across national borders. In south-eastern Nigeria, destinations include local urban centres such as Aba and Port Harcourt, but also Lagos, and Cotonou in neighbouring Benin; and migrants from Mali can move as far away as the main cities on the Atlantic coast of West Africa, as well as Libya and Saudi Arabia. More affordable transport, increasingly extensive migrant networks and demand in destination countries are some of the main factors for this expansion in the scope of movement. More distant destinations mean that migrants are away for longer periods of time (in Mali, this is often between 5 and 20 years) and, crucially, are unable to return home for the farming season, as is the case with intra-regional movement. In northern Mali, labour shortages are increasingly acute and, at the same time, households' dependence on remittances is growing.

Remittances are a crucial component of rural households' incomes and a key element of the continued links between migrants and their home areas, across all wealth groups. However, there is general consensus in all the case study locations that remittances have declined in the past 15 years or so, despite simultaneously becoming increasingly important for rural households. A common reason given for this is the increasing employment insecurity and cost of living in the urban centres; however, despite the decline in financial exchanges, social links between migrants, kin and the wider communities are as strong as ever. For many migrants, this is not only a part of their social identity but also a way of spreading their assets (and risk) across space and maintaining a safety net which helps in times of economic and social insecurity in the cities. This can also be done through migrant associations, which can serve the double purpose of assisting migrants while away and channelling resources to the wider community of origin. In south-eastern Nigeria, it is estimated that the contribution of migrant associations to the construction of facilities such as schools, town halls and water points has, in some cases, outstripped public investment.

Successful migrants can invest in their home areas with a view to returning there upon retirement or earlier; in so doing, they may also inject financial resources and new skills into the local economy. However, not all migrants can develop their asset base in their home area, either because they have limited access to resources – for example, women are often traditionally excluded from inheriting their parental land – or because their limited skills enable them to find employment only in low-paid jobs while away and they cannot put aside savings to invest. Cases of migrants returning to start their own businesses and, in the process, expanding local employment opportunities are relatively rare in the case study locations, and their success often depends on local availability of infrastructure, local institutions and governance contexts.

The role of urban centres in the development of their surrounding region

Governance systems and the institutional set-up are important in defining the nature of the relationship between urban centres and their surrounding region, although this needs to be situated within the broader context of national and supra-national changes in social and economic structures. Like most countries throughout the region, Mali, Nigeria and Tanzania have been undertaking some form of decentralization or deconcentration of administrative and other government functions, although with some significant differences.

In Nigeria, the process of deconcentration started in the early 1960s, and was accompanied by the creation of new states and local government authorities (LGAs). This was largely the result of demands for greater administrative autonomy by different ethnic groups. The federal government retains decision making powers on most matters, while state governments and LGAs are responsible for policy implementation. In Mali and Tanzania, the decentralization process started in the 1990s and more closely reflects the broader shift towards local participation. This is the result of a desire to create a more accountable system, better able to respond to local needs and priorities. It is also the consequence of cutbacks in national governments' budgets and the shifting of some responsibilities and costs away from central government. Some of the major challenges for local governments include: the limited support provided by central government; their limited capacity to carry out their responsibilities; the often conflictive relationship between elected local administration and traditional authorities; and the difficult relations between peri-urban administrations and urban municipalities.

In southern Tanzania, the limited provision and maintenance of essential transport infrastructure is a major bottleneck in the economic development of the region. However, in such under-resourced areas, it is unrealistic to expect local government to take full charge of basic infrastructure without significant support from central government. With decentralization, local government officials are responsible for a wide range of functions – in Tanzania, this includes needs identification, planning, budgeting and implementation jointly with other local institutions. Clearly, significant efforts are necessary to improve the capacity of local councils to fulfil their expanded duties.

The relationship between elected local government and traditional authorities is especially critical where there are tensions between the statutory rights system of land tenure and the customary system. In peri-urban areas, these are underpinned by informal land markets and the resulting conflict of interest between traditional chiefs who attempt to retain control, including over private sales of land under customary tenure, and elected governments whose responsibilities include the provision of infra-structure (roads, sanitation, etc) for which access to land is essential. In Mali, the potential for conflict is much higher in communes with low levels of social and political cohesion among the population, showing that in many cases the boundaries of the new units do not reflect social, economic and political realities.[6] Tensions between rural and peri-urban communes and urban municipalities concern primarily changes in land use, and the management of water resources and of domestic and industrial waste from the urban centre. Increasing competition between agricultural and residential use of natural resources is at the heart of overt conflict around the town of Himo in northern Tanzania, whereas waste dumping from Bamako is a major problem in one of the city's peri-urban settlements. These issues are likely to become increasingly important in many locations, and call for the development of mechanisms for negotiation and collaboration between neighbouring local governments.

Non-governmental organizations (NGOs), local associations and private sector actors also play an important role in local development. They often contribute to the provision of services and of physical and social infrastructure, and influence the role of urban centres in regional development. Following economic reform in the 1980s, public funding for essential services such as health and education, and for basic infrastructure such as water and sanitation, have declined. In many African countries, international donor agencies, NGOs and churches have taken over service provision, often concentrating in the rural areas. The result in Tanzania is that in the two towns of Himo and Lindi, urban residents and especially low-income urban groups have less access to basic education and health facilities than do rural residents. Water availability is also better in rural settlements, thanks to the wells and water pump construction efforts of international agencies, while low-income urban residents rely on irregular and expensive provision from informal vendors. This is not to say that funds should be diverted from rural to urban settlements, but a broader approach encompassing both rural and urban areas would make the targeting of low-income groups more effective.

In south-eastern Nigeria, civil society associations such as town development unions, age-grade groups (a traditional type of association based on age groups) and home-town-based migrant associations have a significant role in the funding and construction of public facilities such as water points and school halls. A better synergy between these actors and the public sector would improve infrastructure development in the urban centres and their surrounding regions. Finally, the private sector can also play an important role in the provision of services such as transport. However, the case of southern Tanzania shows that where there is inadequate provision and maintenance of the road system, operating costs for transporters are so high that they can hamper interest from competing enterprises and result in a monopoly of sorts, with resulting high prices and unreliability. In all three countries, transport is identified as a major bottleneck, along with insufficient processing and storage facilities, both of which affect local production and make it vulnerable to cheaper imports. Local governments' responsibilities increasingly include local economic development, and there is clear scope for the development of a regulatory framework and the provision of incentives to private investors in the areas of transport and processing of local produce. However, this requires improved capacity from local government as well as increased legitimacy.

Conclusions

In the 'virtuous circle' model of regional development, it is usually assumed that urban centres, through the provision of markets and services, can impart the impetus for agricultural growth in their surrounding regions. This will then translate into the expansion of non-farm employment and increased demand for both agricultural and manufactured goods and services. However, the case studies' findings show a more complex picture. Only two urban centres, Aba in southeastern Nigeria and Himo in northern Tanzania, seem to play a role in the economic development of their region. Both are regional market nodes and, perhaps more importantly, both are integrated into national and international trade networks. Both serve as markets for goods produced in the rural areas and as destinations for migrants and commuters engaged in non-agricultural employment. But this is not sufficient to overcome constraints in agricultural production and to make farming attractive to younger generations who are steadily moving out of it.

In the more 'rural' settlements, agricultural production is constrained by limited physical access to markets and processing. The inability of the settlements to attract investment in transport and processing facilities stems largely from a lack of incentives and limited infrastructure. With decentralization, local governments will become increasingly responsible for creating enabling environments for private sector investment, but the capacity to do so will need to be developed. In contrast, farming in the peri-urban areas – where private sector investment is more likely to focus – shows clear trends towards polarization, with wealthier urban residents engaging in commercial farming and displacing undercapitalized small-scale family farmers who, in turn, switch to waged agricultural employment, non-farm employment or migration – and most often a combination of these.

Finally, macroeconomic policies such as the liberalization of international trade can have a considerable impact on local economies. For example, local vegetable oil production by women's groups in Tanzania and traditional cloth weaving in south-eastern Nigeria were important income-generating activities, especially for women, but both have been undermined by cheaper imports. The potentials and limitations of regional economic development, and especially the potential role of local governments in providing an enabling environment for market-led economic growth, need to be understood within this wider context of changing global trade and production patterns.

Notes

1   Toulmin, C. and Quan, J. (eds) (2000) *Evolving Land Rights, Policy and Tenure in Africa*, DFID/IIED/NRI, London.
2   See Tacoli, C. (2002) 'Changing rural–urban interactions in sub-Saharan Africa and their impact on livelihoods: A summary', Working Paper 7 in the *Rural–Urban Interactions and Livelihood Strategies Series*, IIED, London, p13; also Diyamett, B., Diyamett, M., James, J. and Mabala, R. (2001) 'The case of Himo and its region, northern Tanzania', Working Paper 1 in the *Rural–Urban Interactions and Livelihood Strategies Series*, IIED, London; and Kibadu, A., Lerise, F., Mbutolwe, E. and Mushi, N. (2001) 'The case of Lindi and its region, southern Tanzania', Working Paper 2 in the *Rural–Urban Interactions and Livelihood Strategies Series*, IIED, London.
3   Pedersen, P. O. (2000) 'Busy work or real business: revaluing the role of non-agricultural activities in African rural development', ASC Working Paper 46, Africa Studies Centre, Leiden.
4   Ellis, F. (1998) 'Household strategies and rural livelihood diversification', *Journal of Development Studies*, vol 35, no 1.
5   Bryceson, D. F. (1999) 'African rural labour, income diversification and livelihood approaches: A long-term development perspective', *Review of African Political Economy*, no 80, pp171–189; also Bryceson, D. F. (1999) 'Sub-Saharan Africa betwixt and between: Rural livelihood practices and policies', ASC Working Paper 43, Africa Studies Centre, Leiden.
6   Toulmin, C. (2002) 'Keeping an eye on decentralization', mimeo, IIED, London.

Chapter 4

Evolving Rural–Urban Relations and Livelihoods in Southeast Asia

Jonathan Rigg

The context of change in rural lives

Rural Southeast Asia is often paraded as the final redoubt of tradition. That here, in the countryside, away from the factories and tower blocks, we find the Southeast Asia of old. Yet, even a cursory glance at recent work on the region emphasizes that while the visual landscape may sometimes remain unchanged, there has occurred a fundamental transformation in the lives and livelihoods of rural people. Indeed, in some areas it is difficult to know whether 'rural', as a category, is very useful when it comes to under-standing how people, today, manage their lives.

There are two important caveats to note at the outset. First, Southeast Asia is, quite clearly, a diverse place and change is occurring across the region in different ways, some-times markedly so. While certain general statements can be made about the nature of rural change and emerging rural–urban relations it would be foolish not to acknowledge that there are multiple trajectories. The experience of Laos is different from that of Malay-sia, and the experience of, say, a rice farmer in the north of Thailand is different from that of a rubber planter in the south. Second, many of the issues highlighted here are also pertinent to other regions of the world. In some areas – for example, South Korea, Japan, and much of Europe – there are, at a general level at least, well-established and accepted 'wisdoms'. This is not to say that the experience of Southeast Asia merely mirrors the past experience of other, more 'advanced', countries but rather to acknowledge that there is a global dimension that it is easy to ignore in regional (area studies) terms.[1]

The bulk of this chapter is concerned with the impacts of change and how people have responded to them at the individual and household levels. However, it is first useful to take a step back from the minutiae of local existence to map out the wider picture and the context within which these changes are occurring.

The first point to emphasize is that, barring one or two exceptions, Southeast Asia has made the transition from land abundance to land scarcity. Increases in agricultural

Note: Reprinted from *Southeast Asia Transformed: A Geography of Change*, Chia Lin Sien (ed), copyright © (2003) with permission from the Institute of Southeast Asian Studies, Pasir Panjang, Singapore.

output are being generated more through strategies of intensification than through exten-sification. Where large areas of 'un-' or 'under-utilized' land do (apparently) exist, for example, in the Indonesian provinces of Irian Jaya and Kalimantan, in the Malaysian states of Sabah and Sarawak, and in highland Vietnam, land is usually of poor quality and difficult to develop. For example, in the early 1980s Indonesia's transmigration pro-gramme was already having to deal with a shortage of sites. 'The basic reality', Hardjono wrote in the mid-1980s, 'is that large tracts of good land are no longer available [for set-tlement in Indonesia]' (Hardjono, 1986, p34). In a similar vein, Rambo writes that while Vietnam's highland frontier is endowed with apparently 'immense unexploited resources that only await Kinh [ethnic Vietnamese] settlement' there are, at the same time, 'serious unanswered questions about the long-term carrying capacity of upland agricultural sys-tems that make this development potentialy problematic' (Rambo, 1995, ppxi and xv).

A second element in this wider picture relates to mobility, accessibility, and trans-port. As Dick and Forbes (1992) have observed with reference to Indonesia, there has been a 'transport revolution' in Southeast Asia. There are few people in the region today who are isolated from the market or, for that matter, from the tendrils of the state. Booth notes how improving transport networks in Indonesia have helped spread the ideology of economic development (1995, p110) while Dearden suggests that the development of the road network in northern Thailand 'has probably done more to change the land-scape of the North and the mindscape of [its] inhabitants than any other single factor' (Dearden, 1995, p118). Even in countries such as Laos, where the road system is still highly underdeveloped, access by people to the market, and vice versa, is proceeding rapidly (see Rigg, 1997). While it is doubtful whether people even in pre-modern South-east Asia were quite as isolated as commonly imagined, there is little reason to question the importance that improvements in transportation have had on mobility, economic integration, and social change.

Social change is important in a wider sense, and particularly among younger age groups. Education, contact with metropolitan lifestyles and mores, whether directly or indirectly (through the media), have encouraged people to expect 'more' from life. Expectations and aspirations have changed and many younger women and men do not wish to emulate their parents. They wish to avoid the perceived drudgery of farming and the low status which it is accorded in many modernizing Southeast Asian societies. In her work among the Batak of Sumatra, Rodenburg emphasizes that Batak youth 'despise' work in agriculture, and suggests that farming is held in 'increasingly low esteem' (1997, p201). Instead, money is invested in education so that the young can escape from the village. Murray describes how young female slum-dwellers in Jakarta have traded the lives and the livelihoods of their parents for an urban existence far away from agriculture (geographi-cally and metaphorically), an existence which is defined, more than anything else, by a wish to be modern (Murray, 1991). This is a theme that resonates across the region.

The entry of rural people into non-farm work would not be possible without the availability of non-farm working opportunities. This ties in with the process of industri-alization and sectoral shifts in the economies of the region – and in the changing distri-bution of work which has accompanied the process. What, in this regard, is significant about the economic crisis which hit the region in mid-1997 is that in some instances these non-farm opportunities have evaporated, forcing people back to their villages, and back into agricultural work.

Taken together, these four elements of the wider picture – the declining availability of land resources, improving transportation and increased mobility, changing desires and aspirations, and the increasing opportunities for off-farm work created by the process of modernization – provide much of the background that lends itself to understanding the parallel changes occurring at the household level in rural areas of Southeast Asia.[2]

Changing rural livelihoods

Looking at assorted statistical tables, whether produced by international organizations like the World Bank, or national agencies such as the Thai National Statistical Office or the Indonesian Central Bureau of Statistics, one could be forgiven for assuming that Southeast Asia remains a region where most people live in the countryside and derive a living from agriculture (Table 4.1).[3] In assuming this they would be echoing the impression generated by decades of rural research which has tended to '"agrarianize" the countryside' (Alexander et al, 1991, p1), viewing the region as 'quintessentially agrarian' (McVey, 1992, p7). Moerman's study of Ban Ping in northern Thailand illustrates the tenor of many studies:

> In Ban Ping, rice is the main component of every meal, the major source of cash, and the object of most labour. Its production, consumption, and sale are the most common topics of village conversation. All other activities – economic, political, religious, and social – must yield to the rice cycle and the rains that govern it (Moerman, 1968, p10).

However, what village studies since the 1980s almost invariably show is a dramatic diversification in people's livelihoods away from agriculture and into assorted non-farm

Table 4.1 *Residence and occupation, Southeast Asian countries*

	Rural population as % of total, 1999	% of labour force in agriculture 1998
Brunei	40	2
Cambodia	84	74
Indonesia	60	45
Laos	77	78
Malaysia	43	19
Myanmar	73	63
Philippines	42	40
Singapore	0	0
Thailand	79	51
Vietnam	80	71

Note: The labour force figures for Brunei, Cambodia, and the Lao PDR are from the mid-1990s.
Sources: World development indicators, www.worldbank.org; UNDP statistics, www.undp.org

activities.[4] The evidence for this rural diversification from farm to non-farm (or agriculture to non-agriculture) is widespread, and although degrees of diversification vary it is a common theme from Vietnam (Dang Phong, 1995) and Indonesia (Firman, 1994; Cederroth, 1995), to Malaysia (De Koninck, 1992; Hart, 1994), the Philippines (Eder, 1993), and Thailand (Ritchie, 1993 and 1996; Chantana Banpasirichote, 1993). As Hill writes in the conclusion to his review article on agricultural change in Southeast Asia, 'rural people are in many areas less than committed to agriculture having added significant off-farm and non-farm employment to their domestic economies' (1998, p18).

While the nature of the diversification process currently underway in Southeast Asia is arguably something new, the attractions of diversity are not. Historical work has emphasized that multi-stranded livelihoods were the norm in many areas and among some groups of people. People living in environmentally marginal areas such as north eastern Thailand and the Indonesian islands of East Nusa Tenggara traditionally embraced what have been termed 'diverse portfolios' of activities. In North-east Thailand, not only have farmers 'grown different types of rice, planted at different times in different places' but rice cultivation was also just one (albeit the most important) activity among many (Grandstaff, 1992, p138; see also Rigg, 1986). Fox's work on the island of Roti in eastern Indonesia likewise emphasizes the importance of flexibility and variety in maintaining subsistence when, in any one year, a part of the subsistence system might fail (Fox, 1977, p50).[5] It is also true that marginal groups in society have tended towards multi-stranded livelihoods strategies. Whether it be a product of environmental or socio-economic marginality, the buffer of diversity is seen to bring security and stability when households cannot depend on a single crop or activity given a capricious environment or a system of social and economic relations where they are excluded or marginalized.

Despite this long tradition of diversity in rural systems, the current trend in rural livelihoods is, it is suggested here, rather different in its focus and in its effects. It is new non-farm activities, sustained or created by the contemporary process of development, which are underpinning diversification.

One village which has been the subject of study since the early 1970s is Ban Lek in Thailand's Chiang Mai Valley. Writing of Ban Lek in the 1970s, Tanabe describes a 'closed village community remote from the centre' experiencing 'a relatively gradual involvement in commodity relations' where economic activity was 'highly concentrated on agriculture' (Tanabe, 1994, pp107 and 251). While there was a degree of diversification even in the 1970s, this was primarily geared to opportunities in the village and the surrounding countryside (Tanabe, 1994, p112). Ritchie, who built on Tanabe's work and conducted field work in the village in the early 1990s, paints a very different picture of Ban Lek (Table 4.2). By the time of Ritchie's fieldwork, non-farm occupations were no longer supplementary, but essential to household reproduction, and few could be easily classified as 'farming' households (Ritchie, 1996, p279). From the so-styled 'closed village community' of the 1970s, Ban Lek had become a settlement with an extensive network of social and economic relations stretching far beyond the village, and a deep dependence on those relations. Ritchie uses the term 'inter-penetration' to describe the process of change in Ban Lek, a process whereby villagers have not only fanned outwards to exploit opportunities in the world beyond the paddy field, but the world beyond the paddy field, material and non-material, has impinged on village life.

Table 4.2 *Ban Lek, Northern Thailand, 1974–1991*

Occupation	1974	1985	1991
Farming	52.0	47.0	4.8
Farming and wage labour	2.2	17.8	18.3
Farming and other	5.3	2.6	12.5
Wage labour	32.0	26.7	51.0
Self-employed	5.7	4.4	9.6
Government employment	2.6	1.5	3.8
Total	100.0	100.0	100.0

Source: Ritchie (1993), p10

Eder's work in San Jose on the island of Palawan in the Philippines, conducted during two periods in 1970–1972 and 1988, offers another nuanced perspective on processes of agrarian change in the region. He argues that 'increasing supplementation of farm incomes through individual wage and other off-farm employment masks a ... crucial persistence in household-organized economic enterprise, a persistence that, in turn, helps explain why proletarianization does not inevitably bring increased vulnerability and suffering' (1993, p650).[6] The period from the early 1970s through to the late 1980s saw a proliferation of new economic opportunities in the area, for example, market vending, charcoal making, tricycle driving, wage labouring in the Palawan capital of Puerto Princessa City, and overseas contract employment.[7] These non-farm opportunities dove-tailed neatly with agriculture, permitting small farmers to improve their standards of living even while their landholdings were diminishing in size. Small farmers were not, in this case study, squeezed out of agriculture by the process of proletarianization. They creatively combined farm and non-farm work to improve their standard of living.

As these two studies hint, it is not just a case of rural people exploiting working opportunities in urban and peri-urban areas. Factory work and non-farm activities have also come to rural areas, occasionally drawing urban workers (back) to the village. In some instances this can be seen to fit the mould of classic rural industrialization 'involving the growth, development and modernization of various forms of industrial production within the rural sector generally and rural villages specifically' (Parnwell, 1990, p2). Rural industrialization of this type is not just another form of regional development, but village-based industrial development (Parnwell, 1994, p30). In other cases, it reflects a rather more fundamental incorporation of rural areas into the system of global economic relations. Wolf, for example, describes 'ten large-scale "modern" factories, driven by Western machinery and technology ... [squatting] in the middle of the agricultural land of two villages [in Java] that still have neither running water nor electricity' (1992, p109). Tomosugi (1995) writes of piece workers in a village in the Central Plains of Thailand making artificial flowers for a company in Bangkok. In both cases the factories, geared to export, draw cheap rural labour into a global production process where the inputs, other than labour, are sourced extra-locally and the outputs are marketed internationally. This extension of the urban/industrial into formerly rural/agricultural areas, and their incorporation into a wider system of global economic relations, links with recent work on Extended Metropolitan Regions in Asia (see below).

Changing rural livelihoods and the household

At a village level, then, it seems that there is an important process of diversification underway across the region. Studies consistently show an increase in the importance of non-farm activities in rural people's livelihoods. However, this focus on the village as the unit of study does not tell us much about what is occurring at the intra-village level or, indeed, at the intra-household level. Is it a case of a uniform process of diversification occurring? Or are there important differences among households and individuals?

If we consider a crude delineation of households into 'rich', 'middle' and 'poor', it is possible to suggest that each will find slightly different attractions in engagement in non-farm work. While, for rich households, non-farm work may be considered part of a strategy of accumulation, for the poor it is more likely to be part of a survival strategy, and for middle households a strategy of consolidation (see White and Wiradi, 1989; Rigg, 1989) (Table 4.3). Often, non-farm work for the poor is highly marginal, and pay may be equivalent to, or less than, farm work. This is a point emphasized, for example, by White (1991) and Cederroth (1995) in Java and Arghiros and Wathana Wongseki-arttirat (1996) in Thailand. In the latter example, a villager explained that making *ngop*, or farmers' hats, was so poorly paid that 'you can't do it quick enough to eat' (Arghiros and Wathana Wongsekiarttirat, 1996, p131). However, for better-off rural households non-farm work may be a means by which considerable savings can be built up.

To some extent, the division between 'rich', 'middle', and 'poor' relates to demographic issues connected with the life cycle, and family and community dynamics. Eder, in his study noted above, writes of 'core', 'off-spring', and 'migrant' households (Table 4.4). While core households were comparatively well provided for in terms of land holdings, off-spring households were land-poor. Not surprisingly, then, off-spring households were more reliant on non-farm work. But this does not mean that this work is obviously poorly paid compared with core households, or with agriculture (and in this respect Eder's work contrasts with the studies noted in the previous paragraph). Where it is, then, those off-spring households have often come from marginal core households or are educated only to primary level. So far as the group of migrant households is concerned, this shows great variation including, as it does, both relatively wealthy former town dwellers who have moved into San Jose and now commute to work, and poor families from areas of severe poverty, land shortage, and agrarian unrest. This latter subgroup owns the least land of all.

Another study which highlights the importance of viewing agrarian change in the context of household dynamics is Rigg's longitudinal study conducted in North-east Thailand between 1982 and 1994 (Rigg, 1998b). As in Eder's work, non-farm opportunities are critical determinants of wealth and poverty. But the distribution of non-farm work closely relates to the stage in the household life cycle that each family finds itself. 'Young' nuclear households with children below working age are poorly placed to exploit opportunities in the non-farm sector while 'mature' household with adult

Table 4.3 *In-situ non-farm work*

	Occupation	Skills and capital	Entry	Strategy
Land-poor and landless	petty trading	unskilled, little capital required	easy	survival
	basket-making	simple skills, little capital	easy	survival
	garbage pickers	unskilled, little or no capital	contact required	survival/consolidation
	construction sector	unskilled, no capital	contact required	survival/consolidation
Middle income households	transport sector	skill required but probably only little capital	contact required	consolidation/accumulation
	footstall operators	skill required and some capital		consolidation/accumulation
	construction sector	skill required, no capital	contact required	consolidation/accumulation
	factory work	low skills but perhaps secondary level education, no capital	contact desirable	consolidation
Rich households	large-scale trading	skills, entrepreneurship, and considerable capital required	difficult	accumulation
	taxi/bus ownership	skill, entrepreneurship, and considerable capital required	difficult	accumulation

Source: Based on Rigg (1998a)

Table 4.4 *Sources of income for core, off-spring and migrant households, San Jose, Philippines (% of households, 1988)*

	Core households	Off-spring households	Migrant households
Agriculture only	40	26	12
Non-agriculture only	13	42	64
Both agriculture and non-agriculture	48	32	24

Notes: Core households, n = 63; Off-spring households, n = 96; migrant households, n = 119. There are rounding errors in this table.
Source: Eder (1993)

children have much greater potential to benefit. These young households, Rigg suggests, can be categorized as the 'aspiring' poor or 'pre-prosperous'.

The terms 'non-farm' or 'non-agricultural' encompass a great range of activities from well to poorly paid. Entry, similarly, may be difficult – as in the cases of running a taxi service or money lending – or comparatively easy – as in the cases of hawking, petty trading, or wage labouring (Table 4.3). It can be argued that when it comes to understanding the forces behind rural diversification, and the likely outcome of the process, the reductionist farm/non-farm distinction, loses much of its utility – though the terminology is difficult to avoid.

Examining processes of rural change from the perspective of the household, while understandable, does present certain problems and challenges. It is now widely accepted that the household – like the village – should not be viewed as undifferentiated and that the interests of household members may not just be different, they may be at odds. Therefore, to write of household 'strategies' as if collectivism were the norm disguises a good deal of intra-household factionalism and conflict. In particular, work has illuminated the differing interests of men and women, and of different generations. Wolf's study (1992) of factory daughters in Java reveals the degree to which young women resist, contest, and in some cases go against the wishes of their parents in pursuing their desire to take up factory work. On the basis of studies by scholars such as Wolf (1992), Hart (1994) and Elmhirst (1995, 1996), it is possible to delineate a shift in generational power towards the young and, to some extent, in the balance of power between the sexes. This is partly associated with the employment changes noted previously, for many of the better paid non-farm opportunities are geared to the young, and often young women. It is on this basis that Hart argues in her work on the Muda area of Peninsular Malaysia for a 'reconceptualization' of the household. In her view, the 'diversification of "household" income sources is the outward manifestation of shifts in the structure and exercise of power between men and women and between elders and juniors …' (Hart, 1994, p49). There would seem to be parallel processes under way. On the one hand, education and changing mores are permitting and encouraging young women to engage in alternative work; while on the other, alternative working opportunities are providing the means by which young women can negotiate or contest existing household norms.

While most recent work tends to support the view that the household is not just divided, but also fluid, this does not mean that the direction of change is inevitably towards greater freedom and independence for women, and especially young women. Kato (1994) and De Koninck (1992), in their work in the Malaysian states of Negeri Sembilan and Kedah, respectively, note the emergence of the *seri rumah* or 'princess of the house'.[8] Women, relieved of the need to work in the fields due to mechanization and the proliferation of relatively well-paid non-farm jobs, have retreated to the house. It should be added that, according to De Koninck, this process of housewifization is regarded by women as an advance, freeing them from the need to undertake degrading farm work rather than, as commonly imagined, marginalizing them in the home.

Elmhirst's work conducted in a Javanese transmigrant settlement and an indigenous Lampungese village, both in South Sumatra, nicely illustrates the complex interplay at the household level between gender, income status, and non-farm opportunities (Elmhirst, 1995). In the Javanese transmigrant settlement, households cannot meet their livelihood needs from farming alone. Instead, both women and men take up additional work, usually locally, in the logging and plantation industries. There are few constraints on female mobility, and economic necessity, coupled with a flexible view of the role of women, makes for the widespread involvement of women in local non-farm work. By contrast, in the rather richer Lampungese community few women work locally, such work being viewed as shameful and degrading. But while Lampungese women do not work in the fields or in local plantations, unmarried girls do work, and in considerable numbers, in factories in Tangerang, outside Jakarta. Elmhirst postulates that Lampungese girls have been able to negotiate this partly because such work is out of sight – 'there is no shame in what cannot be seen' – and partly because *adat* (local custom) is being reworked. In addition, the financial benefit of extra-local employment to the household is less than that from local employment, even though the return (in terms of wages) may be greater. Javanese households find it easier to make a claim to income generated locally than Lampungese households can to income earned extra-locally, in Java.

Agriculture as a 'sideline'?

What is the future of farming in the context of the processes outlined above, where agriculture is losing its central position in people's lives and becoming just one activity among many? There is, very clearly, not one answer to this question but several. Consider the following perspectives from work conducted in Indonesia, Malaysia, the Philippines, and Thailand between the late 1980s and 1990s:

> industrial expansion has augmented rather than transformed employment opportunities. Farming continues to be the mainstay of the village economy but its capacity to support households financially is diminishing. The population is increasingly dependent on employment in the industrial sector (Guinness and Husin, 1993, p288 on a subdistrict in East Java).

> These structural changes [in Malaysian society] may be comprehended in two broad and interrelated processes of 'de-agriculturalization' and 'de-*kampong*-ization' … Malays

of Negeri Sembilan, especially the young, are simply not interested in agriculture. ...
Former *sawah* [wet rice fields] are covered with bushes and shrubs; rubber smallholdings
too are sometimes full of thick undergrowth which indicates that nobody goes there for
tapping (Kato, 1994, pp167 and 168 on a *kampong* in Negeri Sembilan, Malaysia).

Agriculture and non-agriculture are ... in a dynamic relationship,... but it is a dynamic
which is leading to the 'squeezing out' of agriculture (Kelly, 1999 on Manila's Extended
Metropolitan Region).

While villagers continue to seek opportunities for off-farm income, the villagers and
village leaders still place greater importance upon initiatives to promote the sustained
production of agricultural produce ... [this case study points] to the central importance
of integrated agricultural practices for household livelihoods (Attwater forthcoming on
two villages in upland Phetchabun, Thailand).

The situation in North Tapanuli today is that an increasingly low esteem is attached to
farming. To the extent that households have land at their disposal, the proceeds are
generally invested in children's education and not in increasing the viability of the family farm.... villagers hold firmly to the idea that education is the only way to progress
(Rodenburg, 1997, pp201–202 on a village in the Toba area of North Sumatra).

In many instances, households are reluctant to give up agriculture, or at least their land,
even when they have access to better-paid, and possibly higher status, non-farm work. It
seems that rural people, inured over the years to the risk of instability and collapse, continue to value diversity for the stability it can bring to household livelihoods. The economic crisis in the region merely served to underline this point. In his study of two
villages in upland Phetchabun, which marks the geographic divide between the Khorat
Plateau of Northeast Thailand and the Central Plains, Attwater suggests that Thailand's
economic malaise has highlighted the 'central importance of integrated agricultural
practices for household livelihoods'. With off-farm opportunities evaporating as the
crisis bites, farmers will, he postulates, take refuge in varied village-based activities
(Attwater, forthcoming). But there are also studies which argue almost the reverse,
hazarding that non-farm occupations act as safety valves for the poor, providing them
with work in the face of the marginalizing effects of agricultural modernization (e.g.
Cederroth, 1995, pp111–112).

The interactions between farm and non-farm, and local and non-local, are critical
to understanding many of the key developments in rural areas of the region. In Java, for
example, non-farm work has played an important role in retarding the processes of land
concentration and proletarianization (White, 1991, p65). Farmers with sub-livelihood
holdings have not, in the main, been forced to sell their land and the process of land
concentration, which was expected to be an outcome of technologically-driven agricultural modernization, has not materialized to the degree anticipated. As both Cederroth
(1995) and Maurer (1991) as well as White and Wiradi (1989) and Hart (1994) argue,
to understand the unexpected resilience of poor farmers it is necessary to 'look beyond
the *sawah* [rice field]' (Maurer, 1991, p97). This echoes a key finding of Eder's work in
the Philippines where 'partial reliance on nonagricultural employment has made family

farming itself more attractive' (Eder, 1993, p665). Farming thrives because of non-farm employment opportunities.

Another important outcome of the interactions between farm and non-farm has been in terms of the impact on agricultural methods and cropping patterns. Many village studies, including those from densely settled areas such as Java, the Central Plains of Thailand and Manila's hinterland, describe a situation of labour shortage. Kelly, for example, working in the province of Cavite, south of Manila, details the difficulties that farming households face in sourcing labour during planting and harvesting (Kelly, 1999). Young people have been attracted into factory work creating labour shortages and forcing up wages, while social change has led many young people to avoid farming and farm work altogether. In this instance, a combination of economic and socio-cultural processes are serving to marginalize farming. As Kelly explains, 'there is greater cultural (and economic) capital to be gained from working in non-agricultural sectors' (Kelly, 1999).

The shortage of farm labour and its rising cost has, in turn, created conditions conducive to the mechanization of production. Tractors, rotavators, even transplanters and combine harvesters, are increasingly common. Farmers have also tried to save labour by farming less intensively, the most evident manifestation of this being the widespread shift from transplant to broadcast rice culture. In other areas, farmers have shifted into less labour-demanding crops. Preston, working in Central Java, describes how villagers have replaced vegetables with fruit trees in their home gardens, shifted from the annual cultivation of some crops to their cultivation in alternate years and, in some cases, curtailed the traditional practice of dry season cultivation of padi land with non-rice crops (Preston, 1989). In some instances land has been left idle. Kato, for example, writes of abandoned padi fields 'covered with bushes and shrubs' in Malaysia's state of Negeri Sembilan (see the quote at the beginning of this section). In both the Central Plains of Thailand and in Melaka State, Malaysia, scholars have identified a trajectory where land is abandoned and villages become little more than dormitory settlements or places of retirement (Chantana Banpasirichote, 1993; Courtenay, 1988).

While a common theme in studies such as those noted above is that farmers maintain a farming presence, even when land is just kept ticking over or even left idle, there are also examples of rural households selling up and moving out of farming altogether. To quote Kelly's work in the Philippines once again, he states that even 'older farmers see little point in continuing to work the land when there seems no chance that their children will show any interest in inheriting their tenancy rights'. In the light of this, 'selling up their rights and using compensation money to pay for the completion of their children's education, or building homes for them in the village seem more realistic legacies for the next generation' (Kelly, 1999).

Rethinking social, economic, and spatial categories

It is worthwhile beginning this section with Eder's observation that the 'safest (and most useful) conclusion for the moment ... is that the local dynamics of agrarian change and differentiation are immensely variable, often reflecting unique combinations of complex and even conflicting processes' (Eder, 1993, p649). So, while this chapter has described a development narrative which, it is contended, has currency across the region, it would be wrong not to acknowledge the importance of local particularities creating unique rural geographies. There are areas, households, and individuals in Southeast Asia where the trajectories of change outlined here are only weakly represented and where Elson's perspective continues to apply:

> It is true, of course, that Southeast Asia's populations are still overwhelmingly rural in residence and that the majority of the region's workforces find employment in spheres closely associated with rural production. It is also true that many Southeast Asians still construct their sense of self and community in ways not wildly dissimilar to that of their forebears a century ago (Elson, 1997, p239).

Yet, even in those countries of the region which, until recently, have followed very different developmental paths, namely Vietnam, Laos, Cambodia, and Myanmar, it is possible to discern the beginnings of what appears to be a radical shift in rural life and livelihood. Li Tana (1996) identifies rural–urban migration – 'peasants on the move' – as a key mechanism in Vietnam's national development. Dang Phong also writes of a 'de-rice-ification' in Vietnam – a 'move away from rice cultivation by much of the rural population, a trend that will certainly intensify' (Dang Phong, 1995, p169). Economic reform has opened up far more opportunities for rural people, and many are endeavouring to construct livelihoods that embrace both farm and non-farm.

So, while there are important difference among countries and within each country, not to mention between households within villages, there is sufficient evidence from local studies to trace out a handful of broad parameters of change which would seem to have currency across many parts of the region. These are: the increasing contribution of non-farm activities to rural livelihoods; the increasing reliance of rural households on non-local sources of income; the increasing impact on agriculture of demands generated by non-farm activities; and the increasing spatial fragmentation of the household. Looking at these processes as a whole, it is possible to discern a significant reshaping of three critical elements in Southeast Asia's rural geography, namely: the household, the category 'rural', and agriculture.

The household, perhaps always more fractious and fractured than hitherto assumed, has become more fragmented still. This is true in at least two senses. First, and most clearly, the interests of household members have diverged. Partly this may be a product of contemporary economic and cultural change, where men and women pursue different livelihoods, and young and old reach for different goals. But possibly just as important, social and cultural change has created the conditions in which household members are more likely to challenge established household norms and power structures. This is clearest in work which has focused on the role of young women in the household (e.g. Wolf, 1992; Elmhirst, 1995, 1996, 2000). But while fragmentation may have increased, it would be wrong to describe the household, as a collective enterprise, as 'dead'. The household remains a stage where cooperation and conflict, corporatism and individualism, mutuality and inequality, and consensus and discordance, co-exist. In a sense, and paradoxically, the household is defined by dissonance.

The second sense in which the household has fragmented is in spatial terms. Traditionally the household was defined as a co-residential dwelling unit. It was geographically rooted and had a spatial as well as a familial identity. This notion is increasingly hard to sustain when household 'members' may live and work in a distant place – even abroad. Their membership of the household is founded, in such instances, not on geography, but on psychology and economics. The distant members, the 'shadow household', as it has been termed[9] play a role in the functioning and management of the household. They remit money, for instance, and may often play a part in strategic agricultural decisions. Psychologically they remain a part of the household because they identify it as 'home'.[10] But spatially they might not be 'there' at all. Writing of circulation as a way of life among the Wosera Abelam of Papua New Guinea, but which also resonates in the context of Southeast Asia, Curry and Koczberski argue that 'In many ways, a migrant never really leaves the village in a spiritual and cultural sense, and hence there is no clear distinction between source and destination sites when examining the lived experience of Wosera migration' (1998, p36).

These changes to the household have had ramifications for agriculture, and the place of agriculture within the farm economy. In the past, it was usual to see agriculture at the centre of rural people's livelihoods, with other activities playing a secondary and subsidiary role. This is reflected in the earlier quote from Moerman's study of Ban Ping where he writes that 'All other activities … must yield to the rice cycle …' (Moerman, 1968, p10). Today, it is not unusual for the rice cycle to yield to other activities – farm, so to speak, is in thrall to non-farm. This is reflected in the widespread shift from transplant to broadcast rice culture;[11] the planting of padi land to less labour-demanding crops (e.g. Preston, 1989); and, in some cases, the apparent abandonment of farm land, for example, Kato (1994), Rigg (1995) and Courtenay (1988). In each instance, the changes evident in agriculture must, and can only, be understood within the context of the wider household economy. Kelly writes of the 'tension' between rural and urban as 'different developmental priorities are played out' (Kelly, 1998, p54). On the other side of the coin, patterns of rural social differentiation must be viewed in terms of the household as an enterprise embracing farm and non-farm, local and non-local, and not just in terms of agriculture (Eder, 1993, p651).

Finally, there is the question of whether 'rural', as a category, should be reconceptualized to account for the patterns of change outlined here. Hoggart, for example, has argued that the 'broad category "rural" is obfuscatory … [and] … does not provide an appropriate abstraction' (Hoggart, 1990, p245). McGee, with specific reference to Southeast Asia, also highlights a blurring of the 'rural' and 'urban' worlds as interaction and interpenetration proceed creating, in the process, Extended Metropolitan Regions reaching far beyond the boundaries of what has traditionally been viewed as the city.[12] More widely, Koppel has proposed that the whole rural–urban dichotomy debate is 'ersatz' (Koppel, 1994, p48). This questioning of 'the rural' has occurred for several reasons which have been discussed in this chapter. The fluidity of the human landscape where individuals may work for six months of the year on the farm and six months in urban, factory work. The high and increasing levels of interaction between farm and non-farm livelihoods where agricultural decisions are taken in the light of demands generated by other activities. The difficulty of ascribing a definition of 'home' which is geographically rooted when the psychology of home may still be centred on rural villages but the spatial and economic reality is that people are working and living away from home. And the degree of penetration, in some areas, of urban people and industrial work into rural areas. Taken together, these changes in rural areas of Southeast Asia, and in the agricultural activities that traditionally underpinned livelihoods in the countryside, make a convincing case for arguing that a fundamental transformation is under way.

Implications for development, and development policy

Consider some of the terms that are being used to describe rural change in Southeast Asia. In no particular order, they include: hybridity, persistence, interpenetration, de-agriculturalization, diversification, de-*kampong*-ization, multiplicity, and re-peasantization. There are two issues that come through looking through this list. First is the notion that the Southeast Asian countryside is becoming increasingly differentiated as it becomes more tightly incorporated within the national and international economies. Interpenetration is leading to diversification; and diversification, to hybridity. The second issue is the apparently contradictory trajectories implied in some of the terminology. What can be made of Kato's reference to 'de-agriculturalization' in Negeri Sembilan, Malaysia (Kato, 1994) and Eder's to 'persistence' in Palawan, the Philippines (Eder, 1993)? While, in using these terms, the authors are referring to very different household responses, the explanation for each lies in a surprisingly similar set of processes. For Kato, the availability of renumerative non-farm employment, coupled with a growing aversion to agricultural work, is encouraging people to abandon farming (but not their fields). For Eder, the availability of non-farm work is permitting farmers with sub-viable holdings to maintain a presence in farming. This is also something that Hart refers to when she writes of the remarkable 'tenacity' of tiny holdings in the face of mechanization (Hart, 1994, p57).

Until relatively recently the answers to the two questions 'what does the future hold for agriculture?' and 'what does the future hold for rural households?' would have been, in most cases, very similar. Today, however, while these two questions are still linked, their association is much weaker. This gradual de-linking of 'rural' from 'agricultural' provides a challenge for existing theories of agrarian change and goes some way to account for their limited explanatory power. As Hart points out, it is partly because of their 'preoccupation with production relations in agriculture' that such theories fail to shed much light on contemporary rural change (Hart, 1994, p47). When non-farm issues do enter the equation they are often seen as 'derivatives (and even residuals) of processes of agrarian differentiation' (Koppel and Hawkins, 1994, p18).

These changes in rural areas of Southeast Asia also have profound implications for rural development policy and practice. Take, for example, the key issue of rural poverty and, more widely, rural well-being. In the past, as Koppel and Hawkins emphasize, rural poverty was seen to be a function of agrarian deficiencies: lack of land and capital, low levels of productivity, and poor physical resources, for example (Koppel and Hawkins, 1994, p2). Thus the solutions to rural poverty, in policy terms, were also often conceived in terms of agriculture: cheap credit, land reform, and the development and provision of suitable biochemical and mechanical technologies, for instance. Such an approach is no longer appropriate for it overlooks the fact that for many individuals and households agriculture has become, or is fast becoming, a 'sideline' where it is just one activity within a portfolio. This needs to be recognized if appropriate rural development policies are to be formulated. An agricultural development strategy which assumes that rural households are labour rich and have the labour resources to invest in some new high(er) return, but also labour-intensive crop or technique, may find uptake to be poor. Likewise, investment in irrigation in environmentally marginal areas to extend double cropping may be misguided if farmers use the dry season to engage in non-farm pursuits, whether in situ or ex situ. In other words, not only do theories of agrarian and rural change have to be sufficiently catholic to include factors that lie outside agriculture and beyond the village, but so too do agricultural and rural development policies. If rural areas are not embedded in this wider milieu, then the trajectory of change is likely to be misconstrued.

In the light of the changes described here, what is the future of rural Southeast Asia? Clearly, there are many futures, reflecting the uniqueness of place. At a general level, it seems reasonable to argue that agriculture will continue to decline in importance both in terms of its contribution to national income and to household livelihood. In parallel, we should also expect to see rural economies and livelihoods becoming more diverse or hybrid. This, at one level, may seem obvious given the experience of other regions and the structural changes that appear to be part and parcel of modernization and development. Yet the economic crisis, which afflicted the region from 1997, led to numerous calls for a 'return to the farm'. The King of Thailand, for example, on the occasion of his seventieth birthday, suggested that returning to a self-sufficient, farm-based economy might offer a way out of the crisis (*Bangkok Post*, 1998). 'Whether or not we are a tiger is unimportant', he said, 'The important thing is for the economy to be able to support our people', adding, in populist vein, 'We need to go back so that we can go forward' (TDN, 1997, p12). While economic hardship may lead some people to take refuge in rural life and agricultural work, it is difficult to see this as much more than a short-term crisis response. As the International Labour Organization (ILO) pointed out in a study of the social effects of the economic crisis, there may be considerable scope for absorbing displaced workers in family-based farms but this will be 'at the cost of reduced labour productivity and returns per capita' (ILO, 1998). Increasingly, rural people are constructing livelihoods that either avoid agriculture or they are pursuing multiple occupations embracing farm and non-farm. Agriculture alone does not have the productive capacity to meet the rising needs and changing aspirations of a large segment of the population of the region. Many may maintain a rural and agricultural presence, but this tells only half the story of rural Southeast Asia at the turn of the century.

Notes

1   For studies of rural change conducted elsewhere in the developing world, but which echo points made here, see: Barnes (1983) on Kenya, Berry (1993) on sub-Saharan Africa, Collins (1988) on Peru, Preston (1992) on Bolivia, Racine (1990) on South India, and Zoomers and Kleinpenning (1996) on Central Paraguay.

2   This chapter is concerned more with rural than with agricultural change. For a wide-ranging summary of changes in Southeast Asian agriculture, see Hill (1998).

3   It is also postulated that the official Chinese data 'massively overestimate' the number of farm workers. Rawski and Mead (1998) calculate that there may be well over 100 million 'phantom farmers'.

4   Alexander et al (1991) make the point, with reference to Java, that non-farm activities have probably always been more important than accepted wisdom dictates. Deficiencies in the historical statistical data and the relative invisibility of non-farm work, especially when that work was undertaken by women, has tended to shield the true nature of the rural economy from view.

5   Fox does note a trend towards greater specialization in the Rotinese economy (Fox, 1977, p50).

6   Proletarianization here is used to refer to the shift from self-employment on family farms to wage employment, whether farm or non-farm.

7   Cederroth, in his study in East Java, also notes the proliferation of new non-farm opportunities open to farmers (Cederroth, 1995, p112).

8   The state also has a role to play in the promotion of what has become known, in the Indonesian context, as the culture of 'ibuism' or housewifization. Ibuism embeds modern Indonesian women firmly within the domestic sphere, identifying their role in the modernization effort clearly as mother and wife. Guinness notes how national groups like the Family Welfare Association (PKK or Pembinaan Kesejahteraan Keluarga) map out a clearly defined set of roles for the modern housewife: faithful companion, household manager, producer of children (preferably two), mother and educator, and good citizen (Guinness, 1994, p283).

9   See Tacoli (1996).

10   See Chapman (1995).

11   See, for example, Tomosugi (1995), p63; Wong (1987), p214; Rigg (1995); and Hart (1994), p54.

12   See McGee (1989, 1991) and also Ginsburg (1991) and Luxmon Wongsuphasawat (1995).

References

Alexander, P., Boomgaard, P. and White, B. (1991) 'Introduction', in Alexander, P., Boomgaard, P. and White, B. (eds) *In the Shadow of Agriculture: Non-Farm Activities in the Javanese Economy, Past and Present*, Royal Tropical Institute, Amsterdam, pp1–13

Arghiros, D. and Wongsekiarttirat, W. (1996) 'Development in Thailand's Extended Metropolitan Region: The socio-economic and political implications of rapid change in an Ayutthaya District, Central Thailand', in Parnwell, M. J. G. (ed) *Thailand: Uneven Development*, Avebury, Aldershot, pp125–145

Attwater, R. 'Labour migration in upland Thai communities: Sources of livelihood and local resource management', *South East Asian Review* (forthcoming)

Bangkok Post (1998) 'Back to relying on basics', *Bangkok Post Year End Review*, 15 January, pp8–9

Barnes, C. (1983) 'Differentiation by sex among small-scale farming households in Kenya', *Rural Africana*, vol 15–16, pp41–63

Berry, S. (1993) *No Condition Is Permanent: The Social Dynamics of Agrarian Change in Sub-Saharan Africa*, University of Wisconsin Press, Madison, WI

Booth, A. (1995) 'Regional disparities and inter-governmental fiscal relations in Indonesia', in Cook, I. G., Doel, M. A. and Li, R. (eds) *Fragmented Asia: Regional Integration and National Disintegration in Pacific Asia*, Avebury, Aldershot, pp102–136

Cederroth, S. (1995) *Survival and Profit in Rural Java: The Case of an East Javanese Village*, Curzon Press, Richmond, Surrey

Chantana, B. (1993) *Community Integration into Regional Industrial Development: A Case Study of Klong Ban Pho, Chachoengsao*, TDRI, Bangkok

Chapman, M. (1995) 'Island autobiographies of movement: Alternative ways of knowing?', in Claval, P. and Singaravelou (eds) *Ethnogeographies*, L'Harmattan, Paris, pp247–259

Collins, J. L. (1988) *Unseasonal Migrations: The Effects of Rural Labor Scarcity in Peru*. Princeton University Press, Princeton

Courtenay, P. P. (1988) 'Farm size, out-migration and abandoned padi land in Mukim Melekek, Melaka (Peninsular Malaysia)', *Malaysian Journal of Tropical Geography*, vol 17, pp18–28

Curry, G. and Koczberski, G. (1998) 'Migration and circulation as a way of life for the Wosera Abelam of Papua New Guinea', *Asia Pacific Viewpoint*, vol 39, no 1, pp29–52

Dang, P. (1995) 'Aspects of agricultural economy and rural life in 1993', in Kerkvliet, B. J. T. and Porter, D. J. (eds) *Vietnam's Rural Transformation*, Westview; Institute of Southeast Asian Studies, Singapore, pp165–184

De Koninck, R. (1992) *Malay Peasants Coping with the World: Breaking the Community Circle?* Institute of Southeast Asian Studies, Singapore

Dearden, P. (1995) 'Development, the environment and social differentiation in Northern Thailand', in Rigg, J. (ed) *Counting the Costs: Economic Growth and Environmental Change in Thailand*, Institute of Southeast Asian Studies, Singapore, pp111–130

Dick, H. and Forbes, D. (1992) 'Transport and communications: A quiet revolution', in Booth, A. (ed) *The Oil Boom and After: Indonesian Economic Policy and Performance in the Soeharto Era*, Oxford University Press, Singapore, pp258–282

Eder, J. F. (1993) 'Family farming and household enterprise in a Philippine community, 1971–1988: Persistence or proletarianization?', *Journal of Asian Studies*, vol 52, no 3, pp647–671

Elmhirst, B. (1995) 'Gender, environment and transmigration: Comparing migrant and Pribumi household strategies in Lampung, Indonesia', Paper presented at the Third WIVS Conference on Indonesian Women in the Household and Beyond, Royal Institute of Linguistics and Anthropology, Leiden, 25–29 September

Elmhirst, B. (1996) 'Transmigration and local communities in North Lampung: Exploring identity politics and resource control in Indonesia', Paper presented at the Association of South East Asian Studies' (ASEASUK) Conference, School of Oriental and African Studies, London, 25–27 April

Elmhirst, B. (2000) 'Negotiating gender, kinship and livelihood practices in an Indonesian transmigration area', in Koning, J., Nolten, M., Rodenburg, J. and Saptari, R. (eds) *Women and Households in Indonesia: Cultural Notions and Social Practices*, RoutledgeCurzon, London, pp208–234

Elson, R. E. (1997) *The End of the Peasantry in Southeast Asia: A Social and Economic History of Peasant Livelihood, 1800–1990s*, Macmillan, Houndsmill, Basingstoke

Firman, T. (1994) 'Labour allocation, mobility, and remittances in rural households: A case from Central Java, Indonesia', *Sojourn*, vol 9, no 1, pp81–101

Fox, J. (1977) *Harvest of the Palm: Ecological Change in Eastern Indonesia*, Harvard University Press, Cambridge, MA

Ginsburg, N. (1991) 'Extended Metropolitan Regions in Asia: A new spatial paradigm', in Ginsburg, N., Koppel, B. and McGee, T. G. (eds) *The Extended Metropolis: Settlement Transition in Asia*, University of Hawaii Press, Honolulu, pp27–46

Grandstaff, T. (1992) 'The human environment: Variation and uncertainty', *Pacific Viewpoint*, vol 33, no 2, pp135–144

Grandstaff, T. (1998) 'Environment and economic diversity in Northeast Thailand', in Charoenwatana, T. and Rambo, A. T. (eds) *Sustainable Rural Development In Asia*, Khon Kaen University, Khon Kaen, Thailand, pp11–22

Guinness, P. (1994) 'Local society and culture', in Hill, H. (ed) *Indonesia's New Order: The Dynamics of Socio-Economic Transformation*, University of Hawai'i Press, Honolulu, pp267–304

Guinness, P. and Husin, I. (1993) 'Industrial expansion into a rural subdistrict: Pandaan, East Java', in Dick, H., Fox, J. J. and Mackie, J. (eds) *Balanced Development: East Java in the New Order*, Oxford University Press, Singapore, pp272–295

Hardjono, J. (1986) 'Transmigration: Looking to the future', *Bulletin of Indonesian Economic Studies*, vol 22, no 2, pp28–53

Hart, G. (1994) 'The dynamics of diversification in an Asian rice region', in Koppel, B., Hawkins, J. and James, W. (eds) *Development or Deterioration: Work in Rural Asia*, Lynne Rienner, Boulder and London, pp47–71

Hill, R. D. (1998) 'Stasis and change in forty years of Southeast Asian agriculture', *Singapore Journal of Tropical Geography*, vol 19, no 1, pp1–25

Hoggart, K. (1990) 'Let's do away with rural', *Journal of Rural Studies*, vol 6, no 3, pp245–257

International Labour Organisation (ILO) (1998) 'The social impact of the Asian financial crisis', Technical report for discussion at the High-Level Tripartite Meeting on Social Responses to the Financial Crisis in East and South-East Asian Countries, Bangkok, 22–24 April, www.ilo.org/public/english/60empfor/cdart/bangkok/index.html

Kato, T. (1994) 'The emergence of abandoned paddy fields in Negeri Sembilan, Malaysia', *Southeast Asian Studies (Tonan Ajia Kenky)*, vol 32, no 2, pp145–172

Kelly, P. (1998) 'The politics of urban–rural relations: Land use conversion in the Philippines', *Environment and Urbanization*, vol 10, no 1, pp35–54

Kelly, P. (1999) 'Everyday urbanization: The social dynamics of development in Manila's Extended Metropolitan Region', *International Journal of Urban and Regional Research*, vol 23, no 2, pp283–303

Koppel, B. (1994) 'The rural-urban dichotomy reexamined: Beyond the ersatz debate?', in Ginsburg, N., Koppel, B. and McGee, T. G. (eds) *The Extended Metropolis: Settlement Transition in Asia*, University of Hawai'i Press, Honolulu, pp47–70

Koppel, B. and Hawkins, J. (1991) 'Rural transformation and the future of work in rural Asia', in Koppel, B., Hawkins, J. and James, W. (eds) *Development or Deterioration: Work in Rural Asia*, Lynne Rienner, Boulder and London, pp1–46

Li, T. (1996) *Peasants on the Move: Rural–Urban Migration in the Hanoi Region*, Institute of Southeast Asian Studies, Singapore

Luxmon W. (1995) 'The Extended Metropolitan Region and uneven industrial development in Thailand', Paper presented at the First EUROSEAS Conference, Leiden, 29 June–1 July

Maurer, J.-L. (1991) 'Beyond the Sawah: Economic diversification in four Bantul villages, 1972–1987', in Alexander, P., Boomgaard, P. and White, B. (eds) *In the Shadow of Agriculture: Non-Farm Activities in the Javanese Economy, Past and Present*, Royal Tropical Institute, Amsterdam, pp92–112

McGee, T. G. (1989) 'Urbanisasi or Kotadesasi? Evolving patterns of urbanization in Asia', in Costa, F. J., Dutt, A. K., Ma, L. J. C. and Noble, A. G. (eds) *Urbanization in Asia: Spatial Dimensions and Policy Issues*, University of Hawai'i Press, Honolulu, pp93–108

McGee, T. G. (1991) 'The emergence of Desakota regions in Asia: Expanding a hypothesis', in Ginsburg, N., Koppel, B. and McGee, T. G. (eds) *The Extended Metropolis: Settlement Transition in Asia*, University of Hawai'i Press, Honolulu, pp3–25

McVey, R. (1992) 'The materialization of the Southeast Asian entrepreneur', in McVey, R. (ed) *Southeast Asian Capitalists: Studies on Southeast Asia*, Cornell University Press, Ithaca, New York, pp7–33

Moerman, M. (1968) *Agricultural Change and Peasant Choice in a Thai Village*, University of California Press, Berkeley, CA

Murray, A. (1991) *No Money, No Honey: A Study of Street Traders and Prostitutes in Jakarta*, Oxford Univeristy Press, Singapore

Parnwell, M. J. G. (1990) *Rural Industrialisation in Thailand*, Hull Paper in Developing Area Studies no. 1, Centre of Developing Area Studies, University of Hull

Parnwell, M. J. G. (1994) 'Rural industrialisation and sustainable development in Thailand', *Thai Environment Institute Quarterly Environment Journal*, vol 1, no 1, pp24–39

Preston, D. (1989) 'Too busy to farm: Under-utilisation of farm land in Central Java', *Journal of Development Studies*, vol 26, no 1, pp43–57

Preston, D. (1992) 'Restructuring Bolivian rurality? Batallas in the 1990s', *Journal of Rural Studies*, vol 8, no 3, pp323–333

Racine, J. (1990) *To Migrate or to Stay? Mobility and Retention of Rural Population in South India*, Pondy Papers in Social Sciences no. 5, French Institute, Pondicherry

Rambo, A. T. (1995) 'Defining highland development challenges in Vietnam: Some themes and issues emerging from the conference', in Rambo, A. T., Reed, R. R., Le Trong Cue and DiGregorio, M. R. (eds) *The Challenges of Highland Development in Vietnam*, East-West Center, Hawai'i, ppxi–xxvii

Rawski, T. G. and Mead, R. W. (1998) 'On the trail of China's phantom farmers', *World Development*, vol 26, no 5, pp767–781

Rigg, J. (1986) 'Innovation and intensification in northeastern Thailand: Brookfield applied', *Pacific Viewpoint*, vol 27, pp29–45

Rigg, J. (1989) *International Contract Labor Migration and the Village Economy: The Case of Tambon Don Han, Northeastern Thailand*, Papers of East-West Population Institute, no. 112, East-West Center, Honolulu

Rigg, J. (1995) 'Errors in the making: Rice, knowledge, technological change and applied research in northeastern Thailand', *Malaysian Journal of Tropical Geography*, vol 26, no 1, pp19–33

Rigg, J. (1997) *Southeast Asia: The Human Landscape of Modernization and Development*, Routledge, London

Rigg, J. (1998*a*) 'Rural-urban interactions, agriculture and wealth: A Southeast Asian perspective', *Progress in Human Geography*, vol 22, no 4, pp497–522

Rigg, J. (1998*b*) 'Tracking the poor: The making of wealth and poverty in Thailand (1982–1994)', *International Journal of Social Economics*, vol 25, nos 6–8, pp1128–1141

Ritchie, M. (1993) 'The "village" in context: Arenas of social action and historical change in northern Thai peasant classes', Paper presented at the Fifth International Thai Studies Conference, School of Oriental and African Studies, London, July

Ritchie, M. (1996) 'Centralization and diversification: From local to non-local economic reproduction and resource control in Northern Thailand', Paper presented at the Sixth International Conference on Thai Studies, Chiang Mai, Thailand, 14–17 October

Rodenburg, J. (1997) *In The Shadow of Migration: Rural Women and Their Households in North Tapanuli, Indonesia*, KITLV Press, Leiden

Tacoli, C. (1996) 'Migrating for the sake of the family? Gender, life course and intra-household relations among Filipino migrants in Rome', *Philippine Sociological Review*, vol 44, nos 1–4, pp12–32

Tanabe, S. (1994) *Ecology and Practical Technology: Peasant Farming Systems in Thailand*, White Lotus, Bangkok

Thai Development Newsletter (TDN) (1997) 'IFCT sees poor economic growth', *Thai Development Newsletter*, vol 33, July–December, pp12–13

Tomosugi, T. (1995) *Changing Features of a Rice-Growing Village in Central Thailand: A Fixed-Point Study From 1967 to 1993*, the Centre for East Asian Cultural Studies, Tokyo

White, B. (1991) 'Economic diversification and agrarian change in rural Java, 1900–1990', in Alexander, P., Boomgaard, P. and White, B. (eds) *The Shadow of Agriculture: Non-Farm Activities in the Javanese Economy, Past and Present*, Royal Tropical Institute, Amsterdam, pp41–69

White, B. and Wiradi, G. (1989) 'Agrarian and nonagrarian bases of inequality in nine Javanese villages', in Hart, G., Turton, A. and White, B. (eds) *Agrarian Transformations: Local Processes and the State in Southeast Asia*, University of California Press, Berkeley, CA pp266–302

Wolf, D. L. (1992) *Factory Daughters: Gender, Household Dynamics, and Rural Industrialization in Java*, University of California Press, Berkeley, CA

Wong, D. (1987) *Peasants in the Making: Malaysia's Green Revolution*, Institute of Southeast Asian Studies, Singapore

Zoomers, A. E. B. and Kleinpenning, J. (1996) 'Livelihood and urban-rural relations in central Paraguay', *Tijdschrift voor Economische en Sociale Geografie*, vol 87, no 2, pp161–174

Part 3

Policies that Address, Ignore or Misunderstand Rural–Urban Linkages

Chapter 5

Transitions in Sub-Saharan Africa: Agriculture, Urbanization and Income Growth

Mary Tiffen[1]

Transitions and growth models

Development theory has been preoccupied with providing improved living standards and quality of life either to the great majority, or more recently, to the poorest of the poor. This normally requires economic growth greater than population growth, both to improve incomes directly, and to increase the taxable capacity underpinning good government services.[2]

It is clear that the high-income countries are urbanized and have large industrial and service sectors. Agriculture provides only 2 per cent of their gross domestic product (GDP), compared with 10 per cent in middle-income and 41 per cent in low-income countries (World Bank, 2000b). Most low-income countries have a higher proportion of their labour force in agriculture than its proportion of output value. Many development economists in the 1950s and 1960s therefore urged the need to shift labour into higher productivity sectors, by a structural transformation leading to industrialization of their economies. Rostow (1960) propounded a rapid take-off stage, for which a necessary condition was a rise in the productive investment rate to over 10 per cent of national income. It was generally believed in the 1960s that such investment must be made by government, due to lack of private capacity. In consequence, high taxes on agriculture through marketing boards and export duties had general approval. Helleiner (1966) wrote in relation to Nigeria:

> The disposition of Marketing Board surpluses may not have been perfect, but the rates of return from their investments in research, roads, agricultural schemes, universities, modern manufacturing plants and so forth are unlikely to have been any lower than those on housing, sewing machines, land clearing, and the other small-scale outlets for peasant funds discussed above, let alone so much lower as to offset the difference between savings rates (p184).

Note: Reprinted from *World Development*, vol 31, no 8, Tiffen, M., 'Transitions in sub-Saharan Africa: Agriculture, urbanization and income growth', pp1343–1366, copyright © (2003) with permission from Elsevier, London.

The failure of policies aimed at inducing rapid industrialization discredited belief in a take-off and stages of growth.[3] The importance of the agricultural sector as a supplier of raw materials, food and labour, and as the home market for local industrial output, noted by Johnston and Mellor (1961), was increasingly recognized. The low productivity of many government investments and the outright failure of some became better known. Structural adjustment implied 'a shift away from inward-oriented import-substituting development strategies to more outward-oriented ones' (Alexandratos, 1995), and debt-ridden countries have been urged to increase and diversify agricultural exports.[4]

If GDP rises smoothly as a result of long-term effects of capital formation, labour force expansion and technological change, it can be modelled by econometric analysis, using the 30–40 years of statistical data which are now available for a large number of countries. Kenny and Williams (2001) have shown the limited explicatory power of econometric models, and their often contradictory results. They note several causes, including, importantly, the assumption that the process of economic growth is the same, not only in all countries, but in all periods of time. They suggest therefore, 'that mathematical modeling techniques have invaded territory to which they are ill-suited' (Kenny and Williams, 2001, p14).

This paper uses a few generally agreed principles of economic growth to construct a non-mathematical model that reflects historical experience. The model conforms to the broad thrust of available statistical data, but shows that economies are fundamentally different at different points in time, particularly in the relationship of their agricultural

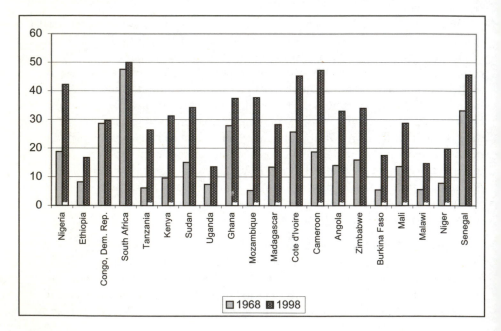

Source: Calculated from World Bank (2002). Countries in this and subsequent figures are arranged in order of population size

Figure 5.1 *Urban population, largest Sub-Saharan African countries as a percentage of total population*

and non-agricultural sectors. Policies therefore need to be varied according to the stage at which the country finds itself, rather than applied universally. The development of the agricultural sector is initially extremely important. However, at a later stage increases in the productivity of towns are required, to improve urban incomes, to provide alternative occupations to the rural poor, and to stimulate agricultural investment through growing demand.

Tomich et al (1995) also returned to a stages approach in their book, *Transforming Agrarian Economies*. The model differs from them in emphasizing the change in markets rather than in labour disposition, and the acceleration of change. They identified countries with abundant rural labour with 50 per cent or more of the labour force in agriculture, but thought that:

> ... it will be decades before they reach the *structural transformation turning point*, when the absolute size of the agricultural work force begins to decline. Until then, poverty can be alleviated only if productivity and employment in the rural economy are increased (pp9–10).

In fact, a number of countries even in sub-Saharan Africa (SSA) are at or near this point. Calculating from World Bank (2002), urban population in SSA increased at an average of 5 per cent per annum and rural at 2 per cent per annum 1968–2000, and averaged 34 per cent of the total in 2000. It is now heading for 50 per cent in some (Figure 5.1). Rural population growth had dropped to 0.4 per cent per annum or less in 8 out of the 20 largest countries in 1998–2000 (Figure 5.2), and not all rural is agricultural. While

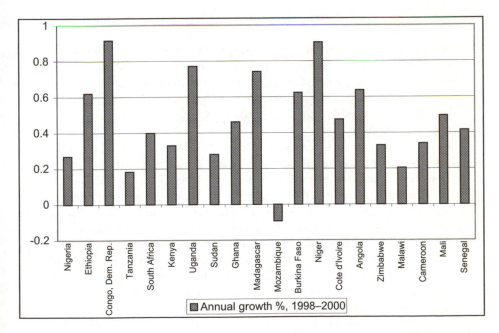

Figure 5.2 *Annual growth rate (%) of rural population, in 20 largest SSA countries, 1998–2000*

policy debates have focused on the pros and cons of exports, the swiftly growing internal market has become much more important to farmers, and is a main generator of change in farming systems, particularly, but not only, in the semi-arid areas. The urban market is attracting not only their products, but also their labour.

The model is delineated and explained in the section below. The section on 'The weaknesses of the statistical base' illustrates the dubiety of much of the population and national income data relating to SSA, which lies behind allegations of low or negative growth rates in income per capita, and falling agricultural output per capita (World Bank, 2000a). Wiggins (1995, 2000) has already discussed the conflict between these statistics and the evidence of change and growth gathered from a limited number of village case studies. As these can be unrepresentative, the section on 'Farmers' investments in response to changing markets in four semi-arid districts of SSA' illustrates the rapidity of change in four semi-arid African districts, 1960–2000. Some 30 per cent of the SSA population live in semi-arid areas (Jahnke, 1982), which provides a difficult environment for agriculture. If there are achievements in these areas it is likely that this is also the case in the better-endowed areas. The final concluding section considers the policies and government services likely to be most important in the near future.

The model

Basis

The model utilizes some of the most basic and durable concepts in economics:

- The division of labour by specialization improves productivity and leads to technological improvements developed out of the skills and experience of the specialists. Adam Smith (1776) gave his famous illustration of pin manufacture. Specialization requires concentrations of population – in villages and to an increasing extent as specialization proceeds, in towns and cities, to facilitate the exchange of services, products and information.
- The division of labour is limited by the extent of the market. The extent of the market is determined in great part by the costs of transport in relation to the value of the product, and also by the numbers and incomes of the potential purchasers.[5]
- Improvements in output per labour day or per hectare require the investment of either or both capital and labour for a delayed reward, but there are diminishing returns to additional units of the same input unless there is also a change in technology or in the nature of the output. Hence sustained growth depends on the combination of investment with new or modified and adapted technologies (Romer, 1989). This applies both in agriculture and industry (Anderson, 1990; Tiffen and Mortimore, 1994). The development of technology is facilitated endogenously by specialization, but is also helped by the openness of society to information from external sources, whether brought in by the written word and other media, or through the mechanisms of external trade, or through the concentrations of people typical of a marketplace.

• Investment, while a necessary condition for improved output and incomes, is not a guarantee of either. A given amount of investment does not and cannot produce a given amount of growth. Investment incurs risk, and is more likely to be successful with good information about the nature of the risks and of the market, and if the investor has been able to develop his/her skills and judgement. The more complex and larger the investment, the larger is the range of specialisms needed to provide information, and the greater the need for qualitative and quantitative skills in managing and assessing it.

Sectoral change over time

There is a symbiotic relationship between the agricultural and non-agricultural sectors of an economy, which changes over time, as illustrated in Figure 5.3. In phase A, almost all labour is absorbed by producing food for its own household, at low levels of output per labour unit. In scattered communities in a period when transport was slow, expensive and difficult, labour has to be spread inefficiently to cope with a variety of needs. As Smith (1776, p338) remarked:

> Without the assistance of some artificers ... the cultivation of land cannot be carried on but with great inconveniency and continual interruption. Smiths, carpenters, wheel-wrights and ploughwrights, masons and bricklayers, tanners, shoemakers and tailors are people whose service the farmer has frequent occasion for.

Farmers are unable to sell any surplus they produce, if all near them are similarly engaged, and they have no access to other centres of demand.[6] Typically, occasional surpluses are spent in feasting and drinking rather than investing to produce more. With low population density, extensive agriculture, using long fallows to restore fertility, is appropriate (Boserup, 1965).

Moving out of this situation is slow and difficult. Figure 5.3 shows that agricultural and non-agricultural labour form each other's market. The respective size of the market, shown by the vertical columns, limits the development of the other sector. Typically the first non-agricultural sectors to develop are those of administration and defence, which often cull any small agricultural surplus that exists without contributing much to the reduction of 'inconveniency' and the interruption of agricultural tasks by other necessities.

The units of time in Figure 5.3 are not standardized. Phase A typically lasted many centuries while the transition Phase B may be accomplished in 50 to 500 years. Its length, often difficult to document in the absence of historical data, depends in part on the technologies available in an external contact economy (Gerschenkron, 1962). In the early slow part of Phase B it is usually assisted by access to external capital and markets to expand the non-agricultural sector and transport facilities. In Britain, generally recognized as the home of the industrial revolution, it began with raw wool exports to only slightly more advanced economies in Europe in the medieval period, and started gathering speed circa 1760–1800. Later developing countries have generally made the transition more quickly than the UK. The most recent examples are in eastern Asia.[7] Change accelerates as productive technologies and technologies for the exchange of goods and

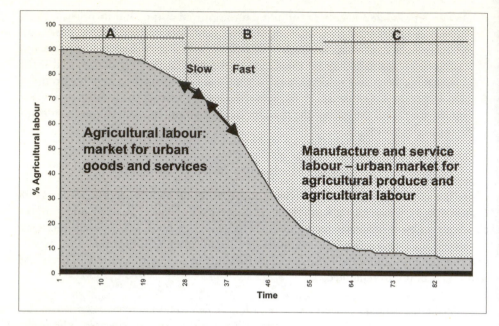

Note: Arrows show positions of low-income and lower middle-income countries in 1960 and 1980, as given in World Bank (1983).

Figure 5.3 *Agricultural, manufacture and service sector over time*

information improve. Concentrations of people facilitate the exchange and development of ideas (Simon, 1977). Countries that cut themselves off from the exchange of goods, ideas and capital, as did China for many centuries (Landes, 1998), and Albania more recently, move more slowly down the curve.

The contact economy also provides a market for farmers hitherto dependent on an extremely small non-agricultural sector. The enlarged market provides a 'vent' for farmers, and stimulates efforts to provide a surplus above family needs in return for desirable consumer goods and inputs, many of which are initially imported. In countries which initially have some underused labour and land the export crop is additional to existing production (Myint, 1967). Hopkins (1973) illustrated this with special reference to West Africa. In countries with large numbers of peasant farmers, their additional purchasing power stimulates the consumer goods and service sectors. This effect is not so powerful in countries where a few people control most of the land and hold down agricultural wages, as in parts of Latin America, as Tomich et al (1995) point out. Fortunately, this does not apply in most of SSA, where small-scale farming predominates.

The external economy may also provide investment capital that begins to expand the local urban sector, with port and transport facilities etc. Smith thought the rapid progress towards wealth of 'our American colonies' in the 17th and early 18th century was due to the fact that their citizens were able to concentrate their scarce capital resources on the development of agriculture (which he saw as its most productive and secure use) because British merchants were supplying the capital for the much more risky export trade – ships and even warehouses (Smith, 1776, p329). The steam ship and railway expanded the reach of export markets in Asia in the 19th century, but, aside from ports, major transport and urban infrastructure investments for SSA only occurred in the first half of the 20th century.

Under the stimulus of export markets for a product which many can supply, agriculture begins to become more productive. Initially, there is vacant land farmers can develop for cropping They are helped by better implements usually brought in by trade – axes, metal hoes, animal-drawn ploughs, etc. These are often locally manufactured once the market is established, though they will only be selectively adopted, according to their suitability for the land-labour ratios and other local conditions (Pingali et al,1987).[8] Farming can therefore begin not only to supply food, but also to release labour to a growing urban sector, which is beginning to produce and supply consumer goods, services and some of the inputs for agriculture, reducing the inconveniency of self-manufacture, and freeing up labour for more intensive farming. The urban sector can begin to grow because farmers are now becoming a local, effective, cash-earning market. The economy is embarking on Phase B, in Figure 5.3.

In turn, a larger, more productive urban sector enlarges the market for farmers and stimulates them to invest in improvements. Without investments to improve productivity a falling proportion in farming would be unable to supply the needs of a greater proportion in the non-agricultural sectors. The internal market becomes very large by Phase C. At this stage the manufacturing and service sectors are no longer limited to the agricultural sector for their internal market, since they are also selling to other specialists in the non-farm sectors. The size of the internal market for farm output depends on the incomes (and therefore productivity) of urban people, as well as actual numbers in towns, since Bennet's Law predicts that as incomes rise, the share of starchy staples in food declines, and diet shifts towards livestock products, fruit and vegetables (Tomich et al, 1995, p163). However, it is also governed by the costs and speed of transport facilities for bulky and/or perishable commodities.[9]

Rural should not be equated with agricultural. While agricultural activities take place almost entirely in the rural areas, rural areas will also develop services and small-scale manufacturing activities to meet local needs. Large scale manufacturing industries will be located in urban areas at nodal points on the transport network, to facilitate distribution to a wide market.[10]

As the manufacturing and service sector increases its productivity and income, it attracts labour out of agriculture, leading to the faster stages of Phase B. At some point, even in populations that are still growing, the actual numbers of people performing agricultural tasks begin to drop, as well as their share in the workforce. There is a growing need for additional capital to substitute for labour. As an example, farmers on a new irrigation scheme in Muda, Malaysia, found themselves obliged, between 1974 and 1979, to begin hiring combine harvesters and other machinery to replace the labour of sons and daughters who had moved into a growing industrial sector.[11] Some farmers are forced out of farming by their inability to finance new capital requirements, or their heirs choose to sell up to transfer into activities perceived as more profitable. A tendency towards larger, capital-intensive farms develops as Phase C approaches. This paper is not examining Phase C, but concentrates on Phase B, as it is likely to develop in SSA.

The importance of investment and the differing nature of investments required to improve agricultural and non-agricultural productivity

While in historical experience the growth of the manufacturing and service sector is generally associated with higher incomes per capita, this desirable outcome has depended on effective investments in all sectors, and, therefore, on policies that have provided incentives and security for investment in and maintenance of new assets, and the availability of information and education to increase ability to select effective investments.

Characteristically, but not exclusively, raising the productivity of the small-scale farming sector requires many repeated small private investments (developing new land, acquiring a new tool or other input, increasing the value of livestock held, planting and nurturing tree seedlings etc). These are barely perceptive to outsiders, though they can have a significant impact on production (Tomich et al, 1995, p21). In some cases the investment can be of work for a delayed reward, rather than actual cash. The cumulative size of these incremental and intermittent investments depends on whether there is an enabling policy environment, which preserves private incentives to invest, spreads information about opportunities and risks, and improves access to markets. Effective private investment in agriculture is most assisted by appropriate public investments outside agriculture, for example, in communications infrastructure[12] to assist marketing and the gathering of new information. State investments in primary education can assist in the uptake and assessment of information.

Although agricultural investments are typically small and incremental, there are exceptions. Government investment in large irrigation facilities has been crucial in Asia, though often beset by difficulties in management and maintenance. The water resources of SSA make it necessarily more reliant on small-scale irrigation to which farmers can themselves contribute resources and management inputs. State investment in research has also been important and can speed up the development of improved crop varieties etc.

By contrast, large increases in the productivity of the industrial and service sector depend characteristically, but not exclusively, on large-scale, lumpy, investments in electricity, water, communications etc, which are typically supplied by state, municipal authorities or by shareholders in large private firms (often foreign in the initial stages). These are being termed collective investments, in contrast to the family-scale investments in farming. Large collective investments, like family investments, need good information and risk assessment to succeed, but, as the demands are more complex, this requires public and private investments in higher education for management as well as in primary education for the workforce.

Goodness of fit with statistical time series

It has already been said that the curve in Figure 5.3 is not based on consistent time units. It is presented to illustrate a pattern, and the steepness of the slope in Phase B will vary according to the circumstances and policies of particular countries. The point at which it levels out will depend in part on the size and natural assets of different countries, and in part on their policies. However, it will always take the form of a backward sloping S, owing to mutually reinforcing and accelerating impacts of one sector upon the other.

These impacts are related to the efficiency and income effect of the investments made in each sector. They will be less where the major element in the service sector is an unproductive civil service, or where the state has invested in manufacturing projects that fail to give an economic return. The World Bank estimates that the productivity of investment in SSA needs to double (World Bank, 2000a).

Nevertheless, the model as depicted fits reasonably well with data on percentage of the labour force engaged in agriculture for 1960 and 1980. The change in their position is shown by the arrows on the curve. Low income countries, less than 18 per cent urbanized in 1960, moved relatively slowly in 20 years from 77 per cent engaged in agriculture to 70 per cent in 1980. Lower middle-income countries, less than 38 per cent urbanized in 1960, moved more rapidly in the same 20 years from 71 per cent in agriculture to 55 per cent. The figures are not exactly comparable, as some countries have moved from one category to the other in the same 20 years. However, they tend to confirm the thesis that urbanization and, by implication, the development of the manufacturing and service sector, accelerate, giving rise to the S-shaped curve depicted in Figure 5.3. They also confirm that this process is associated with increasing wealth per capita. The agricultural labour force figures are somewhat suspect, since they tend to be worked out as a residual after the known workforce in formal sectors have been deducted (Tomich et al, 1995). They include many in the non-formal non-agricultural sector. Hence, the data on urbanization provide a better guide to the scale of change, though there are problems with varying definitions of urban. Figure 5.1 has shown that since 1968 most SSA countries have become over 30 per cent urban and five are over 40 per cent. This implies agricultural labour occupies no more than 60–70 per cent of the labour force, placing them clearly in the transition Phase B of Figure 5.3.

The weaknesses of the statistical base

National statistical data have many weaknesses in SSA (and probably elsewhere).

Population and labour data

While the World Bank population and urbanization figures can be accepted as giving orders of magnitude, they are not safe as accurate inputs into mathematical comparisons between countries. Censuses have been infrequent in many SSA countries.[13] The results are late in entering national and international statistics. The on-going population transition in some countries, and the AIDS epidemic in others, have probably lowered annual growth rates below estimated rates. The most glaring errors are in Nigeria, where the census of 1991 counted 88.99 million. However, the World Bank (2002 was still giving 98.98 million as the 1991 figure, and adding 2.8 per cent annually till 1997, reducing this by stages to 2.4 per cent in 2000. This produced an estimated population of 127 million in 2000, whereas a continuous growth rate of 2.4 per cent from the census figure results in 110 million.[14] The discrepancy in the divisor affects all Nigerian per capita data, and even affects group data for SSA, as Nigeria holds 20 per cent of the SSA population.

Definitions of urban vary by country and by census date. Urban in Nigeria in 1963 was defined as agglomerations over 5000, and over 20,000 in 1991. In Niger, in 1988, 'urban' was places of more than 2500 with a government office (Republic of Niger, 1992). In Senegal, urban in 1988 meant having a municipal commune. The second largest city, Touba, a religious rather than administrative headquarters, was administratively rural, though it counted 183,000 inhabitants in 1988 (Barry et al, 2000). By 1999 it was reported as 500,000 (Coulon, 1999) – not insignificant in a country with a total population of 10,000,000.

Employment by sector is generally acknowledged to be the weakest part of most census data.[15] The percentage living in rural areas can be taken as the upper limit for agricultural labour, since the number of rural people whose main activity is outside farming is almost certainly greater than the number of urban people whose main activity is farming. Many studies have found considerable rural non-farm income. In a review of 25 case studies in SSA, at times varying from 1974 to 1990–1991, Reardon (1997) found its average share of household income to be 45 per cent. Bryceson (2002) found higher levels by the later 1990s in six SSA countries, with 60–80 per cent of income from non-agricultural sources. If carried out only in the off-season these activities are not competitive with farm labour, but some household members give preference to non-farm labour even in the farming season. Demand for local retailing, transport, and manufactures rises when farming areas generate higher output and higher incomes. In five villages in Java visited in 1974 and revisited in 1987, it was observed that farm incomes had improved by possibly 30–50 per cent in real terms, and there was better clothing, wider possession of consumer goods, and better access to education and transport (Prabowo and McConnell, 1993). This obviously meant more employment of rural teachers, drivers, shopkeepers etc, and there were specialized industries in some villages. On the Muda irrigation scheme in Malaysia every additional US$1 earned from improved rice output generated another US$0.74 of activities and earnings off-scheme (Bell et al, 1982). These intersectoral linkages are also noted in SSA (Barrett et al, 2001b) but these often 'informal' activities may not be caught in official statistics.

Agricultural output, food imports and contribution to the GDP

Agricultural output is notoriously difficult to estimate. The amounts consumed on farm or traded domestically are likely to be underestimated. Figure 5.4 shows the value of agricultural exports as a percentage of agricultural GDP for 1995. It is immediately apparent that Zimbabwe and Malawi were not valuing their locally consumed crops and livestock.[16] A survey in a tobacco growing area of Malawi found that just over 40 per cent of farmers' income came from crop sales, of which only 15 per cent in 1990 and 9 per cent in 2000 came from the export crop, tobacco. The field pea contribution was 10 per cent in 1990 and 23 per cent in 2000 but until 1998 this crop was not officially recorded (Orr and Mwale, 2001).

Despite the growing urban population, who, being slightly better off, consume more high value foods and beverages than rural people, food imports have generally remained in a range of US$3–10 per head since 1980.[17] Food import data in countries with limited import routes are likely to be more reliable than food production data, but

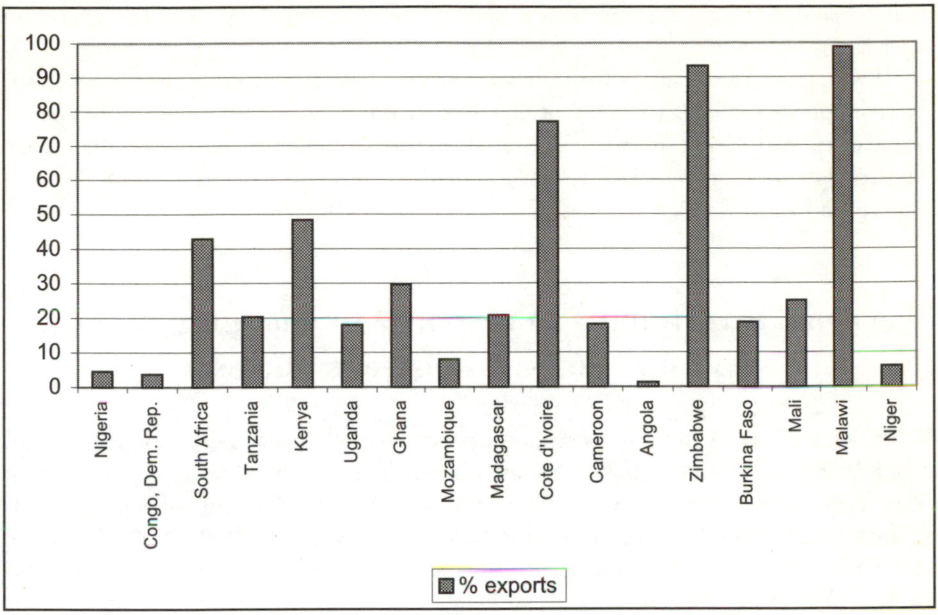

Source: Constructed from World Bank Africa Database (2000) (data not available in 2002 version)

Figure 5.4 *Agricultural exports as a percentage of agricultural GDP in largest SSA countries, in 1995*

not all countries measure imports. Calculations from World Bank (2002) show that among the nine large countries supplying this data, in eight, food imports per capita have been static or falling since the mid-1980s, Kenya being a possible exception. In most they have remained below $10 per capita, in constant 1995 US$. Senegal, where policy favoured rice imports to increase specialization on groundnuts, is exceptional with a level generally above $25 per capita, though it seems to have fallen since the devaluation of the CFA Franc (FCFA) in 1994. Nigeria, up at nearly $35 in 1981–1982, fell back to $4–8 after successive devaluations. Some temporary rises due to droughts can be seen, particularly marked for Zimbabwe, 1989–91. The implication is that in most countries, farmers have kept up with the level of demand, and changes in its nature, with variations in part due to policies, and occasionally to drought. This is incompatible with the calculated volume of food output by major crop given in table 8-6 in World Bank (2002) (which quotes FAO data). This shows annual percentage growth in almost all cases of less than 1 per cent, which is certainly less than population increase. Static per capita production implies an annual growth in food crops equal to population growth, unless imports are rising.[18]

Farmers might meet internal demand without increasing productivity if they transfer resources from export crops to food crops. However, volumes for three main exports, cocoa, cotton and coffee, 1968–97 were maintained (World Bank, 2002). Groundnut exports fell substantially between 1968 and 1978, stabilized 1978–88 and fell again somewhat between 1988 and 1998. Our studies show more of this crop going to meet local demand, but falls in export prices and rosette disease in Nigeria in the 1970s are other factors.

If we ignore the countries with obvious errors in Figure 5.4, most countries are not exporting more than 20 per cent of agricultural production value, so 80 per cent is locally consumed. Crops internally consumed are now much more important than crops exported, as we should expect to happen with countries in the transition Phase B depicted in Figure 5.3.

Farmers' investments in response to changing markets in four semi-arid districts of SSA

Given the deficiencies in national data, the processes of change are best understood and tested against the model in Figure 5.3 at a district level. At this level sample data from villages can be related to district statistics and, therefore, to the national statistics built up from them. This has been done for four semi-arid areas, 1960–2000. These are Makueni District, Kenya, Diourbel Region, Senegal, Maradi Department, Niger and the Kano hinterland, Nigeria.

Farmers in these areas are restricted in the crops they can grow, unless they have access to pockets of irrigable or water-retentive land. The main crops are cereals and pulses, low in value in relation to bulk, but capable also of providing fodder to livestock. In the past the main export crop was groundnuts, and in Makueni, cotton. Three districts have one short farming season lasting three to five months, but Makueni has two wet seasons of about three months each. Rainfall is very variable from year to year, giving a risk of crop failure. Nevertheless semi-arid areas contain large populations, with particularly high densities in the hinterlands of Kano in northern Nigeria and Dakar in Senegal.

In terms of the model, we are particularly interested to see whether there has been escalating growth in urban populations. If so, we need to see if farmers have been making the appropriate private investments to respond to a growing urban market for both their products and their labour, or if they have been held back by deficiencies in policy, or in the government supply of some of the services identified as particularly necessary. Changes in land markets should also occur as land becomes more scarce, and in labour disposition if urban occupations become more attractive. Secondly, we need to see if the collective investments and policies required to make the growing non-farm sector more productive are in place, so that it can both provide jobs for people leaving the farms, and a growing market for higher value farm produce such as livestock, fruit and vegetables.

The studies were carried out by teams of scientists from the countries concerned, profiling particular aspects of change, 1960–2000, using methods and data appropriate to the subject matter. This included literature reviews; collection, discussion and analysis of district data with the appropriate government office; air photo and remote sensing interpretation; and collective interviews and sample surveys of 10–12 randomly selected farmers in 4 representative villages.[19] The country team leaders were Francis Gichuki (Kenya), Abdou Fall and Adama Faye (Senegal) and Yamba Boubacar (Niger), who collaborated with Drylands Research in developing from the profiles three national syntheses, using the findings to trace and understand socio-economic and environmental change in its various interactions over time. The Nigerian study was limited, for financial reasons, to five profiles, which included an in-depth study of the marketing of food crops and livestock in the Kano area and a review of policy. Findings were checked by one or more workshops in which District officials and farmer representatives took part. The Department for International Development, UK (DFID) also provided funds for endorsement exercises in the local constituencies in 2001–02.

Changes in rural and urban population and in urban demand

Rapid growth of the local towns occurred in three of the four study areas, with urban population being now 30 per cent or over in two cases (Table 5.1).

The increase in the urban market over time is particularly visible in northern Nigeria and Senegal, but the outcome in terms of effective demand for local farm produce differed. Table 5.1 shows the increase in local urban grain requirements estimated at 200kg/head. Between 1952 and 1991 the urban population of the two states constituted from the colonial Kano Province increased at about 8 per cent per year, while the rural increase was nearer 1.6 per cent. In 1952 Kano municipality was the only town with more than 20,000 inhabitants; by 1991 it had been joined by 11 others (Tiffen, 2001). To cater solely for the local towns, each rural family needed to supply ten times as much grain to urban markets on average in 1991 compared with 1952. In addition, they were supplying grains and pulses (especially maize and cowpeas) to the even more urbanized southern Nigeria (Ariyo et al, 2001). If Nigerian farmers as a whole had failed to invest, food imports would have increased dramatically, but this has not been the case. In the late 1960s Nigeria's food imports were $2–3 per capita (World Bank, 2000a). These billowed to $30–35 in the 1970s during the petroleum boom and while the currency was overvalued, but in the 1990s they were running at only $5–8 per capita (all in constant 1995 US$). Given that the import figure includes all foods and beverages, this does not suggest a large import of staple grains. The scale of the increased production demanded from farmers is understated in Table 5.1, as not all families living in towns of less than 20,000 are primarily engaged in agriculture. It also takes no account of industrial needs. Maize, sorghum and millet are important inputs into large commercial brewing, flour milling and animal foodstuff enterprises (Swindell et al, 1999).

Crop production data for the Kano area was only available to us 1982–90 (World Bank, OED, 1995), when yields were strongly linked with rainfall (Tiffen and Mortimore, 2002). However, for Maradi, Niger, there is a series of District figures running from 1964 to 1998. These show the expected variation in production per capita (taking the total population) from year to year, under the influence of rainfall variation. They also show that, after recovery from the droughts in the early 1970s, farmers upped their production to average around 300kg per capita, (Mortimore et al, 2001) despite a growing rural population, and despite the virtual cessation of supportive projects after 1985, under structural adjustment (Hamadou, 2000a, Figures 4 and 5). This must mean that they saw an incentive to increase their sales.

The net sellers of grain to the towns are not evenly distributed among the rural population. In a large CARE sample in Maradi in 1996 the families defined as the most vulnerable (56 per cent) produced 125kg cereals per capita, against a moderately poor

Table 5.1 *Population and urban grain demand per rural person in four semi-arid areas*

		Total	Urban[a]	% Urban	Urban growth p.a.	Rural density	Urban grain need, kg per rural person[b]
Kano Province	1952	3,396,350	130,173	3.8		77	8.0
Kano & Jigawa States	1991	8,685,995	2,516,686	29.0	7.9	(Jigawa) 118 (Kano) 169	81.6
Maradi	1960 (estimate)	561,000	–	–		13	
	1977	949,747	44,459	4.7	–	22	9.8
	1988	1,389,443	110,739	8.0	8.7	33	17.3
Diourbel	1960 (estimate)	261,000	n.a.	n.a.		n.a.	
	1976	423,038	120,249	28.4		70	79.4
	1988	620,197	251,799	40.6	6.9	94	136.7
Makueni (dryland only)	1962	170,717	–	–	–	38	
	1989	524,025	–	–	–	102	

Notes: [a] The 1991 Nigerian urban definition as settlements of over 20,000 is here applied to all data, regardless of country and time differences. Makueni has no towns of this size.
[b] Grain need assumed as 200kg per head per year. Urban demand at this level has been divided by rural population. To get demand per rural family it is necessary to multiply this up by family size, which varies by country.
Source: Calculated from census data, summaries in Gichuki (2000a), Barry et al (2000) and Tiffen (2001)

group (27 per cent) who produced 311kg, and a relatively well off group of 17 per cent who produced 580kg per capita (CARE International au Niger and Université d'Arizona, 1997). The average was 252kg per capita, in a somewhat below average rainfall year. Food selling was near universal but if one estimates per capita needs at 200kg per capita per annum, it is apparent that quite large numbers of rural families are net buyers of cereals, and that a minority are net sellers.[20] Maradi town has grown, but important influences on farmers are the large towns across the border in Katsina State, Nigeria. Grains and pulses flow in both directions, depending on harvest conditions, prices and exchange rate differences (Meagher, 1997).

Most Maradi farmers have relatively small farms. Cereal yields are in the order of 300–500kg per hectare, which gives an idea of the modest cropped hectares in families producing 125–600kg per head. The distinguishing characteristic of large sellers is their good management quality, which has enabled them to accumulate resources (from live-stock sales, crop production or non-farm incomes) for investment in intensification. Farmers of one southern Maradi village said, in discussing the findings of the research, that farming was only profitable for those who had the means to invest, and those who could await a favourable moment for selling. Commerce, crop farming and livestock raising could not be disassociated (Boubacar and Ibrahim, 2002).

In northern Nigeria the most efficient farms were found to be most numerous in high-density areas with good market facilities. These had smaller than average farms with 4.4 hectares (ha) as against the average in the sample of 5.8ha (Okike et al, 2001). There are larger farms in the vicinity of some big cities, encouraged by the state, where entrepreneurs, variously from trade, the old aristocracy, modern business or the civil service and army, bought land in the 1980s and invested heavily in mechanized farms using hired labour, in response to a perceived growing and profitable demand for millet and other staples. In the 1990s their average size in the vicinity of Sokoto had been reduced to 20–50ha because of rising costs of fuel, shortage of spare parts, and high wage bills (Swindell et al, 1999), a trend also noted by Balcet (1997). A sudden bur-geoning of large-scale farms was also seen round Kano but they were estimated to account for only 5 per cent of total agricultural production. Mustapha and Meagher (2000) noted that many of these 'modern' enterprises foundered when state support was reduced in the aftermath of falling oil prices. A particular feature in northern Nigeria has been the burgeoning of *fadama* farming (on low-lying or riverine land), utilizing small pumps to raise groundwater, to irrigate wheat and vegetables. This demands large inputs into small areas (generally less than 1ha) but leads to very profitable sales to the towns (World Bank, OED, 1995; Swindell et al, 1999).

Local urban growth was also very substantial in Diourbel, Senegal, due largely to the new city of Touba as well as growth in the two of the three older departmental towns (Barry et al, 2000). In addition, farmers had easy access to the expanding capital, Dakar. However, there was almost no urban market for the grain they could produce, millet, due to the long-established preference for rice. While they maintained output of millet per agricultural worker 1960–92 at around 500kg for family use (weather permitting), output per total population fell to around 100kg (Faye et al, 2001, figure 14). The mar-ket for groundnuts as a local cooking oil and ingredient was distorted by government efforts to channel all groundnuts to state oil mills, whose high processing costs mean that urban consumers preferred cheaper imported oils (Gaye, 2000). Hence, the main local impact of urbanization was on demand for meat, particularly after the devaluation of the FCFA made imported meat more expensive. From erratic figures available from the veterinary department, small livestock increased from 100,000–140,000 1966–72 to 200,000–250,000 in the 1990s (cattle numbers were relatively static; holdings of equines grew somewhat, Faye et al, 2000). Sales were not equally distributed, for it was only the farmers who had the resources to invest in livestock, concentrated among those who did not usually have to buy in grain, who were able to go in for substantial livestock fattening (Figure 5.5). As in Nigeria, there are some much larger, more mechanized farms, operated mainly by religious leaders and businessmen, whom we excluded from the sample. In the early 1970s these only produced a small proportion of the groundnut crop (O'Brien, 1975), but the current position is not known.

The exception to local urban growth was Makueni, in Kenya. This part of the former Machakos District had experienced an influx of rural settlers 1950–1990 (Tiffen et al, 1994). Neither Wote, which was made the capital of the newly formed Makueni district in 1992, nor any of the settlements along the Nairobi–Mombasa highway on its southern edge, had attained a population of 20,000 by the 1989 census. It may be significant that, unlike the district towns in the other three countries, there had been no collective urban investment to 1998 in electricity, telephones etc,[21] so, even on the highway, enterprises were limited to services to travellers, marketing, and such crafts and small industries as can operate competitively without power.

In Kenya as a whole, Figure 5.1 shows that urbanization was estimated at 30 per cent by 2000. Makueni farmers had some access, over poor roads, to Mombasa and

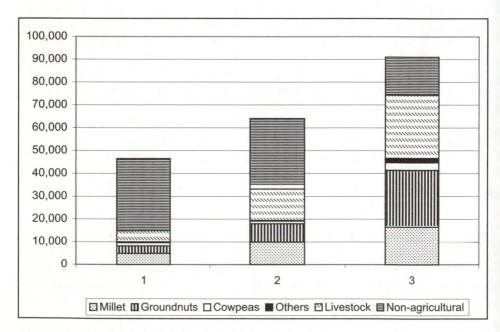

Source: Faye and Fall, 2000 (WP 22), figure 1. Household types as in Table 5.2

Figure 5.5 *Structure of incomes by type of household, Diourbel, 1999–2000*

Nairobi, for their higher value crops such as fruit and vegetables but had no comparative advantage in producing maize for these towns (Gichuki et al, 2000). Mbogoh (2000) found cereal production per person since the district was formed in 1992 varied enormously from year to year, according to district statistics (which are no more than guestimates).[22] The average grain and pulse production 1992–1998 just about met district needs taking all years together. However, in some years farmers were net buyers of cereals and beans (and forced sellers of livestock) while in other years they could sell grains and restock on animals. Unfortunately, livestock disease could wipe out their insurance against crop failure (Fall, 2000). In the worst years, many were dependent on food aid from relatives or the government.

Farmers as investors

As business managers, farmers have to decide how to react to changing product and factor markets, and whether, and in what, to invest.

In northern Nigeria growing food demand has been met by complementary farm investments, despite having to cope with frequent changes and reverses in government policies which have affected the level and competitiveness of food imports, the cost and availability of farm labour, the subsidization or not of fertilizer and other inputs etc (Mustapha and Meagher, 2000). In response to the labour shortage induced by the urban-centred infrastructural petroleum boom in the 1970s, Kano farmers invested to a very considerable extent in buying or hiring ox-drawn equipment, previously rare in the Kano-close settled zone. Maize, a minor crop in 1979, became a major crop in suitable areas by 1989, as farmers adopted a new variety (TZB) that was very responsive to fertilizer, subsidized at the time (Smith et al, 1994). When the fertilizer price was raised, farmers reduced its usage,[23] and reverted to older techniques of maintaining fertility, long practised in the densely settled area around Kano (Mortimore, 1993). They selected and crossed new and old varieties of seed that best matched their ecological niche and changed economic circumstances (Mortimore and Adams, 1999), while also adopting new crops such as soya beans (Balcet, 1997).

Farmers have also responded to the growing demand for meat. The most efficient farms, with the highest gross revenue per hectare and the highest net revenue per farm, were those purchasing in the most crop residues and other inputs, to maintain more than double the average number of livestock in addition to crops, using three times as much manure as the average and more days of animal traction (usually hired) (Okike et al, 2001). Areas of common grazing in the densely settled Kano and Jigawa states are very limited, but 1984 data show the high numbers of livestock kept on farms with some water-retentive land (20– 40 per cent of such households had cattle, and 75–90 per cent had around 15 sheep and goats) (World Bank, OED, 1995, table 3.8). The livestock are penned to maximize manure collection and to fatten up quickly. The high inputs of labour this requires for feeding and watering, as compared with herding (Mortimore and Adams, 1999) is only worthwhile if there is an active market for livestock as well as cereals. There is now an active market for crop residues, with prices higher for groundnut and cowpea hay than for grain (Baba and Magaji, 1998). Farmers have recently shown interest in a new cowpea variety that gives more fodder, though it requires spraying (Singh et al, 2001).

Farmers in Diourbel, Senegal, also calculate the returns to different farm enterprises and technologies and invest accordingly. In the 1960s through to the 1990s, Senegal farmers have been weighing up the value of investing in fertilizer in relation to its price and groundnut prices, and the merits of heavy versus light ploughs, or in buying a plough versus a cart for transport (Faye et al, 2001). In response to the growing urban market for meat, and the rising price of mutton, many in this so-called groundnut basin had by the 1990s decided to go in for animal fattening. Schoonmaker Freudenberger and Schoonmaker Freudenberger (1993) reported how families in a village to the north of Diourbel said it was better to invest in five lambs than to seed an area with 500kg of groundnuts. Livestock have become a major element in farm incomes of the better off, as shown in Figure 5.5. By 1999 much of their groundnut production was not sold for export, but consumed locally as nuts or oil, with the cake and hay providing valuable fodder supporting their livestock enterprises (Faye, 2002; Faye and Fall, 2000). Their investments have followed suit, as shown in Table 5.2. It is not surprising that the poorest spend little on farm inputs, but it is worthy of note that the investments of the middle and better off segments get directed towards livestock rather than crop enterprises.

The way farmers plan, assess, invest over time and juggle resources, was particularly illustrated in the Makueni study. Farmers were asked to identify the three most important past investments contributing to their welfare. Terracing, planting trees, clearing bush, building a house, and educating children topped the charts (Nelson, 2000). Clearing bush and building a house were preliminary investments. Terraces, trees and education came in later stages. On the farms in the sample, the construction of terraces and drains had taken, per hectare, 30–60 man days and Kenya shillings 5000–9000 (Gichuki, 2000b), and had been gradually extended to all their cropped land. All farmers had planted fruit trees, ranging from three on very small farms to over 200 on some larger ones. This involves considerable investment in labour for planting pits and watering during establishment, as well as manure and seedling purchase. Half the sample had made investments intended to improve output even during the difficult 1990s, bunched in years giving a good harvest. All farmers could readily identify the next one or two investments they wanted to make when resources became available. These were mainly related to equipment (67 per cent), inputs (17 per cent) and granaries (13 per cent), needed to increase their output of cereals and pulses (Mbogoh, 2000). A good half of the finance for their investments came from non-farm income (Nelson, 2000), which in bad years gets taken up by consumption needs.

In Maradi, the main investment initially was in clearing new land for cultivation, within the village area while available, later further north. The process is made visible by air photograph and satellite data (Figure 5.6). In one of the four villages, Jiratawa, there was also project investment in an irrigation scheme, but the others were unassisted. Owing to the availability till recently of land that could be fallowed or cleared, investment in intensification is only just beginning. Investments in equipment (Table 5.3) have accelerated since the devaluation of the FCFA, which, as in Burkina Faso (Hoffmann, 1998) and Senegal, has resulted in improved prices for local livestock and grains (Kherallah et al, 2000).

The volume of farm investment in the districts over the 40 years could not be calculated, but it was certainly substantial in Makueni, Maradi and the Kano area. In Makueni and Maradi, credit was unimportant, and finance came from crop and livestock

Table 5.2 *Use of money income by 38 Diourbel farmers (1999–2000)*

Type of household	Type 1	Type 2	Type 3
Household characteristics			
% of sample in this type	29.4	41.2	29.4
Estimated income per head in past year (FCFA)	46,456	64,054	91,019
Months own millet & groundnuts met family needs	<6	6–11	12+
% Income not farm generated	68	48	18
% Family workers absent in farming season	25.0	16.7	18.8
Use of money income (%)			
Consumption			
Buying millet	16.9	7.5	5.4
Buying rice	15.2	13.1	10.3
Buying other food	22.0	11.7	26.6
Clothing	14.3	19.2	9.0
Buying other products	5.6	2.7	3.2
Farm-related expenditure			
Equipment	0.5	0.6	2.1
Buying animals	0.8	12.0	18.9
Buying animal food or medication	1.1	4.4	2.9
Buying crop inputs	1.9	1.9	2.4
Payment for services	1.6	1.8	2.0
Other expenditure			
Health and education	3.6	4.1	2.7
Ceremonial expenses	16.6	21.0	14.5
Total	100.0	100.0	100.0

Source: Faye et al, 2001. Percentage not farm generated calculated from original data not there quoted. The sample was small, being based on 10 randomly selected farmers in four villages but the results are all in the direction expected.

sales, family transfers, and use of non-farm income. We have no data on the role of credit in the Kano area, but some were available. Credit was part of the state-imposed system in Diourbel, circa 1965–1980, when all producers had to belong to a cooperative, which provided inputs on credit, and sold output at controlled, low, prices. In bad years farmers were obliged to default, eventually bringing about the bankruptcy of the responsible state organization (which was also overstaffed, inefficient and corrupt) and impelling Senegal to adopt drastic retrenchment policies (Gaye, 2000).

    The important role of livestock, themselves a form of capital and an insurance substitute, but also demanding capital for replacement and maintenance, was evident in all the districts. However, in lowland Makueni, Kenya, livestock appeared particularly

Table 5.3 *Years in which 40 interviewed farmers acquired new capital equipment in Maradi, Niger*

	Plough oxen	Ox cart	Heavy plough (charrue)	Light plough (houe)	Bicycle	Motor cycle
To 1994	1	8	10	4	2	0
After 1994	18	9	2	34	6	4

Note: The FCFA was devalued in January 1994, and 1994 was counted in the pre-devaluation epoch, on the supposition that its effects on prices might not be immediate. (Shaikh and McGahuey (1996) actually found some pretty immediate increases in water conservation techniques for cereals in western Niger). The heavy plough had been promoted, and credit provided, under a project, which ceased operation in 1987.
Source: Hamadou, 2000b

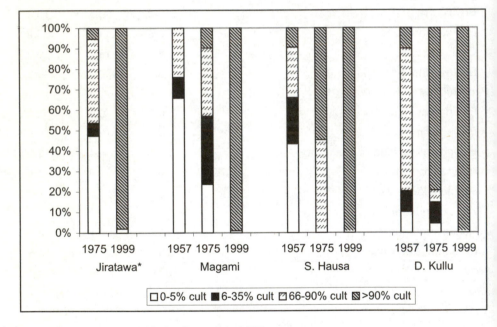

Note: * No data are available for Jiratawa in 1957.
Source: Mahamane, 2001, tables 5, 7, 9, 11. Villages arranged from south to north

Figure 5.6 *Expansion of cultivation in four terroirs, Maradi Department, Niger, 1957–1999, in four cultivation frequency classes (% of area)*

vulnerable to disease, and many farmers had experienced substantial stock losses. Some farmers in the limited areas with suitable topography had built small dams to water crossbred cows, to take advantage of the recently improved milk market when the Marketing Board's monopoly of urban sales was abolished, and these also invested in spraying equipment and veterinary supplies. For most farmers, dairying was too hazardous (Fall, 2000; Mbogoh, 2000).

Exports versus local urban markets

Exports overseas have become less important in the 1990s compared with 1960–70 (Maradi farmers still export, but to towns just over the border in Nigeria). Nigerian groundnut exports fell drastically due to rosette disease in the early 1970s. The crop is now reviving, with the aid of new resistant varieties, there and in Maradi, but sales are oriented to the towns (Hamadou, 2000a; Ariyo et al, 2001). Even in Diourbel, Senegal, where the government has continued to view groundnuts as an export crop, many farmers grow it, but do not sell (Faye and Fall, 2000), and they rank its uses as food, fodder and then cash (Faye, 2002). In Makueni, cotton was briefly promoted as a cash crop under an aid programme 1978–1987 but collapsed due to late payments by the responsible parastatal (Tiffen et al, 1994). Some farmers would be glad if a ginnery could be re-established locally (Gichuki et al, 2000).

Changes in the land market and in income distribution

Land scarcity has developed everywhere, due to a slow increase in rural population and improved market access, which has increased the value of output, and encouraged farm expansion when land was available. As a result, land has become a marketable commodity, in all four of the areas examined. This has been least the case in the Diourbel Region, partly because of the 1964 Senegal statute ascribing ownership to the state and user rights to the user, but also because state policies have in various ways decreased the profitability of groundnut and millet sales, leading to substantial emigration out of farming[24] (Faye et al, 2001). There has not been the same competition to obtain land for young families, or to retain land, as in the other three districts.

In the other three areas the land market is active. Intensification increasingly needs cash to buy labour, inputs, equipment and livestock, in addition to, or in substitution for, labour for a delayed reward. Not all farmers have been able to find the resources and to manage the associated risks. Even in Maradi, where intensification is at an early stage, some poor farmers have had to sell fields to the more successful (Boubacar, 2000). In the Kano area, some farmers have been less able to cope than others with the rapid changes in matters such as fertilizer prices, product prices etc, and Meagher and Mustapha (1997) noted increased income differentiation in one village, between 1989–90 and 1992–93, between small farmers who had to buy in food at rising prices, and larger farmers, who were better able to play the markets. Farmers, or their heirs, who inherit smaller farms, if unable to find the necessary capital to intensify production from a small land holding, are increasingly forced to look to other occupations for a living, and some prefer, or are forced, to sell up. Near Sokoto and Gusau, in north-west Nigeria, some farms have diminished in size to a garden plot, and the main income is earned by agricultural wage labour or other labour. These areas also have many intermediate viable small farms, and some large capitalized farms. In the rapidly changing job and land market of Nigeria, affected by petroleum booms and busts, inflation, import bans and relaxations, voluntary buyers and sellers of land may come to regret their decisions, but the worst sufferers are often those whose land has been forcibly taken over by the state (Iliya and Swindell, 1997), often without compensation, to accommodate urban expansion.

The labour market, specialization and diversification of incomes

In Nigeria, census data showed average family size of 5 in Jigawa, and 5.4 in Kano, with the (male) household head said to constitute 70–80 per cent of its economically active workforce.[25] In Makueni, the resident family was 5.8, including 2 adult workers and children in school. These figures do not suggest an abundance of labour on family farms. In all four countries the farm household was also financially and emotionally linked to adult children and/or spouses who worked elsewhere either as commuters, or for part of the year, or as permanent urban residents. Family labour has to be carefully allocated across occupations, and decisions have to be made as to whether to utilize child labour, or forgo it in favour of sending children to school.

The model in Figure 5.3 was built on the premise that specialization brings benefits. It is apparent that farmer households in semi-arid areas do not specialize in the sense of only growing crops or only rearing livestock, nor in the sense of relying only on farm income. The separation of farming and herding made sense in semi-arid areas in Phase A with low population density and limited access to markets for farm products, but in Phase B, in semi-arid areas, the integration of crops and livestock by smallholders becomes advantageous to provide manure and draught power, the more so as their main crops also provide animal feed.[26] In Maradi, many settled Hausa farmers were acquiring cattle, and many Fulani herders were cultivating crops around a camp that was becoming permanent (CARE International au Niger and Université d'Arizona, 1997; Mortimore et al, 2001). Studies of Fulani livestock raisers in reserves in northern Nigeria show both they and the farmers outside the reserve now combine livestock and cropping, in a variety of ways (Baba and Magaji, 1998; Hassan et al, 1998). If it is not a contradiction in terms, semi-arid farmers have become specialists in mixed farming and crop–livestock integration.

In semi-arid areas with variable rainfall, income diversification, in the sense of combining farming and non-farm activities within one household, has advantages, particularly by spreading risk. A Makueni farmer said 'When there is a drought, I lose as a farmer, but as a teacher, I never experience that drought. I still get my salary and can survive better than if I was only a farmer' (Nzioka, 2000, p12). Ellis (2000, p5) points out that this cuts across the view that specialization and market exchanges are the way to higher incomes and improved welfare, and it might therefore be thought to be in contradiction with the economic logic behind Figure 5.3. However, we must distinguish between household and individual specialization. In the Kenyan case quoted above, the husband concentrated on teaching, and his wife on farming, and they both benefited from sharing resources.[27] In other cases, a second activity may be carried out in a different season – a man farms in the wet season, and trades in the dry, so he can give full attention to each in turn. Indeed, by turning over his capital several times in the dry season, he gains additional resources to buy inputs for the farming season.[28] It is necessary again to distinguish between those who sell small amounts out of necessity, and those who buy in from others and trade on a considerable scale. The latter are generally in the upper echelons of small farmers. CARE International au Niger and Université d'Arizona (1997) found grain sold by even the most vulnerable households (56 per cent of their Maradi sample)[29] who had then to finance by some means or another grain purchases later. A few people in this group and the middle group (27 per cent) were able to buy on a larger scale, as agent of a bigger trader who advanced them money. Wholesaler traders who bought and resold hundreds of sacks of grain on their own account were almost all in the 'riches paysans' category (17 per cent).

It has been observed that diversification does not necessarily level rural incomes. There is often a U-shaped relationship in which the proportion of non-farm in total farm household income is high for both rich and poor, and lower in the middle groups (Iliya and Swindell, 1997; Barrett et al, 2000; Reardon et al, 2000; Toulmin et al, 2000; Bryceson, 2002). When diversification is driven by desperation, families try to cobble together a living by farming, working for others, collecting, hawking, handicrafts etc, and each activity may impede good achievement in the others. Ellis (2000) refers to the key difference between individual diversification and low levels of skill, associated with poverty, and household diversification, in which individuals specialize, which is associated with the better off. In Nigeria, the most successful farmers were those who had within their household someone in well-paid or middling formal sector jobs, or in trading and contracting, which provided a cash flow to finance farm inputs. These households contained individual specialists, backed by accumulated capital or skills, while in poorer households people scramble for casual labour alongside their own farming (Iliya and Swindell, 1997). This was also the case in western Kenya (Hamilton, 2003). In Côte d'Ivoire a middle group of specialist farmers could also be distinguished (Barrett et al, 2001a).

In Senegal, Table 5.2 and Figure 5.5 show that the poorer households in Group 1 scraped a living from a diversity of local occupations. The wealthier households in Group 3, who were investing most in livestock, tended to have most of their non-farm income in the form of remittances from urban-based children. Those in residence concentrated on farming, but in all households, around a fifth of the family workforce was absent in the farming season (Table 5.2). Farmers in Diourbel calculate the opportunity cost of using their sons' labour on the farm or encouraging them to migrate to urban areas or, if they can manage the higher cost, overseas. Some of the ceremonial expenses listed in Table 5.2 support the Mouride leadership in construction and merchant enterprises in Dakar, Touba and overseas, where petty trading, transporting, labouring etc provide income to adherents despite lack of formal qualifications (Wilson Fall, 2000; Babou, 2002).

A remarkable difference between Kenya and the two francophone countries was in investment in education. Makueni parents invested heavily in educating all their children, boys and girls, motivated in part by the hope of qualifying one or more to compete successfully for a skilled or professional occupation (Nzioka, 2000). They were well aware that their children would need non-farm incomes and, despite high costs, sent all boys and girls to primary school, most to nursery school, and 20–30 per cent to secondary school (with an anxious eye on the job market, to see if the latter was cost-effective).[30] Education was regarded as a priority expenditure; and farm investments got what was left over (Nzioka, 2000; Gichuki et al, 2000). On average the household included two non-residents, and while 23 per cent of these worked on family farms elsewhere,[31] 26 per cent were in urban employment in the private sector, and 10 per cent in urban-based government employment. Due to the lack of local towns, rural businesses and government services provided comparatively few jobs (Nzioka, 2000). Educated children in jobs were expected to, and did, assist their parents with emergency expenditures, and, importantly, with financial resources for investments to improve the farm (Nelson, 2000; Nzioka, 2000). This is household diversification, with individual specialization. A similar value was placed on education in western Kenya (Francis, 2000; Hamilton, 2003).

In Diourbel and Maradi the non-farm occupations open to the illiterate young were mainly unskilled labour and petty trading. Rural parents did not see their children as likely to succeed in academically oriented schooling, which starts from day one in French. Hence, migrating rural children can contribute less to the productivity of the urban workforce in Senegal and Niger than in Kenya. With unskilled jobs, their small remittances back home assist subsistence, not farm investment (David and Niang, 1995; Wilson Fall, 2000; Diarra Doka, 2001). Nigeria is an intermediate position, with some families able to access jobs through education, and others investing in traditional client-age relationships to access less skilled work or to get into trade. In Nigeria, as in Kenya, non-farm earnings financed farm investments (Iliya and Swindell, 1997).

The market for farm labour has also become important, as efficient farmers need to buy in labour at crucial times or for special tasks. In Makueni we found wages varied according to demand, level of skill and value of marginal output (Nelson, 2000). Similar wage variation was noted in Nigeria, where the agricultural labour market centres on towns, where it is easiest for seekers of employment and seekers of labour to meet. Farmers with very small farms could intercalate work on these with work for others, and because of their experience, were preferred to cheaper student labour (Swindell et al, 1999).

Conclusions and policy implications

We need to understand the interrelationship of the agricultural and non-agricultural sectors at different points in time as population grows, and redistributes itself between urban and rural. When the current round of censuses has been analysed, we shall probably find more evidence of rapid change, and governments need to be ready with appropriate policies. The growth of the local urban market in SSA has been demonstrated. Policies which increase the purchasing power of local urban communities are becoming more relevant than export-oriented ones. The recent drops in livestock turnover in northern Nigeria due to falling urban incomes (Ariyo et al, 2001) affect not merely farmers' incomes, but also their ability to insure, and to maintain soil fertility.

Farmers have responded to increased demand by a multitude of small investments linked to changes in technologies and in products, but they have been hindered by state control of markets (as in Senegal) or rapidly changing policies, exchange rates and inflation (Nigeria, and to a lesser extent, Kenya). Agricultural output can now only be increased by very efficient combinations of land, labour and capital. Those farmers who cannot invest are increasingly being forced out of farming. Some of the children of even the prosperous farmer will need, or be attracted to, other livelihoods. The rural poorest need a vibrant non-farm sector.

The appropriate areas for government and aid-assisted investment need to be identified bearing in mind both the different types of investment most required by farm and non-farm sectors, and the changing urban–rural balance. For some countries, like Niger, the emphasis must still be the enabling environment to allow small farmers to build up their farms, and become buyers of urban services and manufactures. Other countries now need to give more attention to attracting collective resources to develop the urban sector, while at the same time protecting farmers' capacity to invest to meet urban demand. Priorities for constrained government and aid budgets must be the services and infrastructures which enable citizens to make full use of their own talents, ingenuity and resources (Drylands Research, 2001). Communications infrastructure, (roads and tele-phones), primary education, law and order, and good management of the currency are needed by all sectors, and by farmers as well as industrialists. The interaction between the two sectors depends on good communications. Roads usable by lorries remain vitally important both to farmers (Omamo, 1998) and urban consumers. Education benefits both, if its content and language are appropriate. Farmers in Kenya find education, which starts in local languages worthwhile for their children, and invest their own money in building schools and paying fees (Gichuki et al, 2000; Nzioka, 2000). Swahili, like Hausa, gives access to written information in newspapers, advertisements etc. Their adult children and spouses had a great variety of occupations. Farmers in the Sahel are not convinced of the benefit of free education starting in French, but illiteracy cuts them off from written information (whether on a fertilizer label or in the accounts of their *groupement d'intérêt économique*), and from the better-paying non-farm jobs.

While farmers can usually find their resources for a profitable investment, some services and investments can better be supplied collectively. Examples are preventative veterinary services, some types of water development, and research.

Turning to non-farm sectors, it is clear that rural families, and especially the poorer ones, rely in part on non-farm income, preferably in a nearby town or village, if not, in a more distant city.[32] Premature, state-led industrialization has a poor record. By 1986 most of the state-promoted industries in Maradi town, set up in the late colonial period, or during the uranium boom had closed, and most employment was in the informal sector (Grégoire, 1990; Tiffen, 2001). In Senegal the modern industrial sector was for various reasons uncompetitive, over-regulated, and suffered from 'a domestic market that was highly restricted by low incomes', so failed to expand (Berthélemy et al, 1996, p100). Nigeria has conditions more conducive to successful industrialization, and the modern sector expanded in Kano during the oil boom, with both state and private capital, but import-reliant industries suffered in the 1980s from shortages of raw materi-als, leading to retrenchment of workers, under-utilization of capacity, and closures. While sectors dependent on local raw materials did somewhat better (Olukoshi, 1996), modern industrial establishments fell from 327 in 1989 to 243 by 1993 (Tiffen, 2001). Industry was hindered by rent seeking, deteriorating services and falling demand from consumers hit by inflation (Olukoshi, 1996). Runaway inflation and over-valued exchange rates hindered good management.[33] In turn, the downward pressures on wages reduced effective demand for the higher value agricultural products.

Productive investment in West Africa has been more lacking in the industrial sector, which needs collective investment, than in the farm sector which has responded with family investments. Kenya has a relatively successful modern sector, but concentrated in a few towns. Government investment in providing infrastructure to more towns – elec-tricity, piped water, telecommunications etc – may be more effective than direct state investment in manufacture.

Governments cannot do everything, particularly if they are to avoid taxing away private incentive to invest. They cannot rely on aid, because aid availability per head is going down. Hence, as urbanization proceeds, both aid agencies and national policy makers need to think seriously about appropriate public investments for particular countries at a particular time, and to be conscious that times are changing.

Notes

1   This paper owes much to the collaboration I have enjoyed over many years with Michael Mortimore, and draws upon studies comparing four semi-arid districts in sub-Saharan Africa, which he led for Drylands Research. These were funded by the Department for International Development, UK, which, however, is not responsible for the views expressed. My intellectual debts to others too numerous to mention will be partially apparent in the bibliography. They include an anonymous reviewer who made helpful suggestions.

2   It could be argued that the poorest of the poor could be helped by income redistribution without growth, but this is politically a more difficult option.

3   They have been more successful in Asia than elsewhere. Kriekhaus (2002) has argued that public savings by states with 'high bureaucratic capacity' can successfully allocate resources to strategic industrial sectors. However, in many cases, the need to manipulate resources to reward political supporters has predominated over what capacity there might be.

4   Alexandratos (1995) gives a fuller review of development policy in regard to agriculture than is appropriate here.

5   There are also higher transaction, insurance and information costs in scattered markets (Myint, 1985) – and disruptions from war and disorder.

6   World Bank (2000b, p68) quotes a discussion group in Guatemala: 'We think the earth is generous; but what is the incentive to produce more than the family needs if there are no access roads to get produce to the market?'

7   Malaysia has made a rapid transition in recent decades (Gemmell et al, 2000). Japan is a well-known example of an earlier rapid transition. Land-locked countries tend to take longer than the seaboard countries since initially the most efficient transport for traded goods was water-borne.

8   The local blacksmithing industry seems to have responded to growing demand for more efficient metal tools earlier in West than in East Africa. In Nigeria it is beginning to be replaced by factory-made equipment and parts supplied by state organizations (Iliya and Swindell, 1997).

9   Transport costs consist of fixed and variable costs. The former are relatively small for human and even animal transport, but high for lorries. Studies in Malawi and Benin found traders used logical combinations of transport, using lorries for distances over 12km and 4km respectively. Motorized transport costs were US$0.63 and US$0.28 per tonne per km compared with non-motorized costs averaging US$1.20 and US$1.78. Trading costs were also high in both countries because in the absence of telephones, traders had to travel personally to obtain information, place orders, etc. (Fafchamps

and Gabre-Madhin, 2001). High trading costs apply to what farmers need to buy as well as what they want to sell. Omamo (1998) has shown how walking to purchase maize or sell cotton in a market more than 8km has high opportunity costs, and leads to a preference to earn cash by migratory labour. Poor roads reduce farm incomes, and ability to supply food to the towns, and buy goods and services from urban areas.

10 Exceptions will be industries processing bulky or perishable raw materials that need to be located near the source of supply.

11 IBRD (1981) Impact evaluation of the Muda scheme, consulted by the author for a report to the then Overseas Development Administration on *Improving the Socio-economic and institutional content of irrigation feasibility studies* (Research scheme R4006, ESR 326/307/01, 30 June 1986).

12 Roads and railways, but also telephones and post offices.

13 Most francophone countries had their first circa 1977 and another circa 1988. Some have held or planned a third, at some point 1996–2003 (United Nations Statistics Division, Population and Housing Census, http://unstats.un.org/unsd/demo-graphic/census/cendate, accessed 20 September 2002).

14 FAOSTAT gives a more likely 114 million for 2000. The 1963 census, used as the base for the Bank's calculations, is widely known to have been manipulated upwards for political reasons.

15 The total agricultural labour force is often estimated by reference to the population in a given age range, such as 15–64, from which those known to be in occupations in the formal sector are deducted. The Bank in its Technical Notes to employment tables noted some but not all of the difficulties in estimating unreported economic activity. It ceased to provide agricultural labour statistics after 1990, but the Food and Agriculture Organization (FAO) continues to estimate them in FAOSTAT.

16 Local food production must have been substantial, as their food imports in the same year were only US$6 and US$7 per capita respectively.

17 Import data are fairly reliable for countries with ports, but not all provide them.

18 There is no need to produce more food than locally needed, since crops low in value in relation to bulk can only be exported when transport links are highly efficient – not usually the case in Africa.

19 The sample surveys were not intended to collect data at a level to enable significance testing, but rather to check and update the information available from the district and the literature.

20 It is not just surplus food that is sold, as some households sell off grain after harvest or at other times to meet urgent needs, buying back, often at a disadvantage price-wise, later on.

21 Wote's improved administrative status led to a telephone service and some electricity by 2000.

22 Statistics were only available from 1992, when the District was formed. Agricultural officers were not able to get out much to estimate production due to budgetary constraints.

23 Fertilizer was still available at official prices from state organizations in the 1990s, but tended to be monopolized by big farmers or those with the right connections, who might then sell on at higher prices. Subsidies benefited mainly the big farmers (Iliya and Swindell, 1997; Swindell et al, 1999).

24 Our Senegalese colleagues were particularly keen to test this finding, which had depended mainly on extrapolation from census data, and some reports – Tiffen in Barry et al (2000). Villagers confirmed it.

25 This takes little account of the income-earning activities of wives, but in Hausa areas these generally prefer to pursue their own crafts rather than to work unpaid on the husband's farm.

26 As population density rises, and more pasture land is converted to crop production, farmers need manure to replace fallows, and herders find the advantage of combining farming and herding from a settled base, a change analysed by Binswanger et al (1989).

27 There are also cases in Makueni where the husband works the farm and the wife is a nurse or teacher.

28 As reported to the author by a farmer in Gombe, Nigeria, in the 1960s.

29 CARE interviewed men and women in more than 400 households throughout Maradi District, in 1996.

30 By 1998 there were slightly more girls in secondary. Parents having difficulty with the fees might think sons had a better chance of earning without formal qualifications (Gichuki et al, 2000; Nzioka, 2000).

31 Sons are often given a part of the farm to use on their marriage (but the parent retains the title deed).

32 Long-distance migration seems more disruptive to family structure, judging by Francis (2000).

33 Olukoshi (1996) regarded the stabilization of the macro-policy environment as a necessary condition for the reversal of de-industrialization.

References

Alexandratos, N. (1995) *World Agriculture Towards 2010: An FAO Study*, FAO, John Wiley & Sons, Chichester

Anderson, D. (1990) 'Investment and economic growth', *World Development*, vol 18, no 8, pp1057–1079

Ariyo, J. A., Voh, J. P. and Ahmed, B. (2001) 'Long-term change in food provisioning and marketing in the Kano Region Drylands', Research Working Paper 34, Drylands Research, Crewkerne

Baba, K. M. and Magaji, M. D. (1998) 'Fadama crop residue production and utilisation in north-western Nigeria', in Hoffmann, I. (ed) *Prospects of Pastoralism in West Africa*, Tropeninstitut, Giessen, pp247–262

Babou, C. A. (2002) 'Brotherhood solidarity, education and migration: The role of the Dahiras among the Murid muslim community of New York', *African Affairs*, vol 101, no 403, pp151–170

Balcet, J.-C. (1997) 'Retrospective assessment of farm technology adoption in northern Nigeria (1982–1997): Emerging lessons for technology development and the rural development agenda', unpublished report, World Bank, Washington, DC

Barrett, C. B., Bezuneh, M., and Aboud, A. (2001a) 'Income diversification, poverty traps and policy shocks in Côte d'Ivoire and Kenya', *Food Policy*, vol 26, pp367–384

Barrett, C. B., Bezuneh, M., Clay, D. C. and Reardon, T. (2000) *Effects of Non-Heterogeneous Constraints, Incentives and Income Diversification Strategies in Rural Africa*, Department of Agricultural, Resource and Managerial Economics, Cornell University, New York, Mimeo

Barrett, C. B., Reardon, T. and Webb, P. (2001b) 'Nonfarm income diversification and household livelihood strategies in rural Africa – Concepts, dynamics and policy implications', *Food Policy*, vol 26, no 4, pp315–331

Barry, A., Ndiaye, S., Ndiaye, F. and Tiffen, M. (2000) *Région de Diourbel: Les Aspects Démographiques*, Drylands Research Working Paper 13, Drylands Research, Crewkerne

Bell, C., Hazell, P. B. R. and Slade, R. (1982) *Project Evaluation in Regional Perspective: A Study of an Irrigation Project in NW Malaysia*, Johns Hopkins, Baltimore, MD

Berthélemy, J.-C., Seck, A. and Vourch, A. (1996) *Growth in Senegal: A Lost Opportunity?* OECD, Paris

Binswanger, H., McIntire, J. and Udry, C. (1989) 'Production relations in semi-arid African agriculture', in Bardhan, P. (ed) *The Economic Theory of Agrarian Institutions*, Clarendon Press, Oxford, pp122–144

Boserup, E. (1965) *The Conditions of Agricultural Growth: The Economics of Agricultural Change under Population Pressure*, Allen and Unwin, London

Boubacar, Y. (2000) *Évolution des Régimes de Propriété et d'Utilisation des Resources Naturelles dans la Région de Maradi*, Drylands Research Working Paper 29, Drylands Research, Crewkerne

Boubacar, Y. and Ibrahim, B. M. (2002) *Rapport de Mission de Restitution des Travaux de Recherche dans les Villages de Jiratawa, Magami, Sharken-Hausa et Dan-Kullu (Département de Maradi, Niger)*, unpublished report, Drylands Research, Crewkerne

Bryceson, D. F. (2002) 'The scramble for Africa: Reorienting livelihoods', *World Development*, vol 30, no 5, pp725–739

CARE International au Niger and Université d'Arizona (1997) *Evaluation de la Sécurité des Conditions de Vie dans le Département de Maradi*, CARE-International au Niger, Niamey, Niger

Coulon, C. (1999) 'The Grande Magal in Touba: A religious festival of the Mouride Brotherhood of Senegal', *African Affairs*, vol 98, no 391, pp195–210

David, R. and Niang, O. M. (1995) 'Diourbel, Senegal', in David, R. (ed) *Changing Places? Women, Resource Management and Migration in the Sahel*, SOS Sahel UK, London, pp23–53

Diarra Doka, M. (2001) *Évolutions à Long Terme de l'Organisation Sociale et Économique dans la Région de Maradi*, Drylands Research Working Paper 26, Drylands Research, Crewkerne

Drylands Research (2001) *Livelihood Transformations in Semi-Arid Africa 1960–2000: Proceedings of a Workshop Arranged by the ODI With Drylands Research and the ESRC, in the Series 'Transformations in African Agriculture'*, Drylands Research Working Paper 40, Drylands Research, Crewkerne

Ellis, F. (2000) *Rural Livelihoods and Diversity in Developing Countries*, Oxford University Press, Oxford

Fafchamps, M. and Gabre-Madhin, E. (2001) *Agricultural Markers in Benin and Malawi: The Operation and Performance of Traders*, Policy Research Working Paper 2734, World Bank Development Research Group, Rural Development, Washington, DC

Fall, A. (2000) *Makueni District Profile: Livestock Management, 1990–1998*, Drylands Research Working Paper 8, Drylands Research, Crewkerne

Faye, A. (2002) *Comte Rendu de la Journée de Restitution: Recherches sur les Politiques Publiques et les Investissements Paysans dans la Region de Diourbel; CNRA de Bambey, 19 Février 2002*, unpublished report, Drylands Research, Crewkerne

Faye, A. and Fall, A. (2000) *Région de Diourbel: Diversification des Revenus et son Incidence sur l'Investissement Agricole*, Drylands Research Working Paper 22, Drylands Research, Crewkerne

Faye, A., Fall, A. and Coulibaly, D. (2000) *Région de Diourbel: Evolution de la Production Agricole*, Drylands Research Working Paper 16, Drylands Research, Crewkerne

Faye, A., Fall, A., Mortimore, M., Tiffen, M. and Nelson, J. (2001) *Région de Diourbel: Synthesis*, Drylands Research Working Paper 23e, Drylands Research, Crewkerne

Francis, E. (2000) *Making a Living: Changing Livelihoods in Rural Africa*, Routledge, London

Gaye, M. (2000) *Région de Diourbel: Politicks Rationales Affectant l'Investissement chez les Petits Exploitants*, Drylands Research Working Paper 12, Drylands Research, Crewkerne

Gemmell, N., Lloyd, T. A. and Mathew, M. (2000) 'Agricultural growth and inter-sectoral linkages in a developing economy', *Journal of Agricultural Economics*, vol 51, no 3, pp353–370

Gerschenkron, A. (1962) *Economic Backwardness in Historical Perspective*, Harvard University Press, Cambridge, MA

Gichuki, F. N. (2000a) *Makueni District Profile: Farm Development, 1946–1999*, Drylands Research Working Paper 1, Drylands Research, Crewkerne

Gichuki, F. N. (2000b) *Makueni District Profile: Soil Management and Conservation, 1989–1998*, Drylands Research Working Paper 4, Drylands Research, Crewkerne

Gichuki, F. N., Mbogoh, S. G., Tiffen, M. and Mortimore, M. (2000) *Makueni District Profile: Synthesis*, Drylands Research Working Paper 11, Drylands Research, Crewkerne

Grégoire, E. (1990) *Croissance Urbaine et Santé a Maradi (Niger)*, Université de Bordeaux II, Bordeaux

Hamadou, S. (2000a) *Évolution à Long Terme des Productions Agricoles, du Système de Commercialisation et des Prix des Produits dans la Zone de Maradi*, Drylands Research Working Paper 32, Drylands Research, Crewkerne

Hamadou, S. (2000b) *Politiques Nationales et Investissement dans les Petites Exploitations à Maradi*, Drylands Research Working Paper 33, Drylands Research, Crewkerne

Hamilton, P. (2003) 'Struggling to survive poverty: A survey of small farmers' coping strategies in rural Kenya', *ENABLE: Newsletter of the Association for Better Land Husbandry*, vol 16, March, pp3–30

Hassan, W. A., Hoffmann, I. and Steinbach, J. (1998) 'Sheep and goat keeping under arable farming in the Zamfara Reserve', in Hoffmann, I. (ed) *Prospects of Pastoralism in West Africa*, Tropeninstitut, Giessen, Germany, pp196–210

Helleiner, G. K. (1966) *Peasant Agriculture, Government, and Economic Growth in Nigeria*, Irwin, Homewood, IL

Hoffmann, I. (1998) 'Cattle marketing in Burkina Faso after the devaluation of the Franc CFA', in Hoffmann, I. (ed) *Prospects of Pastoralism in West Africa*, Tropeninstitut, Giessen, Germany, pp127–135

Hopkins, A. G. (1973) *An Economic History of West Africa*, Longman, London

Iliya, M. A. and Swindell, K. (1997) 'Winners and losers: Household fortunes in the urban peripheries of northern Nigeria', in Bryceson, D. F. and Jamal, V. (eds) *Farewell to Farms: De-agrarianisation and Employment in Africa*, Ashgate, Aldershot

Jahnke, H. E. (1982) *Livestock Development Systems and Livestock Production in Tropical Africa*, Wissenschaftsverlag Vauk, Kiel

Johnston, B. F. and Mellor, J. W. (1961) 'The role of agriculture in economic development', *American Economic Review*, September, pp566–593

Kenny, C. and Williams, D. (2001) 'What do we know about economic growth? Or, why don't we know very much?' *World Development*, vol 29, no 1, pp1–22

Kherallah, M., Delgado, C., Gabre-Madhin, E. Z., Minot, N. and Johnson, M. (2000) *The Road Half Traveled: Agricultural Market Reform in Sub-Saharan Africa*, International Food Policy Research Institute, Washington, DC

Kriekhaus, J. (2002) 'Reconceptualizing the developmental state: Public savings and economic growth', *World Development*, vol 30, no 10, pp1697–1712

Landes, D. (1998) *The Wealth and Poverty of Nations*, Little, Brown & Co, London

Mahamane, A. (2001) *Usages des Terres et Evolutions Végétales dans le Département de Maradi*, Drylands Research Working Paper 27, Drylands Research, Crewkerne

Mbogoh, S. G. (2000) *Makueni District Profile: Crop Production and Marketing, 1988–1999*, Drylands Research Working Paper 7, Drylands Research, Crewkerne

Meagher, K. (1997) *Current Trends in Cross-Border Grain Trade between Nigeria and Niger*, IRAM, Paris

Meagher, K. and Mustapha A. R. (1997) 'Not by farming alone: the role of non-farm income in rural Hausaland', in Bryceson, D. F. and Jamal, V. (eds) *Farewell to Farms: De-agrarianiszation and Employment in Africa*, Ashgate, Aldershot

Mortimore, M. (1993) 'The intensification of peri-urban agriculture: The Kano Close-Settled Zone, 1964–86', in Turner, B. L. II, Kates, R. W. and Hyden, H. L. (eds) *Population Growth and Agricultural Change in Africa*, University Press of Florida, Gainesville, FL

Mortimore, M. and Adams, W. (1999) *Working the Sahel: Environment and Society in Northern Nigeria*, Routledge, London

Mortimore, M., Tiffen, M., Boubacar, Y. and Nelson, J. (2001) *Department of Maradi: Synthesis*, Drylands Research Working Paper 39e, Drylands Research, Crewkerne

Mustapha, A. R. and Meagher, K. (2000) *Agrarian Production, Public Policy and the State in Kano Region, 1900–2000*, Drylands Research Working Paper 35, Drylands Research, Crewkerne

Myint, H. (1967) *The Economics of the Developing Countries*, Hutchinson University Library, London

Myint, H. (1985) 'Organisational dualism and economic development', *Asian Development Review*, vol 3, no 1, pp25–42

Nelson, J. (2000) *Makueni District Profile: Income Diversification and Farm Investment, 1989–1999*, Drylands Research Working Paper 10, Drylands Research, Crewkerne

Nzioka, C. (2000) *Makueni District Profile: Human Resource Management, 1989–1998*, Drylands Research Working Paper 9, Drylands Research, Crewkerne

O'Brien, D. B. C. (1975) *Saints and Politicians: Essays in the Organisation of a Senegalese Peasant Society*, Cambridge University Press, Cambridge

Okike, I., Jabbar, M. A., Manyong, V., Smith, J. W., Alinwumi, J. A. and Ehui, S. K. (2001) *Agricultural Intensification and Efficiency in the West African Savannahs: Evidence from Northern Nigeria*, Socio Economics and Policy Research Working Paper 33, ILRI, Nairobi, Kenya

Olukoshi, A. (1996) *Economic Crisis, Structural Adjustment and the Coping Strategies of Manufacturers in Kano, Nigeria*, Discussion Paper 77, UNRISD, Geneva

Omamo, W. S. (1998) 'Transport costs and smallholder cropping choices: An application to Siaya District, Kenya', *American Journal of Agricultural Economics*, vol 80, pp116–123

Orr, A. and Mwale, B. (2001) 'Adapting to adjustment: Smallholder livelihood strategies in southern Malawi', *World Development*, vol 29, no 8, pp1325–1343

Pingali, P., Bigot, Y. and Binswanger, H. (1987) *Agricultural Mechanization and the Evolution of Farming Systems in Sub-Saharan Africa*, Johns Hopkins University Press, Baltimore, MD

Prabowo, D. and McConnell, D. J. (1993) *Changes and Development in Solo Valley Farming Systems, Indonesia*, FAO, Rome

Reardon, T. (1997) 'Using evidence of household income diversification to inform study of the rural nonfarm labor market in Africa', *World Development*, vol 25, no 5, pp735–747

Reardon, T., Taylor, J. E., Stamoulis, K., Lanjouw, P. and Balisacan, A. (2000) 'Effects of non-farm employment on rural income inequality in developing countries: An investment perspective', *Journal of Agricultural Economics*, vol 51, no 2, 266–288

Republic of Niger (1992) *Recensement de la Population de 1988: Analyse des Données Définitives*

Romer, P. M. (1989) *What Determines the Rate of Growth and Technological Change?* World Bank, Country Economics Department WPS, Washington, DC

Rostow, W. W. (1960) *The Stages of Economic Growth*, Cambridge University Press, Cambridge

Schoonmaker Freudenberger, M. and Schoonmaker Freudenberger, K. (1993) *Fields, Fallow and Flexibility: Natural Resource Management in Ndam Mor Fademba, Senegal*, Drylands Paper 5, IIED, London

Shaikh, A. and McGahuey, M. (1996) 'Niger case study: Capitalizing on change', in Clay, D. C., Reardon, T. and Shaikh, A. (eds) *Population, Environment and Development in Africa: Dynamic Linkages and their Implications for Future Research and Development Programming*, Institute of International Agriculture, Michigan State University, East Lansing, MI, pp93–118

Simon, J. (1977) *The Economics of Population Growth*, Princeton University Press, Princeton, NJ

Singh, B. B., Larbi, A., Tabo, R. and Dixon, A. G. O. (2001) *Improvement for Crop-Livestock Systems Development in West Africa*, ILRI-IITA, Ibadan, Nigeria

Smith, A. (1776) *The Wealth of Nations*, reprinted Everyman's Library, 1991, Random House (UK) Ltd, London

Smith, J., Barau, A. D., Goldman, A. and Mareck, J. H. (1994) 'The role of technology in agricultural intensification: The evolution of production systems in the northern guinea savanna of Nigeria', *Economic Development and Cultural Change*, vol 42, no 3, pp537–554

Swindell, K., Iliya, M. A. and Mamman, A. B. (1999) 'Making a profit, making a living: Commercial farming and urban hinterlands in north-west Nigeria', *Africa*, vol 69, no 3, pp386–403

Tiffen, M. (2001) *Profile of Demographic Change in the Kano-Maradi Region, 1960–2000*, Drylands Research Working Paper 24, Drylands Research, Crewkerne

Tiffen, M. and Mortimore, M. (1994) 'Malthus controverted: The role of capital and technology in growth and environment recovery in Kenya', *World Development*, vol 22, no 7, pp997–1010

Tiffen, M. and Mortimore, M. (2002) 'Questioning desertification in dryland sub-Saharan Africa', *Natural Resources Forum*, vol 26, pp218–233

Tiffen, M., Mortimore, M. and Gichuki, F. (1994) *More People Less Erosion: Environmental Recovery in Kenya*, John Wiley & Sons, Chichester

Tomich, T. P., Kilby, P. and Johnston, B. F. (1995) *Transforming Agrarian Economies: Opportunities Seized, Opportunities Missed*, Cornell University Press, Ithaca, New York

Toulmin, C., Leonard, R., Brock, K., Coulibaly, N., Carwell, G. and Dea, D. (2000) *Diversification of Livelihoods: Evidence from Ethiopia and Mali. IDS Research Report*, no 47, Institute of Development Studies, Brighton

Wiggins, S. (1995) 'Change in African farming systems between the 1970s and the 1990s', *Journal of International Development*, vol 7, no 6, pp807–848

Wiggins, S. (2000) 'Interpreting changes from the 1970s to the 1990s in African agriculture through village studies', *World Development*, vol 28, no 4, pp631–662

Wilson Fall, W. (2000) *Région de Diourbel: The Family, Local Institutions and Education*, Drylands Research Working Paper 20, Drylands Research, Crewkerne

World Bank (1983) *World Development Report 1983*, World Bank, Washington, DC

World Bank (2000a) *Can Africa Claim the 21st Century?* World Bank, Washington, DC

World Bank (2000b) *World Development Report 2000/2001: Attacking Poverty*, World Bank, Washington, DC

World Bank (2000c) *World Bank Africa Database 2000*, CD-Rom, World Bank, Washington, DC

World Bank (2002) *World Bank Africa Database 2002*, CD-Rom, World Bank, Washington, DC

World Bank, OED (1995) *Nigeria, Impact Evaluation Report, Kano Agricultural Development Project, Sokoto Agricultural Development Project*, no 14767-UNI, World Bank, Washington, DC

Chapter 6

A Regional Network Strategy for Reciprocal Rural–Urban Linkages: An Agenda for Policy Research with Reference to Indonesia

Mike Douglass

Overcoming the urban and rural divide in planning

Debates on the nature of rural–urban relations hold a prominent position in development theory and planning. Discussions in the 1950s centred on whether towns played parasitic or generative roles in their relations with their rural hinterlands. As originally argued, generative forces of modernization associated with urbanization were hypothesized to outweigh possible parasitic impacts on rural areas (Singer, 1964). The Lewis model of economic development widely adopted at the time also accepted the idea that economic growth and modernization required a transfer of surplus from an assumed moribund agricultural sector to urban industry, thus justifying the appropriation of rural resources, labour and capital by cities in the name of longer-term national economic development (Fei and Ranis, 1964). The general policy prescription derived from the Lewis and related models called for an acceleration of urban industrial growth and the transition to an urban-based society. The concern raised in many Asian countries up to the 1970s was that levels of urbanization were very low and that the push of rural poverty was causing rural–urban migration to create an involuted, distorted urban growth process based on the expansion of low-productivity urban services rather than on the dynamics of industrialization. Whether from a modernization or economic perspective, the prevailing view was that increasing the pace of a more 'authentic' pattern of urban industrial development was needed to compensate for inherent limitations in rural development.

From the late 1950s, an opposing view emerged in a new field of regional planning that was built, in part, on core-periphery and spatial polarization models, which observed

Note: Reprinted from *Third World Planning Review*, vol 20, no 1, Douglass, M., 'A regional network strategy for reciprocal rural–urban linkages: An agenda for policy research with reference to Indonesia', copyright © (1998) with permission from Liverpool University Press, Liverpool.

that in most developing countries the benefits of economic growth increasingly concentrate in one or a few core urban regions. The principal thesis of these models was that the benefits accruing to the core were at the expense of the rural periphery. Cities organized rural areas to serve urban interests, resulting in net capital outflow, brain drain and other resource transfers that lowered rather than raised the potential for rural areas to develop. Cities actively exploited rural areas, with rural poverty and rural–urban migration not emanating from the isolation of rural from urban areas, but rather from the tightening of rural and urban linkages. The further observation that rural areas were often transformed into overly specialized single-crop or natural resource economies to serve urban-based corporate interest fit into the parallel emergence of dependency theory, which argued that the metropolitan nations of the North actively under-developed the agrarian economies of the South. Rural–urban linkages were thus part of global chains of power and control that perpetuated conditions of rural poverty and underdevelopment. Although the idea that cities act as 'theaters of accumulation' inhibiting rather than fostering the development of rural regions (Armstrong and McGee, 1985) has continued to find adherents, the position that gained wider agreement was that the 'backwash' effects of urbanization on rural areas were expected to be only short term, that is, occurring only in the 'early stages of development' (Williamson, 1965). As spatial systems matured, development impulses were expected to naturally become more readily articulated over national territories, thus reversing previously dominant polarization processes.

Although much research was stimulated by this thesis, it did not result in any consistent evidence that polarization reversal has either occurred in a sustained manner in any developing country or that it is an automatic outcome of increasing levels of per capita gross domestic product (GDP) reaching 'mature' stages of development (Douglass, 1990). The general case could still be made, therefore, that if a polarization reversal were to occur, it would be best pursued through government interventions. The question of what kind of policy interventions would be needed was given a single answer: induced urbanization in the periphery, which came to be known as the growth pole or growth centre approach to regional development (Friedmann, 1968). As a strategy, it argued that only the rise of cities in the periphery could challenge the growth of core urban centres. As such, it has no explicit rural content; rural areas are still seen as being developed by the city and remain 'out there' as uninvestigated hinterlands. The absence of any rural development component in this strategy is glaring, but despite this and many other criticisms of the growth pole model (Friedmann and Weaver, 1979), notably those positing that in a transnational age the likelihood that linkage and spread effects will be captured locally is extremely low, this remains the dominant spatial development strategy throughout the world, including Asia.

In the 1970s a new slant on the idea that cities were the cause rather than solution to rural problems received a new thrust under the title of 'urban bias' in rural development, which argued that rural underdevelopment is perpetuated by unrelenting political, social and economic forces favouring cities over the countryside (Lipton, 1977). Subsequent treatments of the same theme cited the development planner as a principal culprit in putting rural development last rather than first. The incentive to be in the capital city for career advancement, the low status of agricultural economics, the avoidance of rural visits during the rainy season when conditions were worst, the disdain of actually staying overnight in a village, and the diplomacy of not asking rural elites embarrassing questions about social cleavages or poorer village residents were part of the systematic biases preventing planners from comprehending rural issues and taking appropriate actions (Chambers, 1985). While most of the debates on rural–urban relations remained abstract and without conclusive empirical evidence supporting either pro- or anti-urban stances, over the decades the cumulative result has been a curious divide in planning. On one side are urban planners who continue to plan for rural development from cities and who know exceptionally little about and give scant regard to the potential for an agriculture- or rural-led development. Their rural landscapes consist of urban nodes and transportation linkages overlaid on topographical maps. For them regional integration through urbanization remains the key. Their policies have a decisive urban bias. On the other side are rural development planners who tend to view cities as parasitic and alien to rural interests. Wary of cities, they rarely put them in their rural landscapes, preferring instead to define rural areas as consisting only of agricultural plots, resource areas and villages. Efforts at integrated rural planning generally use the village and its agricultural land as the highest units of development. The resulting policies typically have a discernible rural bias with little or no interest in investigating how cities might be better brought into rural planning frameworks. To a rural household, however, the landscape of daily life includes both rural and urban elements. Rural–urban linkages are part of the local reality for household members carrying out the diverse tasks of producing income on and off-farm, maintaining a living space in the village, and going to local and even distant towns for shopping, marketing, work, and specialized services. The challenge for rural regional planning is to overcome the rural–urban divide by incorporating this reality into development frameworks and, further, identifying policy measures to foster mutual benefits for both town and village households. The purpose of this chapter is to sketch the outlines of regional planning framework that incorporates rural–urban linkages and can adjust to a variety of local situations. The reference for this discussion is Indonesia. The section on 'Rural–urban linkages and interdependencies' focuses directly on rural–urban relations and argues the case for viewing rural and urban development as being interdependent. The next section: 'Regional networks/clusters as a spatial framework for rural development' places the question of rural–urban linkages into a larger regional network framework that advocates the organization of planning around regional networks (clusters) of rural and urban linkages. The section on 'Regional variations in rural–urban linkages: The case of Indonesia' illustrates the regional network model through examples of types of situations in Indonesia. The final section, 'Towards an agenda for policy research', concludes with an agenda for policy research.

Rural–urban linkages and interdependencies

Formulating comprehensive rural–urban development frameworks to explicitly promote rural development began to receive attention in the 1970s and 1980s. Some attempts, such as the 'urban functions in rural development' approach discussed below, were thinly disguised forms of urban bias. Others, such as the many programmes put forth under the rubric of 'integrated rural development' (IRD), erred in the opposite manner by rarely including explicit urban components. While making the important contribution that rural development must be seen as being multi-faceted, including non-agricultural as well as agricultural activities, IRD was essentially aimed at improving planning coordination through integrated sectoral planning in specific localities (Cohen, 1980; Birgegård, 1988). Although activities continue to be organized under the IRD logo, even where the spatial dimension is implied it is almost always limited to marketing functions; the tendency to treat rural as a village–agriculture question continues. Among the few frameworks put forth that explicitly united rural with urban development was the 'agropolitan' approach (Friedmann and Douglass, 1978; Friedmann and Weaver, 1979; Douglass, 1981). It proposed that rural development could be best pursued by linking rural with urban development at the local level. Setting an agropolitan development process in motion required attention to at least three critical issues: access to agricultural land and water; devolution of political and administrative authority to the local level; and a shift of national development policies in support of diversified agricultural production. Seeing the rural town as a principal site for rural non-agriculture as well as political–administrative functions rather than as an industrial growth pole, the agropolitan approach suggested that in most countries the district scale was the most appropriate unit of development in that it was small enough to afford frequent access to urban functions by rural households yet large enough to expand the scope of economic growth and diversification to overcome the limitations of using the village as an economic unit. It also proposed that local knowledge could better be incorporated into planning processes if it were organized at a level that was close to rural producers and households. While the agropolitan approach has, at best, been only partially applied in practice, its promotion of decentralization and democratization has emerged as the most vital issues in planning in Asia today. The challenge suggested by the agropolitan approach and more fully developed elsewhere (Friedmann, 1992) is how to incorporate local capacity building and popular participation into a programme to foster mutual benefits for rural and urban areas in the course of national development.

The one-sided view of the 'role of cities' in rural development

Although development planning continues to be marked by a divide between rural and urban specialists, over the years a minor tradition focusing on the role of cities in rural development has emerged. In the 1970s the idea that cities could assist in promoting development in rural regions began to focus attention on rural towns at the bottom rather than top of the urban system. With roots in central place theory, a seminal work in this area was that of Johnson (1970), who argued from the case of India that the development of rural towns to fill in the gap between the 'parasitic big city' and the village was a necessary condition for the commercialization of agriculture. The task of the planner was thus one of promoting the growth of market towns. With central place theory as the overall framework, towns also had to be identified in relation to each other to ensure appropriate spacing and functional composition by size and position in the urban hierarchy. Subsequently embellished by Rondinelli as the 'urban functions in rural development approach' (UFRD), Johnson's advocacy of selecting key rural towns as rural development centres was re-interpreted as a set of rural development roles to be played by towns and cities in rural regions. Among the roles identified (Rondinelli, 1979; de Jong, 1988) were:

- consumer convenience centres for purchasing non-durable and durable goods;
- centres for higher order public and private services;
- linkage to (inter-)national markets for selling rural products;
- production supply and support centres;
- agro- and resource-processing centres;
- non-agricultural employment for rural labour;
- centres of information and knowledge.

This listing of roles has received continuing interest among regional planners. The roles have, however, proven to be difficult to translate from abstract generalizations to either real world experiences or policy recommendations. Several reasons account for this difficulty. First, the generalizations are very high off the ground and offer no straightforward way of accounting for the rich variety of (rural) regional contexts within which cities play their developmental roles. The role that a city plays in a rice growing region, for example, can be expected to be quite different than that at the fringe of an industrializing metropolitan region. Thus although the list of potential roles is intuitively appealing, it does not by itself indicate how each role is expected to be manifested in specific contexts and, therefore, how functions should be promoted in different cities.

Second, methods for selecting key rural towns for investments are not clear. Should towns already playing these roles be selected, or should towns with potential for playing these roles be chosen and, if so, how is 'potential' to be defined? Since most of rural Asia has experienced relatively slow rates of economic growth, and since rural towns have not been found to be playing the many roles assumed for them, if towns are to be used for a national programme of rural development, identifying those with high potential becomes a central task. But because such potential can only be defined in relation to the opportunities and needs of each rural region, it follows that the potential role of each rural town or city must arise from the regional context rather than from the study of a town alone. However, the methods developed for selecting key cities focused only on the attributes of the towns themselves, and in the only real world application in the Bicol Region of the Philippines, no study of rural potential was included in the policy research programme (Rondinelli, 1979; Koppel, 1987).

As an example of the severe conceptual and practical problems encountered in mechanistically using central place theory to construct a rigid set of functions for all towns at a given level of the urban hierarchy, a study of rural towns by Cohen et al (1977) showed how town functions varied among four types of regions in Malaysia, that is, regions dominated by the *kampung* (smallholder rice producers) sector, the estate sector, new town settlements in frontier areas, or extensive (forestry) sector. The study found that the assumption that 'town size and urban functional diversity are positively correlated does not hold for those centers which lie at the base of the urban system in developing countries' (p12), and further that (p23), 'The organization of the regional urban space is a function of the form and structure of agriculture – and not the other way around', with differences in agricultural crop regimes and the organizational structure of production being crucial determinants of variation in the functional make-up of rural towns.

Third, and even more problematic, is the assumption that all urban functions are developmental and none has negative impacts on rural areas that outweigh positive ones. Whether the function is that of a bank, a real estate agent, a timber company office or administrative office, if it is located in a rural town, it is assumed to benefit rural hinterlands and all rural households irrespective of social or economic class. In applications of the UFRD approach in the Philippines, it was assumed, for example, that locating a bank in a town would automatically promote rural development by moving formal financial institutions and credit closer to rural areas. Yet, as studies in Thailand have shown, although the majority of bank branches are located in rural areas, the agricultural sector typically receives an extremely small portion of their loans.

The point to be drawn from this observation is that programmes to foster the growth of urban functions for rural development require specific attention to their actual rural linkages and impacts rather than assuming them to be relevant and beneficial in any and all circumstances. Even where urban functions may reach rural households, they may do so in such an uneven manner that they heighten rather than ameliorate problems of rural inequality and poverty. In situations of unequal distribution of land, for example, subsidized government credit institutions set up in rural towns for agricultural development have been found to be biased toward rural elites and large farmers who have channeled loans into further land purchases, leading to increased tenancy rates and widening rural income disparities (Khan, 1979). This is the general case made by Lipton (1977) with regard to urban bias, namely, that urban elites co-opt or give patronage to rural elites as a means of facilitating rural-to-urban surplus transfers, with the net result that urban poverty is perpetuated by the extension of the government into rural development programmes. To put the matter directly: urban functions are not socially neutral. Moving an activity or institution to a rural town may be an important first step toward promoting rural development, but care must be taken to link these functions to the specific tools and means of increasing the spatial and social access by targeted rural households.

Research on the actual roles of towns in rural development

Research on actual roles played by selected towns and growth centres in rural regions in the Philippines, Malaysia, Thailand and Indonesia reveals the limitations of attempting to stimulate rural development solely through promoting the growth of towns. One of the earliest efforts to use selective investments in rural towns as a means to promote rural development was the United States Agency for International Development (USAID) funded UFRD approach noted above. Carried out in the Bicol Region in the late 1970s, the exercise was part of a grand Tennessee Valley Authority-like river basin development scheme that incorporated dam and irrigation development with agricultural projects and urban development into a comprehensive regional development programme. Administered under a special Bicol River Basin Development Authority headquartered in Manila, this ambitious programme was meant to turn one of the Philippines poorest regions into one of its most dynamic and, at the same time, undercut anti-government insurgency in the region.

The programme confronted problems typically associated with central planning, namely, poor coordination among ministries, and was promoted and carried out without any proposal for land reform and other institutional changes either before or during the planning process. Decentralization and participation were given token regard. Instead, the approach taken by the UFRD team was to fill in the supposed missing functions in rural towns to stimulate rural development. No study was done of the conditions or needs of rural hinterlands. A study conducted 10 years after its initiation found that not only were the towns not performing the 'missing' functions, but that they were themselves stagnating (Koppel, 1987).

Some of the contributing reasons for the general failure of this attempt offer constructive thought for rethinking rural–urban relations and provincial urban growth. First, identified functions (e.g. barber shops, cabarets and other entertainment) did not necessarily have much to do with rural development and were, in fact, supported by an unusual presence of national military and civil service personnel in the region. Second, transportation development linking this region to larger towns outside of the region usurped rather than encouraged the expansion of marketing and commercial functions of the local towns. Third, since an advancement of agricultural failed to materialize, the principal source of the growth of central places, that is, rising rural household expenditures for non-agricultural goods and services, also failed to emerge to generate the expansion of towns.

In a related study in Indonesia, three roles were assessed for the Central Java town of Banjarnegara:

(1) consumer shopping and service centre;
(2) antipode to rural–urban migration to metropolitan regions (Jakarta); and
(3) support and marketing centre for agriculture (de Jong et al, 1983; de Jong, 1988).

The investigation found very limited performances in all roles. Concerning (1), consumer shopping and services, a large portion of the district population made no use of the town for shopping, education, health or bank credit services. As a generator of employment alternatives (2), job expansion was, like the town itself, found to be very slow in a region already plagued by high levels of rural underemployment. Finally, as an agricultural support centre (3), although the town was an important node in the marketing chain for fruits and cattle, the more important rural production activities in coconut and vegetables bypassed the town entirely. Furthermore, many of the buyers for fruit and cattle were not town dwellers, but came from outside the region on marketing days, thereby limiting the local employment and related multiplier effects that could have been captured by the town. A similar study conducted in a Malaysian town, Pasir Mas, located along the Malaysia–Thai border drew parallel conclusions (Maude, 1983).

Whether such studies are exceptions to a generally more positive picture of rural towns is an important question in need of further research. Unfortunately, few studies have been carried out on the actual relationships between town functions and rural access to or benefits from them. However, indirect evidence suggested by the generally slow growth of rural towns and persistence of poverty in many rural regions of Asian countries indicates that rural towns have yet to play many of the hoped-for roles assigned to them. Studies carried out in Asia, Latin America and Africa in the early 1980s found that towns in densely settled rural regions located away from metropolitan and frontier regions were growing at rates roughly equal to natural population growth, indicating that employment creation for their hinterland labour force has been close to nil in most cases (Mathur, 1982; Kammeier and Swan, 1984).

Two studies on the northern city Chiang Mai, then Thailand's second largest city, were designed to directly assess specific rural–urban linkages and flows. The first, conducted in the mid-1970s, found that almost all of the economic impacts, including purchase of inputs for Chiang Mai processing and production, demand for services in the hinterland, and increased local incomes and expenditures, were reduced to zero or near zero levels beyond a one-hour travel time distance from the city (Bunchorntavakul, 1976). The major reason for villagers to visit Chiang Mai was shopping, but the frequency of visits even within a 90-minute bus travel range from the perimeter from the centre of Chiang Mai averaged only about one trip per week, and more than one-third of the households said that they very seldom or never went to Chiang Mai.

A decade later a follow-up study of Chiang Mai was carried out using the same methodology pioneered in the earlier research (Ladavalya and Siripool, 1988). Carried out several years after the government had explicitly designated Chiang Mai as one of only a handful of cities to receive top priority planning and investment as a regional growth centre, the study nonetheless found that the spatial spread of economic and social benefits of the city's growth rapid growth was still very restricted. In fact, the expenditures by Chiang Mai factories accrued greater benefits to Bangkok than to the hinterland of Chiang Mai. The study concluded that 'the countryside cannot provide what is needed in a modern, industrializing economy', but it also noted that 'perhaps it could be said that no concerted effort has been made to develop new business that can use what is available, such as agricultural products' (p54). It concluded that villagers residing more than one hour from Chiang Mai 'find practically everything they need in their own villages and immediate areas', with only a few of their total expenditures going to Chiang Mai (p46), and noted the prevalence of itinerant merchants moving by pick-up truck from village to village to sell basic commodities and even luxury goods: 'the people can buy food, clothes, medicine, kitchen appliances, candies' and other goods from the mobile vendors. Thus although in comparison with the earlier study, greater proportions of nearby rural residents were interacting with Chiang Mai, economic multiplier effects were still limited. Related research on five growth centres in five Asian countries (including Surabaya (Indonesia), Jaffna and Kandy (Sri Lanka), Mariveles (Philippines) and Taxila-Wah (Pakistan)) consistently found that diffusion processes and multiplier benefits to rural hinterlands were not significant (Kammeier and Swan, 1984).

These findings show that while planning for a single regional centre over an extended period of time may have pay-offs in terms of generating non-agricultural employment opportunities for rural populations and increased local rural–urban interaction for social and consumer shopping purposes, backward and forward linkages between town and countryside continue to be very spatially limited. Although a focus on a very limited number of cities might save public expenditures on infrastructure and service provisions, the Chiang Mai study suggests that it may not be the most effective means of stimulating the development of rural regions. As a study in the Southern Region of

Thailand concluded, the 'optimistic view that natural forces would create a growth effect from Surat Thani City to its area of influence is, most probably, a dangerous supposition' (Shiann-Far, 1986). This calls into question the strategy of building the urban system in a stepwise down-the-urban-hierarchy manner that, in effect, focuses on such a small number of cities that vast rural areas are left beyond the range of benefits of urban growth. Such a strategy misses numerous opportunities for developing a more dispersed pattern of regional development via a number of smaller-scale rural–urban linkages and regional networks. Finding alternatives to this type of growth pole approach needs to be given greater consideration if towns are to play the development roles assigned to them.

Rural perspective on the role of cities

Most analyses of growth centres in rural development assume the perspective of the city looking outward to its hinterland. Studies from the opposite vantage point in the village reveal quite different insights. A study in Roi-et Province, Thailand, which looked at circular migration as part of rural household economic strategy formulation, found that much of the interaction of rural households with cities is temporary, often a month or two and not simply on an agricultural slack season basis (Lightfoot et al, 1983). Moreover, urban interaction does not characteristically include the poorest of the poor, who are found to be without the necessary resources to be able to move extensively over space. Rural–urban linkages are thus highly selective in terms of access to urban functions as well as timing and duration of stays in urban areas. The implications of such research have been overlooked in most urban policy formulations. Temporary or circular migrants do not tend to show up on annual household registration data and are even less likely to be counted in decennial census-taking. Yet studies on this phenomenon in Asia clearly show that temporary and circular migration is much greater than permanent rural–urban migration. Furthermore, when seen from the household perspective, the view of the urban world is not that of a single urban centre, but is instead one of a network of rural and urban linkages and employment possibilities, including destinations abroad. Rather than specific destinations themselves, it is this network that provides the spatial frame for the formulation and acting out of household economic strategies.

A popular argument put forth in favour of concentrating public investments in only a very limited number of centres is the idea that the principal means of reducing rural poverty is not to focus on 'place prosperity' by trying to develop every region and city; the focus should be on encouraging 'people prosperity' through migration out of lagging rural areas to selected growth centres of high potential. While it might be valid to say that the poor should not be artificially trapped or prevented from migrating from low to high opportunity areas, caution needs to be taken in advancing this view. Rural–urban migrants tend to be young, physically fit and better educated than their village counterparts; the elderly and the poorest people do not leave 'poor' places.

In this regard, the study in the north-east province of Roi-et cited above found that migration to Bangkok tended, over time, to erode village-based networks as migrants became 'captured' by urban-based obligations and remittances to home villages decreased. Villages also experienced losses of scarce labour in peak agricultural seasons. Finally, remittances were not channelled into community infrastructure and thus could not compensate for the decline in labour available for community projects. Thus while some households gained from migration to large metropolitan regions, short-term gains in consumption levels for individuals and their households might be at the expense of the longer-term potential of the local economy (Lightfoot et al, 1983, p41). What is needed, therefore, is a regional development strategy that captures these potentials to their fullest extent. Such a strategy would have regional cities as one component, but would also gain from including a more decentralized approach to rural–urban development at the local level.

Rural–urban interdependencies in regional planning

In view of the limitations of growth centres and urban functions in rural development approaches discussed above, rethinking the role of cities in rural regional development raises the question of how to bring rural and urban development potentials and complementarities together in the planning process. A point of departure for addressing this question is to recognize that the functions and roles played by cities in most rural areas are outcomes of interdependencies that have no one-way urban-to-rural causality. Rather, rural and urban relations need to be seen as being mutually reinforcing. These relationships are summarized in Table 6.1, which shows that for every role of a city, there is a necessary role to be played by its hinterland.

As the table indicates, towns in rural regions act as higher-level market centres of agricultural and rural commodities for both regional and extra-regional sales and distribution. Since the town-centred marketing functions cannot exist without significant levels of marketable surpluses being produced in rural areas, it follows that town and countryside are mutually dependent. To expand production rural producers need mar-

Table 6.1 *Urban and rural linkages and interdependencies*

Urban	↔	Rural
• Agricultural trade/transport centre	↔	• Agricultural production
• Agricultural support services	↔	• Agricultural intensification
– Production inputs		– Rural infrastructure
– Repair services		– Production incentives
– Information on production methods (innovation)		– Education and capacity to adopt/adapt innovation
• Non-agricultural consumer markets	↔	• Rural income and demand for non-agricultural goods and services
– Processed agricultural products		
– Private services		
– Public services (health, education, admin.)		
• Agro-based industry	↔	• Cash crop production and agricultural diversification
• Non-agricultural employment	↔	• All of the above

keting networks provided by towns and the urban system; but without continued expansion of agriculture and agro-based processing activities, rural towns cannot be expected to grow. Similarly, intensification of agriculture will necessitate the appearance of shops in towns to supply increasingly sophisticated inputs and repair facilities that a single village cannot economically sustain.

Continuing down the list of relationships in Table 6.1, a major source of growth of rural towns is increasing demand for non-agricultural commodities for rural household consumption. Research has identified this as the single most important factor for the growth of rural towns (Gibb, 1984). As in the other relations, the ability of towns to act as consumer convenience centres rests on increasing rural prosperity and rising real incomes not just for a few farmers, but for the majority of rural households.

Targeting the impacts of urban development

As the many studies reveal, investing in cities to promote the development of rural hinterlands encounters so many intervening factors that actual beneficial impacts are often much less than expected and unevenly distributed among rural households. Banks may not lend to high-risk rural producers; schools may require informal fees that put them out of reach of poorer households; roads may accelerate environmentally dangerous resource extraction.

Given the likelihood that the realities of rural–urban relations may deflect efforts away from achieving their goals, there is thus a manifest need to more clearly specify who is to benefit from urban investments and what are the means to ensure the desired outcomes. This would not only require more thorough study of rural development potentials; it would also call for closer attention to monitoring programmes to ensure that target groups, such as small farmers, landless workers, and the rural poor are actually reached.

Regional networks/clusters as a spatial framework for rural development

The purpose of the foregoing discussion has been to demonstrate that prevailing theories and policy models do not capture either the realities of or the potential for rural regional development. There is thus a need for a new paradigm of spatial development for policy formulation. Such a paradigm would have to overcome a number of major obstacles, including the dichotomization of planning into rural and urban planning bureaux that promote rivalry rather than collaboration and administrative divisions that separate cities from their hinterlands in planning and management at local levels. In addition, mechanistic models of spatial and development processes, most of which focus on urban nodes rather than rural regions, need to be put aside in favour of efforts to include local variations in rural–urban linkages in identifying components of a national spatial system.

By way of exploring how a new paradigm of rural regional development can be constructed from local level research on rural–urban linkages, Table 6.2 and Figure 6.1

contrast the growth pole concept with an alternative regional network (cluster) concept, the latter of which incorporates rural and village structures with rural–urban linkages and flows. Table 6.2 shows, first, that whereas growth poles have been single-mindedly focused on urban-based manufacturing as the leading sector for regional development, a regional network approach recognizes the multi-sectoral nature of local level development in rural regions and acknowledges the role of regional resource endowments and already existing activities rather than limiting the prospects for local development to inducements to decentralize footloose industries from core regions. Building networks allows for a variety of sources of economic growth and does not assume that each will be urban based. Bulk-losing processing and agro-industry, for example, may be more efficiently located near the fields or along major transport routes, including waterways, rather than in cities or towns.

Second, most growth pole policies adopt an implicit top-down hierarchical view of the world and, in so doing, tacitly assume that city size can be used as the principal

Table 6.2 *Growth pole and regional network models compared*

Component	Growth pole/centre model	Regional cluster/network model
1. Basic sector	Urban-based manufacturing; usually focuses on large-scale 'propulsive' industries and 'footloose' production units headquartered outside the region	All sectors, depending on local regional endowments and conditions; emphasis on local small-medium size regionally based enterprises
2. Urban system	Hierarchical, centred on a single dominant centre, usually identified by population size and associated with the assumptions of central place theory	Horizontal, composed of a number of centres and their hinterlands, each with own specializations and comparative advantages
3. Rural–urban relations	Image of diffusion processes moving down the urban hierarchy and outward from the city/town to its rural periphery. Rural areas as passive beneficiaries of 'trickle-down' from urban growth	Image of a complex rural–urban field of activities, with growth stimuli emanating from both rural and urban areas and with the intensity increasing along regional inter-settlement transportation corridors
4. Planning style	Usually top-down via sectoral planning agencies and their field offices. Regions have 'misty' boundaries determined by economic interaction	Implies the need for decentralized planning systems, with integration and coordination of multi-sectoral and rural and urban activities at the local level
5. Major policy areas	Industrial decentralization incentives: tax holidays, industrial estates, national transportation trunk roads	Agricultural diversification, agro-industry, resource-based manufacturing, urban services, manpower training, local inter-settlement transportation networks

indicator for identifying a region's principal city and, further, that cities of the same size will have the same functions. In contrast, the network concept draws from research in Asia and elsewhere showing that not only is city size an inadequate indicator of either growth potential or local linkages, but also that cities of the same size class can have very different functions and development profiles (Cohen, 1980). Rather than trying to make a single, large city into an omnibus centre for a vast region, the network concept is based on a clustering of many settlements, each with its own specializations and local-ized hinterland relationships. Thus small towns in upland areas or a region may be key marketing centres for estate crops; another may be near an important cultural centre; and yet another may serve as the administrative centre for the region.

Third, growth pole approaches tend to view rural areas as backward and dependent upon diffusion or trickle-down impulses from cities for their development. The network approach takes a more even view by recognizing that appropriate investments in agricul-ture can lead to higher levels of per capita income in that sector and, further, that rural prosperity is a powerful source of urban growth in agrarian regions. At the same time, selected investments in region-serving functions in cities can help to raise the economic growth potential of both town and countryside.

Fourth, a major difference between growth pole and regional network concepts is found in the styles of planning they encourage. In the former, the urban node is the all-important spatial 'actor'. Demarcating its hinterland is presumed to be a fruitless and unnecessary task. Regional boundaries remain 'misty'. In contrast, the multi-sectoral nature of the cluster concept implies the need for a localized capacity to coordinate a large number of interrelated activities. Using existing provincial or district level bound-aries as the level at which coordination and integration of planning is to take place thus becomes an important aspect of the cluster approach.

Finally, the two concepts also differ in terms of the types of policies they are likely to consider. Growth pole policies are built around incentives to attract manufacturing, namely, the public provision of economic infrastructure for urban industry and the expansion of national trunk road expansion linking growth centres with the capital city and, by extension, the international market. In contrast, the regional network concept recognizes the need to expand rural as well as urban infrastructure, and also gives stronger emphasis on local road and transportation linkages among major centres, villages and towns within the region. Equal attention is given to social as well as economic overhead capital. The provisioning of piped water, electricity, sewage, drainage, schools, and improved health services is not merely a matter of 'welfare' but is also important to the upgrading of the quality of regional life needed to sustain economic growth as well.

The contrasts between the growth pole and regional cluster paradigms are sche-matically shown in Figure 6.1. The network concept is based on three principal consid-erations. First, variations in rural–urban linkages are great even among the hinterland of the same principal town; clustering villages and towns into a regional unit of develop-ment can therefore take advantage of the diversity as well as complementarities among various centres and between each centre and its immediate hinterland within a given region. It does not rely on a single centre to lead regional growth. Relations among cen-tres are more horizontal, complementary and reciprocal.

Second, such clusters already exist, even if in a rudimentary form. Interaction among villages and towns, rather than being confined to dyadic relationships between village-town pairs, form localized networks with varying degrees of intensity across the region and beyond. Such clusters can be identified and demarcated in the initial instance by using existing flows of goods and people among settlements. In the case of Indonesia, for example, regional networks were identified by using data showing the frequency of bus, truck and automobile movements among settlements (Douglass, 1984).

The third consideration is that a cluster of well-connected and highly interactive rural and urban settlements may be better able than a single growth pole to provide a level of agglomeration and economic diversity to act as an antipode to the growth of core metropolitan regions. Given the reduction of time distances among settlements made possible by modern transportation and communications systems, somewhat dispersed towns and villages can be linked together to form an effective range of daily interaction that would have been impossible in most rural regions only a decade or two ago. A more robust regional economy covering a wider spatial scale than a single town and its hinterland and offering a wider array of economic activities can also more readily weather the vagaries of external price shocks and shifts in demand and resources. Greater potential would also exist to capture upstream and downstream linkages and multiplier effects in the region.

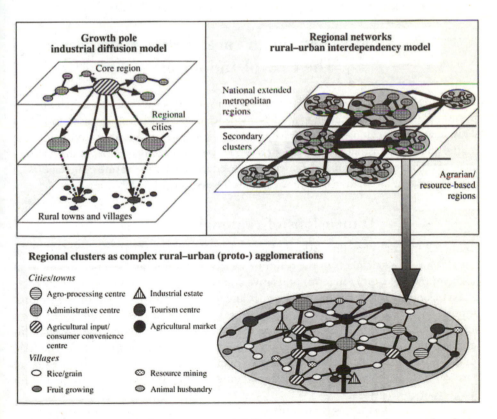

Figure 6.1 *Hierarchical urban-to-rural diffusion versus interdependent rural–urban networks*

In sum, the regional network approach advocates a more decentralized system of planning for working out the dynamics of rural–urban linkages. It challenges many of the precepts of the centre-down diffusion and urban systems models that have dominated policy formulation. It suggests a more diversified, multi-stranded approach to regional development which rests on integrating rural with urban development at the local scale. The approach being recommended advocates a disaggregated and finely-tuned set of policy interventions that allow for variations in regional resource endowments, existing divisions of labour in urban and rural sectors, and local development needs and potentials.

In Indonesia, the transition from a rural to an urban-based economy is now well under way and is reaching into all regions in the country. The timing and pace of this transition is, however, highly uneven over space. If the objective of ameliorating the economic consequences of such uneven patterns of development, which favour very large urban agglomerations and particularly the greater Jakarta metropolitan region (Jabotabek), is to be pursued, the general task at hand is to find ways in which the dynamics of rural–urban linkages and transformations can unfold in a more complementary and reciprocally beneficial manner over the national territory. The regional network model is proposed as a framework for this task.

Regional variations in rural–urban linkages: The case of Indonesia

The regional network paradigm allows for a much wider diversity in rural–urban linkages at the local level than do prevailing models. Evidence from visits to rural areas in Indonesia show how urban-regional systems have much less regularity and uniformity than either central place or industrial diffusion models allow. Historical factors related to the development of each city and region, the presence of government, and the nature of linkages with the national and international economy add to the diversity of possibilities.

Dimensions of regional variations

Figure 6.2 identifies key dimensions of regional variations in rural–urban linkages. On one side are those elements in the realm of society and economy. Socio-economic relations, for example, differ in terms of relative and absolute levels of inequality in income, access to land and other resources, and types and levels of skill attainment by the regional population. These differences may be expressed in terms of class divisions, ethnicity, gender or other socially created cleavages. Unless explicit attention is given to such differences, improving the role of the city may widen rather than close gaps. In Bangladesh, for example, the widely acclaimed Grameen Bank was established principally to reach poor rural women who were without sufficient collateral or social status to qualify for credit from either banks.

Urban functions also vary according to the structure of the rural economy. Fishing villages might require cold storage centres; whereas cattle raising areas might need livestock holding and feeding lots at key transshipment centres. The economic structure of

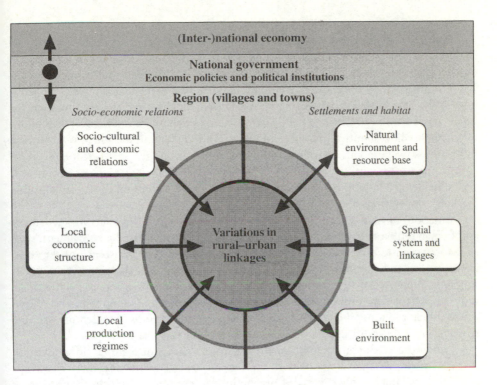

Socio-economic relations
Settlements and habitat

Socio-economic relations
- Basic needs poverty levels
- Inequality in distribution of income and assets
- Level of landlessness, marginal farmers, tenancy
- Basic skills by income groups and gender
- Access to basic social services by income class

Structure of rural economy
Composition of basic sectors (GRDP)
- Primary: mining, fishing, forestry
- Secondary: agro/resource-processing, manufacturing
- Tertiary: tourism, commerce, services

Upstream–downstream multipliers
- Local production of inputs
- Processing/agro-industry
- Commercial sales, producer services, consumer services

Distribution of labour force
- Participation rates and dependency ratios
- Distribution by sector, occupation, status

Rural production regimes
Land distribution and property regimes
- Smallholder vs. large (capitalist/socialist) farms
- Agribusiness: plantations, contract farming
- Common/state/private land distribution
Producer organisations (e.g. cooperatives)

Natural environment and resources
Environment
- Composition and diversity of flora and fauna
- Ecological integrity
- Vulnerability to natural disasters

Resource base
- Soil quality and degree of erosion
- Water availability
- Forest reserves/minerals

Built environment
- Farm (irrigation, drainage, storage)
- Village (roads, bridges, electricity, water supply, communications, housing
- Urban (village–town roads, market centres, water, sewerage, electricity, communications)
- Regional (trunk roads, electricity, communications, market centres)

Spatial system and linkages
- Rural population density
- Levels of urbanisation and complexity of urban system (number of towns/cities, traffic flows, air and water transport)
- Inter-village and village–town access (road quality and frequency of public transport)
- Communications linkages
- Circular migration in the region and with other regions

Note: GRDP = gross regional domestic product.

Figure 6.2 *Factors determining rural–urban relations at the local level*

a town reflects the capacity of the region to capture upstream and downstream linkages and multiplier effects. Thus a regional economy based only on extractive activities with no local processing creates an urban profile markedly different from one of a town in a more complex region.

The organization of production (production regimes) within a given sector or activity will also have a substantial bearing on rural–urban linkages and the requirements for urban services and infrastructure. Plantation versus smallholder cash crop production, for example, show significantly different town profiles. Plantations, which typically use full-time low-wage labour and ship produce in large bulk and may provide lodgings and company stores for workers, may show little demand for local town services; in contrast, a smallholder production regime may depend to a greater extent on towns for supplies, markets, cooperatives, and consumer shopping.

Variations in rural–urban linkages also fall into a second realm covering the habitat and human settlement system of a region. Conditions of the natural environment, such as deforestation leading to constant flooding, may threaten the existence of the town itself, and beyond that it will influence patterns of access and, therefore, the types of functions supported by the hinterland. The natural resource base is perhaps the single most important determinant of a rural regional economy and, therefore, the role of towns in that economy. The classic case of single-resource regions in which towns experience a 'boom-bust' life cycle is an extreme example of this relationship.

Conditions of the built environment are major sources of regional differentiation in rural–urban linkages. Regions with high grade irrigation allowing three rice crops per year have much higher levels of prosperity and commercialization than do most rainfed, single crop regions. Local road networks also profoundly affect rural–urban flows of people, goods and services. Electricity, telephone services, and other linkages add to the physical development of markets and town and village infrastructure to transform the nature, scale and magnitude of rural–urban interaction. Finally, local rural–urban linkages also vary according to relationships to the larger spatial network of towns, cities, transportation and communications flows. As noted, many studies show, for example, that local towns may be bypassed as centres for agro-processing, markets and other urban functions as transportation linkages to more distant, larger towns are improved.

Since this is a dynamic process, so too is the changing functional profile of a town. Activities that were viable at one point in time die out as the larger spatial system develops. More than just a question of access to markets, the connectivity of settlements presents a matrix of competition among regions in terms of comparative advantage and economic potential. Linking up more isolated regions, which are normally characterized by high levels of economic self-sufficiency in their hinterlands, with national and international networks would, for example, be expected to profoundly change the nature and role of towns in the region.

Rural–urban linkages in the contemporary Indonesian context

In giving explicit attention to rural–urban linkages, the Banjarnegara study mentioned previously is perhaps the only one of its kind in Indonesia. Even this study did not, however, cover the range of regional variables summarized in the section on 'Dimensions of regional variations' above. Much research has nonetheless been carried out on some aspects of rural–urban linkages in regional development. Among the more useful studies in this regard is the longitudinal research carried out in eight villages in Java over a 25-year period from the early 1970s. Although not concerned with cities per se, the research contains a wealth of information about rural transformations occurring on Java during a period of intensive urbanization and quantum expansion of rural–urban transportation networks and rural–urban interaction. In one of its most recent reports (Collier et al, 1993), the study found significant differences among villages were the result of not only land capability and other aspects of village potential, but were equally patterned by relative distance from major metropolitan centres. Three types of rural regional contexts were discovered:

1   *Villages within 60km of large rapidly industrializing cities* were characterized by high daily commuting (more women than men, which is reflective of the transnational investment in female-dominated export-processing industries driving metropolitan economic growth in Indonesia) to factory and other work on the urban fringe. Much of lowland Java falls into this category with good roads to most the villages and trucks and buses routinely entering them every hour or more frequently (even every minute). In many instances factories sent buses to pick up workers every day. Communications had become internationalized, with TVs accessible to many village households. Crop regimes had changed in response to increasing labour shortages at peak periods, and wage rates for agricultural labourers had increased. Agricultural land prices were also rapidly increasing in these areas, with land sales increasing to non-village buyers.

2   *Villages in major rice producing areas perhaps near a city but beyond the 60km commuting range of those rapidly industrializing* showed monthly and yearly migration for urban employment and had more full-time farmers operating small plots of land. Agricultural labour shortages existed and were caused by yearly migration. Large farmers were very commercially minded. Wage rates increased in villages having alternative job opportunities; otherwise they were found to have stayed constant. The quality of village housing was improving, but a substantial number still had dirt floors and bamboo walls. Unemployment was found to be low (mostly among more educated males who refused work in agriculture). Most children were finishing at least junior secondary (SMP) education; and slower population growth was leading to a decline in school-age children at lower levels. Electricity had become widely available, but not to all and not to more remote villages; some had TVs; daily newspapers were reaching villages; and at least daily truck and bus services were reaching most villages. Compared with a decade earlier there were major increases in standards of living, although other reports show this to be uneven (Douglass, 1997).

3   *Villages in upland areas distant from large cities* were found to still have poor communications and continued to be dependent on agriculture because of distance to off-farm employment opportunities. The standard of living had fallen in these villages due to dependence on a few crops with declining prices (clove and coffee). Younger and better educated people were migrating out to work as labourers in

factories and construction and as agricultural labourers in lowland areas in rice and sugar cane. Out-migration was leading to a switch to less labour-intensive (tree) crops. Electricity was being extended, but not to the extent of other areas. Village industries were increasing (roof tile, brick making, clove leaf refining, handicrafts; agro-processing (red cane sugar)), but mostly in low-productivity, low-income activities. Televisions had begun to appear, but were not yet widespread.

In light of these findings and the scarcity of other research on rural–urban linkages, visits were made to several villages that have been identified under the special Presidential Decree for rural poverty alleviation (IDT). Unlike other poverty programmes, the IDT programme has two key features. First, it is not aimed at poverty areas as measured by income or basic needs, but rather as having inadequate levels of infrastructure and connectivity with towns and regional transportation networks. Second, it is intended to be highly decentralized, with districts (*kecamaten*) being the level at which projects are to be identified. In September 1996 three candidate IDT villages were visited in the outskirts of Yogyakarta in Central Java; one was visited in eastern Lombok, and another was visited in the hill areas near Bima on the island of Sumbawa.

Three villages near Yogyakarta

Two of the villages near the city of Yogyakarta were actually quite well connected by roads and transportation, had electricity, and were relatively prosperous. The third, located within a 30-minute drive from Yogyakarta and in the hills of the historic Prambanan area of Hindu temples and palaces, had very poor road connections and much lower levels of income and welfare.

The city of Yogyakarta has itself experienced a boost in prosperity in recent years, but not so much from its agricultural hinterland as from its role as a national centre for all levels of education. Schools and universities are still being built in the city, and parents are sending children from across the country to study in this relatively safe city with a high reputation for excellence in education. As a result, the economies of many villages surrounding the city seem to be increasingly specializing in products for the urban population of Yogyakarta as well as for export to other cities. The economy of one nearby village, for example, is dominated by the growing of *salak pondok*, a fruit that can be grown widely throughout Java, but is reputed to have an especially good taste when grown in this village. The growers are not all village people, but also include urbanites who hire villagers to take care of daily management, such as guarding their crop from thieves. The ribbon of development along the principal road through the village is dominated by roadside stands selling the fruit, as is the major village market.

Not very far from this village is another IDT designated village that specializes in pottery. The owner of one of the principal shops told of how in the 1970s the lack of a local market for his wares in the region led him to load his pottery on his bicycle, had it put on a truck and transported to big cities such as Surabaya where he would cycle to sell his products. In the 1980s he decided to stop selling in other cities and to open a shop in his village. He is proud that he now exports not only to other destinations in Indonesia, but even to cities in Australia. Other pottery shops have prospered in the village as well, which is now well known as a pottery village. Somewhat surprisingly, the village has no special clay resources that distinguish it from others in the region. It seems that the entrepreneurial efforts of village residents combined with the growing prosperity of urban residents in the education-driven economy of Yogyakarta have benefited from improvements in connectivity with cities in Central Java to create the market niche for this village.

The third village, located in a dry hilly area without paved roads, was also specialized in a single export, which in this case was limestone slabs quarried from land underneath rice fields and used in urban building construction. A new road had been connected to the village, but it was not yet paved. Nonetheless, it now allowed large trucks to come to pick up the stone. Until that time, each of the large, heavy rectangular stones were carried down the mountain on the heads of village people. Although the trucking may have reduced some of the work, it is not clear that it has resulted in higher incomes. Rough calculations suggest that at the end of the day the villagers earn no more than the going wage for landless labourers in the region even though they own the quarry land. Since they do not own the trucks, there is a likelihood that they face monopsonistic pricing of their cut limestone by the buyers from the city. This pattern of connecting up with larger cities but gaining little economic benefit due to monopolistic and monopsonistic markets is even more pronounced in Eastern Indonesia away from the densely settled rural regions of Java.

Crop production in the upland village near Yogyakarta was severely limited by water availability. Only one crop of rainfed rice could be produced per year, and this was insufficient for household needs; the village was thus a net buyer of rice and other food crops. Limestone sales were the only source of income for these purchases. Given the poor agricultural conditions, IDT funds were used by households to buy calves which are to be raised (but not used for farming) and sold for a profit outside of the village. Households were being equipped with their own cement water storage tanks through government assistance, but most were almost dry in September. Houses were constructed of poorer materials, and consumer durables were limited.

What is somewhat surprising is that although this village is less than 30 minutes from Yogyakarta by automobile, its level of interaction remains low in many important ways. Households reported, for example, that they almost never went to Yogyakarta for any reason. Although work might be available there, they said that for historic reasons they had never developed social relations or networks in the city and thought that without such relations no one would give them a job. This sentiment is consistent with most migration studies, which find that job search through migration follows rather narrow social pathways and that specific job opportunities at the destination are usually known and even agreed upon before migration occurs. In many cities, specific jobs such as pedicab driving or ice cream vending are often associated with migrants from a single region or village.

Children in this village had to walk to school, and due to the lack of water during the long dry season, cattle had to be walked down the mountain for grazing and water. Should the roads be improved and daily transportation be available between this village and Yogyakarta, it is not clear that the results will be a widespread improvement in the village economy. Lack of social contacts in the city, the controlled piece rate of the stone work, and lack of other resources in the village coupled with the lack of water do not suggest that roads will be enough to generate a vital economy. Perhaps if the stone cutters owned their own truck or were able to form a cooperative they might have more leverage over buyers. In any case, direct attention to social and economic factors would need to accompany infrastructure planning if the village is to genuinely benefit from improved rural–urban transport linkages.

'Remote' villages on Lombok and Sumbawa

Lombok and Sumbawa are included in the larger region of Eastern Indonesia, which is considered to cover the most isolated and poorest localities in the island nation. Lombok and Sumbawa are relatively densely settled compared to other major island groups, and in some locations the densities approach those of Java. On both islands, the variations are very great in terms of resource base, economic potential and linkages to the rest of the national and international economy. On Lombok, the most profound economic change now under way is the rise of international tourism centred on the Senggigi beach area, which currently accounts for at least 40 per cent of the economy of West Lombok. Tourism is, however, limited mostly to one or two peak seasons (August and the end-December to early-January period) and is low throughout most of the remainder of the year. Even so, with the many white sand beaches and the proximity to Bali, tourism is likely to be the basic and leading sector of growth for the island for years to come.

For the rest of the island, tobacco is the most widely grown cash crop. Although technical irrigation exists, many of the more arid parts of the island still depend on rainfed irrigation for paddy and other crop growing. Almost none of the tobacco is dried or processed either at the village level or even on Lombok, but is instead shipped directly to Surabaya (Java) for processing and further marketing. As such, very little of the total value added of tobacco is captured on Lombok, leaving the potential for high levels of reinvestment and economic diversification limited. Farmers say they would double their income from tobacco if they were allowed to dry it before selling, but apparent collusion among buyers prevents this.

One of the most significant features of the economy of many Lombok villages is the emigration of workers to Malaysia, which involves professional recruiters and, at least at the present, is allowed by the Malaysian government. In some villages, these migrants account for almost one-fifth of the total labour force. Remittances from these migrants are reportedly important sources of cash in the villages, not a few of which claim to have been depleted of adult men.

Two villages, Menies and Pengkelakmas, located in East Lombok have approximately 700 and 1200 households, respectively. A bridge and secondary road connecting the villages to the kabupaten (regency) road were to have been completed by the middle of 1997, which will for the first time enable trucks to come to Pengkelakmas to greatly improve flows of interaction with the village, including the transport of its agricultural commodities. Currently, it takes one day for villagers to carry their products, such as tobacco, to the main road for delivery to middlemen. Fishermen in the adjacent village also hope to be able to sell their catch to urban centres on the island. With increased market potential, incomes are expected to go up as well as more products can be sold in a shorter space of time. Since even a large increase in the scale of production from the village would not be expected to affect the market price, selling more is not expected to result in lower prices unless certain monopolistic practices among buyers prevail to push prices down.

The villages of Samboir Lama and Teta, located in the hills above Bima in Nusa Tenggara Barat, have just had new roads built that now link them to the kabupaten road. As with all villages receiving road projects, expectations are high that commercial sales of village products (rice, red onions and garlic) will go up and, along with increased access to schools and public services, so will general income and welfare. Minibuses now come three times a day to the villages, although they do not as yet seem to be well timed for the two shifts of school, which takes children about three hours walking one way to reach. The minibus takes only approximately 20 minutes to reach the same lowland vicinity of the school.

The city of Bima itself provides an interesting combination of factors that account for its relative prosperity. As the centre of a Sultanate, it appears to enjoy a higher level of political, and therefore public spending, attention than do many other towns of its size. The city is well laid out and appointed with a high level of road and other infrastructure. It is also the principal point of connection and stopover for tourists going to Komodo Island, home of the huge Komodo Dragon lizards. There are as yet very few hotels, however, but new ones are being constructed and with a more reliable air connection to Mataram and Denpasar, the international tourist economy is expected to enjoy steady growth. One of the hotel managers said that programmes have been organized to recruit and train talented village youth for the hotel industry. Shops in the town include not only numerous clothing and dry goods stores, but also durable goods stores selling televisions, stereos, electronic appliances at a scale that suggests that the town has a sizeable middle class, most of whom come from the more than 2000 public employees in the town, which includes teachers and health workers as well as government planners and administrators.

In sum, although the region exports onions and beef to Java, there is little or no processing of these products in the region, and the vitality of the town appears to depend as much – if not more – on the large size of the civil service and government administration. As with Yogyakarta's education economy, this can, however, have a somewhat catalytic effect in raising demand for staples and higher value added food crops from its rural hinterland than would otherwise be the case if the prosperity of the town were wholly dependent on rural demand for its services.

Summary of observations

Drawing from available case studies in Indonesia and comparing the three villages around Yogyakarta and those on Lombok and Sumbawa, a number of points are revealed that show how regional differentiation occurs at the micro spatial (village) as well as at the macro spatial (region and above) scale:

1   Specialization in markets occurs at the village scale, even in poor villages and even among villages in the same locale.
2   Rural–urban interaction can be very low even with villages located very close to very large cities. This low interaction is the result of poor transportation linkages as well as specific socio-economic conditions of a given village.

3 Improving spatial linkages through, for example, road development, has an indeterminate impact on villages. While access to schools and other services may be heightened, positive income impacts are less certain for several reasons: monopolistic practices may still prevail in buying village products; increases in supply may dampen per unit prices; the village may lack comparative advantage in marketing its products as other villages also begin to enjoy greater access; resources may be depleted in an environmentally unsustainable manner.

4 Village potential is imbedded in both 'absolute space' – the nature of its own human and physical resources – and 'relative space' – its degree of connectivity to larger urban and regional systems. It cannot be solely implied by either natural resource endowments, although these are important, or by past economic histories. The success of the pottery village near Yogyakarta, for example, would not have been predicted on these bases.

5 More successful villages are linked to and interact with more than one urban centre. Access to regional and national urban networks widens market potential and may also help to overcome monopsonistic markets. It also provides a wider range of alternative income-earning opportunities for various members of rural households.

6 Rural–urban linkages are quite specific and do not generally include a full range of activities. In the case of the upland village near Yogyakarta, for example, the major linkage was limestone trade, with limestone being sent out of the village several times per day by truck. In contrast, flows of people and goods between the village and Yogyakarta were highly restricted, as was information about job opportunities.

7 Information about linkages may be more powerful from distant rather than from nearby or even national sources. Recruitment of labour from Lombok for Malaysia did not rely on information coming from cities in Indonesia, but came instead directly through migrant networks from Malaysia to specific villages.

8 Different types of flows between village and town will therefore develop at variant rates with somewhat distinct spatial patterns. The movement of people is unlikely to follow the same paths as the movement of goods or finance. There is, however, a general spatial matrix of interaction within which many of the flows are contained, and within this matrix cities and towns begin to play their own roles. As this matrix expands and changes through local, national and global impulses, so will the role of rural towns.

9 The growth and prosperity of key rural towns, particularly *ibukota* (municipalities) and administrative centres off Java, appears to heavily rely on the size and expansion of the civil service. As such, government sector employment and spending should be included as an important factor in rural–urban linkages. These unexpected sources of local demand can also heighten the potential for rural production of higher value added agricultural products, processed food and village crafts.

10 The emergence of local networks of villages and towns is most easily observed in traffic movements. Two major factors explain these networks. First, as mentioned, crop differentiation at micro levels stimulates local as well as longer-distance exchanges among settlements. Second, public village–town bus systems provide a critical level of daily interaction needed to bring village households into frequent contact with towns and other villages. Port and other types of transport development add to this process.

11 Rural regions off Java seem to have very low levels of backward and forward linkages between village level production and the rest of the economy. Most production appears to be sent to ports for shipment to Java or abroad without even simple processing. National government regulations requiring processing to be done on Java even when it could more efficiently (and with greater regional equity) be done near the source, particularly in the case of bulk-losing processing or processing of perishables which are typical of many rural products, is an often-stated reason for the absence of local processing. The inability to localize these linkages is one of the greatest limitations in promoting a more dynamic process of rural–urban development off Java. This also promotes wider disparities as higher value added in processing is captured in national core metropolitan regions.

12 Financial flows to villages are typically on a people-to-people (e.g. migrant remittances) rather than on an institutional basis (banks and credit associations). Rural household access to low-cost credit is one of the weakest rural–urban linkages.

13 Flows of information have experienced an extraordinary widening of scope through the pervasive diffusion of televisions to even low-income villages in some regions (notably across Java). While this has opened access to national and international information about political, economic and consumer affairs and opportunities, there is little local content, such as agricultural prices or other local producer information, to enhance the knowledge and bargaining position of especially smaller rural producers. Adding local information channels directed toward informing rural producers of vital opportunities and market conditions would be a significant contribution to their economic welfare.

14 The environmental and ecological implications of extending rural–urban linkages seem to be poorly understood or integrated into urban and regional planning. The exploitation of natural resources from distant urban centres is responsible for a great deal of environmental destruction throughout the world, and the expansion of cities into rural peripheries is also cited as a major source of land degradation. Increasing the potential for economic diversity in rural regions could, however, contribute to efforts to move away from dependency on over-exploitation of the natural resource base. In either case, more clearly understanding the environmental implications of rural–urban interaction would make an important contribution to sustaining local development.

15 In general there is a clear sense that rural–urban interaction, particularly that related to road development and television, has experienced substantial increases everywhere in the past two decades. While they have been instrumental in raising levels of welfare, these linkages have not necessarily narrowed either rural–urban or regional disparities in income. Accomplishing this goal would require the creation of virtuous cycles of rural–urban development at the local regional scale (see the section below 'Towards an agenda for policy research'). Infrastructure, while of great importance, is not sufficient for this task by itself.

Towards an agenda for policy research

Insights from real world contexts begin to sketch an agenda for policy research on rural–urban linkages. Figures 6.3 and 6.4 attempt to synthesize the issues they raise by contrasting a virtuous cycle of mutually reinforcing rural–urban linkages with a truncated form of interaction that leads to lower levels of both urban and rural performance at the local level. In the virtuous cycle (Figure 6.3), both (A) international and (B) national conditions are favourable to (C) regional investment in (D) basic/leading sectors and the internalization of three key multiplier effects:

1   employment generation directly through hiring in the export activities and indirectly through hiring in related processing and input supplier firms;
2   processing and manufacturing of basic products are carried out in the region;
3   local purchase of inputs.

Multiple sources of employment generate a widespread increase in household incomes, which in turn generate increased demand for urban services and functions. The economy diversifies and deepens through each cycle, with new leading sectors emerging as older ones run their course. Local planning and producer responsibility combine to renew the environmental base of the region.

In contrast to a virtuous cycle of sustainable development, Figure 6.4 shows what may be the more typical case in rural regions, particularly those located away from major metropolitan centres. Because the region is overly specialized in one or a few primary exports, even somewhat minor swings in international commodity prices have a volatile impact on the local economy. Regional infrastructure and services also typically receive less priority than metropolitan regions and are continuously below needs and potentials. The basic sector has few forward or backward linkages, which greatly limits employment and household income increases. The poor performance of the rural economy has a dampening effect on the local urban economy and its growth potential. Dependence on a narrow resource base leads to over-exploitation and environmental degradation. Low incomes and poverty persist. Towns are often more dependent upon government administration and spending than they are on the rural economy. Even where an enormously profitable mining or other extractive activity, such as forestry, exists, it does not articulate well with its rural hinterlands, which in Indonesia may be composed of small-scale societies that cannot be readily tapped to fill the new labour demands. They remain largely enclave activities more linked to international rather than local markets. While cities around these activities may boom, their impacts on rural areas remain problematic and register striking negative and positive impacts.

While many regions may fall between the extreme examples in Figures 6.3 and 6.4, the diagrams illustrate the ways in which rural–urban linkages can follow quite different trajectories. If one purpose of national planning is to better insure a more reciprocal relationship between rural and urban development, efforts need to be combined to foster a virtuous cycle of development. Research in a number of regional contexts in Indonesia is thus needed to better pinpoint bottlenecks preventing opportunities for these efforts to bear fruit. Towards this end, Figure 6.5 presents a simplified template for research on rural-urban relations. By dividing the research components into structures

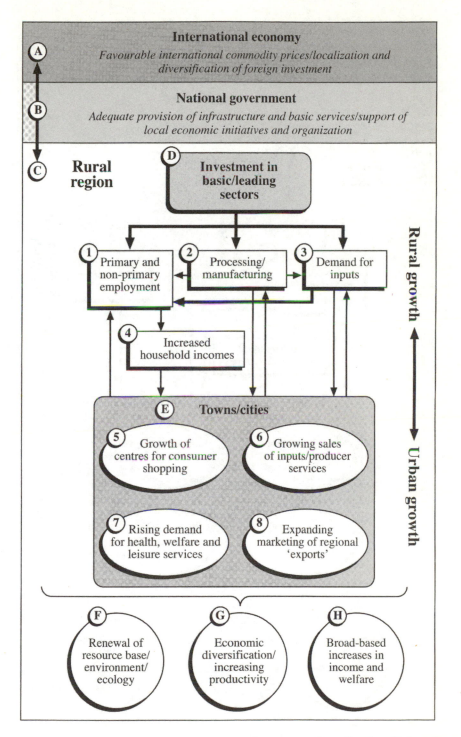

Figure 6.3 *Virtuous cycle of regional development and rural–urban linkages*

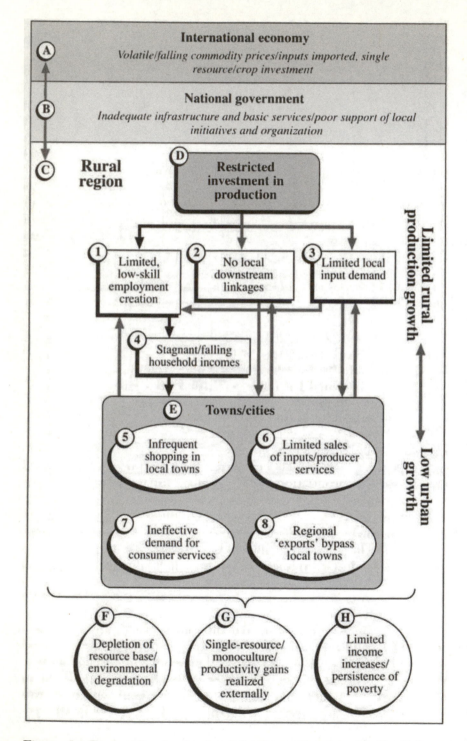

Figure 6.4 *Truncated cycle of regional development and rural–urban linkages*

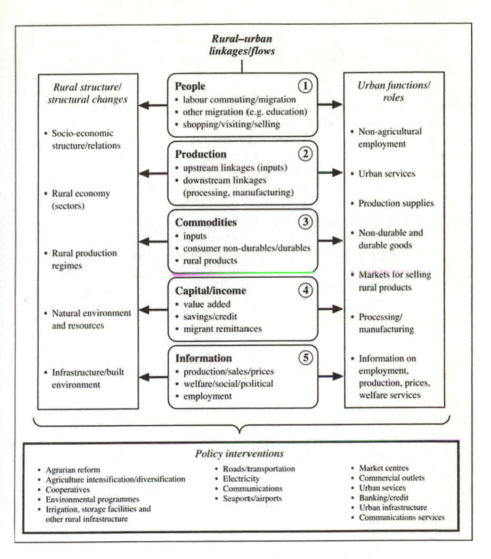

Figure 6.5 *Rural regional development process: Structures, flows and policy interventions*

and flows, it suggests that rural structural change and development is linked to urban functions and roles through a set of flows between rural and urban areas. The task of research is to analyse: (1) patterns of flows; and (2) their combined impact on fostering rural regional development (i.e. both town and countryside).

Five types of flows are identified in Figure 6.5: people, production, commodities, capital and information. Each has multiple components and impacts. Commodities, for example, take the form of production inputs, marketed rural products and daily wage goods (non-durables) and durable goods for final consumption. Each may have quite different spatial linkage patterns as well as variable benefits to rural and urban areas.

If the hypotheses implied by Figures 6.3 and 6.4 are correct, that is, that the flows must lead towards a virtuous cycle of localized (regional) linkages if national objectives of a more even pattern of spatial development are to be achieved, then policy interventions would also be oriented toward improving the chances for reciprocal benefits to accrue from the flows. These interventions would not focus on the flows alone, but would also consider, for example, action in rural socio-economic relations, production, institutional capacity, and environmental spheres.

As an example, a study of the flow of people might find that few go to local towns for employment. Reasons for the low labour absorptive capacity of the town would then be identified and policy options to improve its capacity would be considered. Or, research may find that almost no information is provided from towns on market prices, crop prospects and other vital areas of rural interest. Tracing the value added of a rural commodity from the farm to final consumption would reveal not only how much of the total value added is captured by the region of origin (usually quite low), but also the income implications of locally capturing greater shares of downstream processing and distribution. Conversely, data may show that roads connecting a village have enabled widespread income increases through greater flows of products to external markets, which has led to more frequent visits to towns for shopping and farm inputs, with the further result of spurring the growth of the town.

Structures, flows and policy interventions

Of critical importance in any of these scenarios is not to assume that enhancing the physical connectivity between rural and urban areas will bring either benefits or disbenefits to cities and villages. Rather the task is to study each type of flow to discern the ways in which roads and other infrastructure actually affect the nature and distribution of benefits from rural–urban linkages.

Finally, while research could be conducted between a single village and a single centre, the observation that rural–urban relations generally involve multiple linkages among villages and with local as well as very distant cities suggests that the focus would be better placed in the context of regional networks, with flows studied both from individual villages and among urban centres in an identified regional cluster. In Indonesia, a convenient starting point for the research would be to use a select number of *kawasan andalan*, which are prototype regional clusters identified by the government for priority attention. By studying the dynamics of flows and structural change within these clusters, policies can be better oriented to local conditions to support Indonesia's objectives of creating more symbiotic and reciprocal linkages between rural and urban development.

References

Armstrong, W. and McGee, T. G. (1985) *Theaters of Accumulation*, Methuen, London
Birgegård, L.-E. (1988) 'A review of experiences with integrated rural development', *Manchester Papers on Development*, vol IV, no 1, pp2–27

Bunchorntavakul, D. (1976) *The Impact of the Growth Center on Rural Areas: A Case Study in the North of Thailand*, AIT/HSD, Bangkok

Chambers, R. (1985) *Rural Development: Putting the Last First*, Longman, London

Cohen, J. M. (1980) 'Integrated rural development: Clearing the underbrush', *Sociologica Ruralis*, vol 20, pp195–211

Cohen, M., English, J. and Brookfield, H. (1977) 'Functional diversity at the base of the urban system of Peninsular Malaysia', *Journal of Tropical Agriculture*, vol 45, pp12–25

Collier, W., Santoso, K. and Wibowo, R. (1993) *A New Approach to Rural Development in Java: Twenty-Five Years of Village Studies*, PT Intersys Kelola Maju for ILO, Jakarta

de Jong, W. (1988) *The Role of Towns in Rural Development: A Case Study of Banjarnegara, Central Java*, UGM Press, Yogyakarta

de Jong, W., Palte, J. G. L. and van Steenbergen, F. (1983) 'The role of Banjarnegara as a small regional center in central Java', *The Indonesian Journal of Geography*, vol 13, no 45, pp37–52

Douglass, M. (1981) 'Thailand: territorial dissolution and alternative regional development for the central plains', in Stöhr, W. and Taylor, D. R. F. (eds) *Planning from Above or Below?* John Wiley, Chichester, pp183–208

Douglass, M. (1984) *National Urban Development Strategy Scenarios*, NUDS Project, Ministry of Public Works, Tata Kota dan Tata Daerah, Jakarta

Douglass, M. (1990) *Regional Inequality and Regional Policy in Thailand: An International Comparative Perspective*, TDRI, Background Report 3-3, National Urban Development Policy Study, Bangkok

Douglass, M. (1995) 'Global interdependence and urbanization: Planning for the Bangkok mega-urban region', in McGee, T. G. and Robinson, I. (eds) *The New Southeast Asia: Managing the Mega-Urban Regions*, University of British Columbia Press, Vancouver, pp45–79

Douglass, M. (1997) 'Structural change and urbanization in Indonesia: from the "old" to the "new" international division of labor', in Jones, G. and Visaria, P. (eds) *Urbanization in Large Developing Countries*, Clarendon Press, Oxford, pp111–141

Fei, J. C. and Ranis, G. (1964) *Development of the Labor Surplus Economy*, Irwin, Homewood, IL

Friedmann, J. (1968) 'The Strategy of Deliberate Urbanization', *AIP Journal*, Nov, pp364–371

Friedmann, J. (1992) *Empowerment: The Politics of Alternative Development*, Basil Blackwell, Oxford

Friedmann, J. and Douglass, M. (1978) 'Agropolitan development: Toward a new strategy for regional planning in Asia', in Lo, F. and Salih, K. (eds) *Growth Pole Strategy and Regional Development Policy*, Pergamon Press, Oxford, pp163–192

Friedmann, J. and Weaver, C. (1979) *Territory and Function*, Edward Arnold, London

Gibb, A. (1984) 'Tertiary urbanization: The agricultural market center as a consumption-related phenomenon', *Regional Development Dialogue*, vol 5, no 1, Spring, pp110–148

Grandstaff, S. (1990) *The Role of Demand in Provincial Industrialization*, Thailand Development Research Institute, Bangkok

Hirschman, A. (1958) 'Balanced growth: A critique', *The Strategy of Economic Development*, Yale, New Haven, CN, pp50–75

Johnson, E. A. J. (1970) *The Organization of Space in Developing Countries*, Harvard University Press, Cambridge, MA

Kammeier, D. and Swan, P. (eds) (1984) *Equity with Growth? Planning Perspectives for Small Towns in Developing Countries*, Asian Institute of Technology, Bangkok

Khan, A. R. (1979) 'The Comilla model and the integrated rural development programme of Bangladesh – An experiment in "cooperative capitalism"', in Ghai, D., Khan, A. R. and Lee, E. (eds) *Agrarian Systems and Rural Development*, Holmes and Meier, New York, pp113–158

Khan, A. (1979) 'The Comilla project: An experiment in cooperative capitalism', *World Development*, vol 7, pp397–432

Koppel, B. (1987) 'Does integrated rural development really work? Lessons from the Bicol river basin', *World Development*, vol 15, no 2, pp205–220

Ladavalya, M. L. B. and Siripool, V. (1988) *The Impact of the Regional City Development Project upon Outlying Areas: the Chiang Mai Case*, Chiang Mai University, Chiang Mai, SRI

Lightfoot, P., Fuller, T. and Kamnuansilpa, P. (1983) 'Circulation and interpersonal networks linking rural and urban areas: The case of Roi-et, Northeastern Thailand', Papers of the East-West Population Institute, no. 84, East-West Center, Honolulu

Lipton, M. (1977) *Why Poor People Stay Poor*, Gower Publishing Limited, London

Mathur, O. (ed) (1982) *The Role of Small Cities in National Development*, UNCRD, Nagoya

Maude, A. (1983) 'Do rural towns stimulate rural development?' *Malaysian Journal of Tropical Agriculture*, vol 8, pp40–48

Myrdal, G. (1957) *Economic Theory and Underdeveloped Regions*, Duckworth, London

Richardson, H. (1978) *Regional and Urban Economics*, Penguin, London

Rondinelli, D. (1979) 'Applied policy analysis for integrated regional development planning in the Philippines', *Third World Planning Review*, vol 1, no 2, pp151–178

Shiann-Far, K. (1986) *Growth Relation between Urban Center and Its Hinterland: A Case Study of Surat Thani in Southern Thailand*, Master's Thesis, AIT/HSD, Bangkok

Singer, H. (1964) 'The generative versus parasitic role of cities in development', in Alonso, W. and Friedmann, J. (eds) *Urban and Regional Planning*, MIT Press, Boston, MA

Slater, D. (1989) 'Territorial power and the peripheral state: The issue of decentralization', *Development and Change*, vol 20, no 3, 501–531

Williamson, J. (1965) 'Regional inequality and the process of national development: A description of the patterns', *Economic Development and Cultural Change*, vol 13, no 4, pp3–45

Chapter 7

The Role of Small and Intermediate Urban Centres in Regional and Rural Development: Assumptions and Evidence

David Satterthwaite and Cecilia Tacoli

Introduction

Since the early 1960s, small and intermediate urban centres have attracted the attention of policy makers and planners. Different theoretical approaches have underpinned such interest and the related policy interventions. Early views of the role of small and intermediate urban centres in regional and rural development fell within the general paradigms of modernization and dependency theories. In the first, small urban centres are seen as centres from which innovation and modernization would trickle down to the rural population. Hence, the most effective and rational spatial strategy for promoting rural development is to develop a well-articulated, integrated and balanced urban hierarchy. This network of small, medium-size and larger urban centres is described as '... locationally efficient – it allows clusters of services, facilities and infrastructure that cannot be economically located in small villages and hamlets to serve a widely dispersed population from an accessible central place.'[1]

The pessimistic view echoes the 'urban bias' debate, and originally argued that small urban centres contribute to rural impoverishment and are the 'vanguards of exploitation' of the rural poor and of extraction of natural resources by external forces which, according to the case, may be colonial powers, multinational enterprises, central governments, local administrators and élites. Such exploitation can only be avoided where there is an egalitarian class structure and free access to land, and '... where the stimulus to urban growth results in activity primarily by the people and for the people themselves'.[2]

More recent views adopt a wider perspective and describe uneven development processes as the root of regional inequalities as well as rural–urban and intra-rural dis-

---

Note: Reprinted from *The Urban Part Of Rural Development: The Role of Small and Intermediate Urban Centres in Rural and Regional Development and Poverty Reduction*, by Satterthwaite, D. and Tacoli, C., copyright © (2003) IIED, London.

parities.[3] Although the role of small and intermediate urban centres is not explicitly discussed, the economic and political primacy of large centres and metropolitan regions goes hand in hand with the peripheralization of poorer regions. Recent work in sub-Saharan Africa describes the increasing significance of rural–urban linkages in the livelihoods of rural residents, including occupational and residential transformations, as the mainly negative consequence of pressures on small-scale farming systems accompanied by declining opportunities and high costs of living in the cities.[4] Both views suggest that the role of small and intermediate urban centres in the development of their surrounding rural region is largely dependent on power relations and development strategies at the national and global levels.

Despite the central role often ascribed to small and intermediate urban centres in regional planning, there is little evidence to corroborate or refute their alleged capacity to trigger development or to act as centres of regional extraction. This paper summarizes the potential role of small and intermediate centres, as implicitly assumed by many policies and programmes. This is then discussed in the light of the available, and relatively limited, empirical evidence, with specific attention to small and intermediate centres' roles in more equitable regional development and in rural and urban poverty reduction.

The potential role of small and intermediate urban centres in regional and rural development

The commonly stated spatial aims of regional planning policies assume that small and intermediate urban centres contribute to regional and rural development in four main ways:

- *By acting as centres of demand/markets for agricultural produce from their surrounding rural region*, either for local consumers or as links to national and export markets. Access to markets is a prerequisite to increasing rural agricultural incomes, and the proximity of local small and intermediate centres to production areas is assumed to be a key factor in their potential role.
- *By acting as centres for the production and distribution of goods and services to their rural region*. Such concentration is assumed to reduce costs and improve access to a variety of services, both public and private and for both rural households and enterprises. Hence, services include agricultural extension, health and education (and access to other government services), as well as banking, post, services of professionals such as lawyers and accountants and lower-order services such as bars and cafés, and wholesale and retail sales of manufactured goods from within and outside the region.
- *By becoming centres for the growth and consolidation of non-farm activities and employment* through the development of small and medium-size enterprises or through the relocation of branches of large private or parastatal enterprises.
- *By attracting rural migrants* from the surrounding region through demand for non-farm labour (and perhaps decreasing migration pressures on some larger urban centres).

The empirical evidence available shows great variations in the extent to which small and intermediate urban centres fulfil these roles. Much of this relates to the specific context in which such centres develop, to land-owning structures, to the quality of transport and communications links and to the structural conditions prevailing at the international, national and local levels. In addition, many centres show high levels of economic and population growth but, at the same time, increasing levels of social differentiation and little evidence of poverty reduction.

Small and intermediate urban centres as markets for regional agricultural produce

Whether small and intermediate urban centres develop as markets for rural producers, and especially for small-scale farmers, depends on a number of factors. These include farming systems and access to natural resources and labour; accessibility and affordability of transport, road infrastructure, and storage and processing facilities; the presence of local urban demand (obviously much influenced by population and income levels) and links with a wider network of markets; and the relations between producers and traders. The greatest stimulus for small and intermediate urban centres from agriculture tends to be where crops or other products generate a high income per hectare and where the land-owning structure is not too inequitable (so there are many farmers earning adequate incomes).[5]

In agricultural regions dominated by large-scale commercial agriculture, most small and intermediate urban centres do not have major roles as markets for agricultural produce. Large volumes of cash crops produced under this type of farming system mostly bypasses local centres while the low wages paid to local workers generates little demand for goods and services. This is especially the case for export-oriented cattle-raising and for certain crops which are shipped directly to larger centres and ports, with little or no new economic activities developing in smaller urban centres (see Box 7.1). Even where small and intermediate local urban centres function as administrative and service centres for farmers, fluctuations in world markets can result in stagnation or decline. In Ghana's cocoa-producing Central Region, the collapse of international prices for this commodity triggered population loss in small towns. Where this fell below the threshold of 5000, the settlements were reclassified as villages: as a consequence, between 1970 and 1984 the total urban population of the Central Region fell from 28.5 to 26.5 per cent, while national rates of urbanization continued to grow.[6] Similarly, it is likely that low prices for coffee on the international market have brought serious economic problems to many 'coffee towns' that had originally developed and often boomed during periods when world prices were higher.

Despite the generally limited role of small urban centres in regions dominated by commercial farms, they can nevertheless play an important role as local markets for low-income rural residents, albeit as part of a survival strategy rather than as engines of economic growth. The small town of Banket, in Zimbabwe, lies in a rich agricultural zone. It was established in the colonial era to serve the needs of white commercial farmers, and with a population of 10,000 it still serves as a service centre for the surrounding

Box 7.1 *Cattle-ranching and regional urban centres in Huetar Norte, Costa Rica*

Huetar Norte is primarily a cattle-producing region for foreign markets, although since the implementation of structural adjustment programmes in the 1990s this has been complemented with export-oriented crops. Generous credit facilities were allocated to cattle-ranching in the 1970s, supported by loans from the World Bank, which had made the production of regular quality hamburger meat the keystone of its credit policy in Central America. Large ranchers were preferred over smallholders, increasing inequality in the land-owning structure. Indeed, cattle-ranching caused much rural unemployment, especially among the growing number of landless labourers and evicted smallholders, in turn triggering occupation of forest lands and soil erosion.

Moreover, despite the fact that 21 per cent of national cattle stock grazed in this region, no large slaughterhouses or small rural facilities were located in Huetar Norte. Bypassing the regional centres in favour of the capital city, San José, was the result of a powerful alliance between export ranchers in Huetar Norte and politicians and state bureaucrats in San José. Broadly speaking, government policy induced the rapid exploitation of regional natural resources at the expense of sustainability and of the employment and incomes of a considerable proportion of the region's population. While local centres such as Ciudad Quesada have grown, mainly on the basis of the provision of credit services, this growth can be defined largely as parasitic. The creation of wealth as value added and of employment in the processing of the region's main agricultural produce has, on the whole, bypassed regional small and intermediate urban centres.

Source: Romein, A. (1997) 'The role of central places in the development of regional production structures: The case of Huetar Norte, Costa Rica', in Van Lindert, P. and Verkoren, O. (eds) *Small Towns and Beyond: Rural Transformations in Small Urban Centres in Latin America*, Thela Latin America Series, Amsterdam

rich commercial farms. Waged farm workers are among the poorest of Zimbabwe's population, earning far less than the national rural food poverty line and the total consumption poverty line. When there is a need for quick cash, for example, to pay school fees, finance a funeral or buy basic necessities, farm workers take commodities to the market in Banket. This activity is not regular, however, and because of the tight work schedules, workers often send children or unemployed relatives to town.[7]

In general, small and intermediate urban centres are far more likely to play a role as markets for agricultural produce from the surrounding region in areas where small and medium-scale farming prevail.[8] While these types of farming systems imply some equality in access to and distribution of land, availability of labour can be an equally significant constraint for producers with limited capital to invest in mechanization. Box 7.2 illustrates how in West Africa the issue of labour often overlaps with land tenure systems, and also how strong demand for relatively high-value horticultural produce from nearby urban centres can provide profitable returns from small farm plots.

Demand from urban-based consumers is obviously as important as supply factors. Demand in small urban centres can be limited by incomes and by the fact that, in many

---

Box 7.2 *Secondary land rights and farming in central Mali*

Secondary land rights include sharecropping, tenancy and borrowing of land under customary tenure systems (land management and allocation by traditional authorities such as village chiefs and village councils). Secondary rights are often seen as exploitative, as they do not give permanent tenure rights to users. However, in some circumstances they can benefit both secondary and permanent rights holders. In the village of Baguinéda, in central Mali, secondary rights allow small-scale farmers to hire migrant workers in exchange for temporary rights to cultivate own plots. The system is highly structured, with specific days of the week allocated to working as labourers and others to working on the borrowed land. Two aspects are central to the functioning of the system: first, land tenure in the village is almost exclusively under the customary system and controlled by the village council, allowing for secondary rights allocation. Second, the strong demand from nearby urban markets for horticultural produce, in which the village specializes, makes cultivation of even a small plot relatively profitable and therefore attractive to migrants.

Source: GRAD (2001) 'Potentialités et conflits dans les zones péri-urbaines: le cas de Bamako au Mali', Rural–Urban Working Paper 6, IIED, London

---

instances, residents are likely to grow at least part of the food they consume. But in larger administrative centres, demand from civil servants and government employees can raise demand for staples and higher value-added crops from the surrounding region.[9]

Rural producers' physical access to the markets in small urban centres and the extent of these urban centres' connection to wider networks of regional, national and international urban centres are key influences on their development. Availability and affordability of transport is important not only in connecting producer areas to local urban centres but also in connecting local small and intermediate urban centres to other actual and potential markets. The location of small urban centres is therefore critical. In many cases, urban centres located on road axes, along railways and rivers, or in coastal areas have better links with wider market networks. Indeed, national and regional urban systems always reflect the dominant transport system, although often also showing the influence of transport systems that have been superseded (for instance, the 'railway towns' and 'river ports', even when road transport now predominates[10]). Border centres also often incorporate elements of underground trade networks, especially where pricing policies result in significant price differences for cash crops. This is, for example, the case on the border between Ghana and Côte d'Ivoire, where cocoa and coffee prices are sufficiently different to encourage smuggling.[11]

Recent case studies in northern and southern Tanzania show the importance of regional and national urban networks. Himo, in the north of the country, is a vibrant market for local producers. Most farming is small scale and Himo acts as a collection centre for a large number of small farmers. Produce is then shipped to other Tanzanian towns, including the primate centre, Dar es Salaam, and across the border to Kenya.[12] By contrast, the town of Lindi, in the south, has a very limited role as a market for local produce. This is due partly to the poor state of the roads within its region, making transport costs prohibitive for small farmers, but this also extends to the connection between Lindi and other urban centres in the region, and even with the primate city. Lindi is thus a declining centre, and the main locally produced cash crop, cashew nuts, is exported in its raw form by agents who collect it directly from the villages and ship it to international markets, with little if any value added retained in the region.[13]

However, while infrastructure is certainly important, improving spatial linkages does not necessarily have a positive impact on marketing of agricultural production. The vertically integrated and centrally controlled marketing operations that prevailed in the agricultural sector from the 1960s, and in many cases up to the implementation of structural adjustment programmes, were usually linked to poor prices for local producers – thus limiting farmers' incomes and opportunities to re-invest in farming. In many countries, monopolistic practices still prevail in buying rural produce; moreover, increased supply may dampen prices, and rural settlements may compete against each other if they have no clear comparative advantage in marketing their products.[14]

This points to two key issues: the first is rural producers' access to information on markets, including price mechanisms, fluctuations and consumer preferences; the second, overlapping with this, is the role of traders. Market information can dramatically transform small farmers' practices and help them adapt production to demand while, at the same time, maximizing the use of their resources.[15] Information can be provided by local traders and by migrant relatives with access to urban markets. The recent, dramatic increase in the use of mobile phones facilitates such exchanges and may especially benefit low-income producers. Recent research shows that in villages around Kampala, Uganda's capital city, almost 20 per cent of rural households have access to mobile phones. These same households could not afford the costs of fixed-line phones.[16]

But for the majority of small farmers, traders are the main link with urban markets. Although traders are often perceived as exploitative, they often provide a vital link for small and diversified production flows that are not sufficiently profitable to attract large-scale trading organizations.[17] Moreover, small farmers' limited access to formal credit means that traders often have an increasingly important role as providers of credit. However, with the exception of export crops, trade in agricultural produce is rarely controlled by large, well-capitalized traders. Especially for horticultural produce, the marketing system is often dominated by small-scale traders, even in the case of wholesale dealers and especially in sub-Saharan Africa. In West Africa, traders are usually women who tend to establish personal relationships with both producers and retailers. In this way, financial exchanges are embedded in wider social relations that provide the basic rules for the trust needed for commercial transactions. The major problem confronting most of these traders is limited financial liquidity, which makes them (and, as a result, their creditors) vulnerable to market losses. This problem is compounded by poor physical infrastructure and lack of storage and processing facilities.

The role of traders in the development of small and intermediate urban centres deserves to be better understood. To do so, the category of 'traders' should be broken down to facilitate the identification of specific roles and, eventually, of support interventions. But in many cases, a better understanding is also necessary to regulate the institutional structure of markets, as monopolistic practices or local mercantile oligopolies that control flows of goods tend to bypass local urban centres and re-invest profits outside the region.[18]

The role of small and intermediate urban centres in the distribution of goods and services to their rural region

In this section, we limit the discussion to commercial services, i.e. those that develop based on demand from producers and consumers. By goods we mean both household consumption goods and items related to agricultural production inputs. It should be noted, however, that basic services also have a major impact on livelihoods, as they may improve or negatively affect individuals' and households' capabilities.

The role of small and intermediate urban centres in the distribution of services and goods is at the heart of growth centre and central place policies and programmes. These are based on the concept of urban hierarchy, whereby size plays a key role in the types of services provided by different urban centres. Hence, investments in intermediate urban centres are assumed to spread to and stimulate smaller centres which, in turn, provide a limited range of lower-order services and goods to the rural region. However, empirical evidence does not confirm that the size of urban centres necessarily relates to their economic role within their surrounding region. This is because size tells very little about the economic structures and potentials of the rural region and the nature of the links between urban centres and their surrounding rural region.

Two main factors influence the role of small and intermediate urban centres as providers of services and goods to their rural region. First is the nature of rural economic activities and, related to this, the income levels and purchasing power of the rural population. Second is the capacity of local enterprises to develop to meet this demand and the demand from those living in the urban centre. The quality and nature of the services and goods provided must be able to respond to local demand in the face of competition from elsewhere; even enterprises in thriving smaller urban centres can be undermined by competition from larger urban centres and cities, especially when these are located sufficiently close and transport links are reasonably accessible, efficient and affordable.

A broad-based demand for goods and services depends on rural and urban economic activities that generate adequate incomes spread across the local (both rural and urban) population of the region. Many small and intermediate urban centres (and many large cities) developed because of such a broad-based demand – usually generated by high-value crops. But where incomes are low (because of low-value crops or because prices for formerly high-value crops are depressed), demand is not only constrained in terms of quantity. Since low-income households and individuals usually also have limited time available for purchasing goods and services, they often combine trips to urban centres in order to make the most of their visit. This means that small urban centres which only provide a limited range of such goods and services are often bypassed in favour of larger centres (see Box 7.3).

For most small and intermediate urban centres, increasing rural incomes is a precondition for their development, based on their being focal points in the provision of services and goods to the rural population. This, in turn, is linked to land ownership structures: for example, much of the dramatic decline in rural poverty in Vietnam in the 1990s is attributed largely to land allocation reforms, which have given farmers security of tenure and more freedom to manage and work the land and to determine what crops to cultivate.[19]

Box 7.3 *Market behaviour in a low-income region of the State of Mexico*

The region surrounding the intermediate centre of Tejupilco, about 120km from Mexico City, has very limited socio-economic development, with much of the rural population living at near-subsistence levels. The transport network is also poorly developed. Tenure is a problem, and most rural households have either insufficient land to engage in cash crop production or are landless and rely on seasonal migration for their incomes. Rural settlements are mainly hamlets of less than 1000 inhabitants, interspersed with a substantial dispersed population. A periodic market system, with different prices and goods on offer, takes place in various settlements, the largest of which has a population of 10,000. This small urban centre also offers a range of permanent services, including secondary education institutions, farmer supply agencies, banks, a municipal centre, doctors and dentists, lawyers and accountants.

The structure of periodic markets is the consequence of traders adapting to low demand and trying to maximize profits. Consumers have to adapt to such a system in order to minimize their cash and time costs. As a result, there is no simple correlation between distance to markets and the frequency of shopping trips. Low-income rural consumers adapt by organizing their visits to urban centres to fit in several purposes, including the purchase of goods, the use of services, social visits, in some cases the sale of their own produce, and temporary work. This means that larger regional centres are more likely to be the destination of such trips, as they offer a wider range of opportunities.

Source: Morris, A. (1997) 'Market behaviour and market systems in the State of Mexico', in Van Lindert, P. and Verkoren, O. (eds) *Small Towns and Beyond: Rural Transformations in Small Urban Centres in Latin America*, Thela Latin America Series, Amsterdam

---

To a large extent, the nature of agricultural produce also affects demand for goods and services from the farming population. Labour-intensive and high-revenue produce such as horticulture is more likely to increase incomes for a large number of small and medium-size farmers. By contrast, cattle-ranching requires limited labour but high capital investment for the acquisition of large land holdings. The small labour force cannot provide sufficient demand to stimulate the production of goods and services in local small and intermediate urban centres, while the wealthy few are more likely to rely for household consumption on larger urban centres selling a wider variety of specialized goods and services. Even when the number of those employed in farming is relatively high, their incomes need to be sufficiently high. In Zimbabwe, waged farm workers are among the poorest of the country's population and, although they depend on local small urban centres for essential services such as health care and for the purchase of clothing and other basic items, their purchasing power is so low that it can only support the urban informal sector.[20]

Services and goods for agricultural production rather than for household consumption have been affected by economic reform and adjustment since the 1980s. On the demand side, structural adjustment was meant to increase producer prices and, in some cases and for some commodities, this did occur. For example, in Zimbabwe, maize prices increased in the 1993–1994 season. Since this increase was greater than that of the price of fertilizers, the use of fertilizers also grew. However, this only applied to larger farmers with a marketed maize surplus, whereas small farmers, who rely on subsistence agriculture and non-farm activities and who must purchase at least part of their maize for household consumption, did not benefit from the staple crop's price increase and therefore were not in a position to purchase more agricultural inputs and increase their own production.[21]

With declines in demand, the supply of agricultural inputs by enterprises based in small and intermediate centres has also been affected. Moreover, the impact of rising costs of imports, often compounded by currency devaluation, have hit many activities related to agricultural production: for example, rural transporters, grain grinders, mechanics, welders and photographers have, in many cases, suffered from the high costs of equipment and materials. Indeed, even locally manufactured inputs often have some import content, for example, scrap metal for blacksmiths' tools.[22] Especially in sub-Saharan Africa, the demise of statal and parastatal marketing boards has affected small farmers' access to credit, often severely. With the costs of agricultural inputs and consumer goods rising faster than the prices of agricultural produce, both small-scale farmers and the small-scale urban enterprises that rely on their demand have been affected. To some extent, credit provision has been taken up by local traders, as described earlier.

Overall, trade and services are an important component of non-farm activities in small and intermediate urban centres, and especially in smaller settlements they are often closely related to agricultural production. This may consist of buying farm produce and selling it in local urban and rural markets, or shipping it to other markets outside the region; it may also consist of selling goods, both agricultural and non-agricultural, to farmers and households whose main source of income is derived from

---

Box 7.4 *Urban-based trade and services in northern Tanzania*

Himo is a thriving small market town in northern Tanzania, close to the border with Kenya. It is a collection and distribution point for smaller markets in the Kilimanjaro region, and a large proportion of the produce is sold either directly by producers or by small traders to larger operators, who take it to Dar es Salaam and other regional centres in the country or across the border to Kenya. Himo also receives produce from other Tanzanian regions and manufactured goods from Kenya. On market days, the town is hectic, with produce arriving from near and far, and traders, middlemen, porters and food vendors all trying to cash in on the trade.

Services related to the market are the main source of income for the town's residents, and include about 40 bars, 40 guesthouses and around 70 shops, as well as small slaughterhouses and petrol stations. This concentration of services attracts not only traders but also farmers from surrounding villages, where there are often just a few small shops and no bars.

Source: Diyamett, B., Diyamett, M., James, J. and Mabala, R. (2001) *The Case of Himo and its Region, Northern Tanzania*, Rural–Urban Working Paper 1, IIED, London

farming. Both small and intermediate urban centres also provide recreational services to the population of their surrounding region, including bars, restaurants, hotels and guesthouses, cinemas etc. The link with agricultural production is clear as, in many cases, customers are farmers who come to town to sell their produce or to buy inputs (or, in many cases, do both), and traders travelling between market towns.

The scale and extent of provision of goods and services to rural consumers by enterprises located in small and intermediate urban centres is closely linked to income diversification and to employment opportunities in non-farm activities, which are often located in local urban centres. This is especially important in smaller urban centres, which are unlikely to attract branches of large private and parastatal enterprises due to their limited demand.

Small and intermediate urban centres, livelihood diversification and non-farm activities

Definitions: In this chapter, we define rural non-farm activities as all activities outside the agricultural sector. This excludes wage or exchange labour on other farms (sometimes classed as 'off-farm'[23]) but includes services and manufacturing related to the transformation and processing of agricultural produce, as well as non-related services and manufacturing activities. It also includes all forms of work – self-employment, wage employment, full-time, part-time, formal, informal, seasonal and occasional non-farm income-generating activities. These may take place in a variety of locations: in the home, in rural-based workplaces and urban-based ones requiring workers to commute, and in a number of different places, as is the case for itinerant activities such as trading.

It is generally agreed that in most rural locations, there has been an increase among rural households in the time devoted to, and the income share derived from, non-farm activities, although diversification is not new. Nor is it a purely rural phenomenon, and the reliance of hundreds of millions of urban residents on agriculture, either for household consumption or as an income-generating opportunity, is well documented.[24] However, national employment data tend to underestimate the importance of diversification, as they usually record only people's primary activity. This neglects the fact that individuals are more likely to engage in multiple activities rather than rely on only one, and that there will often be variations over time, either seasonal (and therefore dependent on changes in the labour demands of different activities) or related to individuals' life courses (such as, especially for women, different demands on their time from childcare, caring for older people etc). Recent survey data on employment patterns in southern Tanzania show that 67 per cent of respondents living in villages and in the intermediate town of Lindi are engaged in more than one income-generating activity, including both farming and non-farm activities.[25]

Information on rural households' income share derived from non-farm activities is usually based on relatively small and location-specific household or enterprise surveys. Rarely is there national data, and even where they are available, usually informal sector activities are omitted, including home-based work and petty trade that can be a significant part of non-farm income-generating activities for low-income groups. Available studies show that the proportion of rural households' incomes derived from non-farm sources, including migrant remittances, is between 30 and 50 per cent in sub-Saharan Africa, reaching as much as 80–90 per cent in some regions, such as southern Africa. In south Asia, the proportion is around 60 per cent.[26] In Latin America, non-farm income constitutes roughly 40 per cent of rural households' incomes.[27]

The reasons for the increase in income diversification and non-farm employment

The reasons and determinants of diversification are the subject of intense debate. A key question is whether diversification is the result of growth in both agricultural and non-agricultural sectors or, rather, the result of decline and stagnation in farming.[28] In the regional planning tradition of the 'virtuous circle' of rural–urban economic development, diversification is an essential element of a theoretical model that emphasizes efficient economic linkages and physical infrastructure connecting farmers and other rural producers with both domestic and external markets (see Box 7.5)

As is often the case, there are several variations of this stylized model, although the critical element is that it is agricultural growth that spurs growth in rural non-farm employment. A more sombre view of diversification sees it as one dimension of a wider process of de-peasantization. This is described as an overall sectoral change involving the rapid shrinkage of the proportion of the population engaged in farming and residing in rural settlements. In this context, non-farm activities concentrate in over-competitive and poorly paid services such as petty trade.[29]

Box 7.5 *Income diversification in the virtuous circle of rural–urban development*

The virtuous circle of rural–urban development envisions a mutually reinforcing pattern of linkages between an urban centre and its hinterland, which spurs the growth of both agriculture and non-farm activities. The three main stages in the model can be summarized as follows:

- first, rural households earn higher incomes from the production of agricultural goods for non-local markets, and this increases their demand for consumer goods;
- this leads to the creation of non-farm jobs and income diversification, especially in small urban centres close to agricultural production areas;
- this, in turn, absorbs surplus rural labour, raises demand for agricultural produce and, in so doing, boosts agricultural productivity and rural incomes.

Source: Evans, H. E. (1990) *Rural–Urban Linkages and Structural Transformation*, Report INU 71, Infrastructure and Urban Development Department, The World Bank, Washington, DC; UNDP/UNCHS (1995) *Rural–Urban Linkages: Policy Guidelines for Rural Development*, Paper prepared for the 23rd Meeting of the ACC Sub-committee on Rural Development, UNESCO, Paris, 31 May–2 June 1995

A review of the main reasons behind the growth in rural non-farm employment in different nations and regions suggests that diversification is a response to a variety of factors. These can be divided broadly into 'push' (or constraints) and 'pull' (or opportunities) factors. However, this is more an analytical distinction, and empirical evidence shows that, in most cases, diversification is driven by a combination of both.

For example, in some regions of China and in the densely populated Red River and Mekong deltas in Vietnam, increases in rural non-farm activities are primarily the consequence of large labour surpluses in the agricultural sector. However, it should also be stressed that in both countries, such labour surpluses emerged after the demise of the commune farm system in the 1979–84 period in China, and post-1986 in Vietnam. As households took over responsibility for farming, production levels increased and, in high-potential regions, this contributed to a decline in rural poverty and to increased demand for non-agricultural goods; at the same time, however, land scarcity gave rise to unprecedented migration to small and large urban centres.[30]

In Brazil's central plains, since the early 1970s export-oriented agro-industry has taken hold with highly mechanized crops such as cotton, and has swept aside the traditional production of staples by sharecroppers, small tenant farmers and rural squatters, forcing them to find employment in non-farm sectors.[31] In much of sub-Saharan Africa, the growth in non-farm occupations since the implementation of structural adjustment derives as much from the need for cash to cover user fees for basic services as from the decline in farming incomes and, in some locations, the emergence of new types of employment in services for international tourism.[32] The latter are, in most cases, not the consequence of endogenous development but of the internationalization of trade, production and services. Similarly, the development of many small and intermediate urban centres in northern Mexico, and the related growth in non-farm employment among their populations and that of the surrounding rural regions, is not locally induced but is based on foreign investment and production for international markets in *maquiladoras.*[33]

Diversification patterns, inter-household and intra-household differences

Given the broad variations in the reasons behind diversification, and the ways in which local contexts affect both constraints and opportunities, it is useful to look at diversification patterns in relation to their potential contribution to poverty reduction and to greater equity.

A first distinction can be made between poor and vulnerable households and individuals, and better-off households and individuals. This cuts across both rural settlements and urban centres, as it is increasingly recognized that diversification and access to both rural and urban resources is important for residents of both areas. On the other hand, there are also significant differences in the ways in which different households straddle the rural–urban divide, and in how this contributes to their security and wealth.

Diversification can be described as an accumulation strategy for households with farming assets and with access to urban networks, who often re-invest profits from urban-based activities in agricultural production and vice versa, resulting in capital and asset accumulation. But for other groups, rural non-farm activities can be determined by lack or loss of land, labour or capital in what can be described as a 'survival strategy' that aims to reduce risk, overcome seasonal income fluctuations, and respond to external and internal shocks and stresses.[34] Land ownership can become increasingly unequal, as large farmers and wealthier urban households purchase land rights from smallholders who cannot afford to buy inputs and who have limited access to credit.[35] As a result, the poorest households become less able to spread risk as they lose farming as part of their portfolio of activities. Indeed, reliance on non-farm income sources is much higher than average among rural residents with limited or no access to farming resources, such as, in many nations, women and the landless. But at the same time, households that rely on farming only can be considered a high-risk category, especially in rainfed-agriculture areas where they are susceptible to climatic vagaries.[36]

As wealthier households' diversification of activities consolidates, multi-activity takes place at the household level, where individuals specialize in specific sectors of activity but resources are used to facilitate investments across sectors. By contrast, poor and vulnerable individuals lack the skills and education to specialize in any activity and must engage in a multitude of low-paid income-generating occupations to make ends meet.

At the intra-household level, gender and generational relations are likely to have a significant impact on the ways in which different groups engage in diversification. In Tanzania, domestic trade liberalization has opened up opportunities in local small-scale trade. These have been taken up especially by young women, who are otherwise expected to work as unpaid labour on their family's farm, which they would not expect to inherit; but young men are also moving out of farming, as petty trade replaces agriculture as their main activity. Their reasons for doing so are not only the decline in farming incomes but also frustration at the almost absolute control still held by the older men over land and farming decisions.[37] At the same time, widespread access to information, changing financial expectations and a view of farming as 'un-modern' also have a profound impact on employment patterns in many 'rural' areas. Hence, in densely populated south-eastern Nigeria, which also has a comprehensive network of small and intermediate urban centres, young men in rural settlements are expected to find work, at least for a period of time, in nearby urban centres – should they decide not to do so, they risk being derided for being lazy.[38]

New non-farm employment opportunities can have a profound impact on traditional social structures. For example, in South India, young men from landless low castes who find employment in urban centres openly defy the caste system as they are no longer dependent on their upper caste, land-owning employers for a living.[39] While these transformations should be welcomed for breaking up unequal social relations, their economic and social consequences are still not sufficiently understood. What is clear is that the assumption that rural households and communities are relatively stable units of production and consumption is no longer valid, and that this needs to be taken into account in the formulation and implementation of rural development initiatives.

The nature of rural non-farm employment and the role of small and intermediate urban centres

Only a minor proportion of rural non-farm activities are in the manufacturing sector, usually around 20–25 per cent.[40] Moreover, this is likely to decline due to competition from cheaper imports: for example, in northern Tanzania, labour-intensive vegetable oil-processing by women's groups is undermined by imported oil from Singapore.[41] In south-east Nigeria, traditional cloth-weaving has long been an additional source of income for local women and one which had managed to retain a market niche in the face of competition from imported goods; but lack of backward linkages with agriculture (for example, local production of cotton yarn) and insufficient local infrastructure (such as unreliable electricity supply in the rural settlements) are major constraints on production.[42]

Services and trade typically provide a much larger share of employment and income. Both tend to concentrate in small and intermediate urban centres and have benefited from liberalization and the demise of central marketing boards for agricultural commodities, which controlled trade as well as most transport services between rural settlements and urban centres.[43] Manufacturing in small and medium-size enterprises has also increased in response to the contraction of large formal sector enterprises, although many rural non-farm enterprises employ fewer than five workers and suffer from constraints which can hamper their growth. These range from shortage of capital, limited demand, poor marketing ability, inadequate space, and lack of information, technology, skills and management capability.[44]

Small and intermediate urban centres can help overcome such constraints, and may stimulate the growth of these enterprises by offering markets large enough to capture economies of scale and agglomeration for many types of non-farm enterprises. Higher levels of infrastructure also help reduce production costs and facilitate access to markets and communications. This fits well with the current growing interest in clustering and industrialization and in local economic development, where local and regional institutions, usually located in small and intermediate centres, can play a key role in supporting local actors and connecting them to national and international agencies and markets.[45]

Clusters are defined as sectoral and spatial concentrations of firms, which benefit from a range of localized external economies that lower costs for clustered producers. These include: a pool of specialized workers; easy access to suppliers of specialized inputs and services; and quick dissemination of new knowledge. Clustering is thought to be particularly relevant in the early stages of industrialization by helping small enterprises to grow in small steps, as producers can concentrate in stages rather than on the whole production process, and rely on horizontal linkages with other specialized enterprises to complete the process.[46] But a proactive, consciously pursued joint action around issues and problems of common concern is essential for positive cluster development, and collective efficiency is the critical concept.

Emerging issues in the literature now identify trade networks that give access to non-local markets, and effective sanctions and trust as key elements for clusters to develop. In Indonesia, clusters are often located close to roads and rural centres, and traders and middlemen link producers to distant markets, provide materials and equipment, pass on essential technical information and offer advances for labour. In countries with poor infrastructure, weak information systems and cultures that place high value on face-to-face communication, geographical location is a key element of clusters.[47]

Much of the literature on industrial clusters in low- and middle-income countries draws from Asian and Latin American experiences and, while the consequences of clustering for inter-firm production and social relations and, ultimately, for sustained economic growth is extremely mixed, it is even more so for African nations (see Box 7.6). For example, growth can vary widely, from artisanal clusters serving only local markets to highly dynamic clusters with deep inter-firm division of labour, entering international markets. Moreover, clusters are internally differentiated and, in many instances, large firms emerge and have important roles, raising the issue of the need for vertical, as well as horizontal, integration.

Box 7.6 *Limitations to cluster development in Africa*

The ability of small enterprises to achieve agglomeration economies through clustering (and therefore through collective efficiency or collective action) has been widely documented and discussed in the Latin American and Asian literature. In Africa, experiences have been generally much less impressive. There seem to be a number of reasons for this.

First, small African enterprises seem to cluster primarily to reduce the costs of attracting more customers. This, however, is done in a passive way, as there is no collaboration in marketing and most enterprises continue to sell directly from the workshop. Traders and middlemen are missing in these clusters, and so is their role in knitting together successful clusters and as agents of change.

Second, African small enterprises rarely specialize vertically. Enterprises specialize in specific products and cover the full production process. Exceptions are sharing large orders with other enterprises, although still covering the whole process, and renting out excess capital equipment capacity to other enterprises. The lack of vertical division of work is likely to be due to the often extreme market instability in which the small enterprises operate.

Third, successful Asian and Latin American clusters often comprise a whole town and include large and small enterprises, traders and service providers. African clusters are more narrowly described as small enterprise areas within a town, which limits access to new technology and larger markets – mirroring the limited interactions between large formal sector enterprises and small informal sector ones so common in Africa.

Source: Pedersen, P. O. (2003) *The Implications of National Level Policies on the Development of Small and Intermediate Urban Centres*, IIED, London

---

Key issues in non-farm employment in small and intermediate urban centres

Empirical evidence shows that diversification of income sources is not a transitional phenomenon but, rather, a persistent one with great potential for poverty reduction. This means that while support is necessary for the development of non-farm activities, and especially that of small and medium-size firms which represent the majority of such activities, it is also important to ensure that at the same time, households are able to retain a foothold in farming. Indeed, diversification into commercial agriculture by wealthier urban residents suggests that farming as a secondary activity is an essential part of accumulation strategies.[48] The nature and form of non-farm activities depend on a combination of macro-economic environment at the international and national levels and local conditions, including governance. A pre-condition for the effectiveness of local governance is its integration with national planning. The key issues for policy are summarized as follows.

Recognize the potential that often exists for forward and backward linkages with agriculture to support non-farm enterprises' activities. There are often possibilities to stimulate regional economic growth and development through a closer linking of the non-farm sector to agriculture (especially particular high-value crops that have possibilities for local value added), especially where agriculture remains the main occupation for much of the population. Far too little attention has been given to this in 'small and intermediate urban centre' policies, which tend to give little attention to agriculture. Farming and personal services, as well as simple consumer durables, should be an essential output of non-farm enterprises located in small urban centres.

Ensure that small and micro-entrepreneurs have access to markets, to outside capital sources, to basic education and to essential technical knowledge. Small and especially intermediate urban centres can be key providers of such services. However, different types of small enterprises have different requirements for policy support. For micro-enterprises, access to working capital is often key, while for larger enterprises non-financial constraints are often more critical, especially those relating to access to markets and marketing skills. Entrepreneurs' gender may also affect the type and needs of enterprise, and women may want to fit their business plan around domestic responsibilities.[49] Local policy making and implementation is more likely than national planning to respond to the locally specific variety of needs, especially where local governance systems make local politicians and bureaucrats more responsive and accountable to local citizens.

Respond to competition from larger and international firms by identifying local opportunities. Globalization and market liberalization can negatively affect small and micro-enterprises that cannot compete with cheaper imported goods. Small and micro-enterprises usually do not have the capacity or the information to identify bottlenecks and comparative advantages for the whole sector. Institutional support is therefore key to enabling them to better understand constraints and opportunities in local and non-local markets and, where possible and desirable, become better integrated in national and international supply chains.[50]

Support trade and networking activities based in small and intermediate urban centres to encourage links between the local and rural economy and the national and global econo-

mies. Traders are a vital link between farm and non-farm enterprises, and between local markets and national and external ones. They also often provide credit and technological advice to producers. Many small urban centres function primarily as market towns, but more support should be given to traders as agents of change rather than merely seeing them as exploiters of both producers and consumers.

Ensure that natural resource management responds to the needs of both farming and non-farm activities. In many instances, there is latent or even open conflict in the use of natural resources such as land and water for agriculture or for urban residential and non-farm productive activities. Especially for small urban centres in the proximity of large urban conurbations, competition for natural resources can benefit large urban-based firms and higher-income residents at the expense of low-income 'rural' residents. For example, industries relocated in peri-urban areas can occupy agricultural land or discharge polluting effluents into water used for domestic and agricultural use by rural settlements and small urban centres.[51] Non-farm enterprises located in small and intermediate urban centres can also have a negative impact on the local environment. In China, in the mid-1980s, township and village enterprises were responsible for one-third of gas emissions, one-sixth of water pollution and one-sixth of solid wastes produced in the country.[52] In Vietnam, rural industrial zones are planned to facilitate small enterprises' access to infrastructure and environmental protection measures such as water treatment for weaving firms; however, there is a real risk that home-based micro-enterprises may not afford to move to these zones.[53] Local governments are in the best position to assess local needs and priorities and implement a wide range of initiatives to respond to them, provided they have the legitimacy, the resources and the capacity to do so.

Small and intermediate urban centres and regional rural–urban migration

One of the key potential roles of small and intermediate urban centres is that of attracting rural migrants from their surrounding region through demand for non-farm labour. This would increase local opportunities for income diversification and, at the same time, decrease pressure on larger national urban centres. But the credibility of this role has often been undermined by unrealistic government policies that seek this as an end, but without the policies to strengthen their economies that would actually make this happen.

Since migrants tend to move to centres where they have more chances of finding employment (and reasonably priced accommodation), flows towards small and intermediate urban centres are influenced by national macro-economic strategies and public investment patterns. In many nations, infrastructure and other basic facilities have been provided principally to areas which are judged to have high growth potential; even where they existed, explicit dispersal policies that were meant to support smaller urban centres were often undermined by spatial biases in macro-economic and sectoral policies, including trade, industrial and agricultural policies.[54] For example, the development of export-oriented industries, which are normally located close to major ports and large cities, function as major poles of attraction for migrants.[55]

It is also important to note that migrants are not usually the poorest groups, especially for long-distance migration. This is because moving requires resources: financial means are needed to pay for transport, and social networks are as, if not more, necessary to provide migrants with information on opportunities at destination and with a safety net during the first period there, including accommodation and learning new skills. Hence, the poorest rural residents tend to move locally or, at most, within the region.[56] Their destinations are often other rural areas, where they can sell their labour in agricultural work, often on a seasonal basis. In recent years, networks and demand from employers have stimulated international migration directly from the villages; for example, in northern Mali it is not unusual for men to move to West African coastal destinations several hundreds of kilometres away and, increasingly, to overseas destinations such as the Middle East and North African countries. Since this involves substantial financial costs, migrants tend to stay away for several years before returning home, which can result in labour shortages on their family farms.[57]

An essential pre-condition for migrants moving to small and intermediate urban centres within their region is the availability of employment, especially in non-farm sectors such as trade, services and manufacturing. Indeed, the growth of many such centres is historically linked to their role as market towns for the surrounding agricultural regions and, in many cases, this role also explains the economic and demographic decline of some towns (see Box 7.7).

Many small and intermediate centres show fluctuations similar to those of Dimbokro, which underline their vulnerability to macro-economic changes or changes in transport systems. One of the reasons for demographic decline is that migrants stop moving to these urban centres, or indeed move out of them in search of better opportunities in more dynamic locations. However, the exact contribution of migration to urbanization, including the growth of small and intermediate urban centres, is usually underestimated. This is due in part to the fact that migrants may not be officially reg-

---

Box 7.7 *The interlinked fortunes of a small town and its rural region in Côte d'Ivoire*

The town of Dimbokro, in Côte d'Ivoire's 'cocoa belt' was founded less than a century ago and developed out of 'sheer luck and political will'. It was first chosen by the colonial army as a stopover point on the way north; and despite the unhealthy location, it was selected as one of the very few railway towns while other, busier centres were not included in the network. In the 1940s, production of cocoa and coffee for export in the surrounding region transformed the small administrative district town into an important commercial crossroads busily involved in import–export activities. However, dependence on the plantation economy was the downfall of Dimbokro, when production moved towards the western 'frontier' and road transport replaced rail transport. After growing from fewer than 10,000 to over 31,000 inhabitants between 1956 and 1975, the population of the town stagnated in the following decade.

Source: Bredeloup, S. (1997) 'Dimbokro, the typical Ivorian town or the absence of rural–urban interaction?' in Baker, J. (ed) *Rural–Urban Dynamics in Francophone Africa*, Nordiska Afrikainstitutet, Uppsala

istered as urban residents, either because they consider their stay as temporary or because of administrative restrictions (the population of China's urban centres has long been under-counted because 'floating populations', who have no formal right to work there, are not included); and in part because the availability and reliability of national-level data for the calculation of estimates of the components of urban growth – natural growth, internal migration and reclassification – are limited. In many nations, population censuses do not include specific questions on movement.[58]

Factors affecting destination choices

Despite these problems, migration is increasingly recognized as an essential component of the livelihoods of most households in low- and middle-income nations.[59] While migration can be considered as a household income diversification strategy involving the spatial movement of at least one of its members (with different individuals engaging in farm and non-farm activities in different locations), in some cases the choice of destination underlines the need to rely on both rural and urban resources in the same location. For example, research in sub-Saharan Africa suggests that movement of retrenched formal-sector workers from large urban centres to small and intermediate ones in the 1980s may have been determined by the better opportunities provided by less densely populated centres to combine urban and peri-urban agriculture with other urban-based non-farm occupations.[60]

Another recent significant transformation in migration patterns is the increase in the number of women, especially young unmarried ones, moving independently – that is, not following male relatives. In part, this is because of demand in 'new' sectors, such as export-oriented manufacturing firms and the growing service industry. The first are often located in major urban centres, hence migrants from rural areas bypass local urban centres.[61] Demand for workers in the service industry is more evenly distributed across space, since it includes waitressing in local bars and restaurants (often major employers in small and intermediate urban centres, especially market towns) and work in international tourist resorts. This category also includes the 'entertainment' industry, often a euphemism for prostitution. Whatever the reality of the job, however, there is often a strong stigma attached to female employment in places which are mostly considered disreputable. As a result, many young female migrants tend to move to places further away from their home areas and avoid the local urban centres, so that they will not risk ruining their own and their family's reputations.[62]

Gender also affects decisions to migrate from rural to urban areas for women who, through widowhood or separation, head their own households. For rural women who find themselves without a male partner, economic survival can be problematic since they usually have only limited access to land, and work in rural non-farm activities is often confined to the most marginal and low-paid sectors.[63] In Honduras, 26 per cent of female heads of households in urban *barrios* are migrants who arrived in the cities alone with their children. Young, separated women find it most difficult to survive alone financially in rural areas since, on separation, rights to land tend to remain with men. Their main options are thus to move to areas with better non-farm employment oppor-

> **Box 7.8** *The impact of accommodation restrictions on poor migrants in Brazil's central region*
>
> Brazil's medium-size urban centre of Rio Verde is located in the agri-business central region. While the growth of the centre has attracted many white-collar, middle-class workers from larger urban centres, the majority of migrants are expelled tenant farmers struggling to find local housing and employment. Since the early 1980s, with increasing urban growth and competing demands for urban space from middle-class migrants, local authority officials have introduced restrictions on the size of plots and the ways in which the land can be used in low-income housing projects. This negatively affects residents' opportunities for diversification through renting, secondary housing, small shops or restaurants, subsistence plots or orchards.
>
> *Source:* Chase, J. (1997) 'Managing urban settlement in Brazil's agro-industrial frontier', *Third World Planning Review*, vol 19, no 2

tunities or return to live with their parents as embedded sub-families, if resources are sufficient.[64] This does not exclude migration to the local urban centres, provided local non-farm work opportunities exist. In Biharamulo, a small urban centre with a population of 20,000 in north-western Tanzania, almost 30 per cent of urban households are headed by women, compared with only 7 per cent in the surrounding villages.[65]

Other considerations affect the choice of migration destinations and are also closely related to the different priorities of different groups. In Mexico, the migration of middle-class households from Mexico City to intermediate urban centres is explained as a response to both increased economic opportunities for skilled workers, following the relocation of many firms, and to negative perceptions of the capital city's environmental conditions and air pollution levels. By contrast, low-income households' concerns with access to land and home ownership, which may be more easily achieved in some peri-urban settlements of large urban centres, eclipses any other environmental perceptions, and movement continues to be directed largely towards the capital city.[66] Indeed, particularly in Latin America, spatial control by planners and local élites can be much tighter in small and intermediate urban centres than in larger ones, and informal settlements and alternative land use by the urban poor may not be tolerated (see Box 7.8).

Employment in small and intermediate urban centres, migration and mobility

Whether migrants move to small and intermediate urban centres rather than to larger cities depends on the income-generating opportunities (both 'formal' and 'informal') available locally and on the reasons why migrants move in the first place. In areas where tenant farmers and smallholders are expelled from rural areas because of increasing concentration of land in large, mechanized commercial farms, migrants tend to come from the surrounding region essentially because they often lack the networks and financial means to reach larger, more distant urban centres. A comparative study of migrants in three small and medium-size urban centres in northern Mexico, Costa Rica and Bolivia shows that migrants from the surrounding rural areas, who have limited skills and education, are overwhelmingly concentrated in low-skilled and low-income occupations – hence they have little job stability, limited purchasing power and lack the propensity to save. These very poor migrants have recently arrived in the urban centres and several members of their households engage in a variety of income-generating activities, often more than one in the case of adults. By contrast, these towns also attract a significant group of professional migrants coming from other urban centres, and whose presence in small and intermediate urban centres is part of a career path, usually as employees of large private and parastatal firms who run branches in such centres.[67]

While low-income rural households who lose their farming assets and have no access to alternative income-generating activities have little option but to move to urban centres, in most cases rural residents prefer to live in their home villages and benefit from the opportunities provided by the local urban centres by increasing their mobility.[68] This, of course, requires the availability of affordable transport. In south-east Nigeria, low-income people commute regularly from the villages to the intermediate town of Aba to work as domestic workers, gardeners and so on.[69] This allows them to grow their own food and generally to spend less cash than they would need to by living in the town. Commuting also helps avoid labour shortages during specific times in the farming season, which are often associated with migration.[70] In China, research in Jiangsu Province in the mid-1980s showed that although the change in migration regulations attracted migrants to small towns, especially from within a small radius, the number of commuters was more important than the number of those who had actually moved. Daily commuters from the surrounding rural villages accounted for up to 43 per cent of the daytime urban population.[71]

Better transport facilities are a key element of livelihood strategies based on diversification of activities and reliance on both rural and urban resources. The latter is such an important aspect of how poor groups reduce their vulnerability that poverty reduction policies should focus primarily on increasing the opportunities for diversification. Recent research on mobility in Uganda and Zimbabwe suggests that while planning should include far greater attention to access to services, work and basic needs where people reside, thus cutting down on time-consuming, energy-draining and disruptive movement, there is also a need for more sensitivity in addressing the mobility needs of poor groups. Since low-income groups tend to move primarily by walking, this should include the construction and maintenance of dedicated safe walking paths; moreover, efforts should be made to lower the cost of public transport to increase access to poor groups, with local authorities preventing the development of monopolistic or oligopolistic conditions within public transport services.[72]

Conclusions: the role of small and intermediate urban centres in equitable regional development and poverty reduction

There is a considerable potential role for small and intermediate urban centres in regional and rural economic development. However, their capacity to trigger equitable regional development – that is, balanced across different regions and benefiting all groups – is much influenced by the region's internal characteristics (including the natural resource base, population density and infrastructure), land ownership patterns and economic, social and cultural transformations at the local, national and international levels. At the international level, the positive role of small and intermediate urban centres is supported by access to international markets for small and medium-size producers, with stable commodities prices; and by foreign investment that supports local production and imports that do not compete with locally produced goods. At the national level, important factors include a not too unequal distribution of and access to land; regionally balanced growth strategies, including satisfactory provision of infrastructure, credit facilities and advisory and training services for small and medium-size producers (both in agriculture and in trade and manufacturing); and basic service provision reaching small and intermediate urban centres, adapted to local needs. They also include revenue support to local governments (smaller urban centres' potential to attract new investment being considerably influenced by the competence of its government) and a regulated institutional structure of markets that restricts monopolistic and oligopolistic practices.

At the local level, governance that is accountable and with adequate resources and capacity is essential to identifying local needs and priorities and responding to them. This includes supporting forward and backward linkages between agriculture and services and industry located in local urban centres; and the regulation and management of local natural resource use.

Most successful small and intermediate urban centres have developed when most of these conditions were present, although of course there are also many cases of such centres growing in contexts which can be described as exploitative of the surrounding rural region. These centres are usually more vulnerable to the vagaries of international markets, and in many cases suffer economic and demographic decline after periods of growth. Figures 7.1 and 7.2 summarize the interrelations between the international and national contexts and local governance, and their impact on rural–urban linkages and small urban centres' roles.

However, even successful small and intermediate urban centres may not play a significant role in poverty reduction unless specific attention is given to the needs and priorities of poor and vulnerable groups.

With regard to *small and intermediate urban centres' role as markets for agricultural produce*, it is certainly true that access to markets is essential for small-scale farmers. However, this could remain limited to very low-level transactions unless farmers are able to respond to demand from urban-based consumers (and traders). This implies stable access to natural resources (land and water), labour, financial resources and affordable agricultural inputs. Small and medium-scale traders often play a crucial role in collecting

International context: access to international markets for small and medium-sized producers, with stable commodities prices. Foreign investment supports local production, imports do not compete with locally produced goods.
National context: equitable distribution of and access to land; regionally balanced growth strategies including satisfactory provision of infrastructure, credit facilities for small and medium-sized producers, and basic services (education, health, water and sanitation); revenue support to local government; regulated institutional structure of markets.
Local governance: accountable, with adequate resources and capacity; identifies local needs and priorities and responds to them; supports forward and backward linkages between agriculture and services and industry located in local urban centres; regulates local natural resource management; integrated with national planning.

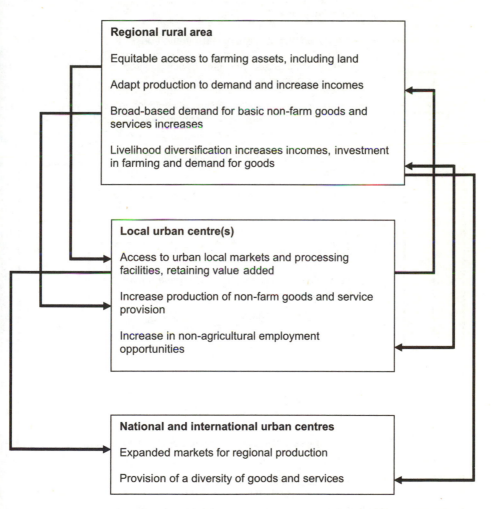

Regional rural area

Equitable access to farming assets, including land

Adapt production to demand and increase incomes

Broad-based demand for basic non-farm goods and services increases

Livelihood diversification increases incomes, investment in farming and demand for goods

Local urban centre(s)

Access to urban local markets and processing facilities, retaining value added

Increase production of non-farm goods and service provision

Increase in non-agricultural employment opportunities

National and international urban centres

Expanded markets for regional production

Provision of a diversity of goods and services

Figure 7.1 *Positive rural–urban interactions and regional development*

International context: limited access to international markets for small and medium-sized producers, unstable commodities prices; foreign investment concentrates in large-scale export production, imports compete with locally produced goods.
National context: inequitable distribution of and access to land; regionally imbalanced growth strategies including limited provision of infrastructure, credit facilities for small and medium-sized producers, and basic services (education, health, water and sanitation); lack of support to local government; unregulated institutional structure of markets.
Local governance: unaccountable, with inadequate resources and capacity; not integrated with national planning.

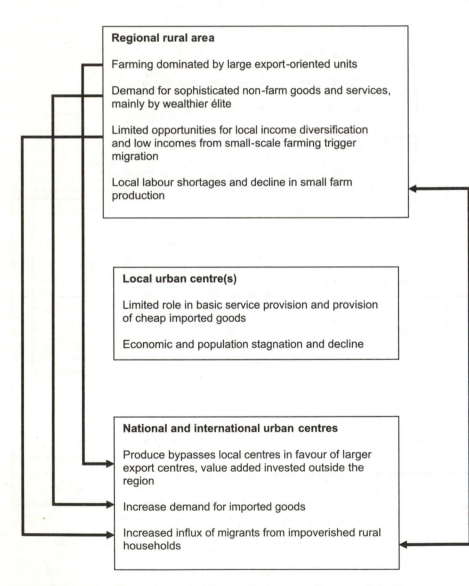

Regional rural area

Farming dominated by large export-oriented units

Demand for sophisticated non-farm goods and services, mainly by wealthier élite

Limited opportunities for local income diversification and low incomes from small-scale farming trigger migration

Local labour shortages and decline in small farm production

Local urban centre(s)

Limited role in basic service provision and provision of cheap imported goods

Economic and population stagnation and decline

National and international urban centres

Produce bypasses local centres in favour of larger export centres, value added invested outside the region

Increase demand for imported goods

Increased influx of migrants from impoverished rural households

Figure 7.2 *Negative rural–urban interactions and regional development*

and channelling produce from diverse and often geographically dispersed small farms; in many cases, they are also a major source of credit and information for small farmers. But small traders are often ignored or viewed with suspicion by policy makers, and the lack or limitation of affordable transport and storage facilities make them especially vulnerable to losses.

Small and intermediate urban centres' role in *the distribution of goods and services to their rural region* only becomes significant where there is a broad-based demand, that is where the income levels and purchasing power of the region's population are sufficiently high and stimulate local production, trade and services. Where incomes are low, households tend to combine several activities in their visits to urban centres, which means that small centres are often bypassed in favour of larger towns that offer a wider range of goods and services. Moreover, in regions with highly skewed income distribution, demand from the wealthy few also tends to bypass local centres, since these cannot provide the specialized goods and services demanded by this group.

Livelihood diversification and non-farm activities are important for all income groups, although a useful distinction is that between the wealthier households who diversify for accumulation and the poorer individuals or households who diversify as part of their survival strategies (often because they have lost their job or income source in agriculture). As a result of rising cash needs and of generally declining revenues from farming, income diversification into non-farm activities is increasingly significant in rural settlements, especially among younger generations and often (although not always) revolving around local urban centres. Especially where the majority of the region's population remains involved primarily (but not only) in smallholder agricultural production, non-farm activities based on forward and backward linkages with agriculture are more likely to stimulate regional growth and to benefit all groups. It is also important to ensure that small and micro-enterprises, where low-income groups concentrate, have access to markets, outside capital sources, basic education and technical knowledge, and are given institutional support to identify local opportunities that enable them to respond to competition from imports. And finally, since the diversification of income sources is so important in the livelihoods of poor and vulnerable groups, it is crucial to ensure that they have access to opportunities both in farming and in non-farm activities – and, in many cases, this involves careful management of natural resources by local governments, for example, by making sure that land and water are not allocated to residential and industrial use at the expense of farming.

Regional rural–urban migration often concentrates in small and intermediate urban centres, although there are many exceptions to this. Since migration requires financial and social resources (migrant networks), it is usually the poorest groups who move locally. Small and intermediate urban centres are able to attract rural migrants if they offer employment opportunities – although the poorest rural migrants usually also have limited education and skills other than farming, and end up in the lowest paid urban jobs. Constraints on accommodation in local urban centres can severely limit poor migrants' ability to diversify their income sources, for example, through subsistence agriculture and home-based income-generating activities. Many rural residents (from both higher- and lower-income groups) prefer to commute into town rather than move, as this helps retain a foothold in farming. Where distances between rural settlements and local urban centres are not too great, investment in transport facilities that respond to the needs of low-income groups are likely to benefit them by increasing their options, and will to some extent reduce pressure on small and intermediate urban centres – and by extension on larger towns and cities.

Notes

1   Rondinelli, D. (1985) *Applied Methods of Regional Analysis: the Spatial Dimensions of Development Policy*, Westview Press, Boulder, CO.
2   Southall, A. (1988) 'Small towns in Africa revisited', *African Studies Review*, vol 31, no 3.
3   Parnwell, M. (ed) (1996) *Uneven Development in Thailand*, Avebury, Aldershot.
4   Bryceson, D. (1999) *Sub-Saharan Africa Betwixt and Between: Rural Livelihood Practices and Policies*, ASC Working Paper 43, Afrika Studiecentrum, Leiden
5   See Hardoy, J. E. and Satterthwaite, D. (eds) (1986) *Small and Intermediate Urban Centres: Their Role in National and Regional Development in the Third World*, Hodder and Stoughton, London, especially Chapter 6; also Satterthwaite, D. and Taneja, B. (2003) *Agriculture and Urban Development*, paper prepared for the World Bank and available at www.worldbank.org/urban/urbanruralseminar/.
6   Songsore, J. (2000) *Towards a Better Understanding of Urban Change: The Ghana Case Study*, Urban Change Working Paper 2, IIED, London.
7   Kamete, A. K. (1998) 'Interlocking livelihoods: Farm and small town in Zimbabwe', *Environment and Urbanization*, vol 10, no 1.
8   See, for instance Manzanal, M. and Vapnarsky, C. A. (1986) 'The development of the Upper Valley of Rio Negro and its periphery within the Comahue Region, Argentina', in Hardoy and Satterthwaite (eds) op cit.
9   Douglass, M. (1998) 'A regional network strategy for reciprocal rural–urban linkages', *Third World Planning Review*, vol 20, no 1.
10 However, in part this is because many of the urban centres that developed because they were on the railway or river were also among the first centres in their region to be connected to developing road systems.
11 Stary, B. (1997) 'De la rente agricole à la rente frontalière: Niablé, une petite ville ivoirienne à la frontière du Ghana', in Bertrand, M. and Dubesson, A. (eds) *Petites et Moyennes Villes d'Afrique Noire*, Karthala, Paris.
12 Diyamett, B., Diyamett, M., James, J. and Mabala, R. (2001) *The Case of Himo and its Region, Northern Tanzania*, Rural–Urban Working Paper 1, IIED, London.
13 Lerise, F., Kibadu, A., Mbutolwe, E. and Mushi, N. (2001) *The Case of Lindi and its Region, Southern Tanzania*, Rural–Urban Working Paper 2, IIED, London.
14 Diyamett et al (2001) and Douglass (1998) op cit.
15 Rengasamy, S., Devavaram, J., Marirajan, T., Ramavel, N., Rajadurai, K., Karunanidhi, M. and Rajendra Prasad, N. (2002) *Farmers' Markets in Tamil Nadu: Increasing Options for Rural Producers, Improving Access for Urban Consumers*, Rural–Urban Working Paper 8, IIED, London.

16 Bryceson, D. F., Maunder, D. A. C., Mbara, T. C., Davis, A. S. C. and Howe, J. D. G. F. (2003) *Sustainable Livelihoods, Mobility and Access Needs*, TRL, London.

17 Pedersen, P. O. (2000) *Busy Work or Real Business: Revaluing the Role of Non-Agricultural Activities in African Rural Development*, ASC Working Paper 46, Africa Studies Centre, Leiden.

18 Harriss-White, B. (1995) 'Maps and landscapes of grain markets in South Asia', in Harriss, J. J., Hunter, J. and Lewis, C. M. (eds) *The New Institutional Economics and Third World Development*, Routledge, London.

19 NCSSH (2002) *Vietnam Human Development Report 2001*, Hanoi.

20 Kamete (1998) op cit.

21 Pedersen, P. O. (1997) 'Rural diversification in Zimbabwe', in Bryceson, D. F. and Jamal, V. (eds) *Farewell to Farms: De-agrarianisation and Employment in Africa*, Africa Studies Centre, Leiden and Ashgate, Aldershot.

22 Meagher, K. and Mustapha, A. R. (1997) 'Not by farming alone: The role of non-farm incomes in rural Hausaland', in Bryceson and Jamal (eds) op cit.

23 Ellis, F. (1998) 'Livelihood diversification and sustainable rural livelihoods', in Carney, D. (ed) *Sustainable Rural Livelihoods: What Contribution Can We Make?*, DFID, London.

24 Baker, J. (1995) 'Survival and accumulation strategies at the rural–urban interface in northwest Tanzania', *Environment and Urbanization*, vol 7, no 1; Kamete, A. (1998) 'Interlocking livelihoods: Farm and small town in Zimbabwe', *Environment and Urbanization*, vol 10, no 1.

25 Lerise et al (2001) op cit.

26 Ellis (1998) op cit.

27 Reardon, T., Berdegué, J. and Escobar, G. (2001) 'Rural non-farm employment and incomes in Latin America: Overview and policy implications', *World Development*, vol 29, no 3.

28 Ibid.

29 Bryceson, D. (1999) 'African rural labour, income diversification and livelihood approaches: A long-term development perspective', *Review of African Political Economy*, vol 80.

30 Kirkby, R., Bradbury, I. and Shen, G. (2000) *Small Town China – Governance, Economy, Environment and Lifestyle in Three Zhen*, Ashgate, Aldershot; Douglass, M. et al (2002) *The Urban Transition in Vietnam*, UNCHS and University of Hawai'i, Honolulu.

31 Chase, J. (1997) 'Managing urban settlements in Brazil's agro-industrial frontier', *Third World Planning Review*, vol 19, no 2.

32 Bah, M., Cissé, S., Diyamett, B., Diallo, G., Lerise, F., Okali, D., Okpara, E., Olawoye, J. and Tacoli, C. (2003) 'Changing rural–urban linkages in Mali, Nigeria and Tanzania', *Environment and Urbanization*, vol 15, no 1.

33 Beneker, T. and Verkoren, O. (1998) 'Reception centre and point of departure: Migration to and from Nuevo Casas Grandes, Chihahua, Mexico', in Titus, M. and Hinderink, J. (eds) *Town and Hinterland in Developing Countries*, Thela Thesis, Amsterdam.

34 Baker (1995) op cit.

35 GRAD (2001) *Potentialités et Conflits dans les Zones Péri-urbaines: Le Cas de Bamako au Mali*, Rural–Urban Working Paper 6, IIED, London.

36 Baker (1995) op cit.

37 Lerise et al (2001) and Diyamett et al (2001) op cit.

38 Okali, D., Okpara, E. and Olawoye, J. (2001) *The Case of Aba and its Region, South-eastern Nigeria*, Rural–Urban Working Paper 4, IIED, London.

39 Anandhi, S., Jeyaranjan, J. and Krishnan, R. (2002) 'Work, caste and competing masculinities', in *EPW Review of Women Studies*, 26 October 2002; available on www.epw.org.in.

40 Haggblade, S., Hazell, P. and Reardon, T. (2002) *Strategies for Stimulating Poverty-Alleviating Growth in the Rural Non-Farm Economy in Developing Countries*, EPTD Discussion Paper 92, IFPRI, Washington, DC.

41 Diyamett et al (2001) op cit.

42 Okali et al (2001) op cit.

43 Pedersen, P. O. (2003) *The Implications of National Level Policies on the Development of Small and Intermediate Urban Centres*, IIED, London.

44 Thanh, H. X., Dang, A. N. and Tacoli, C. (2005) *Livelihood Diversification and Rural–Urban Linkages in Vietnam's Red River Delta*, Rural-Urban Working Paper 11, IIED, London.

45 Helmsing, A. H. J. (2001) *Partnerships, Meso-institutions and Learning: New Local and Regional Economic Development Initiatives in Latin America*, Institute of Social Studies, The Hague, Netherlands.

46 Schmitz, H. and Nadvi, K. (1999) 'Clustering and industrialisation: Introduction', *World Development*, vol 27, no 9.

47 Schmitz and Nadvi (1999) op cit; Weijland, H. (1999) 'Microenterprise clusters in rural Indonesia: Industrial seedbed and policy target', *World Development*, vol 27, no 9; McCormick, D. (1999) 'African enterprise clusters and industrialisation: Theory and reality', *World Development*, vol 27, no 9.

48 Bah et al (2003) op cit.

49 Rogerson, C. M. (2001) 'In search of the African miracle: Debates on successful small enterprise development in Africa', *Habitat International*, vol 25.

50 Rogerson (2001) and Haggblade et al (2002) op cit.

51 Benjamin, S. (2003) *The Role of Small and Intermediate Urban Centres Around Bangalore: Their Impact on Local Economies, Rural Development, Poverty Reduction and Pro-Poor Politics*, IIED, London; Okali et al (2001) op cit.

52 Kirkby et al (2000) op cit.

53 Thanh et al (2005) op cit.

54 Hardoy and Satterthwaite (eds) (1986) op cit; Parnwell, M. (1996) 'Introduction: Uneven development in Thailand', in Parnwell, M. (ed) *Uneven Development in Thailand*, Avebury, Aldershot.

55 Thanh et al (2005) op cit.

56 Skeldon, R. (2002) 'Migration and poverty', *Asia–Pacific Population Journal*, December.

57 GRAD (2001) *Potentialités et Conflits dans les Zones Peri-urbaines: La Cas de Mopti au Mali*, Rural–Urban Working Paper 8, IIED, London.

58 Bilsborrow, R. (1998) 'The state of the art and overview of the chapters', in Bilsborrow, R. (ed) *Migration, Urbanization and Development: New Directions and Issues*, UNFPA and Kluwer Academic Publishers.

59 For a comprehensive review of the literature, see de Haan, A. (1999) 'Livelihoods and poverty: The role of migration. A critical review of the migration literature', *Journal of Development Studies*, vol 36, no 2.

60 Songsore (2000) op cit; for Tanzania, Bryceson, D. (1997) 'De-agrarianisation in sub-Saharan Africa: Acknowledging the inevitable', in Bryceson and Jamal (eds) op cit.

61 Afsar, R. (1999) 'Rural–urban dichotomy and convergence: Emerging realities in Bangladesh', *Environment and Urbanization*, vol 11, no 1.

62 Ouedraogo, J.-B. (1995) 'The girls of Nyovuuru: Dagara female labour migration to Bobo-Dioulasso', in Baker, J. and Akin Aina, T. (eds) *The Migration Experience in Africa*, Nordiska Africainstitutet, Uppsala; Chant, S. and McIlwaine, C. (1995) *Women of a Lesser Cost: Female Labour, Foreign Exchange and Philippine Development*, Pluto Press, London; GRAD (2001) (note 57) and Diyamett et al (2001) op cit.

63 Seppala, P. (1996) The politics of economic diversification: Reconceptualizing the rural informal sector in south-east Tanzania', *Development and Change*, vol 27.

64 Bradshaw, S. (1995) 'Female-headed households in Honduras: Perspectives on rural–urban differences', *Third World Planning Review*, vol 17, no 2.

65 Baker, J. (1995) 'Survival and accumulation strategies in the rural–urban interface in north-west Tanzania', *Environment and Urbanization*, vol 7, no 1.

66 Izazola, H., Martinez, C. and Marquette, C. (1998) 'Environmental perceptions, social class and demographic change in Mexico City: A comparative approach', *Environment and Urbanization*, vol 10, no 1.

67 Beneker, T., van Lindert, P. and Verkoren, O. (1997) 'Migrant–native differences in the labour markets of Latin American towns', in van Lindert, P. and Verkoren, O. (eds) *Small Towns and Beyond – Rural Transformation in Small Urban Centres in Latin America*, Thela Latin American Series, Amsterdam.

68 Baker (1995) op cit.

69 Okali et al (2001) op cit.

70 GRAD (2001) (note 57) op cit.

71 Kirkby et al (2000) op cit.

72 Bryceson et al (2003) op cit; Lerise et al (2001) op cit on transport monopolies in southern Tanzania.

Chapter 8

The Small Town and Urban Context in China

Richard Kirkby, Ian Bradbury and Guanbao Shen

The pattern of China's small towns

In the China of the Ming and Qing dynasties, the myriad small towns scattered throughout the countryside played a vital role as centres of both administration and economic exchange. Towns played host to the periodic fairs and festivals which bound the society of rural China; they were in every sense the central places for China's great farming population. Most prominent in the hierarchy of rural settlements were the over 2000 seats of *xian* (county) government. From these places, law was administered, taxes levied, and the larger-scale agricultural processing and service functions were discharged. They, along with the tens of thousands of smaller rural centres were also host to a range of off-farm trades and activities – carpenters, builders, blacksmiths, masons, as well as shops and small mills for grain processing, oil-seed pressing and beancurd making. Such enterprises were an indispensable mainstay of China's field agriculture.

Prior to the Communist Party's assumption of power in 1949, China had endured a century of civil war and foreign invasion which had destablized the rural economy, and undermined the economic and administrative functions of the rural settlement system. The tentacles of the foreign imposed Treaty Port system – that modern hem on the ancient Chinese garment – had further reduced traditional agrarian activities and their small town marketing nodes. The ravages of the first decades of the 20th century, culminating in a decade of brutal Japanese occupation, plunged the rural economy into unparalleled disorder. The tragic lapse of the Great Leap Forward apart, China's rural economy enjoyed relative stability and the nation's huge farming population a low but survivable degree of material security after 1949. This, and the new state monopoly of foreign trade, promised good conditions for the restoration of the fortunes of the 50,000 or so small towns (Luo Maochu, 1988, p24). However, the policies of the People's Republic in its first three, Mao-dominated decades proved inimical to the revival and blossoming of the small town economy, dependent as it was on the petty capitalism of

Note: Reprinted from *Small Town China: Governance, Economy, Environment and Lifestyle in Three Zhen*, Kirkby, R., Bradbury, I. and Shen, G., copyright © (2000) with permission from Ashgate, Aldershot.

trade and handicrafts. Already by 1957, prior to the formation of the communes and the consolidation of state power in the countryside, the new regime had cut a swathe through the web of small town economic life. When the celebrated social anthropologist Fei Hsiao-Tung (Fei Xiaotong) returned to the Jiangnan village of his pre-war research, he found that traditional small industries and household sidelines were in a state of desuetude (Fei Xiaotong, 1994). As for the cycle of ritual and custom, following the formation of the people's communes in 1958, town fairs, festivals and street entertainment, not to mention collective religious activities, were more or less suppressed. Yet during the Mao era there was at a different level an official espousal of a national urbanization strategy which favoured smaller over larger settlements. The anti-metropolitan tendency was innately endorsed by the Mao faction. It signified a fear and suspicion of the great cities which reeked still of foreign overlords, and it was in tune with their determination to restrain urban investments which were 'non-productive' – in housing and social infrastructure – to the lowest levels compatible with the targets of an intense industrialization programme.

On a larger canvas, the objective was to maximize survivability of the new state, encircled as it was perceived to be by a revanchist US, and after 1960, by a hostile Soviet Union too. 'When the enemy attacks, retreat!': the reflexes of the guerrilla struggles of the Communist Party were now once more invoked (Houkai, 1997, p1). Mao's repeated injunctions on the dispersal of China's industrial infrastructure under the *san xian* (Three Fronts) implanted a vast complex of industrial and research enterprises in the remotest regions of the central south-west, far away from the great urban centres of coastal China. But Mao's grand regional strategy, though it discriminated against already urbanized seaboard China, did not amount to a harnessing of China's rural settlements in any coherent national plan. The lack of any renaissance and positive reformulation of the small town economy for the new era was a clear outcome of the orthodoxies of centralized economic planning which began to take shape from the mid-1950s on. The state's determination to squeeze as much surplus for industrialization as the countryside could yield required a bureaucratic vice on the rural economy. Thus, for most of the period of the rural collective economy (1958–1984), the state's exclusive right to procure and market agricultural goods was rigidly exercised. The farm product of local tradition, more or less diverse, was squeezed by the Maoist obsession with grain. Household handicrafts and service trades, however pettifogging, were severely restricted in favour of state-dictated collective use of the farm slack season. For the Maoists, the 'restoration of capitalism' in China would come not so much from any untoward cosying to the forces of capital – by definition external – but rather from a feared coalescence of petty trading in China's countryside. 'Cutting off the capitalist tail' was the strident purpose of Party power in the countryside, and 'capitalism' was any activity, tangible or merely ideological, which failed to correspond with the Party's diktat. Official antipathy to the 'tail' could be extreme: in the mid-1970s we witnessed peasants being rounded up by bayonet-wielding militia for a crime no greater than tendering a solitary cabbage for sale on the village street.

Such prohibitions denied to China's small towns their function as points of production and exchange for the range of goods and services required by any agricultural community. Instead, the towns were officially construed as mere administrative, social control, and official storage and distribution points. It is nonetheless the case that for many regions, the rural development policies of the Cultural Revolution (1966–1976) did breathe some new life into the small towns. Efforts to improve rural life chances found expression in new schools and hospitals sited in the administrative centres of the people's communes – these numbering some 53,000 towards the end of the Mao era.

In the early 1970s, the rural industrialization movement begun in the Great Leap Forward was once more applied, this time more judiciously. The emphasis was direct utility to agricultural production, the national plan aiming to equip every county with cement and fertilizer plants, with off-farm activities at commune level encompassing farm machinery, pesticides and power generation. The impact of the 'five small industries' programme was mainly seen in the county towns and the richer people's communes. The great majority of small towns remained virtually untouched.

This deficiency was recognized by a policy forum of September 1970. The North China Agriculture Conference of September 1970, convened to promote rapid agricultural mechanization, also called for significant efforts to develop non-agricultural enterprises in rural areas, both at commune and production brigade levels. Again, off-farm developments at these levels were far more successful in richer regions – that is those in the metropolitan hinterlands of the coastal region. An arch example of the late Cultural Revolution was that of the Huaxi production brigade, which by 1978, derived over three-quarters of its total output value from non-cultivating operations, including several industrial workshops (Kirkby, 1982). At the inception of the post-Mao reformation in 1978, those places representing the lowest level of China's formal urban system – the designated towns (*jianzhi zhen*) – numbered some 2200. Yet in 1961, almost two decades previously, these *zhen* had totalled 4429. While the rescindment of almost half China's *zhen* was in formal terms a function of the 1963 adjustment in designation criteria (aimed at reducing the state's burden in the supply of grain to the population), it is nonetheless indicative of the low priority accorded to the small settlement sector. This is further indicated by the figures for total population of the *zhen*: in 1961 they encompassed 44 million, while almost two decades later the total had risen merely to 50 million.

Questions of urbanization strategy and small towns after 1978

The emergence of surplus rural labour

From the early 1950s to the early 1980s, China's urban population enjoyed the considerable advantages of state subsidy – providing secure labour based on a clear wage system, food and other supplies, and relatively generous housing and social welfare provision. As for the over 80 per cent of the population who were rural dwellers, administrative measures effectively confined them to a precarious existence in the villages and small towns. It is now widely accepted that the collective system of the people's communes, though it maintained a basic standard of livelihood in most areas and at most times, concealed considerable rural underemployment. With the introduction of the household responsibility system in place of the communes in the 1979–1984 period, it became evident that a large proportion of the rural population was not needed in crop production.

By the early 1980s, policy analysts were estimating that almost one-third of the rural workforce (then numbering some 350 million) was basically surplus to requirements. Since that time, China has witnessed an unprecedentedly large migration of its rural population. It is estimated that by the mid-1990s, around 80 million persons had effected a migratory shift, about half this number moving permanently to the small towns and cities (World Bank, 1997, p45). By the late 1990s, however, with the rural population growing and per capita land ratios constantly falling, it was estimated that the surplus rural population still constituted 35–40 per cent of the agricultural workforce. Thus after nearly two decades of increasingly flexible employment and residence measures, the pool of labour surplus to the requirements of crop production numbered between 120 and 140 million persons. Here lies China's most pressing challenge – the largest rural-to-urban transition which any nation has ever faced (World Bank, 1997, p45). As China's Action Plan for Human Settlements 1996–2010 acknowledges '… at the heart (of the urbanisation question) is how to handle surplus labour while appropriately distributing the country's non-agricultural population' (Ministry of Construction, 1996, p18).

Establishment of a national strategy for urbanization

The post-Cultural Revolution government's determination to pursue a small towns policy was first formally expressed in 1978 at the National Conference on Urban Work, and later confirmed at the 1980 National Conference on Urban Planning. The objectives were, simply put (Zhou and Li, 1989):

- strictly control the development of the large cities;
- rationally develop medium-sized cities;
- vigorously promote the development of small cities and towns.

Subsequently, in 1989, when China published its first comprehensive set of laws on urban planning, the 1978 slogan was incorporated in a modified form, which gave greater emphasis to the role of small cities. In 1996, when the United Nations staged its second great Conference on Human Settlements (HABITAT II), the 20-year-old policy slogan was blithely reaffirmed (Ministry of Construction, 1996, p14). The guiding principle was the relocation of surplus rural labour within a diversified agriculture, and in township industries located in towns and cities in the region.

The long-pressed notion of limiting urban scale and preventing the development of unmanageable super-cities is not one peculiar to China. Wherever planners are supposed to plan, whether it be in post-war Britain's new towns, in the Soviet Union of the 1960s, or in World Bank policy of the 1980s (with its 'small and intermediate settlements' programmes), a 'smallist' policy preference is the order of the day. And when the Chinese government's strategy was laid down in the late 1970s, the incentive was particularly great to restrict urban development and to exclude the great majority of the rural population from a big city existence. After several decades of investment neglect, the physical fabric of China's cities was extremely poor.

The housing crisis was severe, and the larger the city, the worse the situation. While per capita housing living space was still at 1950s levels – that is less than 5m^2 – in the great cities such as Shanghai it was very much lower. Transportation, utilities and educational and health infrastructure were also operating at their limits. Above all, the central authorities were anxious not to increase what they saw as their major burden of guaranteeing grain supplies to the urban population. With the beginnings of reform of the collective system of agriculture, and the prospect of large numbers of underemployed rural dwellers requiring relocation, it was imperative to affirm an urbanization strategy which deflected them from the great cities of China.

Advocacy of the small towns urbanization strategy

The most visible and eminently argued case in favour of a small town strategy derives, surprisingly, from social scientists with a primary interest in making relevant to present-day needs the historic experience of China's small town network. It was the foremost social scientist of the older generation, Fei Xiaotong, who by the early 1980s had become the undisputed champion of China's small towns. Many years before China's liberation, Professor Fei had built an academic reputation as much in the West as in China based on his advocacy of small towns in China's economy and culture. In 1936, he and his sister Fei Dasheng were drawn to their home area on the shores of Lake Tai in Jiangsu province, the one to conduct social research and the other to assist in the rural cooperative development programme of that time. Fei's investigations in Kaixiangong – his archetypical '*Jiangcun*' ('River Village') – became in turn a thesis at the London School of Economics, and a book published in the late 1930s (Fei Hsiao-Tung, 1939). Seven years after the Liberation of 1949, Fei returned to Kaixiangong. In his own words, 'I was very much worried about the situation that sideline production was neglected and rural industry had failed to be restored' (Fei Xiaotong, 1994, p4). Professor Fei pondered over the reason why the lives of the local people had failed to improve, despite a lead of 60 per cent in agricultural production. Such thoughts were, however, dangerous ones, and contributed to Fei Hsiao-Tung's (Fei Xiaotong) impending isolation as a 'bourgeois rightist'. It was not until 1981 that Fei could once again visit Kaixiangong: he was to rejoice in the restoration of family sideline enterprises and the newly formed collective non-agricultural enterprises which were bringing new wealth. In all this, Professor Fei saw the renaissance of traditional rural pursuits in a new era in which China was liberalizing its overall economy and engaging as never before with the global system.

     Why are the endeavours of one eminent scholar significant to this discussion of China's small town experience? In the early 1980s, Professor Fei and his research team (among whom is one of the present authors) produced a series of studies under the Chinese title of '*Small towns, big issues*' (Fei Xiaotong, 1986). In the approved manner, the work was both investigative and prescriptive – that is, it spelt out and advocated policies which would further promote China's small towns strategy. It might be added here that if there is one clear case in which China's incipient social science community has had a direct influence on national policy, here it must surely lie. As Fei saw it, the long-established restrictions on migration remained the crucial bar to take-off in the non-farming enterprise sector. The rigid urban–rural divide of the household registration system stultified city and village economies alike. Fei strongly advocated a new regime whereby villagers should have the opportunity to concentrate their commercial and industrial enterprises in the small towns nearby to them. Consequently, in 1984 the government introduced a new measure to permit migration to small towns, particularly to those other than county towns. The main proviso was that migrants should undertake to maintain responsibility for their own grain supplies (the *zili kouliang* transferees).

Anticipating the coming increase in China's surplus rural population, Professor Fei called for a far more diverse pattern of rural life. The main consideration was that the small towns should become effective 'dams', preventing the flood of migrants to the cities where large numbers of newcomers would be bound to lead to human misery on a large scale. Thus we have Fei Hsiao-Tung's (Fei Xiaotong) now famous formula, *litu bu lixiang* ('leave the land but don't leave the countryside'). The phenomenon of dual employment for China's rural workforce – an individual at the same time being both worker and farmer (*yigong yinong*) was already emerging in the early 1980s, particularly in Jiangsu province.

The small towns strategy: Contrary voices

The relevance of such grand strategy guidance, and indeed whether or not it has actually influenced outcomes, has aroused considerable debate among scholars and policy makers. It is clear that one of the first problems is vagueness: 'control' and 'rationally develop' are obviously value-loaded and relative terms. A further problem arises because of the rigid size categories implicit in the slogan: 'large cities' – those over 500,000 – medium-sized cities (200,000–500,000), and small cities (up to 200,000) – these are abstract notions which do not take into account the particularities of place. In the words of Zhou and Li (1989, p85), 'The selection of China's urbanization policy should not be based on the size of cities'. We have seen that the most cogent arguments against the small towns strategy as it emerged in the 1980s turn on economics. In the 1990s, an increasing number of analysts inside and outside China questioned whether the small town strategy in its present form is sustainable from the standpoint of land resources and the agro-ecological environment. Opposition to the small towns strategy on economic grounds came in a number of forms. Some evoke a supposedly Marxist idea of historical development through stages: at its present condition of development, China is said to be not yet ready for a spatially dispersed economy. The nation is 'still at the primary stage of socialism' and as in the economic and social spheres, inherent in this dictum is the notion of inequality between places, in terms both of urban size and of economic prowess. When the time is ripe, the argument goes, such concentrations will gradually dissolve through a trickle-down process.

There are thus those who on grounds of 'historical inevitability' see urban concentration as an unavoidable stage. There are those too who advocate a course completely at odds with the official line: further development of China's 'extra-large' cities – those with core populations of over 1 million – is the only rational path (see, for example, Zhao Xiaobin and Li Zhang, 1995, p835). Typically, such analyses rely on statistical correlations suggesting a linkage between urban economic performance and urban scale. Most find it strongly positive, though there are some who maintain that the greatest returns will be from further investment in the more 'manageable' cities in the 200,000–500,000 range. These arguments in favour of a less rigid formulation of urbanization strategy rely on familiar Western concepts of economy of scale and comparative advantage. By the late 1990s there were signs that a new orthodoxy was consequently – and seamlessly – emerging. It was one diametrically opposed to the explicit strategy of two decades. A 'correct' urbanization strategy newly expounded by the State Development Planning Commission went as follows: 'China's guiding principle of urbanization is to plan and develop super-large and large cities, expand medium-sized cities and improve small cities and towns...' (*China Daily*, 18 October 1999).

This volte-face in official line bears the stamp of economistic thinking: China's urbanization level is regarded as 'lagging' by world standards, and a correlation is made between the acceleration of urbanization and the expansion of domestic demand. 'Such an expansion rate calls for shifting 85 million of the rural population into cities within the next five years', proclaims the new line. There is no explanation offered as to the means of employing such huge numbers at a time when the crisis in the state economy means shedding tens of millions from the urban economy.

Urbanization outcomes since 1978: An overview

Transformation of the urban system

The question of measurement of China's urbanization rate is notoriously difficult, mainly because of changing official criteria (Kirkby, 1985). But in broad outline, and according to the reasonably acceptable standards established by the 1990 census, in 1980 the total urban population stood at 135 million, 13.6 per cent of China's total. By the end of 1995, the figure had risen dramatically to 349 million – 28.9 per cent of China's total (Ministry of Construction, 1996, p14). Most of the growth has been accounted for by the sub-municipal rural settlements, especially the designated towns (*jianzhi zhen*). China's officially recognized urban places include designated municipalities (*shi*) and designated towns (*jianzhi zhen*). Since the 1990 census, the precise parts of *shi* and *zhen* populations which can be counted within the urban total have been closely specified according to affiliation to various administrative units (Kirkby, 1994, p135, Figure 8.1). At the sub-municipal level, China's smaller settlements divide into two broad groups – those administered by county (*xian*) governments and those under township governments. The former group are designated towns – *jianzhi zhen* – and include those county seats without municipal status, and other designated towns coming under county control (*xian shu zhen*). The latter, far more numerous group includes the seats of *xiang* government (very often former people's commune headquarters), as well as the large number of places simply referred to as 'rural market towns' (*nongcun jizhen*). The three sites in the present study (Neiguan in Gansu, Yuantan in Anhui and Shengze in Jiangsu) share the status of designated town.

The 15 years after 1984 have seen a quantum leap in the designation of *zhen*. In 1984, the central government significantly eased the official criteria whereby *zhen* could be established. This coincided with a major adjustment in taxation on enterprises owned at *zhen* level. Prior to January 1984, their income tax was set at the rate of 55 per cent, as opposed to 20 per cent for township (*xiang*) and village-owned enterprises. Thereafter, taxation for all rural enterprises owned by *zhen, xiang* and *cun* was equalized at 55 per cent (Lee, 1989, pp778–780). It was, above all, this incentive which spurred thousands of small towns to apply for *zhen* status. While at the end of 1983 there were 2781 *zhen* (only a few hundred more than in 1978), by 1984 year-end the figure had more than doubled, to 6211. Despite some fluctuation (for example, small reductions in the total *zhen* numbers in 1987 and 1989), by the time of the 1990 census there were 11,937 of these designated towns. By 1995 the sector had expanded remarkably, with a total of almost 17,000 (Kirkby, 1994, p131, Table 8.1; Ministry of Construction, 1996, p14). There is no doubt that *zhen* designation brings a greater political and economic influence on the surrounding rural territory. Just as China's municipalities have taken on the role of regional centres under the 'city control counties' (*shi guan xian*) system, so the *zhen* have enlarged their boundaries to incorporate the entire territories of the *xiang* which they usually replace (the *zhen guan cun* or 'town control villages' system), thus allowing greater direct control over human and material resources. All three *zhen* in the present study have considerable rural territory under their jurisdiction.

Other determinants of urban scale

As the October 1999 about-turn in official urbanization strategy acknowledges (and indeed, celebrates), it is manifestly clear that despite the small towns strategy, it has not merely been the sub-municipal settlements which have grown in physical, economic and population terms. Year-on-year double digit growth of the economy, and the weight of % attraction of China's primate cities towards domestic and overseas capital, have ensured a thoroughgoing transformation of all first tier and many lesser ranking cities too. Between 1980 and 1995, the number of cities with core populations of over 500,000 increased from 45 to 75; of these, the 'million' cities went up from 15 to 32 (Ministry of Construction, 1996, p14). The many factors which cause the larger cities to be growth poles cannot be given consideration here. It can be surmised, however, that had there been a completely laissez-faire policy towards the complex issues which surround urban growth, including migration policy, the larger cities would undoubtedly have increased in population far more than has actually occurred. It can also be judged that under such circumstances, the conditions of life for a sizeable proportion of China's urban citizenry would be far inferior to those which now prevail.

While the major cities have grown enormously, this does not mean that the smaller cities and the towns have failed to live up to the role assigned to them in official policy. And indeed, there have been many elements of that policy which have positively encouraged town growth. Two have already been mentioned above: the change in migration rules in 1984 which permitted farming families to move to nearby towns (usually the non-county seats), provided they take responsibility for their own grain supplies (*zili kouliang*), and secondly, the easing of official criteria for town designation. As for the former, research by Ma and Ming Fan (1994, p1625) suggests that its effects are significant within a small radius of the town core. Eighty per cent of *zili kouliang* migrants originated within 5km of the *zhen*. Research in Jiangsu province in the mid-1980s showed that more important numerically than those who have actually shifted to town residence, were daily commuters from the surrounding rural villages who account for up to 43 per cent of the daytime population. These people were either self-employed or working in town-run enterprises. In addition to the registered town population (made up of both non-agricultural persons and agricultural persons) there was a significant proportion (over 10 per cent) of the population made up of unregistered migrants (Ma and Ming Fan, 1994, p1625). The latter, the registered *zili kouliang* migrants, and the daily commuting population, are a direct function of the liberalization of China's rural economic policies following the demise of rigid collectivization. Official data supplied to the 1997 World Bank Report on China (World Bank, 1997, p46, Box 4.2) shows that in the mid-1990s, the cities of over half-a-million received 23 per cent of all migrants. Though this speaks of high absolute numbers, and represents a considerable increase on the mid-1980s figure of 8 per cent, it also demonstrates the resilience of the small town sector in anchoring the rural population to the countryside.

Rural economic transformation off-farm

Regional growth patterns in a number of south-east Asian nations demonstrate the attraction of rural regions on the fringes of great cities to domestic and international capital – a phenomenon characterized by McGee (1989) as 'desakota'. For its part too, China's reinvigoration and expansion of the small town sector could not have occurred in the absence of the required economic factors. Since 1978, a whole series of policy reforms has influenced small town growth. The primary reforms were those which addressed the organization of agriculture. The process of decollectivization and the replacement of the people's communes by contract farming under the various 'household responsibility systems' was matched by a retreat of state organizations from procurement and marketing of farm produce. The state still required households to produce and supply agricultural goods, primarily grain, at stipulated prices. However, quotas were considerably less arduous than in the past. Further, in 1979 and on a number of occasions subsequently, the state has raised procurement prices. The question of an inequitable pricing system between agricultural outputs and industrial inputs remains, as discussed elsewhere (Kirkby, 1998). But in the metropolitan hinterlands at least, encompassing much of the coastal provinces and the Yangzi basin, in general the burden on China's farming communities has been eased. Diversification, specialization, and household marketing of non-quota produce have been freely permitted in the post-1978 system.

As we have noted, during the two decades of the people's communes, petty trading and service activities were largely outlawed and the state's marketing organs held unchallenged sway. During this period private entrepreneurship on even a derisory scale brought down official wrath. But all this was to change in 1984; the reforming government for the first time since the early 1950s sanctioned almost unrestricted private operation of non-agricultural enterprises. These were meant to be on a small scale, with fewer than five employees. In 1982 there were 1.36 million rural enterprises nationwide, with 31 million employees – 9.2 per cent of the rural workforce. The official count for the end of 1986 showed 15 million enterprises (henceforth referred to in the standard way as 'township and village enterprises' or TVEs) with almost 80 million employees. Ninety per cent of the units were privately owned, and these accounted for between one-third and one-half of all the employees.

The remarkable – indeed miraculous – rise of China's TVEs has been the subject of many detailed investigations, including a major World Bank study (Byrd and Lin Qingsong, 1990). Some headline figures attest to the enormous scale of growth: between

1978 and 1994 rural enterprises owned collectively at town, township (*xiang*) and village levels:

- increased their share in gross national industrial output from 9 per cent to 42 per cent;
- increased their share in gross national social output from 7.2 per cent to 32.2 per cent;
- increased their share of gross rural social output from 24.3 per cent to 66 per cent;
- increased their contribution to total state revenue from 4 per cent to 22 per cent.

By the mid-1990s (the period of our study) the TVE sector was thought to employ around 125 million – or over one-quarter of China's entire rural workforce. Considerable diversity exists in China's off-farm economy, with many regional variations. In the early 1980s, researchers identified at least three different 'models' of growth – the south Jiangsu type (diversified collective enterprises established and run by local government organs), the Wenzhou (Zhejiang) type (characterized by household level enterprises and home-working), and the heavy industry-linked type seen particularly in north-east China's Liaoning province (Tan, 1988). The situation today is far more complex and diffuse; the identification of regional models of rural urbanization is no longer straightforward, and nor is it relevant. The rich coastal province of Jiangsu, location of our study site of Shengze, illustrates the most advanced (and atypical) regional development of rural enterprises. Two main factors have determined the high degree of rural industrialization in Jiangsu – firstly, historically favourable natural conditions for agriculture, and secondly, the existence of a mature network of major cities. A diverse and dense communications system, relying heavily on waterways, is an associated factor. By 1994, agriculture accounted for only 15 per cent of Jiangsu's rural economy. Primary and tertiary industries in the rural sector accounted for 15.3 per cent and 30.1 per cent respectively of the province's totals. Most remarkably, in a province with a well-developed urban industrial sector, non-municipal secondary industries accounted for well over half of Jiangsu's total. In Jiangsu's case, the rapid rise of the rural non-farming sector has not been at the expense of agriculture. In the richer parts of the province, such as Suzhou, it is the tendency towards specialisation in larger units which has been key. Among the over 4 million rural citizens of Suzhou, it is not now uncommon to find farms of up to 7ha, enormous by traditional standards. There is a close association between unit size and farm yield. There is also a close link between rising agricultural surpluses and the ability of local communities to invest in non-agricultural enterprises.

Constraints upon the small towns/rural industries strategy

Since 1978, the Chinese state has significantly decreased its role in economic affairs. Central state planning agencies now directly control the variables of production and distribution of just dozens of key commodities. The far greater role for the market, and the privatization of much of the state sector, was clearly signalled by the 15th Party Congress of September 1997. In the process of increasing hegemony of the market, the factors of scale economy, linkage and technological level would in theory give a strong comparative advantage to enterprises in the larger urban centres. In the early to mid-1980s, the proliferation of small rural production units in sectors in which the subsidized state sector remained prominent caused severe conflicts. For example, in cotton growing areas, the newly established rural-based units would monopolize the local crop and transform it into an inferior product. Larger state mills in the cities, often with the latest technology, would find themselves starved of raw materials. In such circumstances, the central ministries would be inclined to intervene, issuing sectoral injunctions to cease production in TVE plants.

The first phase of rapid growth of the TVE sector, beginning in the mid-1980s, was within the context of a volatile national economy. In the aftermath of the 1988–1989 period, when economic instability found expression in political unrest, there were moves afoot by the prevailing conservative forces in the Party leadership to drastically curtail the TVE sector. However, the eventual pragmatic judgement was that any attack on the TVEs would risk enormous social costs as well as structural disequilibria in the economy. Thus, in the 1990s, the re-consolidation of the sector was to proceed. It did so particularly rapidly after Deng Xiaoping's unqualified clarion calls to entrepreneurship associated with his 1993 'southern tour'. The key enhancing factor for the industrial TVEs was horizontal linkage to more advanced urban enterprises, to technological and market chains stretching even beyond China's borders. The tradition of enterprise branch elaboration had roots stretching back to the 1950s. It was strongly advocated for the TVE sector already in the early 1980s, when the case of the city of Weihai, Shandong, was nationally promoted (Kirkby, 1985, Chapter 6). Horizontal linkage renders rural-based production units far less vulnerable to the cold winds of market competition.

Occasionally, by the late 1990s, with the state-owned urban enterprises increasingly unable to sustain levels of output under declining government support, mature rural sub-units were able to attain a position stronger and even superior to that of their urban mother plants. In some cities, laid-off state enterprise workers have sought employment in peripheral collectives, thus reversing the historical relationship between the 'iron rice bowl' of the city and the fragile earthenware vessel of the traditional agrarian life. The TVE sector, though always a fluid arena of start-up, closure, and merger, seemed by the mid-1990s to have reached a plateau of stability. Certainly in the 9th Five Year Plan (1996–2000) the sector was judged as fulfilling an essential role in the national economy: without it there could be no possibility of absorbing the bulk of the surplus rural labour force. In fact, the 9th Five Year Plan emphasized a cycle of continuous rationalization of the rural enterprise sector, and close monitoring of its appetite for rural land.

Despite the enormous achievements in the development of the off-farm sector, its structural sustainability over the long term remains a matter of doubt. We argue elsewhere that crop production and thus agricultural land has been structurally undervalued (Kirkby and Zhao, 1999). Thus the newly proliferating rural enterprises have an unfair economic advantage – a headstart over agriculture. This also encourages inefficiencies, in both production and the use of land. The irruption of a rural surplus workforce – China's most prominent social and economic issue – is greatly increased by the inequities inflicted on agriculture.

It has been observed that more so than for other developing countries, small town production may well be chain-linked to national and even global markets. Among other negative factors, this implants in a technically unsophisticated rural environment many production processes which are dangerous to both the workforce and to local agricultural environments. At the same time, the interface between local industrial production and local agricultural systems is not well served. Rural industries aim to look outwards, over the heads of local farming communities. A long-term strategic solution, difficult to implement because it invokes huge questions of relocation and restructuring, is to maintain and develop that part of the rural enterprise sector which is clearly oriented towards agriculture. Simple consumer durables, farming and personal services meeting the demands of local agricultural communities should be retained. Other manufacturing, particularly that serving national and international markets, should be concentrated in larger urban centres where external and scale economies, higher technologies, and managerial skills are superior. Here there is more likely to be effective state regulation in addition. Such ideas imply also a more rationally developed network of small towns, with surplus rural population concentrating in fewer and larger rural settlements.

The impact of an increasingly deregulated national economy, and the penetration of regional and global capital into China's countryside may yet bring about a renewed phase of instability to the industrializing small towns. By the late 1990s, much of the product marketed in the domestic economy was feeling an increasingly chill wind: the consumer durables which account for a good part of production do not have a limitless market, even in China. Indeed, warehouses were glutted with intermittently purchased household durables, much of which derive from the TVE sector. It was estimated in mid-1998 that some 15 per cent of all township enterprises were significantly loss-making.

Rates of growth of the sector as a whole were also slowing, reflecting a tightening of bank credit. Already in late 1995, such impacts were evident in our study site of Shengze, where textile markets were in the doldrums and whose smart hotels, once the haunt of droves of affluent buyers from every province, were begging for guests. The alternative escape route from the land – migration to the cities – was also becoming obstructed. With the crisis of employment of the state-owned enterprise sector, major cities were beginning to debar rural migrants from a range of employment previously their natural destination ('Migrants go home', *Far Eastern Economic Review*, 26 February 1998, p12). And with at least one-quarter of the township manufacturing sector's product entering overseas markets, the impacts of the undermining of purchasing power and the competitive pressures due to devaluations in the Southeast Asian market after 1998 are, at time of writing, still working their way back to China's myriad townships. For the first time, in the late 1990s, the TVE total labour force showed signs of shrinkage.

The scale of China's contemporary transition from an essentially subsistence agriculture to an urban economy is unprecedented in the history of industrial revolutions. The particular features which make China's current experience so dramatic are the sheer scale of population and territory, combined with the ascendancy of the external capitalist economy to a new spiral of globalization unimaginable even two decades ago. In the post-1978 period there is clearly close dialectical linkage between China's massive integration within the world economy and the new cycle of global penetration of capitalism's production and marketing. This penetration itself reflects significant technological advances in communications, both physical and electronic. Linking globalization to environmental deterioration, one recent analyst writes bleakly: 'China now joins other countries in a struggle for world position that places nation and region in a cascade of economic relations at the bottom of which lies the rural environment' (Muldavin, 1998, p291).

Media accounts and official studies of the impacts of rural industrialization upon the agricultural and living environments are by now almost too numerous to mention. According to no less an authority than Qu Geping, father of China's National Environmental Protection Agency, already by the mid-1980s township industries were responsible for one-third of the nation's gas emissions, almost one-sixth of the polluted water, and a similar proportion of solid wastes (Qu Geping and Li Jinchang, 1994, p161). The growing problem was accorded considerable attention in the 1994 publication *Action Plan for China's Environmental Protection*, 1991–2000 AD (NEPA and State Planning Commission, 1994). A major survey of 1996, conducted by NEPA and the State Statistical Bureau and involving 2 million rural enterprises, chronicled an ever deteriorating state of affairs (see 'Survey to measure rural pollution', *Beijing Review*, 29 April–5 May, 1996, p5).

Though its degree and scale have diminished considerably over the past two decades, rural poverty is still widespread in parts of the country where terrain and climate are unfavourable. In the pre-reform period, strict migration controls combined with far higher living standards in the urban sector created a psychological environment in which rural people yearned for improvements to their lives. Once the controls of the old regime began to ease, and with an increased awareness of the benefits enjoyed in the newly resurgent urban sector, China's rural population were eager to join the bandwagon of 'getting rich' regardless of the price. In a situation of relatively stagnant agriculture, the means to a new life of affluence was perceived as through the development of local off-farm enterprises. In this, local government officials themselves also had a stake, in terms both of prestige and actual material benefit. The universal opinion in China's countryside was now *wugong bufu* 'without (local) industry there is no affluence' (Ma and Ming Fan, 1994, p1642). Thus for villager and local cadre alike, the trade-off between greater affluence on the one hand, and deterioration in customary lifestyle – including local environments and ecosystems – was likely to be settled very much in favour of the former. It was this key issue which prompted our investigations in three towns in three very different regions of China.

References

Byrd, W. and Lin Qingsong (eds) (1990) *China's Rural Industry Structure, Development and Reform*, Oxford University Press, Oxford

Fei Hsiao-Tung (Fei Xiaotong) (1939) *Peasant Life in China: A Field Study of Country Life in the Yangtze Valley*, Routledge, London

Fei Xiaotong (ed) (1986) *Small Towns in China; Functions, Problems and Prospects*, New World Press, Beijing

Fei Xiaotong (1994) 'The road to China's urban and rural development: A subject of my lifetime's research', *China City Planning Review*, March, pp2–11

Houkai, W. (1997) 'Economic result of urban size and location planning policies in China', unpublished paper, *European Agriculture and Rural Development Conference*, Manchester, May

Kirkby, R. J. R. (1982) 'Settlement policy for a modernising China', in Taylor, J. and Williams, D. (eds) *Urban Planning Practice in Developing Countries*, Pergamon Press, Oxford, pp189–214

Kirkby, R. J. R. (1985) *Urbanization in China: Town and Country in a Developing Economy 1949–2000 AD*, Croom Helm, London

Kirkby, R. J. R. (1994) 'Dilemmas of urbanisation: Review and prospects', in Dwyer, D. (ed) *China: The Next Decades*, Longman, Harlow, pp156–185

Lee, Y-S. F. (1989) 'Small towns and China's urbanization level', *China Quarterly*, vol 120, pp663–668

Luo Maochu (1988) 'A review and evaluation of China's policy for the development of small towns', *China City Planning Review*, vol 4, pp22–37

Ma, L. J. C. and Ming Fan (1994) 'Urbanisation from below: The growth of small towns in Jiangsu, China', *Urban Studies*, vol 31, pp1625–1645

McGee, T. G. (1989) 'Urbanisasi or kotadesasi? Evolving patterns of urbanization in Asia', in Costa, A. et al (eds) *Urbanization in Asia: Spatial Dimensions and Policy Issues*, University of Hawai'i Press, Honolulu

Ministry of Construction (1996) 'China: Report on the development of human settlements', *China City Planning Review*, vol 12, pp12–22

Muldavin, J. (1998) 'The limits to market triumphalism in rural China', *Geoforum*, vol 28, pp289–312

National Environmental Protection Agency (NEPA) and State Planning Commission (1994) *Zhongguo Huanjing Baohu Xingdong Jihua 1991–2000 Nian (Action Plan for China's Environmental Protection, 1999–2000)*, China Environmental Science Press, Beijing

Qu Geping and Li Jingchang (1994) *Population and the Environment in China*, Lynnee Rienner, Boulder

Tan, K. C. (1988) 'Regional variation in the growth patterns of Chinese small towns', unpublished paper, *4th Asian Urbanization Conference*, Nanjing, August

World Bank (1997) *China 2020*, The World Bank, Washington, DC

Zhao Xiaobin and Li Zhang (1995) 'Urban performance and the control of urban size in China', *Urban Studies*, vol 32, pp813–842

Part 4

Mobility and Migration Between Rural and Urban Areas

Chapter 9

Environmental Perceptions, Social Class and Demographic Change in Mexico City: A Comparative Approach

Haydea Izazola, Carolina Martínez and Catherine Marquette

Introduction

Since pre-Colombian times, Mexico City has exerted a strong power of attraction both economically and demographically. As in other large urban areas, transformation as well as deterioration of the city's physical environment have been an outcome of this process. The historical concentration of industry, increased vehicle use and greater energy consumption, combined with the city's high altitude and natural valley setting,[1] are some of the specific trends behind the deterioration in air quality in Mexico City despite government efforts.[2] Centuries of disruption to the series of ancient lakes upon which the city rests have also resulted in extreme situations of water shortage or (during the rainy seasons) floods.[3] Meanwhile, the city's rapid rate of population growth, which reached more than 5 per cent during the 1960s and more than 3 per cent in the 1970s,[4] and the resulting current population size of approximately 16 million have made it impossible for urban infrastructure to keep pace. Water and sanitation services and solid waste disposal are neither sufficiently extensive nor efficient and further contribute to the deterioration in the city's physical environment. Furthermore, rapid land use change, due to clearing and the integration of land for housing as well as industry, has further added to air and water problems as well as to those of soil degradation.

It is compelling to wonder what kinds of different coping strategies Mexico City's large and diverse population has developed in response to these deteriorating environmental conditions. This paper begins to explore that question by comparing two groups, namely middle-class households who have out-migrated from the city and low-income households who continue to live in the urban periphery. The analysis is based on the assumption that the way each group perceives environmental change, or 'environmental perceptions', as well as household, community and societal level factors shapes the responses they make. We aim to more closely consider why and how groups exposed to the same basic types of environmental change may respond differently. Since the most obvious response which might be made in the face of environmental deterioration is to move, particular emphasis is placed throughout on migration as a response to environmental change.

Conceptual frameworks for considering environmental change and population responses

Consideration of the impact of Mexico City's physical environmental deterioration on its population has focused mainly on passive responses such as changes in health and morbidity in relation to air and water pollution (respiratory, skin, eye and water-borne infectious diseases).[5] It is only more recently that active population responses to environmental change (for example, out-migration) have begun to be explored.[6] The role played by environmental perceptions in shaping these active responses is important yet little explored. Although demographers have attempted to recognize the links between psychological factors and fertility behaviour (e.g. through the plethora of KAP 'Knowledge, Attitudes and Practice' – studies in the 1970s and 1980s), the psychological dimensions of migration decision making remain far less analysed and have generally not gone beyond vague discussions of push and pull forces[7] or of economic rationality.[8] Recent consideration of the concept of 'environmental refugees', however, has led to recognition that migration in response to environmental change (even acute environmental change such as floods or natural disaster) necessarily involves some interplay of individual, household, community and societal level factors.[9]

Concern with the links between perceptions of the external world (phenomenology) and the interaction between individual perceptions and higher-level determinants of action (household, community, societal) have been a constant concern in modern sociology and psychology.[10] Within anthropology, the sub-disciplines of social linguistics and semiotics,[11] as well as ethnoecology and ethnobotany,[12] have also placed an emphasis on understanding how different social groups perceive the natural world as well as organize and act on these perceptions. Together, these studies point to the way in which individual perceptions of the environment (created by past experiences, future expectations, individual personality, emotions and bodily instincts) interact with higher-level social dynamics linked to households, communities, and larger societies and cultures in order to shape responses.

Social demography in Latin America has produced some useful concepts which attempt to synthesize the varying roles played by individual perceptions and higher-level factors in shaping population responses to changing conditions. Concepts such as social reproduction, household survival strategies[13] and the life course[14] have focused attention on the way in which individual perceptions and intentions interact with household characteristics (size, age structure, income level) and community and societal level factors (e.g. economic opportunities and socio-economic class) to determine migration and fertility responses to macro level and structural social and economic changes such as modernization and urbanization. More recently, changing environmental conditions

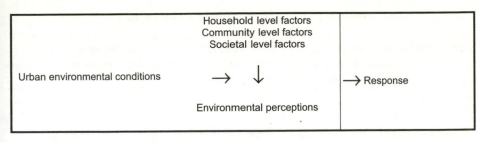

Figure 9.1 *Conceptual framework*

have been suggested as yet another macro level or structural factor which, in addition to economic or social change, may provoke population responses such as migration.[15] The importance of considering the perceptions of the physical environment held by different social groups has also recently been emphasized in relation to understanding population responses to deforestation in southern Mexico.[16]

The above combined currents of thought may be applied to obtain a fuller understanding of the central question of this analysis, that is, why and how different groups within Mexico City are responding to the same deteriorating environmental conditions. As the conceptual framework in Figure 9.1 suggests, household, community and societal level factors, as well as environmental perceptions, may help explain why the study groups make different (or similar) responses in the face of Mexico City's deteriorating physical environment.

Comparative analysis of the study groups

Characteristics of the study groups

This study focuses on information collected in 1994 from two groups of households:

- forty middle-income households which had previously lived in central or nearby suburbs of Mexico City but which later had migrated to medium-size cities in central Mexico (Cuernavaca, Querétaro, Pachuca, San Luis Potosí and Toluca);
- twenty lower-income households currently living in one suburb to the south of Mexico City, Xochimilco.

Comparative information on the two study groups is given in Table 9.1. A study of environmental perceptions and of social, household and community level factors requires the collection of qualitative data. In the case of the middle-income households, five focus groups involving wives from each household were used to collect information, while for the lower-income groups, information was gathered through in-depth interviews with each household member. Basic demographic and economic quantitative data were also collected from each group.

The household, community, and societal characteristics discussed below relate to either the study households as a group, the communities in which these households

Table 9.1 *Characteristics of the groups studied*

Characteristic	Middle-income households (suburb higher region)	Low-income households I (suburb lower region)	Low-income households II
Number of households	40	10	10
Educational level of household head	10 years or more	less than 10 years	less than 10 years
Setting	Out-migrants from Mexico City living in medium-size cities in central Mexico	Hilly long-settled region in Xochimilco, a southern suburb Mexico City	Lower area in Xochimilco, less long settled, greater proportion of recent in-migrants from rural Mexico

reside in Mexico City, or the wider society, that is, the urban environment of Mexico City or the country of Mexico. Perceptions implicitly relate to individuals as the unit of analysis. Because of the different purposes for which the comparative data used here were originally collected, 'environmental perceptions' and their unit of analysis differ slightly between the middle- and low-income households considered. As noted above, information from the middle-class households was collected from focus groups of wives who were used as informants to get some idea of the collective perceptions of their household regarding the environment in Mexico City. This derives from the fact that the original study on this group was aimed specifically at considering household level determinants of middle-class migration flows from Mexico City to medium-size cities.[17] The discussion of this group's environmental perceptions refers to the individual perceptions of wives as representative of their households.

With respect to the low-income households, however, information was collected from all individual household members since the original study on this group focused on the role of individual level, rather than household level, characteristics such as sex, age, personal history and psychological characteristics on their perceptions.[18] For the purposes of the present study, the individual environmental perceptions of all low-income household members were analysed as a whole to arrive at a representative common 'household' perception. Thus, environmental perceptions in the context of this study refer to a representative household level perception of the environment which is based on the perceptions of individual member(s). Clearly, a diversity of environmental perceptions may exist within households and we return to consider this possibility in the concluding discussion.

The middle-income households were identified on the basis of the household head and their spouse having 10 years of education and being engaged in a 'professional' occupation – the latter being defined as an occupation generally known to require at least 10 years' education.[19] Furthermore, the middle-class households studied had out-migrated from Mexico City to a medium-size city in central Mexico and had indicated that deteriorating environmental conditions played some part in their decision to leave. This selection of households was done on the basis, as noted above, that the original study for which they were chosen[20] was aimed specifically at considering determinants of middle-class migration flows from Mexico City to medium-size cities. It does, however, provide us with a clear group for whom environmental conditions in Mexico City played some role in out-migration.[21]

In contrast, the low-income households in Xochimilco were current residents of the metropolitan area of Mexico City. Low-income status was established from direct information about income level as well as direct observation of material living conditions (housing type, access to services etc) and average education levels among household heads and their spouses was less than 10 years. The low-income households from Xochimilco provide a useful contrast to the middle-income households not only in terms of their socio-economic status but also through representing a distinct group who had not out-migrated in response to environmental conditions. It is important to note, however, that the study group in Xochimilco, particularly in the lower areas, does contain a large number of households which are recent in-migrants from rural areas in the surrounding states of Mexico, Puebla and Oaxaca.

In addition, the study group in Xochimilco actually includes two sub-groups from two distinct locations: a higher, hilly long-settled area where subsistence agriculture is combined with wage employment (low-income Group I); and a lowland region where wage employment predominates and which has been subject to more recent waves of in- and out-migration resulting in a less stable population over the last 20 years (low-income Group II). Overall, households in both areas combine wage labour with some agricultural activity.

Environmental conditions

Table 9.2 summarizes the environmental conditions associated with Mexico City which characterize each of the settings in which the groups live. (In the case of the middle-income households, these conditions refer to their experience while still resident in Mexico City, while in the case of the low-income groups these refer to current condi-

Table 9.2 *Environmental conditions among the study households*

Characteristics	Middle-income households	Low-income households I (suburb higher region)	Low-income households II (suburb lower region)
Major physical environmental conditions responding to in Mexico City	• air pollution • poor water quality • solid waste pollution	• air pollution • water shortage • poor water quality • loss of tree cover • solid waste pollution • land degradation linked to land use change	• air pollution • water shortage • surface water pollution • solid waste pollution • land degradation linked to land use change

tions.) Air pollution and water-related problems were common physical environmental conditions faced by all groups.

Households in Xochimilco, however, were subject to some additional problems relating to the suburb's particular history and development. Both study locations in Xochimilco are undergoing rapid land use change as this once rural agricultural area is being integrated into the metropolitan area. Xochimilco also attracts in-migrants from the rural states of Mexico, Puebla and Oaxaca. These trends have led to loss of tree and vegetation cover ('green spaces') as fields make way for residential buildings, particularly in the upper regions. At the same time, demand for water in Mexico City's central and northern industrial areas has triggered shortages in surrounding areas such as Xochimilco.

These trends may have had an even greater impact on the lowland areas than on the highland areas. Historically, the lower region of Xochimilco was the centre of a traditional water and agricultural management system based on *chinampas* and is located on one of the few remnants of the ancient system of lakes which once occupied the entire valley where Mexico City is situated. The *chinampa* system drew on the water from this lake to create a well-adapted and productive mud-mulch bed system for growing crops.[22] The channelling of water from the lake towards the urban centre and the urbanization of Xochimilco have inevitably disrupted this ancient agricultural system and reduced its scale in the area.[23] With this breakdown, dysfunctional parts of the canals system have led to surface water pollution and water shortages. Because of its historical significance, the lower region has been designated a protected area, complicating the tenure status of the people who currently live there. We will now consider important household, community and societal level conditions which are also affecting the study group.

The household, community and societal context

Table 9.3 presents information on household, community and wider social conditions affecting the two study groups. Socio-economic status based on income level is clearly a primary characteristic differentiating the two study groups. However, as Table 9.3 indicates, differences also existed with respect to household structure and life cycle stage; the middle-income households were fairly homogenous, consisting of mainly young couples with young children while the low-income households showed greater diversity.

Distinct community level factors, or factors relating to the immediate social groups with which the study groups interact, are also apparent. The focus groups with the middle-income households revealed a shared sense of the value of the family and of the quality of family life (*convivencia*) as well as a general awareness of environmental issues, which is undoubtedly connected to the increased attention given to these issues in the media in recent years. The low-income groups at both the household and community level were clearly undergoing extensive social and economic changes. The upper region in Xochimilco, which traditionally had been a cohesive and tightly organized community, has been increasingly affected by generational differences, the decreasing importance of agriculture, and increased wage employment and levels of education among younger groups. At the same time, in-migration to this traditionally stable area has caused tension over land resources. In the lower area, designation of the area as a protected region combined with continued in-migration has also led to uncertainty and

Table 9.3 *Household, community and wider social conditions among the study households*

	Middle-income households	Low-income households I (higher region)	Low-income households II (lower region)
Household level	• higher socio-economic status • nuclear households in early stages of household formation with young children	• lower socio-economic status • diverse household structures at diverse life cycle stages with children of diverse ages • breakdown of traditional family structures	
Community level	• traditional emphasis on family (*convivencia*) • increased awareness of environmental issues	• breakdown in traditionally strong community identity • increased in-migration and social segmentation • value still placed on landowning and agriculture	• diversity due to history of in-migration • designation of region as protected area and uncertainty in land tenure • value still placed on landowning and agriculture • value placed on home ownership
Societal level	• decentralization of economic activity to medium-size cities	• urbanization: transition from subsistence agriculture to wage-based modes of production • poverty differentials and migration processes: differentially greater landlessness, low material standards of living and their linkages to rural–urban migration trends	

tension over access to land. Both regions still value land ownership and agricultural activity. In the lowland area, the generally worse-off conditions many households have recently left behind in their rural areas of origin have also led this community to place a high value on home ownership.

At the societal level, several wider country trends also emerged as important in a consideration of environmental perceptions and responses. Middle-income households' decision to migrate to medium-size cities was related to changing economic opportunities which, in turn, may be linked to increased decentralization of economic activity away from Mexico City. For low-income households, the general expansion of the urban area of Mexico City, the broader economic trends driving this urbanization process and their impact on the transition from agricultural to wage employment in the urban periphery have been important. At the same time, urban–rural poverty differentials, lower overall standards of living in rural areas and the resulting rural–urban migration have also affected the low-income households, particularly in the lowland areas where in-migration was a significant on-going dynamic.

Environmental perceptions

Table 9.4 considers some of the main environmental perceptions which the study groups reflected. The middle- and lower-income groups presented contrasting overall perceptions of the concept of 'environment'. The middle-income group reflected a wide notion of the environment which encompassed physical conditions such as air pollution as well as less tangible factors relating to the overall 'quality of life' (e.g. traffic, noise, distance to place of work, aggressiveness of city residents). Among the lower-income households, environmental perceptions focused more narrowly on those aspects most linked with daily existence, e.g. land quality.

Turning to perceptions, the middle-income group reflected a specific focus on the negative effects of air pollution on household health whereas the low-income groups had a much vaguer notion of environmental changes. Air pollution and its negative impacts on health did not figure extensively in their perceptions. In the higher region in Xochimilco, despite extensive obvious loss of tree cover, households seemed unaware of the scale of the problem and only remarked that the environment was generally not the same 'as it used to be'. However, a clear connection was made between this vague notion of change and the arrival of migrants, who were seen as the cause of any deteriorating environmental conditions. In the lower region, there was wide variation in terms of positive and negative perceptions of environmental conditions (e.g. water shortage and pollution). However, households in the lowland areas generally shared a common perception of the value of their surroundings based on their feelings of pride regarding land

Table 9.4 *Perceptions of environmental conditions*

	Wives from middle-income households	*Collective family members from low-income households I (suburb higher region)*	*Collective family members from low-income households II (suburb lower region)*
Overall	• Integrated and wide concept of environment linked with idea of broad 'quality of life'	• Narrower conception linked to daily survival	
Specific	• Deterioration in air quality and negative effects on health	• Vague sense of loss of 'old' environment • No sense of extent of actual loss of trees • In-migrants perceived as cause of environmental degradation • Passivity, look to state for action with some distrust	• Contradictory and varied • Varies from positive to negative • 'Pride' of landholding transcends only unifying ecological concern • Politically active in defence of land and home ownership

and home ownership. Households in this area actively compared their status before coming to Xochimilco, where they frequently had neither land nor housing, to their conditions after migrating, where they had both land (no matter how little) as well as a home (no matter how precariously constructed).

Discussion

As Figure 9.1 suggests, differences in environmental perceptions and, ultimately, responses linked to these perceptions exist between the two study groups which can be traced to the influence of multiple factors at the household, community and societal level. We focus for the moment on the middle-income households studied.

As noted at the outset, this group indicated that their out-migration from Mexico City was partly in response to deteriorating environmental conditions. The previous discussion provides specific insight into the many factors which propelled them towards this action as well as some factors which may have facilitated it. The higher socio-economic status, and thus expectations, of the middle-class households are no doubt linked to their broader perception of environmental conditions in Mexico City in terms of overall 'quality of life' issues.

At the household level, their early life cycle stages, contingent with having young children who are more vulnerable to respiratory and other illnesses, may be linked to their focused perceptions on air pollution and its health effects. At the same time, the common values of their immediate community, which emphasize the family as well as a certain degree of awareness of environmental issues and their health impacts, may also reinforce their sensitivity to the effects which general negative environmental trends in Mexico City may have had on their households. At the societal level, decentralization of industry out of Mexico to medium-size cities is a structural factor which has probably created additional employment opportunities and which middle-class households may be best poised to take advantage of given their generally higher levels of education and technical training. Household, community and societal level factors together thus help at least partly to explain why and how the middle-class households responded to changing environmental conditions through migration.

The low-income households in Xochimilco present a much more complex picture. First, because of their diversity, household level factors such as life cycle stage and type do not provide any insight into observed general patterns as they do among the middle-income households. Income level, however, is likely to play a key role, and their less specific and more practically oriented overall perceptions of the environment are consistent with the struggle for daily survival. The more positive perceptions the lower-income groups have of their environment (or rather their lack of clear negative perceptions as, for example, the middle-income group holds vis-à-vis air pollution) are no doubt linked to their values and concerns regarding land and home ownership – both of which they have achieved in Xochimilco. Their overall environmental perceptions thus also reflect the impact of their distinct community settings as well as the broader social trends (see Table 9.3) which both stimulate and maintain these values.

However, differences between the high and lowland regions in Xochimilco point to the fact that perceptions as well as responses may differ within as well as between socio-economic groups. Differing community level characteristics between the two low-income groups provide some insight into why this is the case. Households in the lowland areas, which are made up mainly of recent in-migrants, reflect a diversity of positive and negative perceptions contingent with the multiple backgrounds from which they come. In contrast, the threat to community homogeneity presented by in-migration to the highland area has led this group to perceive in-migrants as the cause of negative environmental changes in Xochimilco. Moreover, the traditional cohesion of the highland community may make them relatively intransigent and passive (when compared to the lowland group) in recognizing environmental changes and ultimately in organizing to improve their environment. In contrast, the lowland community's overriding concern with land and home ownership eclipses any other environmental perceptions and leads it to greater activism in pursuit of these interests. This type of proactive attitude among poor urban communities in Mexico, motivated by concerns over land and housing, has been noted elsewhere.[24]

The discussion above shows the complex role migration may play in relation to population responses to environmental change as well as environmental perceptions. Among the middle-income households studied, out-migration is a response to negative environmental conditions in Mexico. In the case of the low-income households, however, the process of recent in-migration to Mexico City is a household or community level factor which conditions the way in which these groups perceive and respond to their environmental conditions. Besides the obvious function of migration as a 'response' in terms of avoiding negative environmental conditions (e.g. middle-income group), the migration process itself (being a recent in-migrant) may also affect the way one perceives the environment (e.g. low-income groups). Migration, thus, may have multiple functions within the scheme presented in Figure 9.1, serving sometimes as a response to environmental change, sometimes as a household or community level factor which may shape environmental perceptions.

One implication of the above observation is that the question 'why might middle-income households migrate out of Mexico City in response to deteriorating environmental conditions while lower-income populations in Xochimilco cannot?' is not one which can or should be explained simply in terms of household economic characteristics. The fact that better-off households have the resources (professional skills, economic resources, etc) to allow them to find employment elsewhere clearly facilitates their migration response. However, a lack of such resources among lower-income households does not similarly explain why they do not out-migrate in response to the same environmental conditions. Rather, many low-income households are themselves recent in-migrants who thus have made a recent migratory move – to Mexico City – where they expect to find a better life for themselves. This status, itself, then becomes a key element shaping their perceptions of the environment in Mexico City and, ultimately, their response to it. In this regard, future study of other and perhaps larger groups of in-migrants to Mexico City, for example, those settling in the more industrialized northern suburbs, is important and may reveal different or similar patterns of perceptions and responses among different in-migrant groups.

Still, the current study does raise the important question of what determines whether individuals may migrate out of, or remain in, urban areas in the face of urban environmental deterioration. The issue of out-migration from cities in developing countries has generally not been a concern, given the rapid rate at which they have continued to grow for the last few decades. However, in the case of Mexico City, as with other cities in Latin America, rates of urban growth are in fact slowing down and out-migration flows have increased.[25] In this context, issues normally associated with urban dynamics in cities within Northern countries (for example 'white-flight', 'gentrification', 'sub-urbanization', 'counter-urbanization', etc) may be useful in beginning to think about similar processes which may be occurring in places such as Mexico City. In this context, future research among middle-income households that have developed other strategies (e.g. continue to live in Mexico City and do not migrate or undertake 'temporary' weekend migration) will yield additional insight.

The present study takes only a preliminary look at what is ultimately a very complex notion – 'environmental perceptions'. One critical set of factors shaping environmental perceptions, which was probably not sufficiently addressed above, is that of individual personality factors. We have treated households as being integrated and have presumed that general household level environmental perceptions can be derived and interpreted. In fact, individual household members, depending on their age, sex and relationship, may hold very different perceptions of the environment. The role of this individual heterogeneity, its relationships in the creation of shared perceptions and responses among households, communities and larger social groups (including migration responses), remains to be explored. The notion of 'environmental perceptions' captures multiple processes which take place at that point where objective reality, individual personality, and household, community and societal level forces collide. Further exploration of these processes represents an important step in understanding not only responses to environmental change, as considered here, but also population impacts on the environment.

Notes

1   Manmade causes of air pollution synergistically interacted with the city's geographic setting to make matters worse. Mexico City is naturally subject to higher dust and suspended particle concentration due to the erosion of the ancient system of lake beds on which the city rests. Its location within a valley also results in weak wind patterns which cause an insufficient dispersion of air contaminants. This valley location also predisposes the city to thermal inversions whereby the lower layer of warm air (where contaminants are most heavily concentrated) fails to rise or disperse in the upper atmosphere and remains trapped over the city. In addition, the city's high altitude (2240m above sea level) is associated with greater amounts of ultraviolet radiation which enhance the conversion of primary air pollutants into secondary pollutants such as ozone. Furthermore, motor vehicles function less efficiently and produce greater amounts of polluting carbon monoxide and hydrocarbons due to the city's high altitude – see Herrera, A. (1990) 'Contaminación en aire, agua y suelo en la ciudad de México', in Leff, E. E. (ed) *Medio Ambiente y Desarrollo en México* vol 2, Centro de Investigaciones Interdisciplinarias en Humanidades – UNAM, Mexico City, pp547–580.

2   Bravo, H., Roy Ocotla, G., Sánchez, P. and Torres, R. (1992), 'La contaminación atmosférica por ozono en la zona metropolitana de la ciudad de México', in Restrepo, I. (ed) *La Contaminación Atmosférica en México. Sus Causas y Efectos en la Salud*, Comisión Nacional de Derechos Humanos, Mexico City; also Legorreta, J. and Flores, A. (1992) 'La contaminación atmosférica en el Valle de México', in Restrepo, I. (ed) op cit; Lacy, R. (ed) (1993) 'La calidad del aire en el Valle de México' in *Documentos de Trabajo No. 1*, Programa de Estudios Avanzados en Desarrollo Sustenable y Medio Ambiente, El Colegio de México; see also Note 1, Herrera (1990); and Pérez, R. (1993) 'Estadísticas de energía y contaminación atmosférica en México. Hacia un sistema de estadísticas ambientales', in Izazola, H. and Lerner, S. (ed) (1993) *Población y Ambiente. Nuevas Interrogantes a Viejos Problemas?* Sociedad Mexicana de Demografía, El Colegio de México, The Population Council, pp105–130.

3   Ezcurra, E. (1990) 'The basin of Mexico', in Turner, B. et al (eds) *The Earth Transformed by Human Action*, Cambridge University Press, New York, pp577–588; also Mazari, M. and Bellón, M. (1995) 'Sustentabilidad del desarrollo urbano: Agua', in Aguilar, A., Castro, L. J. and Juárez, E. (eds) *El Desarrollo Urbano de México a Fines del Siglo XX*, Instituto de Estudios Urbanos de Nuevo León-Sociedad Mexicana de Demografía, Monterrey, pp165–178.

4   Partida, V. (1994) 'La ciudad de México. Nuevo derrotero en su ritmo de crecimiento', in *Demos. Carta demográfica de México*, vol 7, Fundación Mexicana para la Planeación Familiar, A.C., Mexico, pp13–14.

5   Finkelman, J. (1990) 'Medio ambiente y desarrollo en Mexico', in Leff, E. (ed) *Medio Ambiente y Desarrollo en México*, vol 2, Centro de Investigaciones Interdisciplinarias en Humanidades, Mexico City, UNAM, pp581–630; also Castillejos, M. (1991) 'La contaminacion ambiental en México y sus efectos en la salud humana', in Schteingart, M. and d'Andrea, L. (eds) *Servicios Urbanos, Gestion Local y Medio Ambiente*, El Colegio de Mexico, Mexico City, pp187–204; Santos Burgoa, C. and Rojas, L. (1992) 'Los efectos de la contaminación atmosférica en la salud', in Restrepo, I. (ed) *La Contaminación Atmosférica en México. Sus Causas y Efectos en la Salud*, Comisión Nacional de Derechos Humanos, Mexico City; and Rivero, O. and Ponciano, G. (eds) (1996) *Riesgos Ambientales para la Salud en la Ciudad de México*, Programa Universitario del Medio Ambiente, Mexico City, UNAM.

6   Izazola, H. and Marquette, C. (1995) 'Migration in response to the urban environment: Out-migration by middle-class women and their families from Mexico City after 1985', in Clarke, J. and Potrikowska, A. (eds) *Population and Environment in Industrialized Regions*, *Geographia Polonica*, vol 64, Polish Institute of Geography and Spatial Organization, Polish Academy of Sciences, pp225–256.

7   Ravenstein, E. G. (1885) 'The laws of migration', *Journal of the Royal Statistical Society*.

8   Todaro. M. (1995) *Economic Development*, 5th edition, Longman, p260 forward.

9   Suhrke, A. (1993) 'Pressure points: Environmental degradation, migration and conflict. Environmental change and acute conflict project', Occasional Paper Series No 3, International Security Studies Program, American Academy of Arts and Sciences and Peace and Conflict Studies Program, University College, University of Toronto, Toronto, Canada; also Suhrke, A. (1997) 'Environmental degradation,

migration and the potential for violent conflict', in Geditsch, N. P. (ed) *Conflict and the Environment*, Kluwer; and Richmond, A. (1993) 'Environmental refugees and reactive migration: A human dimension of global change', Paper presented at the International Union for the Scientific Study of Population (IUSSP) General Meeting, 24 August–1 September, Montreal.

10 Gregory, D. (1978) *Ideology, Science and Human Geography*, Hutchinson, London; also Seamon, D. (1984) 'Philosophical direction in behavioral geography with an emphasis on the phenomenological contribution', in Saarinen, T., Seamon, D. and Sell, J. (eds) *Environmental Perception and Behavior*, University of Chicago, Chicago, IL; Schutz, A. (1967) *Fenomenología del Mundo Social*, Paidós, Mexico; Berger, P. and Luckmann, T. (1968) *La Construcción Social de la Realidad*, Amorrortu, Buenos Aires; Lowenthal, D. (1975) 'Past time, present place: Landscape and memory', *The Geographical Review*, vol 65, pp1–36; Sell, J., Taylor, J. and Zube, E. (1984) 'Toward a theoretical framework for landscape perception', in Saarinen et al op cit; and Merleau-Ponty, M. (1985) *Fenomenología de la Percepción*, Planeta, Barcelona.

11 Lévi-Strauss, C. (1963) *Structural Anthropology*, translated by Jacobson, C. and Schoepf, B., Basic Books, New York.

12 Frake, C. (1962) 'Cultural ecology and ethnography', *American Anthropologist*, vol 64, no 1, part I, pp53–59; also Conklin, H. (1969), 'An ethnoecological approach to shifting cultivation', in Vaydya, A. P. (ed) *Environment and Cultural Behavior*, University of Texas Press, Austin, Tex, pp221–233.

13 Mertens, W., Przeworski, A., Zemelman, H. and Mora y Araujo, M. (1982) *Reflexiones Teórico-metodológicas Sobre Investigaciones en Población*, El Colegio de México; also PISPAL (Programa de Investigaciones Sociales sobre Población en América Latina) (1986) *Problemas Metodológicos en la Investigación Sociodemográfica*, El Colegio de México; and Oliveira, O., Pepin Lehalleur, M. and Salles, V. (1988) *Grupos Domésticos y Reproducción Cotidiana*, UNAM Coordinación Humanidades, El Colegio de México and Grupo Editorial Miguel Angel Porrúa, Mexico.

14 Tuirán, R. (1993) 'Vivir en familia: hogares y estructura familiar en México 1976–1987', *Comercio Exterior*, vol 43, no 7, July.

15 See Note 6.

16 Arizpe, L., Paz, F. and Velázquez, M. (1993) *Cultura y Cambio Global: Percepciones Sociales Sobre la Deforestación en la Selva Lacandona*, Centro Regional de Investigaciones Multidisciplinarias, UNAM and Grupo Editorial Miguel Angel Porrúa, Mexico.

17 See Note 6.

18 Martínez, C. and Vargas, L. (1997) 'Ambiente y salud en Xochimilco: Una aproximación cualitativ', *Estudios de Antropología Biologica*, vol VIII, pp393–421.

19 Jusidman, C. and Eternod, M. (1994) *La Participación de la Población en la Actividad Económica en México*, INEGI-IISUNAM, Mexico.

20 See Note 6.

21 Complete details of the study methodology for the middle-income households are given in Izazola and Marquette (1995), see Note 6; see also Note 18.

22 Coe, M. (1964) 'The Chinampas of Mexico', *Scientific American*, vol 211, pp90–98; also Outerbridge, T. (1987) 'The disappearing Chinampas of Xochimilco', *The Ecologist*, vol 17, no 2–3; and Moncada, O. (1982) 'Evolución y problemas actuales

de la zona de chinampas del distrito federal', *Boletín del Instituto de Geografía*, vol 12, pp211–225.

23 Chapin, M. (1991) 'The practical value of ecodevelopment research', in Oldfield, M. and Alcorn, J. (eds) (1991) *Biodiversity: Culture, Conservation and Ecodevelopment*, Westview Press, San Francisco, CA; also Canabal, B., Torres, P. and Burela, G. (1993) *La Ciudad y sus Chinampa*s, Universidad Autónoma Metropolitana (Xochimilco), Mexico.

24 Moctezuma, P. (1984) 'El movimiento urbano popular Mexicano', *Nueva Antropología*, vol 6, no 24, pp61–88.

25 González, L. and Monterrubio, M. (1992) *Tendencias de la Dinámica y la Distribución de la Población, 1970–1992*, Consejo Nacional de Población (CONAPO), Mexico City.

Chapter 10

Improved Livelihoods in Improved Watersheds in India: Can Migration Be Mitigated?

Priya Deshingkar

Introduction

Contrary to mainstream views on rural livelihoods, a growing number of 'rural' people have lives that are inextricably linked with urban areas. A large number of village studies from different parts of the country conducted in the last five years show a marked increase in temporary migration for work. This includes seasonal migration, circular migration and other forms of short-term migration. While some of these studies are based on resurveys of villages (see for instance the work by Singh and Karan (2001); Karan (2003) in Bihar et al (2003) for Jharkhand) others have used recall to arrive at this conclusion (Rao (2001) for Ananthapur; APRLP (2004) in Khandelwal and Katiyar (2003) for South Rajasthan; and Grameen Vikas Trust (pers comm Meera Shahi) for Madhya Pradesh; Rogaly et al (2001); and Rafique and Rogaly (2003) for West Bengal).

While it is certainly true that people migrate out because there is not enough work locally, interpretations of this phenomenon have varied. The policy and academic discourse has remained rather negative (see, for example, Breman (1985) on migration in Gujarat, and Reddy (1990) on migration in Andhra Pradesh), viewing migration as 'forced' and a symptom of rural distress. However many poor people perceive migration as an opportunity that has opened up to them with improved roads, communication networks and the expanding informal economy, not least because it allows them to escape highly exploitative patron–client relationships[1] in the village. Many erstwhile disadvantaged communities earn far more through migration than they would ever be able to in their own villages (see especially Deshingkar and Start (2003); Deshingkar (2004a and b), Deshingkar and Anderson (2004), Deshingkar and Grimm (2004), Karan (2003), Rao (2001)).

Note: Reprinted from *Watershed Management Challenges: Improved Productivity, Resources and Livelihoods*, Sharma, B. R., Samra, J. S., Scott, C. A and Wani, S. P., copyright © (2005) with permission from International Water Management Institute, New Delhi.

An interesting dimension is the relationship between agriculture, natural resources and migration. A common assumption that underpins many rural development programmes including watershed development programmes is that deteriorating agriculture leads to out-migration, and improving the natural resource base and generating employment in rural areas can reduce or reverse migration. This paper synthesizes the available evidence on migration patterns in watershed development areas and how policy should address continuing migration. The chapter begins with a brief overview of watershed development programmes, in terms of their objectives and coverage. It then provides an overview of watershed evaluation studies that have assessed the impact on migration patterns. Following on from this is a discussion of the factors which cause migration. Finally policy recommendations are presented.

Watershed development in India

Currently US$1000 million is invested yearly in watershed development programmes (WSD) that are implemented by a range of Departments at the centre and state level. The Department of Agriculture and Cooperation implements the National Watershed Development Projects for Rainfed Areas (NWDPRA). The Ministry of Rural Development implements the Integrated Wasteland Development Programme (IWDP), the drought prone area program (DPAP) and the desert development program (DDP). The watershed approach has been adopted in other schemes for the development of catchment areas, flood prone areas and control of shifting cultivation in North-Eastern regions. In addition to the Centrally Sponsored Schemes several state governments are also implementing schemes for soil and moisture conservation on watershed lines. There are also a number of donor-funded and research oriented watershed development projects.

The goal of most watershed projects is to increase agricultural productivity through soil and water conservation and rainwater harvesting at the micro-watershed scale. There are effectively three routes through which the rehabilitation and development of water scarce watersheds is expected to contribute to rural development: increased agricultural productivity; improved natural resource conservation; and, more equitable and sustainable management of common property resources.

Halting migration has been an important objective of watershed development programmes

In addition to the above objectives, watershed development aims to increase employment through labour-intensive soil and water conservation. Besides the short-term effects of watershed development on rural employment, there is a widespread belief that if WSD programmes succeed then they will reduce the flow of migration. WSD implementation can affect migration through an increase in short-term employment as well as long-term productivity gains. The evidence indicates that many WSD programmes do succeed in reducing migration rates at least during the implementation phase. For example, a study by the Central Research Institute of Dryland Agriculture (CRIDA) of 37 watersheds located across different agro-ecological zones and managed by a range of different project implementing agencies (PIAs) showed that migration rates had been reduced in nearly all of them and the reduction ranged from 22 per cent in the Ministry of Rural Development (MORD) implemented watersheds to 42 per cent in non-governmental organization (NGO) implemented ones (Sastry et al, 2003). Additional employment generated ranged from 20 days/person/year in government implemented watersheds to 25 days/person/year in NGO implemented ones. This was attributed to the improvement in physical and biological factors: groundwater tables improved by 1.05m in arid, 1.57m in semi-arid and 1.38m in humid areas. The improvement was better in non-government/donor supported PIAs compared with government supported watersheds. Soil erosion and water run-off improved by 25 and 33 per cent. Employment generation improved from 12.5 per cent in arid areas, 25 per cent in semi-arid areas and 21 per cent in humid areas. Another large evaluation of 2000 odd watersheds in Andhra Pradesh by the State Water Conservation Mission between 1998 and 1999 showed that migration declined between 10 and 40 per cent. Other examples are the study by Dilasa, an NGO, in six DPAP WSD programmes in western India launched in 1996, which found a reduction in migration rates (Hanumantha Rao 2000). Similarly the WSD programme in Jhabua, Madhya Pradesh has shown a reduction in migration.

Migration reduction impacts seem to be more marked in intensively treated, NGO managed watersheds during non-drought years as shown by preliminary results from the International Water Management Institute (IWMI) Livestock, Environment and Development Initiative (LEAD) project (Jetske Bouma, pers comm) Only in a handful of cases has a near complete halt or reversal of migration been achieved. Examples include the Indo-German watershed Development Programme in Maharashtra and the Integrated Micro Watershed Development Programme of the N.M. Sadguru Water and Development Foundation in Gujarat where very high migration rates of 78–80 per cent were reduced to a 'trickle' of around 5 per cent. The duration was also reported to have decreased from roughly nine months to two months. While these successes may be testimony to the outstanding performance of the NGO, there may also be exceptional circumstances as in the case of Ralegan Sidhi where heavy expenditure and the importing of water from other areas made it possible (Sastry et al, 2003). Shah's (2001) work in Gujarat also shows that a significant reduction in migration was achieved only in the case of households which had benefited from a substantial increase in irrigation. She also notes that employment gains during the project implementation phase may not be sustained afterwards.

On the whole, the impacts of WSD on long-term migration appear to be disappointing; Shah and Memon's 1999 (quoted in Hanumantha Rao, 2000) study of WSD programmes being implemented in Gujarat since 1995–1996 observed that although employment opportunities had increased, migration rates had not come down. Similarly a recent review of several watershed programmes in Karnataka and Maharashtra conducted by the Centre for Interdisciplinary Studies in Environment and Development (CISED) and the Society for Promoting Participatory Ecosystem Management (SOPPECOM),[2] has concluded that the impact of WSD on livelihoods and on migration and employment patterns has not been as significant as the impact on soil conservation.

If viewed against the stated objective of controlling or reversing migration,[3] this could be perceived as a widespread failure of WSD programmes. But given the state of flux in Indian agriculture and urban areas, it is not surprising that migration has continued or even increased. It is important to understand these trends in the overall development context where strong new 'pushes' and 'pulls' have emerged.

Migration trends

In addition to the villages studies mentioned before, there are plenty of other examples, many of which continue to be regarded as 'anecdotal' and remain undocumented. Project staff and local government officials who are involved in rural livelihood programmes frequently mention the growing incidence of seasonal migration. For example, staff of the Department for International Development (DFID) funded Western Orissa Livelihoods Project estimate that around 300,000 labourers migrate from Bolangir every year. Bolangir is one of the poorest and drought prone districts in the state. Similar numbers have been reported by staff on the Andhra Pradesh Rural Livelihoods Project from Mahbubnagar, a poor and dry district in Andhra Pradesh.

In sharp contrast to the narrative that is developing through micro studies, macro level data sets and studies based on these tend to underemphasize the importance of migration and may even draw the conclusion that population mobility is decreasing. For instance, the 2001 National census and 1999–2000 NSS data show a slowdown in permanent or long-term rural–urban migration rates despite increasing inter-regional inequalities (Kundu, pers comm, 2003). Kundu calculates that rural–urban migration has declined by 1.5 percentage points, even allowing for a decline in the fertility rate, increases in urban boundaries and the emergence of new towns.

The main problem with conventional surveys is that they are unable to capture information related to temporary movement and part-time occupations. This is illustrated very nicely by the Panchmahals study (Shylendra and Thomas, 1995) where the village was supposedly completely dependent on agriculture according to official statistics (98.4 per cent of the households and 97.7 per cent of the labour force reported agriculture as their primary occupation in the National Sample survey of 1993–1994), was actually highly diversified. Roughly 90 per cent of the households were engaged in non-farm activities and migration rates were very high.

It is very likely that short-term migration will continue to increase due to a variety of new pushes and pulls that have become apparent recently. Apart from the constraints in traditional agriculture there are new forces of change such as acute population pressure, commodity price crashes, improved infrastructure and urbanization all of which, as we discuss in the following paragraphs, add to the flow of migration.

The 'push': Declining opportunities in agriculture

Situations of surplus labour arising from the scarcity of cultivated land, inequitable land distribution, low agricultural productivity, high population density and the concentration of the rural economy almost exclusively on agriculture have led to a continuous increase in out-migration. Having little access to land in a predominantly agrarian society leaves the landless with few alternatives to migration. In India 80 per cent of the holdings are now small and marginal and per capita net sown area is less than 0.2ha.

Drought

Drought is the classic push affecting a growing number of people which exacerbates the problems described above. Nearly two-thirds of the arable land in India is rainfed and low potential and this is where the effects of drought are most severe. Natural drought is exacerbated by manmade drought: groundwater exploitation in western and southern India has reached unsustainable limits (see several reports by IWMI).

A majority of the villages in the dry areas stretching across eastern Maharashtra, eastern Karnataka, western Andhra Pradesh and southern Madhya Pradesh, have very high rates of migration. A typical case is the drought prone Mahbubnagar district in Andhra Pradesh which has had high migration rates for several decades. It is now well known for the legendary *Palamur* labourers who work in construction all over India. The neighbouring district of Ananthapur is also highly drought prone and is one of the poorest districts in India. There too seasonal migration has become routine (Rao, 2001). In a study in Madhya Pradesh Deshingkar and Start (2003) found that more than half the households in four out of six study villages had migrating members. The proportion was as high as 75 per cent in the most remote and hilly village with infertile soils. In Andhra Pradesh, while average migration rates were lower, the most remote and unirrigated village had 78 per cent of the households with migrating members. Similarly a study by Mosse et al (1997) of the first phase of the DFID funded Western India Rainfed Farming Project (Madhya Pradesh, Gujarat and Rajasthan) revealed that 65 per cent of households included migrants. Another later study in the same area found that in many villages up to 75 per cent of the population is absent between November and June (Virgo et al, 2003). The dry areas of Bihar, Orissa, Gujarat and West Bengal are also known for high migration rates. Bolangir, a very poor and drought-prone district in Orissa, is a striking example. An estimated 60,000 people migrated out during the 2001 drought (Wandshcneider and Mishra, 2003) alone and as mentioned before current informal estimates are in the region of 300,000. The situation in the arid Panchmahals district of Gujarat (Shylendra and Thomas, 1995) is similar where seasonal migration was so high that 44 per cent of the labour force was migrating and the average number of persons migrating from each household was 2.2 including women.

The situation in most of the backward and dry areas of India (nearly two-thirds of the country) is increasingly resembling this because of the low levels of diversification and deteriorating access to common property resources.

Poor mountain and forest economies

Out-migration has also been historically high from poor mountainous areas which suffer similar problems of low agricultural productivity, poor access to credit or other prerequisites for diversification and high population densities. A recent increase in migration has been reported from Uttaranchal by Mamgain (2003) as the fragile mountain ecosystem cannot support increasing populations. The poor mountainous districts of Nepal also have high rates of out-migration (Bal Kumar, 2003). More or less the same factors create a push from many forested areas where population pressure has increased and common property resource (CPR) based livelihoods have become unsustainable. A study on linkages between the degradation of CPRs, and out-migration in arid and semi-arid regions by Chopra and Gulati (2001) found a significant positive relationship between land degradation[4] and out-migration. The very high rates seen from forested tribal areas of Madhya Pradesh are an example of this.

Other push factors

The most recent push factor appears to be a fall in agricultural commodity prices brought about by macroeconomic reforms linked with liberalization and globalization policies. Fresh evidence of this has emerged across India. For example, recent research by Ghosh and Harriss-White (2002) in Birbhum and Bardhaman districts of West Bengal suggests that paddy producers are facing heavy losses as prices fell sharply by over 50 per cent since 1999. This situation was created by the reduction of subsidies as well as the de-restriction of inter-state transport which has allowed cheaper paddy to come in from Bihar, as well as from Jharkhand and Orissa where distress sales were occurring. Another example is that rubber prices fell to a third of what they used to be five years before because of cheap imports. This has adversely impacted on the 900,000 rubber growers in Kerala of whom 90 per cent are small farmers with less than 2ha of land.[5] Similar stories are being reported about tea, groundnuts, rice and many other commodities that were previously remunerative. But there are few other academic studies in this area because it has emerged very recently. Press coverage however, has been extensive.[6] More research is urgently needed in this area.

The 'pull': New opportunities in urban-based industry and services

In the 1950s, development economists viewed the demand for labour created by 'growing modern industrial complexes' and the gap in rural and urban wages as the main 'pull' factor. There have since been many models and debates on what motivates people to migrate including theories of 'expected' as opposed to actual wage differentials. Other pull factors include the desire to acquire skills or gain new experiences. In the case of voluntary migration of the poor for economic reasons, the wage gap is probably the most important pull and the most important recent determinants of this appear to be urbanization and the spread of manufacturing.

Urbanization

Urbanization has become a major driver of internal migration Rates of urbanization influence rural–urban wage differences: an increase in the demand for labour in urban areas can push up urban wages and increase migration. Rural–urban differences in average incomes increased in many South and East Asian countries during the 1990s, especially in China and fell in most African countries (IFAD, 2001; Eastwood and Lipton, 2000). Current Economic and Social Commission for Asia and the Pacific (ESCAP) projections are that urbanization rates in South and south-west Asia will soon exceed other regions in Asia (Guest, 2003). This is already beginning to be reflected in the growing importance of rural–urban migration. While rural–rural migration[7] still accounted for roughly 62 per cent of all movements in 1999–2000 according to National Sample Survey data there has been a sharp increase in rural–urban migration recently (Srivastava and Bhattacharyya, 2003) as more young men travel to work in construction and urban services. For example, studies in areas of Bihar that have experienced a doubling of out-migration rates since the 1970s show that migration is now mainly to urban areas and not to the traditional destinations in irrigated Punjab where work availability has declined (Karan, 2003). In dry parts of Gujarat it was seen that urban incomes were so lucrative that not even government employment schemes such as the Jawahar Rozgar Yojana (JRY) and irrigation could reduce outmigration.

Will migration in WSD areas continue to increase?

Given the deteriorating situation in heavily populated rainfed areas of the country it is quite possible that migration rates will continue to increase despite efforts to create employment locally.

In addition to the pushes and pulls mentioned previously, there could be other reasons for continuing migration including:

- The additional employment created through watersheds is not keeping pace with population growth (and additional labour availability). For example, an estimated 1 million workers are added to the workforce every year in Andhra Pradesh and it is unlikely that watershed programmes can absorb all of these.
- WSD benefits only richer farmers and excludes the growing population of landless and marginal farmers.
- The labourer/household no longer wishes to pursue a livelihood system based on agriculture.
- Migration has occurred post-WSD because it has improved the asset base of the household and actually *enabled* it to migrate and explore other more lucrative opportunities beyond the village.

This is starting to become apparent in some areas. For example, Reddy et al (2001) in a study of WSD in Andhra Pradesh found an increase in the extent of migration when before and after scenarios were compared in all the watersheds studied except one. Even though significant employment was generated during the project period, migration increased afterwards. Their explanation is that this occurred because labour participation increased consequent to the increased demand for watershed works which was then released into the labour market after completion of the works. Earlier studies on watershed development in Maharashtra (Deshpande and Reddy, 1991 quoted in Reddy et al, 2001) also found the same.

How migration can contribute to poverty reduction and agricultural development

Seasonal migration is often linked to debt cycles and the need for money for repaying debts, covering deficits created by losses in agriculture, or meeting expenditures of large magnitude on account of marriages, festivals, ceremonies etc. Earlier research was very optimistic about remittances being invested in improving agriculture (Oberai and Singh, 1980). Indeed a link between migration money and investment in tubewell irrigation has been suggested by Shah (2004) – in fact earning additional income for developing irrigation facilities has often been reported as the main reason for migration from the dry land regions.

But it is very difficult to separate spending on 'consumption' and 'production' uses at the household level and the two are very interchangeable. Several studies appear to show that consumption needs to take precedence over any investment in productive uses. However, spending on consumption may not be a cause for worry in itself as it can contribute to the overall increase in the well-being of the household through for instance better nutrition, education etc.

On the proportion of remittances in overall household income, it was believed by many scholars for a long time that remittances form an insubstantial part of household income. A major proponent of this theory was Lipton (1980) who based his argument on the widely quoted Indian village studies conducted by the Institute of Development Studies at Sussex in the 1970s (Connell et al, 1976) which estimated remittances at 2–7 per cent of village incomes, and less for poor labourers. However, new evidence suggests that this is not necessarily the case. Deshingkar and Start's (2003) research in unirrigated and forested villages of Madhya Pradesh showed that migration earnings accounted for more than half of the annual earnings from labour. In the more prosperous State of Andhra Pradesh, the overall contribution was much lower but in the village that was in the unirrigated and poor north-western corner, migration contributed 51 per cent of household earnings. Research by Mosse et al (1997) of the first phase of the DFID funded Western India Rainfed Farming Project (Madhya Pradesh, Gujarat and Rajasthan) notes that 80 per cent of cash income in project villages was derived from migration. Even where remittances are irregular and small they may play an important role in reducing vulnerability and improving food security.

Box 10.1 *Migration as a survival or accumulation strategy*

While many studies on migration have tended to emphasize the impoverishing effects of migration they have rarely posed the question of what these households and individuals would have done in the absence of the opportunity to migrate. In Indian writings, the term *distress* migration and migration for survival have often been used; explaining migration by the poor as a response to natural calamities and other shocks (Murthy, 1991; Reddy 1990; Rao, 2001; Mukherjee 2001 who calls it 'distressed' migration). Distress migration has also been noted in a variety of African contexts by the Participatory Poverty Assessments (PPAs) though not necessarily using the same terminology.

But there is compelling evidence showing that the returns from migration can improve over time as migrants acquire more knowledge, confidence and skills; when they can cut out exploitative middlemen and contractors. The concept of *accumulative* migration (Deshingkar and Start, 2003) has been gaining acceptance. Rao's (2001) study of Andhra Pradesh distinguishes between migration for survival and migration for additional income. He observes that people from Rayadurga district were migrating for survival in the 1970s but changed to migration for additional income in the 1990s. Another example is Bihar where earlier studies described distress migration and more recent ones such as the one by Karan (2003) describe migration in much more positive terms. In the PPAs synthesized in Voices of the Poor (Narayan et al, 2000) migration was identified by both men and women as an important factor leading to upward mobility: the importance of migration was greatest in Asia, followed by Latin America and the Caribbean and less so in Africa.

When migration is bad for WSD

A reverse relationship between migration and watershed development has also been shown to exist where migration adversely affects the incentives for community resource management and participation. Concern has also been expressed in the past over the potentially detrimental effects of out-migration on the productivity of sending areas due to the depletion of labour. While some studies have certainly shown a worsening of poverty levels due to the large-scale male dominated migration as in remote areas of Nepal and Africa, more recent research has shown that some of these impacts may be offset in situations where wages in the destination are high and remittance and communication mechanisms are improving as in several parts of India, Southeast Asia and China.

An important implication of livelihood diversification is that natural resource-based activities may become part-time and this could have negative consequences particularly for participatory resource management such as watershed and community forestry programmes. Those who are away for long periods of time may not be able to participate in community activities and decision making and their access to resources may be compromised. Adverse effects of migration on watershed development have been documented by Turton (2000) and *Samuha* in Karnataka. Also, in a recent conference on common property resource management,[8] a session was devoted to discuss the adverse impacts of migration on the management of common resources such as forests, water and pasture lands (pers comm, Jetske Bouma, Rahman 2004; Reyes Morales and Pacheco, 2004; Lopez, 2004).

Policy implications, knowledge gaps and research needs

The present review shows that the WSD-migration link has been addressed by only a few researchers and that too indirectly. Not many have examined the relationship in its entirety: the (positive) effect of additional income; the (negative) effect of labour depletion and reduced collective action and the effect of changing preferences and household behaviour.

What the examples and possibilities illustrate is that the relationship between watershed development and migration is complex and by no means straightforward. In fact any assumptions to that effect are not only inaccurate but could also be damaging by leading to erroneous policy prescriptions. It is therefore important to be able to understand exactly what is likely to occur in particular contexts. Given the increases witnessed recently in migration rates, and the associated increase in the proportion of household income derived from migration, this merits some serious study; a need that has also been noted by other researchers in the field (see, for example, Shah, 2001).

In this, attention needs to be paid to the broader context in which changes are taking place. India is currently going through a transition from an economy that consisted of very large numbers of viable small and marginal farms to one where the structure of agriculture and industry is changing rapidly in response to globalizing forces, environmental limits and stresses and population pressure. While new industries and informal sector jobs have emerged in urban areas creating a considerable pull for poor labourers, a stronger push is also being experienced in many rural areas with land fragmentation, drought, groundwater scarcity and falling agricultural commodity prices.

It is very likely therefore that the increases in productivity that are brought about by WSD may not be sufficient alone to stem the tide of migration. A few studies have begun to observe this; for example Reddy et al (2004) document that watershed development alone is not a *sufficient* condition for sustaining rural livelihoods.

Probably the most important implication for policy is to recognize that migration will continue and this does *not* represent a failure of WDPs. Migration should be viewed as an inevitable part of unequal regional development and although not the perfect way of providing employment to the poor in rainfed farming it is arguably an important mechanism by which the fruits of agricultural development in more prosperous areas are redistributed. There is therefore an urgent need to understand how WSD can become a part of efforts to support more diverse livelihood portfolios where a win–win situation can be created say, through improving the resource base which creates a more conducive environment for investing remittances leading to an overall increase in growth, employment and poverty reduction.

Since roughly 66 per cent of the arable land area in India is limited to dryland agriculture due to climatic factors, soil erosion, poor water retention capacity etc and it is in such areas where migration and watershed development appear to overlap heavily, it is time to find a way of creating a win–win situation where migration is viewed as a viable livelihood option and WSD programmes are designed with that in mind. Therefore plans for participation need to take into account that part of the population will be absent for periods of time. This creates a different requirement in terms of who is represented in local village institutions and who is given what role in local resource management. The gender implications may be greatest especially where male out-migration is high. It also raises the issue of what the goals of WSD should be – creating an improved natural resource base may actually enable more people to migrate.

Mobility and the positive impacts of remittances are being viewed as an important route to poverty reduction and economic development in Southeast Asian and East Asian countries such as Indonesia, Vietnam, Cambodia and China (Deshingkar and Grimm, 2004). Temporary migrants represent much untapped potential in India too and the time is ripe to start thinking about ways of mainstreaming migrant support programmes and migrant incomes into rural development programmes such as watershed development.

Notes

1   Although many Marxist analysts such as Olsen and RamanaMurthy have argued that migrant employment contracts are equally exploitative, the bargaining power of labourers has increased significantly where the availability of work has increased vis-à-vis the labour pool.

2   Report of the workshop is available at www.cised.org/research_programmes.htm.

3   See, for example, the report of the Working Group on Watershed Development, Rainfed Farming And Natural Resource Management for the Tenth Five Year Plan.

4   Land degradation was measured through increases in the proportion of sheep and goats in total livestock. Out-migration was measured through increased sex ratio (in favour of female). Among other important factors, irrigation was found to have a significant negative impact on out-migration.

5   India is the fourth largest producer of rubber in the world. www.hinduonnet.com/thehindu/thscrip/pgemail.pl?date=2002/05/19.

6   Several articles have been published in *The Hindu* a respected English newspaper in India, particularly by P. Sainath, an internationally recognized journalist writing on drought, poverty and migration who is known for his book *Everybody Loves a Good Drought*.

7   Workers from backward states like Bihar, Uttar Pradesh, Orissa and Rajasthan routinely travel to the developed green revolution states of Maharashtra, Punjab and Gujarat for the transplant and harvesting season.

8   The bi-annual conference of the International Association for the Study of Common Property (IASCP), 9–13 August 2004 in Oaxaca, Mexico.

References

APRLP (2004) 'Role of migration in people's lives. A qualitative study of four villages in Maha-boobnagar and Anantapur districts', Project Support Unit, Andhra Pradesh Rural Livelihoods Project, Hyderabad

Bal Kumar, K. C. (2003) 'Migration, poverty and development in Nepal Ad Hoc Expert Group Meeting on Migration and Development', Ad Hoc Expert Group Meeting on Migration and Development, organized by the Economic and Social Commission for Asia and the Pacific, Bangkok, 27–29 August

Breman, J. (1985) *Of Peasants, Migrants and Paupers: Rural Labour Circulation and Capitalist Production in West India*, Oxford University Press, Oxford

Chopra, K. and Gulati, S. C. (2001) *Migration, Common Property Resources and Environmental Degradation: Interlinkages in India's Arid and Semi-arid Regions*, Sage Publications, New Delhi

Connell, J., Dasgupta, B., Laishley, R. and Lipton, M. (1976) *Migration from Rural Areas: The Evidence from Village Studies*, Oxford University Press, Delhi

Dayal, H. and Karan, A. K. (2003) *Labour Migration from Jharkhand*, Institute for Human Development, New Delhi

Deshingkar, P. (2004a) 'Rural–urban links in India: New policy challenges for increasingly mobile populations', Paper presented at World Bank Rural Week 2 March, Washington, DC, Session on Rural–Urban Change 'Ditching the Dichotomy: planning and development based on understanding continuous rural and urban space'

Deshingkar, P. (2004b) 'Understanding the implications of migration for pro-poor agricultural growth', Paper prepared for the DAC POVNET Agriculture Task Group Meeting, Helsinki, 17–18 June

Deshingkar, P. (2004c) 'Livelihood diversification in developing countries', Hot Topic Paper, DCD/DAC/POVNET/A(2004)5/RD2, POVNET Agriculture Task Team Consultation, Organisation for Economic Co-operation and Development, Development Assistance Committee

Deshingkar, P. and Anderson, E. (2004) 'People on the move: New policy challenges for increasingly mobile populations', *Natural Resource Perspectives*, no 92, June, Overseas Development Institute, London

Deshingkar, P. and Grimm, S. (2004) 'Internal migration: An update', Paper commissioned jointly by the Urban and Rural Change and Migration PD Teams of DFID, London

Deshingkar, P. and Start, D. (2003) 'Seasonal migration for livelihoods, coping, accumulation and exclusion', Working Paper no 220, Overseas Development Institute, London

Deshpande, R. S. and Reddy, V. R. (1991) 'Differential impacts of watershed based technology: Some analytical issues', *Indian Journal of Agricultural Economics*, vol 46, no 3, pp261–269

Eastwood, R. and Lipton, M (2000) 'Rural–urban dimensions of inequality change', Working Paper 200, World Institute for Development Economics Research, Helsinki

Ghosh, P. K. and Harriss-White, B. (2002) 'A crisis in the rice economy', *Frontline*, vol 19, no 19, pp14–27

Guest P. (2003) 'Bridging the gap: Internal migration in Asia, Population Council Thailand', Paper prepared for Conference on African Migration in Comparative Perspective, Johannesburg, South Africa, 4–7 June

Hanumantha Rao, C. H. (2000) 'Watershed development in India, recent experience and emerging issues', *Economic and Political Weekly*, 4 November, pp3943–3947

IFAD (International Fund for Agricultural Development) (2001) *Rural Poverty Report 2001: The Challenge of Ending Rural Poverty*, Oxford University Press, Oxford

Karan, A. (2003) 'Changing patterns of migration from rural Bihar', in Iyer, G. (ed) *Migrant Labour and Human Rights in India*, Kanishka Publishers, New Delhi, pp102–139

Khandelwal, R. and Katiyar, S. (2003) *Aajeevika Bureau. An Initiative to Upgrade Labour and Migration Opportunities for the Rural Poor in South Rajasthan Sudrak*, 283 Fatehpura, Udaipur Rajasthan

Lipton, M. (1980) 'Migration from rural areas of poor countries: The impact on rural productivity and income distribution', *World Development*, vol 8, p227

Lopez, R. (2004) 'Impacts of migration on social capital and community forest management', Paper presented at the bi-annual IASCP conference in Oaxaca, Mexico, 9–13 August

Mamgain, R. P. (2003) 'Out-migration among rural households in Uttaranchal: Magnitude and characteristics', *Labour and Development* (special issue on migration), vol 9, no 2, pp259–287

Mosse, D., Gupta, S., Mehta, M., Shah, V. and Rees, J. (1997) 'Seasonal labour migration in tribal (Bhil) Western India', Report to DFID-India, New Delhi, KRIBP Working Paper, Centre for Development Studies University of Wales, Swansea

Mukherjee, S. (2001) 'Low quality migration in India: The phenomena of distressed migration and acute urban decay', Paper presented at the 24th IUSSP Conference, Salvador, Brazil, August

Murthy, R. R. V. (1991) 'Seasonal labour migration in semi-arid areas: A case study of palamuru labour', MPhil Dissertation, Department of Economics, University of Hyderabad, Hyderabad

Narayan, D., Chambers, R., Shan, M. K. and Petesch, P. (2000) 'Voices of the poor: Crying out for Change', World Bank Report, Oxford University Press, New York

Oberai, A. and Singh, H. K. (1980) 'Migration, remittances and rural development: Findings of a case study in the Indian Punjab', *International Labour Review*, vol 119, no 2, pp229–241

Olsen, W. and Ramanamurthy, R. V. (2000) 'Contract labour and bondage in Andhra Pradesh (India)', *Journal of Social and Political Thought*, vol 1, no 2, www.yorku.ca/jspot

Rafique, A. and Rogaly, B. (2003) 'Internal seasonal migration, livelihoods and vulnerability in India: A case study', Paper presented at Regional Conference on Migration Development and Propoor Policy Choices, 22–24 June, Refugee and Migratory Movements Research Unit, Dhaka

Rahman, A. (2004) 'Migration and demographic change in the context of commons management in Bangladesh', Paper presented at the bi-annual IASCP conference in Oaxaca, Mexico, 9–13 August

Rao, G. B. (2001) 'Household coping/survival strategies in drought-prone regions: A case study of Anantapur district, Andhra Pradesh', India SPWD-Hyderabad Centre

Reddy, D. N. (1990) 'Rural migrant labour in Andhra Pradesh', Report submitted to the National Commission on Rural Labour, Government of India

Reddy, V. Ratna, M, Reddy, G., Galab, S., Soussan, J. and Springate-Baginski, O. (2004) 'Participatory watershed development in India: Can it sustain rural livelihoods?' *Development and Change*, vol 35, no 2, pp297–326

Reddy, V., Ratna, M., Reddy, G., Galab, S. and Springate-Baginski, O. (2001) 'Watershed development and livelihood security: An assessment of linkages and impact in Andhra Pradesh, India', Draft report, CESS/University of Leeds, Leeds

Reyes Morales and Pacheco, A. (2004) 'Common resource use in Oaxaca, Mexico, related to international migration, social capital and production', Paper presented at the bi-annual IASCP conference in Oaxaca, Mexico, 9–13 August

Rogaly, B., Biswas, J., Coppard, D., Rafique, A., Rana, K. and Sengupta, A. (2001) 'Seasonal migration, social change and migrants rights, lessons from West Bengal', *Economic and Political Weekly*, 8 December, pp4547–4559

Sastry, G., Reddy, Y. V. R. and Prakash, O. (2003) 'Impact of watershed management practices on sustainability of land productivity and socio-economic status (ROPS-14&14A)', National Agricultural Technology Project, Central Research Institute for Dryland Agriculture (ICAR), Hyderabad

Shah, A. (2004) *Land Degradation and Migration in a Dry Land Region in India: Understanding the Dynamics*, Gujarat Institute of Development Research, Ahmedabad

Shah, A. (2001) 'Water scarcity induced migration: How far watershed projects can help?' *Economic and Political weekly*, vol XXXVI, no 35

Shah, A. and Memon, G. (1999) 'Watershed development project in Gujarat: A quick review' (mimeo), Gujarat Institute of Development Research, Ahmedabad

Shylendra, H. S. and Thomas, P. (1995) 'Non-farm employment: Nature, magnitude and determinants in a semi-arid village of Western India', *Indian Journal of Agricultural Economics*, vol 50, no 3, pp410–416

Singh, M. and Karan, A. K. (2001) *Rural Labour Migration From Bihar*, Institute For Human Development, New Delhi

Srivastava, R. and Bhattacharyya, S. (2003) 'Globalisation, reforms and internal labour mobility: Analysis of recent Indian trends', *Labour and Development* (special issue on migration), vol 9, no 2, pp31–55

Turton, C. (2000) 'Enhancing livelihoods through participatory watershed development in India', Working Paper 131, Overseas Development Institute, London

Virgo, K., Yadav, R., Kanugo, Y. and Bond, R. (2003) 'Agriculture or livelihoods? Experiences of practitioners and beneficiaries of the DFID-funded Western India Rainfed Farming Project', *Tropical Agriculture Association Newsletter*, vol 23, no 3, pp13–17

Wandschneider, T. and Mishra, P. (2003) 'The role of small rural towns in Bolangir District, India: A village-level perspective NRI Report No: 2750', DFID-World Bank Collaborative Research Project on the Rural Non-Farm Economy and Livelihood Enhancement, London

Chapter 11

Taking Advantage of Rural Assets as a Coping Strategy for the Urban Poor: The Case of Rural–Urban Interrelations in Botswana

Fred Krüger

Urbanization in Botswana

Botswana is not an ideal model of urbanization processes in Africa. Most of its population of some 1.5 million still live in rural areas and less than one-third were officially classified as 'urban' in 1996.[1] Although the growth rates of Botswana's urban settlements lie between 5 and 10 per cent per year and are among the fastest in sub-Saharan Africa, the cities are still small compared with those in most other African countries. The largest urban settlement is Gaborone, the capital of Botswana, with a population of some 160,000 in 1997. It is followed by Francistown with about 80,000 inhabitants while all other urban centres have less than 30,000 residents.

Urban centres' population growth rates lie well above the rate of natural increase. In Botswana's cities, there is some evidence that the rates of natural increase are not above the national average. For the country as a whole, mortality rates are almost similar in rural and urban areas but the Total Fertility Rate in urban regions is significantly lower than in rural areas.[2] Thus it must be assumed that urban growth is still largely due to in-migration from rural areas. This is especially true for Gaborone. Gaborone was designed on the 'drawing-board' in the early 1960s to become the capital of the newly independent Botswana. Under colonial rule, only a small British police camp and a railway station existed on the site of the future capital. Almost all of the population of new Gaborone consisted of people from rural villages who came to look for lucrative jobs on one of the numerous building sites of the evolving capital. After all of the capital's necessary infrastructure had been set up, the migration streams did not subside. One major push factor for the migrants to leave the rural areas has always been the

Note: Reprinted from *Environment and Urbanization*, vol 10, no 1, Krüger, F., 'Taking advantage of rural assets as a coping strategy for the urban poor: The case of rural–urban interrelationships in Botswana', April, copyright © (1998) with permission from IIED, London.

threat of drought, to which Botswana is extremely susceptible, and, before government relief programmes were established, the risk of famine was high. When designing the capital, the planners had estimated that Gaborone's final size would reach around 20,000 inhabitants in 1990. This figure was reached in 1970 and today, it is more than eight times this figure. The continuous flow of people to Gaborone has led to an average increase of its population of about 8 per cent a year.[3] The likelihood of a food crisis has been mitigated by the relief programmes but drought still threatens the economic basis of rural dwellers and continues to be one of the causes of extensive rural–urban migration.

In Gaborone, most migrants from rural villages move to degraded housing areas which show signs of slum or squatter existence, mainly to Old Naledi in the southern part of the city. Feddema described the residents of these areas as 'small farmers, herdsmen and unwed mothers'.[4] While perhaps too condensed a summary, since many in-migrants have found work in town, and many were or have become husbands or wives, Feddema's statement clearly indicates both the former and the current socio-economic background of many urban households in Botswana. As will be shown below, a considerable number of these households continue to engage in farming activities even when working in the formal or informal urban employment sector on a more or less regular basis. A lot of migrants still look upon the city only as their second home, their true home being the village where they were born. A survey conducted by the author in 1992–1993 and research carried out by Feddema[5] and others show that this attitude towards the city persists for a very long time after arrival in town and over great distances: most members of urban households who had come to Gaborone or Francistown more than 15 years ago still referred to their village of origin as their first and true home, even if it lay hundreds of kilometres away. Many indicated that they had always planned, and would still like, to move back as soon as possible although they had in fact already been in the city for decades.

When these strong mental links to the countryside persist for so many years, then parts of a traditional, rural value system must have been brought to the city and kept there despite the presence of 'modern', urban lifestyles. How is this preservation of rural attitudes possible and in what ways does it contribute towards sustaining or weakening the urban and rural livelihood systems of these households? These are questions that are considered in this paper. It draws on a survey conducted by the author in Gaborone and Francistown in 1992–1993, with additional field work carried out in 1996. The aim was to analyse the living conditions and survival strategies of vulnerable urban population groups in low-cost, self-help and squatter settlements in Botswana. The empirical part of the survey was carried out in five low-cost/low-income housing areas (Old Naledi, Extensions 31, 32 and 48 and Somerset West) and included semi-structured household interviews. The systematic sample was based on cadastral maps with indicated plot boundaries. Every 15th plot was visited and all households living there were interviewed. Additional households (e.g. living on informal plots not on the maps) and experts were interviewed where appropriate. The overall sample size was approximately 230 out of some 5000 households living in these areas. Although the sample size was rather small, the systematic method used for drawing the sample implies that it is possible to generalize for Old Naledi and even most other urban low-income housing settlements in Botswana.[6]

Preservation of rural lifestyles

There are at least three reasons why rural attitudes are preserved in the cities and close linkages to the home villages of migrants remain present and active for many years:

- Normally, not all family members migrate at once. Usually, only a few members of rural households, mostly men, move initially to the cities.[7] If migrants are married, they may be followed by their spouses and children a couple of years later. In most cases, the household will be divided, with some members of the family remaining in the village and others living on their own in town. Members who have migrated not only face a 'new way of life' in town but must also cope with the fact that the rest of their family, household or clan probably live hundreds of kilometres away. This in itself puts a strain on those who have migrated, making it *desirable* for them to keep in touch with those left behind in the home village. But maintaining strong links with the rural areas is also a *necessity* for the new, urban way of life: although many migrants have moved to the urban centres in order to find employment and send some remittances or goods to their home village, a considerable number of them have difficulties in generating enough income to survive in the cities, let alone to support their families back home. Deprived of direct access to rural in-kind income such as food produced on a subsistence basis, and pushed into an almost entirely monetary market economy, it becomes vital for the new urban residents to have cash available. But it is also extremely beneficial if they can rely on rural assets to safeguard their livelihoods in the cities. When rural assets serve as safety valves for urban dwellers, this is one element of what has often been called 'ruralization' of the African city. This process of ruralization has been described sometimes as something totally new, and assumes that African cities were not under rural influence earlier in the century and have never before been part of intense urban–rural interactions. It must be argued, however, that cities in sub-Saharan Africa have *always* been somewhat ruralized, as will be pointed out in the case of Botswana below. Social groups affected by this process have sometimes been described as 'displaced'[8] or as groups or households living in dual worlds,[9] thus stressing the fact that their true home is neither town nor village or, in other words, that the close linkages to their home village make it impossible for them to become properly integrated into urban society.

- In many African countries the gap between real rural incomes and real urban incomes has narrowed considerably in the last years,[10] thus increasing the necessity for some urban dwellers to fall back on rural assets for their own well-being in town instead of supporting their families in the countryside. This is certainly the case in Botswana, as the author's own findings from a survey conducted in 1992–1993 reveal. By maintaining close ties to the home villages, rural attitudes are nourished and kept alive in the cities despite the existence and influence of what might be called 'typical' urban lifestyles.

- A society which has always been basically rural (in the case of Botswana one which has always been a cattle-breeding society) and which experiences urbanization and the emergence of cities as something very new will always value rural lifestyles as natural and obvious even in urban surroundings which are heavily influenced by

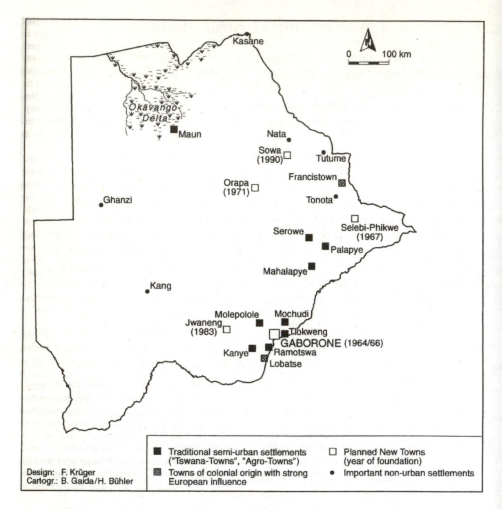

Figure 11.1 *Botswana: Urban settlement types by origin and function*

westernized or globalized conditions. In Botswana, cities in a modern sense are very young. Only two towns, Francistown and Lobatse, date back to colonial British influence (see Figure 11.1). Most of the urban settlements in Botswana were founded as new towns in the 1960s, 1970s and 1980s. The traditional, pre-colonial Tswana settlements were large villages with often more than 10,000 inhabitants. These settlements are often referred to as 'agro-towns' in the literature[11] and they had not only had housing functions and were centres of agricultural activities but also served as commercial and political nodes for large regions. From some of these Tswana settlements, the chiefs exercised control of their states. The agro-towns were functionally divided into overlapping economic, social and administrative units (wards), and the pattern of their socio-spatial differentiation was based on social rank, kinship and tribal membership and showed clear traits of contemporary intra-urban structures. These ward divisions are still recognizable today and most functions have remained intact. The agro-towns acted and still act as growth centres and sources of diffusion and, in general, combined a lot of functions which, today, we would possibly divide into 'rural' and 'urban'. Many of these agro-towns are now officially classified as 'urban' and serve as primary or secondary centres within the settlement system of Botswana[12] but a clear definition as 'city' from a geographical viewpoint remains impossible because many rural elements are still present, too. With the structure and functions of these agro-towns as part of its culture, Tswana society – which has been confronted with what we call urbanization only for the last few decades – still easily preserves traditional rural attitudes and a rural value system under modern urban conditions.

The transition from rural to urban life in Botswana

But what exactly happens to rural lifestyles when migrants move to the city? What are the 'modern' urban conditions these migrants confront? Larsson[13] has argued that in Botswana many of these changes take place in the housing context. She developed a set of keywords to describe different aspects of traditional and modern housing in order to gain a better understanding of the transformation process relating to rural–urban migration. However, a focus on housing alone is not sufficient to explain the transition from rural to urban life. In a society where livelihood systems are under constant threat from drought, entitlement declines, health hazards etc, variables which describe income-generating activities and the provision of food must be considered as well. Figure 11.2 illustrates some of the variables under change. It must be pointed out, however, that the keywords presented form the extremes of a continuum. Many intermediate stages of the transition process are possible and – in the case of the agro-towns – likely.

The figure shows three major spheres: the cultural, social and economic setting; the use of space; and the elements of housing and income provision. Characteristic attitudes, gender issues and lifestyles mingle with the socio-economic variables. It becomes clear that monetarization and commodification are probably the most important features of the rural–urban transition. Attitudes towards the use and function of space also change significantly. As space is scarce in the overcrowded low-income housing areas in the cities, a lot of privacy is lost and the use of space for one's individual needs is usually limited to a few square metres. Many activities that traditionally take place outside (for example, cooking, chatting, etc) have to be shifted indoors (where there is not much room either) and a trait of African lifestyle which Larsson summarized as 'outdoor living' is lost.

One important element of the cultural, social and economic context is that of identity. As mentioned earlier, migrants often lack a clear definition of what is their home. Many will refer to the villages of their ancestors as their home village even though they moved away long ago and have lived in town for decades.

Another key variable is the housing issue, which represents the transition process very well. In the rural context a dwelling is always an integrated part of the household. To sell a house or a plot of land or to rent out accommodation is usually unheard of. There is also a clear definition of shared responsibilities when constructing or maintaining

Rural areas  Urban areas

Cultural, social and economic context

Mainly traditional rural setting	Mainly modern urban setting
Subsistence economy	Market (cash) economy
Indigenous knowledge system	Knowledge system based on transferred technology
Custom law	Official legal system
Village identity	No clear identity
Dwelling integrated part of household	Dwelling regarded as commodity

Use of space

Mainly outdoor living	More indoor living
Lots of space	Limited space
Space may be used according to one´s needs	Space can rarely be used according to individual needs
Much privacy, dwelling for owner´s household only	Little privacy, dwelling often includes rooms for tenants

Housing, provision of food and income

Housing

Household has much knowledge of constructing a house and lots of influence on its design	Household has little knowledge of constructing a dwelling and little influence on its design
Low building costs because of use of natural materials	High building costs because materials have to be purchased
Time and manpower most important resources	Money most important resource
Women and men build houses	Men build houses

Income-generating activities

Agricultural activities, mainly cattle-breeding and small-scale subsistence farming	Activities based on cash economy, often in informal sector, some subsistence home gardening
Mainly regular, periodic activities	Often irregular, temporary or casual activities
Extremely vulnerable to drought events	Some vulnerability to drought
Most food is produced	Most food must be purchased

Sources: Larsson, 1990; Krüger, 1997, altered

Figure 11.2 *The transition from rural to urban life in Botswana: Housing and income generating activities*

a dwelling. Both men and women collect materials and engage in the construction of the house but it is the task of women to keep the housing compound in good repair and to take care of the *lolwapa*, an open space in front of the huts which is surrounded by a low, often richly decorated mud wall serving as outdoor kitchen and living room. In the urban context, households are often separated and clear gender definitions and responsibilities break up. Dwellings are mostly built and maintained by men alone. Rooms or shanties are frequently rented out, dwellings become a commodity for which money has to be paid and cash income be provided.

A detailed analysis of the living conditions in low-income urban housing areas in Botswana showed that over 40 per cent of the sample households had to pay rent for their dwellings – even for temporary shelters and backyard shacks made from cardboard, plastic or corrugated iron sheets.[14] Renting out temporary dwellings for cash is something almost never encountered in rural areas of Botswana.[15] The rent absorbed so much of their cash income that one-fifth of these households were left with practically no money for food or clothes. Up to 15 per cent of the landlords, on the other hand, had no cash income other than the little rent they received from their tenants, leaving them in the same bleak economic state as their lodgers.

The transition from subsistence to cash economy and the need for a monetary income particularly relates to access to food. Food entitlements in Botswana are above all a question of having cash available. Although Botswana's domestic food grain production is low, and more than two-thirds of the annual grain requirement has to be imported,[16] there has never been a critical supply shortage in recent years due to very efficient drought relief programmes. These relief measures (employment schemes, feeding programmes etc) focus on rural areas where some additional food can be produced on a subsistence basis. In the cities, however, there are neither drought relief schemes nor enough possibilities for growing food. This does not mean that people in rural areas are generally better off than those in urban centres but it implies that a lot more food has to be *purchased* in the cities than in the countryside. Alternatives are scarce: horticultural activities and home gardening, which are often found in urban and peri-urban areas in other African countries, still contribute little towards securing an urban food supply in Botswana. The growing of food by urban households is limited: irrigation is almost impossible due to a lack of water, the fertility of the mostly sandy soils is low, and gardening and the growing of vegetables generally have been of little importance in the traditional Tswana society where cattle-breeding dominates. However, the number of urban home gardens has slowly increased in the past years. Field assessments carried out by the author in 1993 and 1996 revealed that on 5–10 per cent of all plots in low-income housing quarters and site-and-service areas in Gaborone and Francistown home gardens can be found, where a small variety of vegetables (mainly pulses and cabbage) and sometimes maize or sorghum are grown during the rainy season. In all cases, production was for subsistence only and the output was small. In the peri-urban area around Gaborone, some cultivated patches for the market production of vegetables were found but their number is still almost insignificant.[17]

In terms of transition, it must be noted that the (still slow) increase in urban home gardening in Botswana is *not* a classical transfer of rural activities to the cities and therefore does not stand for a preservation of rural lifestyles. As noted above, home gardens have a comparatively small role in traditional Tswana society. Horticulture and home gardening must be seen as an innovation in order to obtain sufficient food rather than as a survival strategy of rural dwellers which is being transferred to urban areas.

The relative unimportance of urban subsistence agriculture makes the purchase of food inevitable. But the necessity to have cash available is aggravated by the fact that food is expensive in Botswana's cities. Apart from a small number of street vendors who sell small quantities of maize, fruit or vegetables, there are hardly any public markets, unlike so many cities on the African continent. This lack of open markets may be explained historically by Tswana society traditions: in pre-colonial and even colonial times, kings (*kgosi*) and village chiefs planned and organized inter-tribal trade while intra-tribal trade activities were often prohibited. Open markets did not exist. Following good harvests, all surplus yields had to be stored for times of drought and crop failure, a simple yet effective survival strategy. If at all, livestock and food were, and often still are, obtained from fellow tribes members by barter.[18] Many of these restrictions have ceased to exist but what may be called the development of a 'trading mentality', or the encouragement of public food marketing, set in relatively late. The small number of open markets and food stalls in the towns today is remarkable. Official efforts to promote open food trade by building market squares and halls have partly failed. In Gaborone alone, two or three market halls built by town planning institutions a couple of years ago to attract food vendors have remained vacant since construction.

Major trade activities have always been dominated by Indians, the British and South Africans, and it is in the branches of South African chain stores and supermarkets where most food has to be purchased. Their assortment of goods meets all 'western' standards but so do their food prices. Cheaper alternatives are not easily found and even the urban poor are often compelled to shop in these supermarkets in order to buy food. Apart from that, prices are not only high but fixed – haggling or buying on credit is impossible. The absence or scarcity of petty markets, which traditionally acted as a survival strategy, now serves to increase the vulnerability of low-income urban households.

Interactions between urban and rural livelihood systems

To manage the change in economic conditions, i.e. the increasing importance of monetary income and assets, most rural-urban migrants have to develop numerous survival strategies. Some of these have been well documented in the literature over the past years and include all kinds of diversification of income-earning opportunities (supplementary cash-earning activities in the informal sector in particular) as well as the formation of new social self-help networks. Many of these coping strategies can be found in Botswana, too; the author's own research findings reveal that more than 50 per cent of all households living in low-income and squatter areas in Gaborone and Francistown are, in one way or another, involved in these activities. Of these, about half of all households interviewed have family members who engage in informal cash earning through vending activities like street hawking. In over 30 per cent of the households women were found brewing and selling beer. Other households offer services such as hairdressing or carpentry. Men often hire themselves out as unskilled builders whenever workers are needed to erect new houses. Women frequently form small neighbourhood groups and engage in what might be called a 'rotating credit association' (*motshelo*): each participant regularly pays a small amount of money into a cooperative 'savings' account', and every weekend one partner is paid out and may use the money to organize a party where beverages (often home brew) and some food are sold. The earning may be kept by the partner so once in a while she has some spare cash available to spend on food or clothes. The variety of these activities is very large. This chapter, however, focuses on the rural–urban interface. If typically rural attitudes and lifestyles are being preserved in the cities, they will certainly contribute in some way to strengthening the livelihood systems of the urban poor.

We have seen that home gardens are one, although not a major, element of urban food security. Much more important are long-lasting rural–urban linkages. In Gaborone alone, some 50 per cent of all low-income urban households maintain pastoral and/or arable farming activities in their former home villages. This is especially true for Old Naledi. This low-income housing area emerged as an informal settlement for workers who were employed during the course of the construction of the new capital. In 1971, it already had about 6000 inhabitants.[19] After some reluctance the government legalized the settlement and began with upgrading measures, mainly a restructuring of plots and an improvement of public sanitation facilities. The living conditions did improve at first, but during the 1980s the settlement began to degrade again. Today, according to official census data, over 20,000 people live in an area not much larger than the original settlement, and the actual number of inhabitants in Old Naledi probably is much higher. The area is over-populated and now shows clear signs of a 'slum' quarter.

In Old Naledi, more than one-third of all household heads are cattle holders (see Table 11.1) and of these, one-third moved to town more than 20 years ago. About half of the Old Naledi households own or have access to a plot of land which is ploughed and cultivated regularly. Overall, about 25 per cent of the households hold both cattle *and* land. The results of the survey show that these numbers also apply to households living in other low-cost housing areas in Gaborone or Francistown.

While some households possess fewer than 15 cows, the average herd size is well over 20 animals (see Table 11.2). The cattle herds are usually kept at grazing-posts (so-called 'cattleposts') which are often situated hundreds of kilometres away from the city. In most cases, herdsmen are hired to look after the cattle and they are usually paid not in monetary terms but 'in kind' (milk and meat). Arable farming is done mostly by family members or relatives in the home village and, occasionally, external workers are employed.

Having to pay herdsmen or other hired persons is a burden for all those urban dwellers who have only small incomes themselves. But the great advantage of these rural

Table 11.1 *Households in Gaborone – Old Naledi: Cattle and land ownership and length of stay in town*

Duration of stay in town	(%)	Still holding land (%)	Still owning cattle (%)
Less than 10 years	37.8	57.1	42.9
10 to 19 years	30.7	52.9	23.5
20 and more years	31.5	37.1	2.9
All households	100.0	47.8	36.9

Source: Own survey 1992–1993

Table 11.2 *Livestock holders in Gaborone – Old Naledi: Size of cattle herds*

Up to 15 animals (%)	16–24 animals (%)	25–34 animals (%)	35 and more animals (%)
25.7	38.4	7.7	28.2

Source: Own survey 1992–1993

assets is that they serve as a safety reserve for the urban poor: if all other means in the city fail to provide enough income or food, then a goat or cow can be slaughtered or sold, or one can fall back on grain and vegetables produced in the home village. The average market price for a cow depends on the actual rainfall situation but is usually in the region of 600–800 Pula (c. US$180–250). If minimum living standards are assumed, then it can be estimated that this sum is sufficient for one person to survive in town for three to six months. A goat may be sold for about 40–80 Pula (US$12–15). Of course, selling livestock means a reduction in assets so it is normally only done when there are no other coping options.

The maintenance of rural–urban linkages and of rural assets as an emergency reserve is almost ubiquitous in sub-Saharan Africa and has been widely reported and documented in literature.[20] However, the fact that migrant households successfully maintain these linkages and rely on them even decades after moving away from the countryside is surprising. There appears to be little correlation between cattle or land ownership and the length of stay in the city. Table 11.1 reveals that access to land seems to decrease over the years but cattle ownership does not. Long-lasting ties also exist over large distances: indeed, the distance between city and home village does not seem to influence the existence of, and access to, rural assets. The case of Gaborone – Old Naledi shows that not only the majority of migrants from neighbouring districts own cattle or land but also the majority of households whose home villages lie in remote parts of the country. Figure 11.3 proves that there is no correlation between the actual migration distance and the number of migrant households who hold cattle or land.

Access to these rural assets is at least a supplementary if not an essential element for securing and stabilizing the livelihood systems of many vulnerable urban households. Without cattle or land, many urban residents would face severe problems of income and food security. The importance of keeping a rural economic base over large distances and long periods must not be underestimated in the context of material safety within a commodified, commercialized and monetarized urban sphere of life. But there is more than just the material aspect of safety. Animal husbandry plays a central role in Tswana society. To own livestock implies reputation and influence in society and the number of cattle in one's possession is directly associated with one's social power. Those who do not own cattle are not without power or influence but those who do are regarded socially with more esteem and respect. This is particularly important in an urban environment where in-migrants are losing some of their social influence and participation because extended family relations are deteriorating over distance and time and social networks are being reconfigured. Particularly in the urban low-income or squatter areas where most migrants settle, cattle ownership helps sustain an individual's dignity and authority in the group. Therefore, to own cattle not only has financial advantages but is also

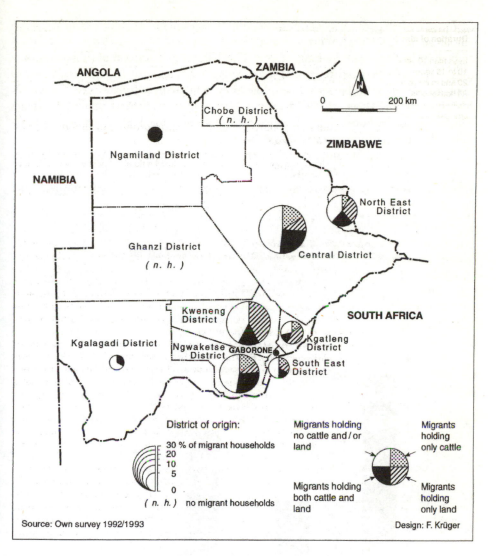

Figure 11.3 *Cattle and land ownership of migrants in Gaborone – Old Naledi*

morally sustaining which, in turn, may have positive effects on well-being because it reduces some of the frustration of having to live in rundown and degraded surroundings with little money or food.

Livestock ownership and land tenure also contribute to strengthening or sustaining urban–rural social links which otherwise would probably decline more easily. An indicator to prove this is the frequency of home visits: urban dwellers who own cattle or land travel home more often than those who do not have any rural assets. Figure 11.4 illustrates the results of a sample taken in Gaborone. It is clear that all migrant households who own livestock or have access to land travel back home on a more or less regular basis. This is in order to look after their cattle or to help with ploughing and cultivating activities. What Figure 11.4 does not show, but which can be concluded from interview samples, is the tendency towards increased home visits and prolonged stays in the rural areas at the beginning of the rainy season. This has led to distinct monthly or seasonal movement cycles between town and home village or cattlepost. In any case, however frequently or seldom these visits take place, they help preserve urban–rural ties which, themselves, must be seen as both a coping strategy in case of urban income shortages and as some sort of buffer network which cushions a probable ineffectiveness, malfunction or disruption of urban social networks.

It may be argued of course that the term 'urban poor' does not apply to cattle owners or land holders. How can an individual or household be termed 'poor' or 'vulnerable' if there are assets and access to emergency reserves? It must be noted, however, that

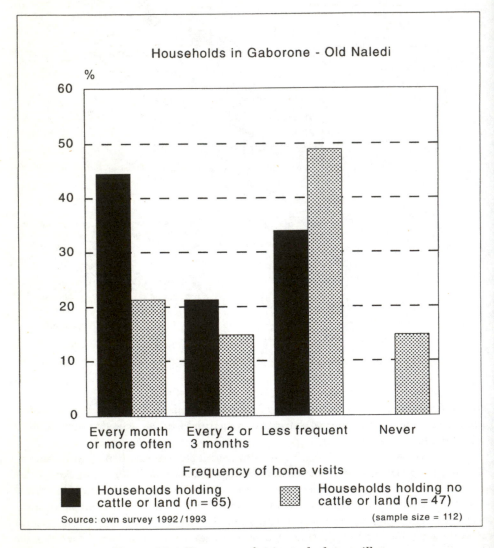

Figure 11.4 *Frequency of visits to the home village*

many in-migrants from rural areas have *nothing else*, that is, no decent dwelling, no regular employment, no balanced food intake, etc. This is the case in most site-and-service ('self-help') and low-income housing quarters in the cities of Botswana. It must also be considered that rural assets are never really safe. On the contrary, arable land and livestock are severely threatened by drought, and cattle or harvest losses do occur frequently. Moreover, in cases of loss, urban residents find it difficult to benefit from government drought relief measures which focus exclusively on rural areas. Unfortunately, the impact of non-urban factors – for example, drought – on urban livelihoods has received little attention in the literature and has as yet not been taken into account when designing drought relief schemes in Botswana. A number of town dwellers who were interviewed stated that a drought related loss of crop yield or livestock would be particularly devastating because it would mean the end of their last potential food or income reserves.

Urban households holding livestock or land may face another entitlement decline if the cattle or landowner dies. In this case – depending on the laws of succession – sometimes the land rights and cattle are not automatically inherited by those left behind but have to be given either to members of the family who still live in the home village or to the village or tribal community. This problem has to be viewed in the context of Botswana's legal system: legal questions are handled by both customary and common law and sometimes there is choice between the two. In practice, customary law is more often employed in rural areas and usually involves all private issues such as matters of inheritance. Whenever legal questions arise about their rural assets, urban dwellers will want to settle the issue according to tribal customary law. In the case of the death of a person who owned livestock or land, the bereaved family members who live in town have to apply to the village headman or tribal chief to regain access to these resources. The necessary negotiations may take one or two years and even after that period may not be successful. It is obvious that women are particularly affected because, according to customary law, they are usually not entitled to inherit a deceased person's property of value, such as cattle,[21] and access to land is also not granted automatically. In the past years, some changes in these customary rules of succession have taken place but, in general, they still leave women in an unfavourable position. If the worst comes to the worst, the bereaved spouse and children have not only lost a family member (and – in terms of urban livelihood systems – an actual or potential provider of cash income) but are also deprived of their last emergency resources.

When the point was made that although households have rural assets they must, in certain cases, still be categorized as vulnerable, this does not mean that there are no other urban social groups in equal or even greater distress. About 45 per cent of all the urban poor have neither access to arable land nor own cattle. In cases of entitlement decline, for example, when income-generating opportunities collapse, family members fall ill etc, these households have no means left for coping. The survey undertaken in Gaborone and Francistown showed that of those town dwellers who cannot secure a foothold in the rural economy or who cannot fall back on urban–rural social networks, about 10–15 per cent must be classified as living under severe risk. The base of their livelihoods is highly unsafe. What is pointed out in this chapter is that functioning rural–urban linkages are an invaluable safety element for many vulnerable groups but they do not guarantee a secure sustenance.

Conclusion

At the beginning of this paper, it was suggested that rural–urban migrants are displaced because they live in two worlds. The transition from rural to urban life expresses itself in many forms and generally includes maintaining rural coping strategies in order to survive in the city. In fact, for those who can successfully preserve ties to their home village and make use of back-up resources, being displaced stands for having the means to survive. The fact that linkages are kept up over decades, that there are regular movement cycles between town and country, and that rural assets are valued both in monetary and in social terms all stress the point that any disruption of these rural–urban interactions may easily become a severe threat to many urban households. At best, their living standards will decrease, at worst they will lose the economic means of surviving in the city.

Whilst the persistence and adaptation of rural–urban interrelations as an integrated part of the urbanization process in sub-Saharan Africa has been widely recognized, their impact on urban livelihoods has received little consideration. In Botswana, most relief and aid measures have been designed exclusively for rural dwellers. There are numerous programmes for so-called 'remote area dwellers', drought affected rural households, smallholders and large-scale commercial farmers but, up to now, only one major scheme (an extensive self-help housing programme) has been set up in support of low-income urban residents. The political implication is that more attention should be paid to the rural–urban interface. To have access to rural assets does not automatically stand for being invulnerable. Further studies have to be undertaken, especially to analyse the negative effects of drought, and drought related damage to rural assets, on urban households. Drought relief programmes have been particularly successful in Botswana (although a number of shortcomings have been revealed in the past years) but if measures were developed to further mitigate the risk of declining incomes after loss of rural assets, this might lead to a considerable reduction in social vulnerability not only in rural but also in urban areas.

Note

1   FAOSTAT Statistics Database (1997) http://apps.fao.org/lim500/nph-wrap.pl? Population&Domain=SUA.
2   VanderPost, C. (1992) 'Regional patterns of fertility transition in Botswana', *Geography*, vol 77, no 335, Part 2, pp109–122; also Diamond, I. and Rutenberg, N. (1995) 'Recent trends in fertility in Botswana', *Journal of International Development*, vol 7, no 1, pp145–161.
3   Census data from Central Statistics Office (1991) *Stats Brief*, no 91/4, Gaborone.
4   Feddema, H. (1990) 'Survival through cooperation in Naledi', *The Botswana Society Occasional Paper*, no 4, Gaborone.
5   See Note 4.
6   The study was funded by the International Geographical Union (IGU) and by the German Research Council (DFG). For a detailed report see Krüger, F. (1997) *Urbanisierung und Verwundbarkeit in Botswana*, Centaurus, Pfaffenweiler.

7   Latest census data in Botswana do not look into migration patterns in detail. These assumptions are based on experts' estimates from the Central Statistics Office in Gaborone and on household interviews carried out by the author in both rural and urban regions of Botswana.

8   *Zeitschrift für Wirtschafts-geographie* (1992) vol 36, no 1–2, special issue focusing on urbanization processes and demographic change in sub-Saharan Africa.

9   Among many others, this term has been used by Gugler, J. (1991) 'Life in a dual system revisited: Urban-rural ties in Enugu, Nigeria, 1961–1987', *World Development*, vol 19, pp399–409.

10   Potts, D. (1995) 'Shall we go home? Increasing urban poverty in African cities and migration processes', *The Geographical Journal*, vol 161, Part 3, pp245–264.

11   Silitshena, R. (1990) 'The Tswana agro-town and rural economy in Botswana', in Baker, J. (ed) (1990) *Small Town Africa*, The Scandinavian Institute of African Studies, Uppsala, pp35–50.

12   See Note 3.

13   Larsson, A. (1990) *Modern Houses of Modern Life*, University of Lund, School of Architecture, Report R1, Lund.

14   See Krüger (1997) in Note 6.

15   For a detailed report on low-income rental housing in the Republic of South Africa and a list of other rental studies, see Gilbert, A., Mabin, A., McCarthy, M. and Watson, V. (1997) 'Low-income rental housing: Are South African cities different?', *Environment and Urbanization*, vol 9, no 1, pp133–147.

16   See Mokobi, K. F. and Asefa, S. (1988) 'The role of the government of Botswana in increasing rural and urban access to food', in Mandivamba, R. and Bernstein, R. (eds) *Southern Africa: Food Security Options*, University of Zimbabwe, Harare; also Ministry of Finance and Development Planning (1992) *Aide Memoire: The Drought Situation in Botswana and the Government Response*, Gaborone (unpublished paper).

17   Small livestock, especially goats and chickens, are of some importance for food security in the peri-urban regions. In the cities they play no role in urban micro-farming.

18   Schapera, I. and Comaroff, J. (1991) *The Tswana*, revised edition, Kegan Paul International, London; also Schierholz, P. (1989) *Bauern im Transformationsprozeß*, Breitenbach Publishers, Saarbrücken.

19   Ministry of Local Government and Lands (1971) Gaborone Planning Proposals, Gaborone.

20   See Note 10; also Vorlaufer, K. (1992) 'Urbanisierung und stadt-land-beziehungen von migranten in primat – und sekundärstädten Afrikas: Dakar/Senegal und Mombasa/Kenya', *Zeitschrift für Wirtschaftsgeographie*, vol 36, no 1–2, pp77–107.

21   The Botswana Society (ed) (1993) *Changing Roles of Women in Botswana*, Gaborone.

Part 5

Beyond the City Boundaries: Peri-Urban Areas and Environmental Issues

Chapter 12

Urban Agriculture in the Metropolitan Zone of Mexico City: Changes over Time in Urban, Suburban and Peri-Urban Areas

H. Losada, H. Martínez, J. Vieyra, R. Pealing, J. Rivera,
R. Zavala and J. Cortés

Introduction

This chapter describes the transformation of agriculture in Mexico City from a conventional rural form to a new urbanized model, as a reaction to urban development and the availability of waste products from the city as well as a response to the demands of recreation and tourism. From this has emerged a new concept of the rural producer or urban farmer who now has access to an urban infrastructure, to education and research. The development of these new production systems has also influenced spatial organization, with the introduction of new crops to meet a changing urban demand. The final part of the chapter looks at the development of these urbanized systems within the context of sustainability.

Historical Aspects of Mexico City's agriculture

The valley of Mexico is made up of many different regions and sub-regions, each with its own distinctive natural conditions and diverse ecological characteristics.[1] It is situated at an altitude of 2429m above sea level, covers 9600 square km and is surrounded

Note: Reprinted from *Environment and Urbanization*, vol 10, no 2, Losada, H., Martínez, H., Vieyra, J., Pealing, R., Zavala, R. and Cortés, J. 'Urban agriculture in the metropolitan zone of Mexico City: changes over time in urban, suburban and peri-urban areas', October, copyright © (1998) with permission from IIED, London.

by a volcanic mountain range. It includes parts of the states of Mexico, Tlaxcala, Puebla, Hidalgo and the federal district of Mexico City. The climate is temperate humid in the south, temperate dry in the centre and the north, with permanent snow in the mountains, and the natural vegetation consists largely of pine forests and grasses.

The first inhabitants of the valley appeared 22,000 years ago and consisted of nomadic groups who were hunter/gatherers.[2] The change to a sedentary population, in approximately 8000 BC, coincided with the introduction of an incipient agriculture.[3] These populations formed the first human settlements (c. 700 BC) and gave rise to highly complex and organized urban environments such as once existed at Teotihuacan. At the beginning of the Christian era, urban structures increased in both number and organization, which led to the formation of important political, economic, religious and administrative urban centres, culminating some time between AD 1200 and 1500 when the greatest cultural changes occurred.[4] At this time, there was an estimated population of 20 million in Mexico.[5] The sustenance of such a variety of urban cultures was undoubtedly related to the complex pattern of intensive agriculture and to the different forms of production that existed. These were closely linked to the environmental conditions and topography of the region. Within this complex agricultural landscape, six models of production stand out:

• the *chinampas* (floating plots) in the wetland zone, a form of intensive agriculture that used silt and human excrement as a source of organic matter;
• slash, fell and burn;
• slash and burn;
• the terraces of the highland zones;
• the family orchard (or kitchen garden);
• the backyard, where a mixed cultivation of maize, vegetables, flowers, fruit, turkeys, ducks and dogs existed.[6]

The conquest of Tenochtitlan by the Spanish in 1524 brought with it fundamental changes for the valley of Mexico, with the incorporation of new species of vegetables, domestic animals and grains, and the introduction of European technologies.[7] These new techniques had an important effect on the ecological conditions of the valley. The growth of mining activities, a new politico-administrative structure and the devaluing of native agricultural technologies were among the factors that had a detrimental impact on the environment. Examples of these impacts include:

• the draining of the system of lakes into one single lake (Xochimilco-Chalco), inevitably affecting the *chinampas*;
• the deforestation and intensification of labour in the highest areas of the valley, restricting the development of the terraces and the slash, fell and burn agricultural systems, and replacing them instead with permanent agriculture.

There were, however, some positive impacts. For example, new species of plants were very successfully introduced (indeed, Mexico has been described as 'an adaptation laboratory for new species'[8]) as were some important species of livestock such as cattle and horses, sheep, goats, pigs and poultry.

Over time, agriculture in the valley of Mexico maintained a mixed form of production that both supplied the urban population and met subsistence needs. There were some basic changes in land tenancy but these did not affect the organization or distribution of goods. During the first half of the 19th century, three major zones of supply could be identified:

- the area to the north and west, where the *haciendas* supplied the urban centre with maize, wheat, barley, beans, potatoes, livestock and their products;
- the area to the east, which supplied maize, wheat, barley, beans, fruit and *pulque* (a partially fermented drink produced from the agave);
- the region to the south of the city, which supplied vegetables, horticultural products and other fresh goods such as meat, milk, butter and cream. This region was also very important as a major producer of *pulque*.[9]

At the end of the 19th and the beginning of the 20th century, within the context of the country's programme of modernization under president Porfirio Díaz, the development of urban or industrial land use was favoured at the expense of the agricultural sector. This resulted in the displacement of agricultural land, the diversion of water for domestic or industrial uses, and the strengthening of the paper, wood and charcoal industry. The exploitation of the forest related to the latter stimulated the development of a new form of agricultural production, the *tlacolol*, made up of small parcels of land within the forest which allowed the seasonal cultivation of maize, beans, squash and chillis, for subsistence use.[10] These models of production, which were supplying the metropolis, prevailed until the middle of the 20th century, at which stage urban growth entered a new phase, bringing about profound changes in the way agricultural activities were carried out in the region.

Expansion of the metropolis and environmental degradation linked to the agricultural sector

The period of the Mexican Revolution (1917–1919) and the Lázaro Cardenas régime (1930s) saw the realization of promises of agrarian reform and support for the development of a rural infrastructure within Mexico. The end of the 1940s saw the Green Revolution[11] and the resulting phase of agricultural prosperity known as 'the Mexican Miracle'. Associated with the success of the Green Revolution was a steady migration from rural areas to the metropolis. As a result, Mexico City began a phase of enormous population growth and developed 'western' aspirations that were to have serious repercussions on the regional models of agriculture. To illustrate this, data available[12] for the period 1940–1980 show an expansion of the urban zone from 11,753ha to 100,000ha, the city's greatest growth since its foundation by the Spanish in 1524. This growth was, undoubtedly, connected to migration and to the demographic explosion that occurred during this period (see Figure 12.1).

In contrast to the major contemporary urban centres in other parts of the world, where vertical development has occurred, the nature of the sub-soils and the high water

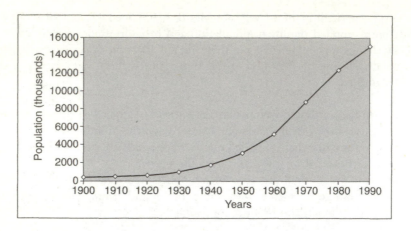

Figure 12.1 *Population growth in Mexico City*

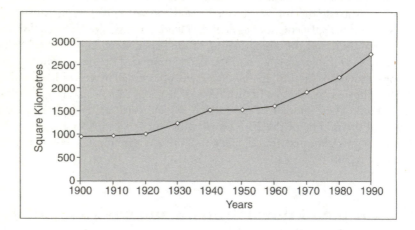

Figure 12.2 *Urban expansion of Mexico City*

table in the valley of Mexico determined that the growth of Mexico City should be predominantly horizontal, occasioning the invasion of agricultural land and rural outskirts that had previously made up a natural 'green belt' around the city. The three previously mentioned zones of agricultural supply were replaced, with the areas to the north and west of the city being developed as industrial zones, and the areas to the east and south being diverted towards housing. The changes that have taken place in this latter area have affected the ancient system of canals and impeded the natural flow of water. This, in turn, has led to the irreversible process of salinization, causing stagnation of the Xochimilco-Chalco lake. The lake's deterioration has been further exacerbated by the diversion of its natural water sources to meet the city's growing need for potable water; also, liquid waste disposal from the expanding urban and industrial zones has increased the concentrations of heavy metals, detergents and pathogenic organisms in the water.[13] These new conditions caused the water hyacinth to flourish, making navigation of the canals difficult and inhibiting the growth of endemic flora. These changes have also substantially altered the land use patterns of the *chinampa* zone. Sensitive crops such as tomatoes have disappeared and the conditions that enabled cultivation could only be maintained with the use of chemical fertilizers, insecticides, herbicides and fungicides, further augmenting the levels of water, soil and air pollution.[14] Furthermore, the paper manufacturers and timber companies, who were located in the adjacent highland zones, have initiated an irreversible process of deforestation leading to extensive areas of erosion. This has been exacerbated by indiscriminate use of the area by city dwellers in their pursuit of 'open space' and countryside activities. The cultivation of *maguey* for the production of *pulqe* has been affected by climatic changes, and the temporal lands where subsistence crops such as maize, beans, wheat etc, were cultivated have been abandoned due to a shortage of water.

At the beginning of the 1970s, a presidential order reclassified the city's administrative and political regions into 'urban' and 'agricultural'. Of the city's 16 political regions, only seven were allowed to develop as agricultural zones.[15] This new classification led to important changes in land prices, with land becoming more valuable for its potential for urban development than for its original agricultural use, thus stimulating the urbanization of any remaining areas of 'green belt'. Within this process of uncontrollable urban growth, livestock production and agricultural activities that had previously taken place in these regions were either displaced (and relocated in neighbouring zones) or engulfed by the urban mass to remain as 'islands' of agriculture within the metropolis (such as the dairies of Iztapalapa[16]). This phenomenon has been strengthened by the creation of large distribution centres where agricultural products from the surrounding states are collected and redistributed within the city. Such centres include the metropolitan food supply depot in Iztapalapa which, constructed on an ancient area of *chinampa*, generates huge quantities of fruit and vegetable waste.

The general effect of urbanization has been the generation of urban pollution as shown in Table 12.1. This has inevitably affected the resources – water, soil and air – and the agricultural environment, reducing the production of traditional crops such as maize. This situation has been compounded by the abandonment of agricultural activity in favour of steady work within the city, leading to a vicious circle of deserted farmland, urban expansion and pollution. The extent of the detrimental effects of these pollutants on humans, animals and plants has not yet been well evaluated. In order to hide the real effects of air pollution, the government produced an awkward system of measurement called the Metropolitan Index for Environmental Contamination (MIEC) based on an arbitrary scale as shown below.

Urban expansion was such that outlying villages became incorporated into Mexico City, forming the concept of a municipal conurbation or metropolitan zone. The metropolitan zone is defined as the area containing the city centre and the political and administrative functions. Its characteristics are typically urban, representing the place of work and residence of non-agricultural workers. The process of urbanization 'burst' the political boundaries of the politically defined federal district and a number of municipalities from the state of Mexico were incorporated into the city, engulfing livestock production, causing the abandonment of other agricultural activities and leading to further deterioration in the environment. The neighbouring regions of these degraded areas, such as what remains of the old lake Texcoco, have started to generate new forms

Table 12.1 *Indicators of air, soil and water pollution*

Air pollution: mean values of air contaminants in the city

Pollutant	MIEC*(one year average)
Nitrogen dioxide	40
Carbon monoxide	47.5
Sulphur dioxide	32.5
Suspended particulates	142.5
Ozone	103.5

* Metropolitan Index for Environmental Contamination. The scale used to express concentration of air pollutants is as follows:

MIEC value	Health effects
100	Good – no danger to health
200	Unhealthy – people with heart/respiratory problems should reduce physical activity
300	Very unhealthy – as for 200; also applies to elderly people
400	Dangerous – healthy people to avoid outdoor exercise
500	Very dangerous – people advised to avoid physical activity and use of vehicles

Mean values of contaminants of soil and water in Xochimilco's lake (which is used for agriculture)

Soil contamination		Water contamination Heavy metals (parts per million)	
		Metal	Mean value
Aluminium	7000ppm	Ferrum	144.25
Mercury	0.90ppm	Copper	11.67
Cadmium	0.49mg/l	Magnesium	3.5
Nickel	13ppm	Zinc	104.18
Chromium	14ppm	Lead	18.61
Lead	5.98mg/l	Chromium	2.77
Zinc	1.28mg/l	Cobalt	4.13
Copper	0.44mg/l	Nickel	2.88
Iron	9000mg/l	Cadmium	0.758

Sources: Departamento del Distrito Federal (1994), *Red de Monitoreo Ambiental de la Zona Metropolitana,*México; also Peralta, M. (1983), *Determinación de algunos metales pesados en suelos agrícolas de Xochimilco,* Tésis de QFB, ENCB, IPN, México; Miramontes, B., Arroyo, L. y J.M. Tarín (1988), *Informe final del proyecto de investigación: estudio edafológico de la zona lacustre de Xochimilco-Tláhuac,* Departamento de Producción Agrícola y Animal, UAM-Xochimilco, México; and Moreno Y., Méndez T., Arana F. and A. González (1995), *Estudio preliminar sobre la concentración de metales pesados en tres de las especies de carpas más importantes en la zona lacustre de Xochimilco: memorias del 2do. Seminario de Xochimilco Tomo II,* México D.F.

Coliforms in water, vegetables and soil of Xochimilco

Source	Faecal coliforms per 100ml	Total micro-organisms per 100ml
Irrigation water	1600	13,000
Vegetables	1000	3200
Soil	1300	100,000

Source: Coutiño, M. (1981), *Evaluación bacteriana en vegetales irrigados con aguas negras en la zona de San Gregorio, Xpchimilco,* Tésis de Biología, Facultad de Ciencias, UNAM, México

of pollution made up of dust and excrement storms (suspended particles). These reached such a level in the 1980s that the government implemented its first 'ecological rescue plan' aimed at eliminating the dust excrement storms and returning the lake to its original role as a habitat for migrating birds. Nevertheless, the urban spread continued, inevitably affecting certain ecosystems (e.g. the forest regions) not only because of building but also because of new uses for these resources as a result of urban demand. Examples include the demand for Christmas trees, the extraction of leaf mulch for use in urban gardens and the collection of firewood for heating wealthy urban homes. This degradation of the forest environment has culminated in a devastating plague of bore worms which, to date, has proved impossible to eradicate.

The local authorities have attempted to stall the process of environmental degradation with ambitious reforestation plans, proposing the use of non-native species such as eucalyptus. However, rather than helping, this policy has accelerated the deterioration of natural habitats with the eucalyptus inhibiting the growth of native vegetation and consuming large quantities of water while failing to fulfil its role in erosion control and timber production.

By the end of the 1980s, the pressures of urbanization and the threats to the traditional agricultural zones were on-going. This was particularly evident in the area of *chinampa* on Xochimilco. Here, the problem was exacerbated by modifications to Article 27, which legitimized the sale of *ejidal* land (lands vested in peasant communities by agrarian reform), which was considered the last vestige of 'green belt' containing the urban spread. A government proposal focusing on 'ecological rescue' and the prohibition of construction in ecologically sensitive areas was their attempt to halt this movement and loss of 'green belt'.[17]

The 1990s marked the end of this stage of urban expansion – checked by economic crisis and a concern to conserve what natural resources remained. The result of this excessive urban growth is reflected clearly in the city environment, where the average area of open space per person is $2m^2$ compared with an international urban average of $10m^2$. During this same stage of urban growth, 73 per cent of the forest area, 99 per cent of the wetlands and 71 per cent of the soil was lost; and it has been calculated that 700ha of agricultural land is engulfed by urbanization every year.[18]

The adaptation of agricultural production to a new environment

In spite of the environmental degradation and expanding metropolis which have put great pressure on the traditional forms of agriculture, the powerful pre-Hispanic antecedent whereby lifestyle and culture are strongly linked to agriculture has ensured the survival of these traditional systems of production. This survival has been reinforced by the relationship between western urbanization and agriculture as illustrated, for example, in the activities of gardening or keeping pets. New ways of using agricultural space have emerged, starting with the creation of a network of socio-economic relations that have had a qualitative impact on regional agriculture. It is within this context that three

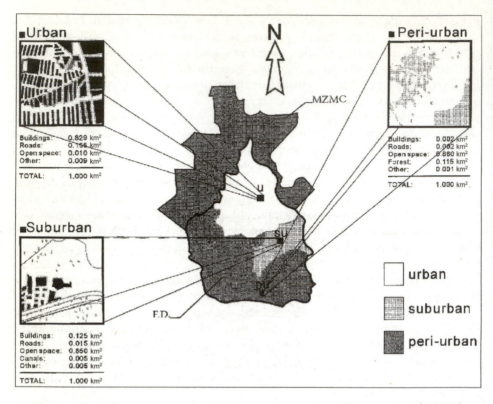

Figure 12.3 *Characterization of the metropolitan zone of Mexico City (MZMC) including the federal district (FD) in terms of land use in an urban, suburban and peri-urban space*

agricultural spaces have been identified: urban, suburban and peri-urban. Figure 12.3 shows the metropolitan zone of Mexico City (MZMC), including the federal district (FD), characterized in terms of the three new land use spaces (indicated as: U, SU and PU). An area of 1km² was randomly chosen from the official street map[19] to illustrate land use characteristics of the new spaces by means of several indicators relating to urban development.

The urban space

The urban agricultural production space is derived from the livestock practices that existed before the process of urbanization. An important characteristic of this model is that the farming systems are framed within the 'urban' concept, with access to infrastructure and public services causing a rise in land prices. The increases in land value occasioned the combination of the home with the processes of production and stimulated an intensification of land use for agricultural purposes. An extension of this is the reversion of urban spaces, for example, using the flat roofs of houses to keep animals and using public gardens and sidewalks for grazing. However, the most important characteristic of the urban model is its foundation on two fundamental premises: first, the availability of vegetable wastes from the city's large markets and food-processing plants as a supplement to the animals' diet; and second, the sustained demand from the local population for the resulting agricultural products. A further consideration is the additional pressures of producing within an urban environment that do not exist within the rural equivalent. This is most clearly illustrated by the problem of agricultural waste, the pressure of disposal of which within the urban environment has, by necessity, led to the development of a 'chain of use' whereby the waste produced by the cattle and pigs of the urban agricultural model is used as a source of organic material in the suburban and peri-urban models of agriculture.[20]

The dominant population in the urban space is a heterogeneous local or migrant one which has maintained its own culture, and the lack of agricultural space has ensured that animals are culturally and socially linked to the human environment. The main systems of this model include backyard livestock with chickens, turkeys, ducks, geese, pigeons, ornamental birds and 'sporting' birds (e.g. fighting cocks), rabbits and pigs; dairy cattle for milk and meat production; a system of pig production derived from conventional mechanized farming systems; and, finally, a system based on the traditional agricultural orchard, the family garden which allows the cultivation of vegetables and herbs, medicinal and ritual plants, and decorative plants. Table 12.2 denotes the presence of livestock in the three different spaces of the MZMC. Actual figures for urban zones are likely to be higher since it is 'illegal' to raise livestock in urban areas and, in some delegations, the census thus tends to ignore their presence. Also, people are likely to under-report the amount of livestock they own for fear of taxes or legal action. It is interesting to note that there is a larger number of hens in the urban space than in the peri-urban one despite the latter's much greater area and thus potential for keeping livestock. This phenomenon confirms the hypothesis discussed above that urban spaces are suitable for livestock production.

The suburban space

A second agricultural production space resulting from the urban environment is the suburban model. Here, the new urban infrastructure has been superimposed upon the original rural setting, forming a new frontier to agriculture. Despite an intensive use of space, derived from the pressures of urbanization, land prices fluctuate between agricultural and urban levels, acting as an indicator of the viability of an agricultural land use. These areas tend to be the 'reception' areas for provincial migrants looking for permanent employment in the city while still retaining ties with their original communities. The result is a multicultural social structure.

The best example of suburban agricultural space is the *chinampa* of Xochimilco, where a traditional form of agriculture has been modified in order to function within a degraded environment. Traditionally used for the production of vegetables and flowers, the *chinampas* are now used for the cultivation of maize in order to meet the demand from the city's inhabitants for *elote* (corn-on-the-cob) and grass turf for use in urban gardens.[21] An alternative is the cultivation of *romero*, a species well adapted to degraded conditions and which reflects the traditional culture of the region (being used in the celebrations of Lent, Day of the Dead and Christmas). Also, the availability of contaminated water and silt and the lack of productivity have led to a system based on

Table 12.2 *Distribution of livestock in the three zones of the metropolitan zone of Mexico City (MZMC) in 1990*

	Cattle	Goats	Pigs	Hens	Turkeys	Broilers	Quails	Rabbits	Beehives	Bullocks	Horses	Mules	Donkeys
Urban zone													
Total	2931	25	1541	132,902	310	101	–	4271	200	10	16	9	24
Mean per delegation/ municipality	420	7	81	10,260	50.5	14	–	264	25	10	8	2	12
SD*	475.7	4.1	445.3	31,331	94.0	30.1	–	962.4	53.5	–	2.8	1.2	15.5
Suburban zone													
Total	6597	209	12,992	411,191	4010	1302	315	9780	2789	49	527	389	248
Mean per delegation/ municipality	3293.5	104.5	6492	162,921	1926	650.3	156.6	4859	1149	24.08	262.4	193	122.5
SD*	256.6	0.7	308.3	177,349	787.7	43.8	23.3	783.5	1117	6.3	34.6	34.6	26.8
Peri-urban zone													
Total	13,591	2042	43,807	189,842	15,500	4682	488	15,101	3738	516	2770	1421	1379
Mean per delegation/ municipality	482.084	111.8	1634	7247.5	698.3	245.3	29.65	763.5	90.09	19.35	115.6	55.37	71.79
SD[a]	1331.4	164.2	3701	25,645	1013	272	32.8	1002	670.2	74.6	278.7	132.2	111.6

Note: [a] Standard Deviation
Source: INEGI (1990) *Censo Agrícola, Ganadero y Forestal,* Instituto Nacional de Estadística, Geografía e Informática, México

greenhouses and market gardens which can respond to increased demand for such goods from the growing middle- and upper-class sectors of the city. These changes in the modes of production have led to a reorganization of the *chinampa* space, allowing traditional systems such as dairy production, backyard production and family orchards to exist alongside new uses of large areas of previously degraded land, thereby improving the quality of life for the local residents.

Another factor influencing the reorganization of the *chinampa* space is the traditional role of Lake Xochimilco as a recreational resource, attracting tourists from both Mexico and overseas. This has led to a new use of the suburban space as a centre of family recreation and as a place to discover nature and the culture lost in the process of urbanization. This combination of tourism and agriculture has provided the impetus for a revitalization of pre-Hispanic and colonial traditions, which is reflected. in the market in Xochimilco where both traditional and consumer goods can be found.[22] In this way, tourism has been responsible for the rescue of ancient forms of production such as the consumption of *mextlapiques* (fish roasted in maize leaves) and also for the stimulation of new forms of production to meet tourist demand such as the cultivation and sale of the Christmas Rose. Finally, it has opened the door for products coming in from neighbouring regions such as the *nopal*-legume and timber products from Milpa Alta.

Table 12.3 shows areas of crop land in the urban, suburban and peri-urban zones. As mentioned above, land available for crops in the urban zone is very scarce, with larger areas being available in the suburban and peri-urban zones. During the spring/summer season, the suburban zone shows larger areas of crop land use than the peri-urban zone.

Table 12.3 *Seasonal use of crop land in the three zones of the metropolitan zone of Mexico City (MZMC) in 1990*

Area (hectares)	Spring–summer	Autumn–winter	Perennial	Not sown
Urban zone				
Total	303,334	6303	2618	25,922
Mean per delegation/municipality	18.4	2.6	1.2	1.6
SD[a]	108.5	2.3	0.5	18.1
Suburban zone				
Total	12,174.8	920.9	739.3	2698.8
Mean per delegation/municipality	1038.6	40.8	68.3	226.8
SD[a]	1232.3	131.6	68.2	268.3
Peri-urban zone				
Total	10,931.5	338.7	12,300.2	3477.5
Mean per delegation/municipality	525.9	17.5	131.3	169.6
SD[a]	2129.5	61.7	4129.7	710.0

Note: [a] Standard deviation.
Source: INEGI (1990) Geneo Agricola, Ganadero y Forestal, Instituto Nacional de Estadistica, Geografia e Informática, México

This is due to the presence of the *chinampas* in the suburban space, which is mainly devoted to vegetable production during the rainy season (May–September). In the peri-urban zone, in contrast, perennial crops constitute the greatest land use.

The peri-urban space

A third agricultural production space is the peri-urban model. This consists of the last remaining rural spaces in the metropolitan zone and, although there is an urban infrastructure and clear indications of an urban influence, there remains a predominantly rural ambience. The meeting of rural and urban has created a new concept of the 'metropolitan village', where a rural way of life is mixed with a city culture. This, in contrast to the suburban model, has allowed agricultural land use to remain sufficiently profitable vis-à-vis urban land use and is due to the existence of a mono-cultural society which has prevailed despite immigration. However, it is clear that the influence of the city has affected the manner of agricultural production. One such change is in the pattern of land tenancy whereby, in recent years, private ownership has been granted to land which has, traditionally, been communal.

A second important change is the predominance of small properties rather than the large areas of cultivation characteristic of the conventional rural sector.[23] This is associated with the potential use of the land for urbanization and with the preoccupation of individual producer activity over the communal activities of the past. In relation to the form of production, the peri-urban model maintains a pattern of production dependent on income from both the land and urban employment so that family incomes are likely to be the sum of several activities: agricultural and commercial activities and permanent employment within the city. An additional factor which has reinforced the urban link is the introduction of an urban transport system which has made possible commuting from the 'metropolitan village' to the city centre. Inevitably, this has had a strong cultural influence. The principal activity continues to be small-scale arable farming while livestock not for self-consumption serves to reduce 'risk', that is, in periods when there is high availability of employment in the city, the number of animals decreases and vice versa.

The agricultural systems which are dominant in the peri-urban model are terraced agriculture in the hills to the south of the city and valley agriculture in the adjacent areas. The terraced system, with its pre-Hispanic roots, represents an agricultural system which demonstrates a long and close relationship between environment and topography and has determined the different uses of different spaces. One of the most important changes to take place in the terraced zone occurred in the 1980s and coincided with an increasing awareness of health that focused on the value of high-fibre vegetables and the effect of hypoglutens. In this respect, *nopal*-legume represented a food of great importance[24] and this international preoccupation with health stimulated the expansion of its production in the terraced zone, with an increase from 1600ha at the beginning of the decade to in excess of 7000ha today. This, together with a reappraisal of *nopal*-legume within the well-off population and its export to Japan and the US, has further promoted a growth in production. This has caused prices to rise and, consequently, has improved living standards for the producers.

The expansion of *nopal*-legume production has caused a reorganization of space, such as has occurred in the *chinampa* zone, and has given rise to a new use of agricultural space. The backyard, the family orchard, draught animals and milk production have remained within the villages while *nopal*-legume is grown in a ring around the villages, along with some vegetable cultivation, and has displaced maize as the dominant crop. There is then a ring of agro-forestry systems which include natural and introduced crops, sheep, *maguey* (for *pulque* production) and leaf mulch. Finally, there is the forest itself, providing a number of resources for the community (resin, firewood, timber, fungi, compost, etc). Although an impressive range of production systems exist within this zone, the most important (economically) is *nopal*-legume, as shown by its location in the areas closest to the 'metropolitan village'. *Nopal*-legume, perhaps more than any other crop, illustrates the close association between agriculture and the metropolis. Its enormous demand, from people from all social strata, has caused an expansion in its production area, the only crop where this has occurred. A second indication of this link is the adaptation of *nopal*-legume production to available technology, that is, the intensive use of animal manure produced from the urban and suburban agricultural models, and from the village dairies.

A similar pattern of change, responding to the city's influence, can be seen in the maize-bean-squash crop complex, traditionally characteristic of the rural sector. The traditional black bean has been substituted by the broad bean which is sold to meet the urban demand for *tlacoyos* (a Mexican snack prepared with maize and broad bean). Likewise with maize, the popularity within the city for products manufactured from blue maize has led to its cultivation in preference to the white varieties. In contrast to *nopal*-legume production, maize is cultivated largely for own consumption or retail sale but, as in the case of *nopal*-legume, the majority of maize producers use manure as their main fertilizer.[25]

In the peri-urban production space, an important place is occupied by systems linked to recreation. These zones are particularly popular with the urban low-income

Table 12.4 *A summary of the main productive processes found in the various urban spaces of the metropolitan zone of Mexico City (MZMC)*

Space	Model of production	Productive processes	
		Agriculture	Livestock
Urban	New	Family garden	Backyard animals (poultry and pigs) Dairy cattle Beef cattle Pig production
Suburban	*Chinampa*	Legumes and flowers Family orchard Greenhouse Market gardens	Backyard animals Dairy cattle
Peri-Urban	Terrace	*Nopal* production Family orchard Maize Forestry Grasslands	Backyard animals Draught animals Dairy cattle Bees Sheep

groups who, at weekends, visit the area in search of rural isolation and traditional foods. Within this model, two commercial systems can be identified, namely the barbecue-wool system and the *mole* system.

The barbecue-wool system is a form of production well adapted to the forest zones south of the city. It is based on the traditional consumption of mutton steam-cooked in a wood-fired oven and has developed two aspects, namely the preparation of barbecued food to meet local tourist demand and the supply of various markets within the city. These markets include the meat market (for which up to 2000 sheep per week are slaughtered) and the local wool market close to the village of Gualupita.

The second commercial system is the preparation of *mole* which is based in the village of San Pedro Atocpan. It represents the cultural adaptation of a traditional technology, that is pre-Hispanic cuisine, but with the components of today's production originating far from the agricultural areas of the zone.

The agriculture of the valley zones is a reminder of conventional management of the rural sector. The system is dominated by the cultivation of maize, either as a mono-crop or with squash and broad beans. Cultivated to a lesser extent is *amaranto* (a pre-Hispanic grain) which is used in the preparation of *alegrías* (a sweet) and *atoles* (a maize drink). Another relatively important system within this zone is cut-fodder production. Alfalfa is one example, managed intensively on a small scale. Another example is oats which are an important source of feed for fattening small flocks of sheep and small herds of cattle. A final example comes from the less fertile areas (due to salinity) where natural grassland vegetation has established and which is used for occasional grazing.

Perspectives of agricultural development in urban systems

The persistence of agricultural activity within and close to the metropolis is a clear example of the strong cultural link between the inhabitants of the valley of Mexico and their agricultural antecedents of 8000 BC. An innovative population, facing the problems of serious environmental deterioration brought about by urbanization, has found ways of adapting to these new conditions and has developed new technologies allowing it to continue agricultural activities within a new pattern of production. Furthermore, this 'ability' to improvise has implications within the search for a sustainable relationship between the natural environment, socio-economics and the welfare of animals.

Contrary to what might have been hoped for, city development proposals have been based on a 'western model' of development, dominated by concrete, automobiles and the concept of 'green spaces' within the city, such as parks and gardens, as controlled 'imitations' of nature. At the same time, agriculture (historically important in supplying food to the urban centres) has been considered counter to the ideal of modern, urban life, giving rise to a curious 'corruption' whereby animals exist only as pets, as 'exhibition pieces' (e.g. in zoos) or for sport; and agricultural livestock is seen as an agent of pollution – to be prohibited or for the extortion of bribes.

In analysing the problems that confront the agricultural sector within the metropolitan zone, it is important to understand the leading role adopted by the local authorities. The federal district of Mexico, like the political authorities of many Mexican states, entrusted its agricultural development to the Coordinated Commission for Agricultural Development. The commission's proposals focused on the seven agricultural delegations of the federal district which are typified by suburban and peri-urban agricultural spaces, while those delegations where urban space production is practised failed to receive any government support. This means that although, clearly, animals are found in these urban delegations, they are not recognized at government level. This problem was further exacerbated by the commission's promotion of mechanized agriculture, linked to the agricultural developments of the 'Green Revolution', ignoring both natural resources and the producers. Their policy failed. The supplied technology depended on the intensive use of external inputs and the cooperation of the producers which never materialized. The result of this badly implemented policy was the loss of the notion of a metropolitan agriculture. As a consequence, what might have been used for agricultural support was redirected towards plans for 'ecological rescue' – one recent example being the ecological park of Xochimilco.[26] The plan consisted of isolating a small part of the wetland zone and implementing a canal cleaning programme, prohibiting further urbanization and substituting untreated waste for treated waste within the area. Yet, however well-intentioned, the plan represents an example of the loss of the aforementioned concept of 'agriculture' and the producers, who are the agents responsible for any changes towards sustainability, continue to use agro-chemicals, contaminated water and silt etc, leaving much to be desired regarding a plan of 'ecological rescue'.

In contrast to the blinkered view of the government, the enormous imagination and capacity of the new urban farmer has made possible agricultural production within the urban environment. This phenomenon introduces a very important dimension, demonstrating the capacity of the unprotected sectors (i.e. the urban farmer) to generate alternative solutions in the face of the ecological 'catastrophe' presented by the uncontrolled growth of the city. They have reorganized space, devised new ways of using degraded land, modified conventional agricultural systems in response to the demands of the urban sector and have realized the potential for utilizing large volumes of waste as a source of food for animals and/or plants. An example of this adaptation and development of a 'new' technology can be found in the delegations east of the city. Here, the metropolitan food supply depot produces huge volumes of fruit and vegetable wastes which allow the dairy stables, considered illegal by the local authorities, to exist and expand (albeit within a medium of bribes and fines). The excreta from the livestock is transferred to the terraced and valley agricultural systems (which typify the peri-urban model) and is used as an organic fertilizer, as a temperature regulator and as a water provider, thus forming a chain of recycling never considered by official programmes.

Despite some more enlightened attitudes relating to sustainability, the large urban centres are generally regarded as generators of contaminants, destroyers of natural ecosystems and high consumers of external inputs. But in the light of this article, this is clearly too narrow a vision of the urban situation. The growth and development of the urban centre has led to the establishment of new markets, directly influencing traditional systems of production. One example is that of ornamental birds, which have generated a new industry supplying cages, food and drink dispensers, and other accessories, while the demand for seed, fruit and insect feed has promoted new sources of agricultural work and reduced the flow of migrants from the countryside to the city.

Another example is gardening which has assimilated a significant number of urban farmers and which constitutes a new industry in commodities such as compost, flower-pots, turf, ornamental plants, tools, furniture, etc. A third and very significant example is that of *nopal*-legume. The increased demand from the city for this product has stimulated a need for labour and a re-evaluation of land values, to such an extent that *nopal*-legume growing land is of sufficient value to provide a 'green' barrier to contain city growth.

A change in outlook by the authorities is currently taking place as a result of two factors. The first, namely the economic crisis, has limited development opportunities and therefore reduced the pressure to purchase land for construction. This has been reinforced by a government policy to increase the cost of living within the metropolitan area in a strategy to reduce migration from the countryside. Similarly, the second factor, that of environmental degradation and pressures on natural resources, has increased a general awareness of the need to conserve 'rural' spaces. This changing attitude has generated an urban phenomenon characterized by projects of 'action-rescue'. Examples of these include projects implemented in the former Lake Texcoco area in the 1980s and, more recently, in the *chinampa* zone of Xochimilco. Here, in spite of the limitations of this type of 'ecological rescue' project, urban development has been stalled and research aimed at diminishing pollution and regenerating production has been supported.

Within this context, the opportunity arises to find an alternative form of agricultural development for the metropolis, switching from mechanized forms of production that endanger the environment to traditional urban systems of agriculture characterized by 'self-conserving' technologies which avoid pollution and ecosystem degradation, and that allow increased income generation thereby benefiting large sections of the population who have scarce economic resources. An additional objective concerns animal welfare and the search for a method of production which respects the well-being of the livestock while maintaining a reasonable standard of living for the producers. The suggestion that agricultural development within the city should base itself on the existing urban systems is supported by the fact that a close working relationship has developed between different systems, forming a complex agricultural structure in which, for example, the wastes of one system (i.e. excreta) are used as a source of organic material and nutrients in another system (i.e. arable production). This allows, in the medium term, an improved, more efficient use of renewable natural resources and the abandonment of those forms of production based on the use of fossil fuels such as oil. It is necessary to stress that urbanization has only been a problem since the beginning of the modern era although cities have existed long before this. Bookchin[27] pointed out that we need to be aware of the social and ecological relationships that exist within cities beyond the economic processes of production and consumption.

Accepting a proposal such as the one presented in this work will not be easy to achieve. In the first place, it is necessary to establish a working relationship between researchers and the city authorities, in which modifications to the city environment and the emergence of a new generation of urban farming systems are acknowledged. Recognition of these systems of production would enable the implementation of relevant research, focusing on the integration of these systems with their environment, improving their management and reducing the obstacles presented by the politicians. It is also clear that the urban agricultural producer has responsibilities and an obligation to follow certain 'rules' such as acceptable animal management and the elimination of the foul smells, flies and rats that are frequently associated with livestock production. In conclusion, it is clear that we need to reconsider what sort of city we really want – and this may involve a rejection of the 'western' model of development where animals are nothing more than pets, in favour of a new model which searches for a development in harmony with nature and based on a system of production which originated in the valley of Mexico.

Notes

1 Cardoso, M. D. and García, E. (1982) 'Vegetation and climate in the basin of Mexico', Latin American regional conference IGU, Brazil, Geographical Topics of Mexico City and its Environs, Instituto de Geografía, UNAM, México, pp19–24.

2 Armillas, P. (1949) *Notas Sobre Sistemas de Cultivo en Mesoamérica. Cultivos de Riego y Humedad en la Cuenca del Río Balsa*s, Anales INAH, México.

3 Clavijero, F. (1979) *Historia Antigua de México*, Porrua, Colección Sepancuantos, México.

4 Ixtlixóchitl, F. (1975) *Obras Histórica*s, Ed. O'Gorman, UNAM, México, Instituto de Investigaciones Históricas: Historiadores y cronistas de indias 2, México.

5 Semo, E. (1995) 'México, un pueblo en la historia. De la aparición del hombre al dominio colonial', Alianza Editorial, Séptima edición en El libro de bolsillo, México.

6 Rojas, T. (1990) 'La agricultura en la época prehispánica', in *La Agricultura en Tierras Mexicanas Desde sus Orígenes Hasta Nuestros Día*s, Consejo Nacional para la Cultura y las Artes, Grijalbo, México.

7 Romero, M. A. (1990) 'La agricultura en la época colonial', in *La Agricultura en Tierras Mexicanas Desde sus Orígenes Hasta Nuestros Día*s, Consejo Nacional para la Cultura y las Artes, Grijalbo, México.

8 Hernández, X. E. (1985) 'Exploración etnobotánica y su metodología. Xolocotzia', *Revista de Geografía Agricola*, vol 1, pp163–188, Universidad Autónoma de Chapingo, México.

9 Miño, G. M. (1991) *Haciendas, Pueblos y Comunidades. Los Valles de México y Toluca Entre 1530 y 1916*, Consejo Nacional para la Cultura y las Artes, México.

10 Bataillon, C. (1972) *La Ciudad y el Campo en el México Central*, XXI Siglo Veintiuno Editores, México.

11 Reyes, C. P. (1981) *Historia de la Agricultura. Información y Síntesi*s, AGT, México.

12 Departamento del Distrito Federal (DDF) (1985) *Imágen de la Gran Capital*, *Enciclopedia de Méxic*o, S.A. de C.V. Almacenes para los trabajadores del Departamento del Distrito Federal, Ciudad de México, MCMLXXXV. Source: Departamento del Distrito Federal DDF (1985) 'Imagen de la gran capital', *Enciclopedia de México*, México; also INEGI (1994) 'Estadísticas históricas de México', Instituto Nacional de Estadística, Geografía e Informática, México.

13 Balanzario, Z. R. (1976) *Contaminación de las Aguas en los Canales de Xochimilco*, UNAM, Facultad de Filosofía y Letras, Colegio de Geografía, México.

14 Canabal, C. B., Torres-Lima, P. A. and Burela, R. G. (1992) *La Ciudad y sus Chinampas. El Caso de Xochimilco. Primera Parte. La Expansión Metropolitana y el Medio Rural del Distrito Federal*, Colección Ensayos, UAM, México.

15 Sánchez, L. (1982) *Comisión Coordinadora para el Desarrollo Agropecuario del Distrito Federal. Memoria 1978–1982*, Fuentes Impresores, S.A. Departamento del Distrito Federal, México.

16 Losada, H., Cortés, J., Grande, D., Rivera, J., Soriano, R., Vieyra, J., Fierro, A. and Arias, L. (1996a) 'The production of milk from dairy herds in the suburban conditions of Mexico City. I. The case of Iztapalapa', *Livestock Research for Rural Development*, vol 8, no 4, p53.

17 DDF (1989) *Rescate ecológico de Xochimilco*, Folleto, DDF, México.

18 Schteingart, M. (1989) 'The environmental problems associated with urban development in Mexico City', *Environment and Urbanization*, vol 1, no 1, April.

19 García, C. (1992) *Guía Roji, Ciudad de México, Area Metropolitana y sus Alrrededores*, 59ava Edición, México.

20 Losada, H., Grande, D., Vieyra, J., Arias, L., Pealing, R., Rangel, J. and Fierro, A. (1996) 'A suburban agro-ecosystem of nopal-vegetable production based on the intensive use of dairy cattle manure in the southeast hills of Mexico City', *Livestock Research for Rural Development*, vol 8, no 4, p66.

21 Camacho, P. R. (1995) 'La situación actual de la agricultura chinampera de Xochimilco, distrito federal', in Rojas, T. (Co-ordinator), *Presente, Pasado y Futuro de las Chinampas*, Patronato del Parque Ecológico de Xochimilco, A.C. y CIESAS, México.

22 Losada, H., Pealing, R., Soriano, R., Rivera, J., Cortés, J., Vieyra, J. and Martínez, H. (1997) 'The rapid appraisal of the sustainable region of Xochimilco by the study of local markets in the southeast of Mexico City', *Livestock Research for Rural Development*, vol 9, no 3 (in press).

23 See Note 10.

24 Losada, H., Neale, M., Rivera, J., Grande, D., Zavala, R., Arias, L., Fierro, A. and Vieyra, J. (1996) 'Traditional agricultural and animal production in the southeast of Mexico City as a resource for sustainable agriculture. The presence and experimental utilisation of the nopal vegetable *(Opuntia ficus-indica)* as an important sustainable crop of terraced areas', *Livestock Research for Rural Development*, vol 8, no 2, p40.

25 Fierro, A., Losada, H., Rangel, J., Rivera, J., Vieyra, J., Arias, L., Cortés, J. and Grande, D. (1996) *La Tecnología de la Producción de Maíz de Auto-Consumo como un Agroeco-Sistema Sustentable del Sureste de la Ciudad de México*, Memoria, II e Simposio Internacional y III e Reunión Nacional sobre Agricultura Sostenible, una contribución al desarrollo agrícola integral, CSLP, FIUASLP, CEA, CP México.

26 Stephan-Otto, S. (1995) *Sustentabilidad de los Parques Ecológicos: El Caso del Parque Ecológico de Xochimilco*, Segundo Seminario Internacional de Investigadores de Xochimilco, Memorias, Asociación Internacional de Investigadores de Xochimilco, México.

27 Bookchin, M. (1992) *Urbanisation Without Cities: The Rise and Decline of Citizenship*, Institute of Policy Alternatives of Montreal (IPAM), Black Rose Books, Montreal/ New York.

Chapter 13

The Politics of Urban–Rural Relations: Land Use Conversion in the Philippines

Philip F. Kelly

Introduction

Urban–rural relations have conventionally been understood in terms of social and economic interactions and linkages between two distinct modes of production and reproduction.[1] These relationships might be in the form of household livelihood strategies that straddle the two sectors;[2] flows of commodities, capital and migrants; or, more recently, in new forms of 'urbanization' that embody elements of both the urban and the rural.[3] While each of these approaches provides useful insights, they essentially overlook the politics of rural–urban relations both in terms of the policy choices that are made relating to the use of land and with regard to the political processes (broadly conceived) that facilitate land conversion.

This chapter examines some of the developmental priorities and political processes involved in land conversion in the Philippines, and the region around Manila in particular (see Figures 13.1 and 13.2). It is in the agricultural provinces of Manila's extended metropolitan region that some of the country's most productive farmlands also form the core region of an industrializing and globalizing national economy. The result has been a process of regionalized urbanization in which urban–rural relations are primarily constituted in the encroachment of urban land uses and employment into rural settings. Large swathes of irrigated agricultural land in the 'rice bowl' provinces of the Central Luzon and Southern Tagalog regions have been converted to a variety of urban and industrial uses: export processing zones and industrial estates; institutions such as hospitals and universities; leisure landscapes such as golf courses, resorts and theme parks; and, most significantly in terms of the area involved, residential sub-divisions. The result is a reworking of the social and economic, as well as the physical, landscape of formerly 'rural' areas, such that even within the same household the urban–industrial economy might co-exist with agricultural production. Thus, while urban–rural economic rela-

Note: Reprinted from *Environment and Urbanization*, vol 10, no 1, Kelly, P. F. 'The politics of urban–rural relations: Land use conversion in the Philippines', April, pp35–54, copyright © (1998) with permission from IIED, London.

tions elsewhere in the country might operate across a distinct spatial divide, in the mega-urban region of Manila (and other primate cities of Southeast Asia), the traditional dichotomy between the 'rural' and the 'urban' has become less meaningful.

This blurring of boundaries is, however, an intensely political process. In the Southern Tagalog region in particular, the process of land conversion from agricultural to urban uses has been an issue of contentious public debate in recent years. It precipitates emotive issues relating to national food security, the priority given to industrial versus agricultural development, and the rights of tenant farmers and agricultural labourers. It is, therefore, an inherently political process in which decisions are made and options are exercised concerning land use and developmental priorities.

This chapter examines the political contestation and negotiation of the land conversion process and suggests that rural–urban relations in Manila's mega-urban region must be seen as politicized at three interconnected levels of social relations – the national, the 'local' and the personal. At a national level, specific policy frameworks exist that regulate the land conversion process but they are frequently circumvented and undermined by developmental strategies geared towards industrialization rather than agricultural modernization. At the level of local municipal governments, legislation allows considerable flexibility in interpreting zoning by-laws and therefore determining land uses. More importantly, this flexibility is applied in a context where the boundaries between public and private roles, and between regulatory responsibilities and vested interests, are frequently blurred. Finally, the 'everyday politics' of relations between landlords, tenants and other local power brokers creates a context in which tenant farmers find it difficult even to assert their legal rights to adequate compensation or land redistribution through agrarian reform.

The chapter is structured in the following way. The first section outlines the dimensions of land conversion in the Philippines and then focuses on Manila's mega-urban region in particular. Using unpublished government data, it is suggested that official figures may significantly underestimate the extent of land conversion. The second section will then highlight some of the social, economic and environmental issues that are associated with land conversion and which form the basis for opposition to the process. The subsequent three sections of the chapter then describe the political processes, negotiations and resistance that have emerged around the issue of land conversion at the national, local and personal level.

The chapter draws upon a total of nine months of fieldwork in 1994–1995 both in Manila and in the adjacent province of Cavite to the south. The field research was based on surveys and interviews in two villages in the small market town of Tanza. More than 400 residents were surveyed for basic socio-economic data and more than 60 detailed interviews were conducted with farmers, ex-farmers, government officials, developers, youth leaders and other local residents. It should be added, however, that the information concerning the politics of land conversion that is presented here is drawn from a variety of experiences in Cavite as a whole and is not intended to imply the culpability of particular individuals.

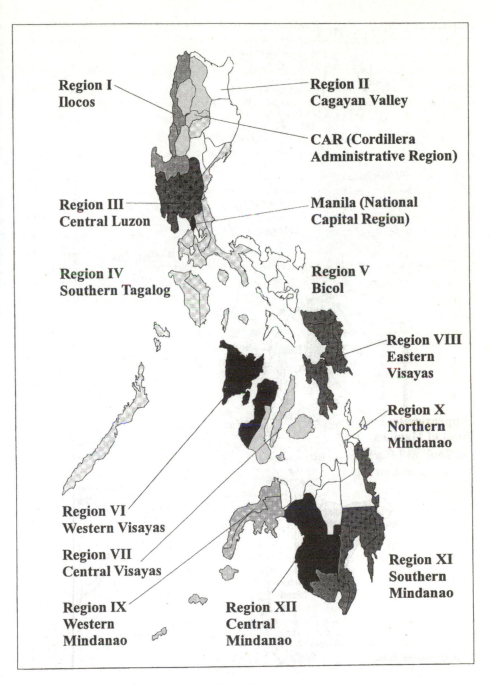

Note: Regional divisions were modified in 1995.
Source: Map No. 25, Republic of the Philippines, NAMRIA, Makati

Figure 13.1 *The Philippines by region*

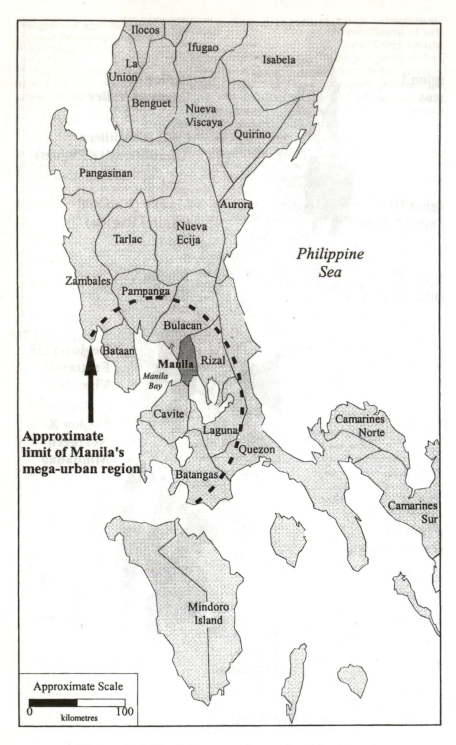

Figure 13.2 *Manila's mega-urban region (sketch map)*

The dimensions of land conversion

In the 1990s, growing political concern and protest over land conversion in the Philippines has reflected the intensification of the process itself. The Department of Agrarian Reform (DAR), the government agency responsible for recording and regulating the land conversion process, started systematically recording conversions in March 1988.[4] Table 13.1 provides DAR figures between 1988 and the end of June, 1995. Figure 13.1 indicates the parts of the country that correspond to each region.

Table 13.1 shows that, according to DAR records at least, over a seven-year period a total of 33,707ha of agricultural land were converted to other uses, either with legal clearance from DAR, without such clearance or exempted from clearance. Recent press reports suggest that the rapid rate of conversion continued and even accelerated in 1996. By June 1997, DAR's cumulative conversion total (approved, illegal or exempted) since 1988 had reached 56,965ha, an increase of 23,258ha in just two years.[5]

The figures in Table 13.1 also indicate that the process of land conversion has a distinctive geographical pattern within the Philippines. Looking at the approved conversions alone, approximately half of the national total was accounted for by Region IV (Southern Tagalog). This pattern reflects the mega-urbanization of Manila into its surrounding agricultural provinces – particularly Cavite and Laguna to the south. Significant, but much lower, levels of conversion were also experienced in Region III (Central Luzon) immediately to the north of Manila.

The importance of mega-urbanization in these figures can be illustrated by taking the province of Cavite as an example. There, the process of conversion has been driven

Table 13.1 *Philippine agricultural land area (hectares) converted, March 1988–June 1995*

Region	Approved	Disapproved[a]	Exempted[b]	Total
CAR	38	0	9	47
I	70	2	20	72
II	166	7	26	198
III	2223	348	703	3274
IV	7029	305	13,022	20,358
V	178	59	45	281
VI	1325	227	431	1984
VII	208	164	6	378
VIII	76	90	302	468
IX	241	0	38	279
X	913	201	2576	3690
XI	1971	217	99	2286
XII	300	0	92	393
Philippines	**14,739**	**1619**	**17,348**	**33,707**

Notes: [a] Disapproved for conversion but converted anyway.
[b] Exempted through Department of Justice Opinion 44. Exemption figures are updated only to July 1994.
Source: Unpublished data from Department of Agrarian Reform, Quezon City, July 1995

by the development of large industrial estates across the province, mostly over the last five years. By 1995, the province had 11 major industrial estates employing almost 55,000 workers. To house these workers, and to accommodate commuters employed in Manila, housing estates started to proliferate across the province in the 1990s. This process of urbanization is reflected in dramatic increases in the cost of land in Cavite. In the province as a whole, the cost of home lots increased by an average 20.4 per cent each year between 1990 and 1993 (this compares with a 5.5 per cent increase in Metro Manila).[6] Table 13.2 indicates the conversions that were registered with the provincial government between 1988 and mid-1995 and illustrates the importance of residential and, to a lesser extent, industrial activities in the process of land conversion. It is significant to note that between 1989 and 1993, the recorded area of irrigated rice land in Cavite fell from 14,710ha to 12,800ha – a decline which would imply a substantial impact from land conversion to other uses.[7]

There are, however, reasons to suspect that these figures from the DAR represent only a fraction of the land actually taken out of agricultural production. The figures do not include, for example, land that is lying idle because its owners have removed the tenant farmers and are waiting for a more profitable moment to convert the land to other uses. In addition, many lands have simply been converted without the knowledge of the DAR.

An indication of the extent to which land conversion goes unrecorded can be gleaned from data recorded at the municipal level using Tanza in Cavite as an example.[8] Data at the municipal offices show 248ha of agricultural land as being approved, or exempted from approval, for conversion between 1989 and 1994, and a further 119ha as having been forwarded to the provincial DAR office for processing. These figures indicate a significantly higher rate of conversion than that shown by data held by the national DAR office which records just 214ha of land converted over the same period and none being processed. Furthermore, local figures also record 222ha of land as having been converted without permission, the vast majority for residential sub-divisions.[9]

Table 13.2 *Land conversions in Cavite approved by DAR, 1988–1995*

Year	Residential	Industrial	Institutional	Farm lot	Unknown	Total
1988	7.0			21.0		**28.0**
1989	17.4	25.0				**42.4**
1990	159.8	160.8	14.8			**335.4**
1991	73.0	35.0	148.7			**256.7**
1992	209.5	266.6	12.4	67.8	53.8	**610.1**
1993	99.9	24.8	10.0	12.0		**146.7**
1994	125.3	7.9				**133.2**
1995*	286.6					**286.6**
Total	**978.5**	**520.1**	**185.9**	**100.8**	**53.8**	**1839.1**

Note: * January–June.
Source: Unpublished Data, Department of Agrarian Reform, Quezon City

These conversions do not feature anywhere in national DAR records. Separate data on rice lands in Tanza, gathered by local Department of Agriculture extension workers, suggest that over 400ha of irrigated rice land were lost to other uses between 1989 and 1995.[10] Putting these figures together suggests that official national figures for a town such as Tanza should be almost doubled to match locally collected data on legal *and* illegal conversions. Furthermore, it would seem that irrigated rice land accounts for almost all of the total conversion.

Contested territory: The politics of land conversion

The landscape of 'rural' towns such as Tanza is characterized by a patchwork of urban development and continuing agricultural production. In more remote villages, agricultural land is still farmed although water supply for irrigation and labour supply at harvesting and planting times represent perennial problems for farmers.[11] In more accessible areas, however, large swathes of land have been converted to industrial uses or residential sub-divisions. Alternatively, land may simply lie idle, with cattle grazing on grassed-over rice fields whose owners await either development permits or more propitious market conditions.

When residential development occurs, there are several different types of sub-division that might be constructed. A 'first class' sub-division includes house lots and full service provision – septic tanks for household sewage, concreted roads, pavements, rudimentary basketball courts and perhaps even a chapel. In such sub-divisions, house lots are sold to buyers who then construct their own homes on the site. At the opposite end of the spectrum is the 'low-cost' sub-division in which one-room, one-storey terraced units are constructed to a standardized design when a purchaser is found. These sub-divisions are designed as 'social' housing and most are purchased through contributions to the government service insurance scheme or social security system, or to national savings schemes such as Pag-Ibig. Whatever the style of sub-division, house lots remain empty until a buyer is found or until the new owner decides to construct a house on the lot. The result is often a bleak landscape of occupied houses interspersed with vacant units or empty lots strewn with garbage.

The incursion of the 'urban' into the 'rural' in this way has implications at various levels. At the village level, socio-economic and environmental changes are experienced that have, on several occasions, led to outright resistance to land conversion. At a national level the politics of resistance to land conversion are motivated by broader issues of food security and development priorities. Each of these issues is discussed in turn.

Social change

The residents of new sub-divisions tend to be a mixture of young families related to long-standing villagers, and migrants from outside the *barrio*, most of whom have arrived to work in the emerging local industrial sector. In one such sub-division in Cavite, a survey conducted in 1995 of 301 residents revealed that approximately two-thirds were born outside the municipality in which it is located.

Profound social changes have resulted from this recent influx of migrants to expanding villages in Cavite. During interviews in one village in 1995, those who were born in the *barrio* spoke of the breakdown of formerly tight social networks and a growing feeling of *anomie* and 'urbanness':

Q: Are there big differences from when you were growing up in Mulawin?

A: Big ones! Of course it's not the same as before, the camaraderie is different. Those who are really from here are different. Everybody was like a relative. Unlike now, when the trend is for those people from other provinces [to come here], it's as if it's every man for himself. Not like before, when if someone was sick you would visit them because they are relatives and friends. It's like Manila now. Manila lifestyle (Cavite villager, 1995, translated from Tagalog).

Others too talked of changing interpersonal relations (*pakikisama*) and a growing unease with the anonymity of their social milieu. Evidently, the tightly woven social fabric that has been the norm in rural areas is becoming unravelled. The sheer number of new people in the village means that they cannot be absorbed into existing social networks. A personalized system, through which relationships were structured ranging from personal disputes to business arrangements, has been broken down by the influx of newcomers. Inevitably, tensions and suspicions result:

When sub-divisions were constructed it became disordered, with lots of different kinds of people here. It's difficult to get along with different people, and that's why it's become very difficult since we've had these sub-divisions (Cavite villager, 1995, translated from Tagalog).

The social consequences of land conversion also include issues of equity and justice. As will be described later, conversion is frequently used as a means of circumventing agrarian reform, so that an opportunity for redistribution of rural income is lost.[12] But displaced tenant farmers will, at least, receive disturbance compensation. The biggest losers in the process of land conversion are landless agricultural labourers who do not have tenancy rights that must be compensated, who are dependent on agricultural work for their livelihoods and who have little formal education or experience that might offer opportunities in the urban-industrial economy. For this group, already the most marginal in rural society, land conversion represents a profound dislocation. Many in the farm lobby point out that the agricultural sector has the ability to absorb such labour in a way that the manufacturing industry is incapable of doing on a similar scale.[13]

Environmental impacts

The environmental consequences of land conversion have been widely criticized.[14] Vicente Ladlad, for example, highlights the impact of land use conversion in Laguna on the biological productivity of Laguna de Bay, a freshwater lake to the south-east of Manila.[15] Elsewhere, urban and industrial development are in direct conflict with agricultural activities. In Cavite, for example, farmers complain that irrigation canals have become silted up with eroded material from local building sites, thus impeding water supply. In other cases, water supply is also blocked by household refuse as new residents respond to inadequate service provision by simply discarding their waste into nearby canals. Farmers also complain that crop pests have become an increasing problem with the development of residential areas in the midst of farmland.

Food security

The concentration of land conversion in some of the country's most productive agricultural areas has raised the issue of national food security.[16] Total rice production in the Philippines continues to fall short of national demand. Over the last five years, the country has imported between 200,000 and 900,000 metric tonnes annually.[17] In the first half of 1997, 650,000 metric tonnes of rice were imported to safeguard against diminished yields.[18] Every decision to purchase rice has been met with condemnation from opposition politicians and agrarian advocacy groups. Official figures indicating that 50,000ha of land have been converted since 1988 would seem to represent only a fractional impact upon the country's total rice land area which is in excess of 2 million hectares. But many groups believe that the concentration of conversions in the most productive rice-growing regions of Southern Tagalog and Central Luzon has compromised national food security and necessitated imports.

Developmental priorities

A broader theme, incorporating many of the issues already described, concerns the relative importance given to agricultural development versus industrialization. The Philippines' economic and social development programme during the Ramos administration has been guided by the Medium-term Philippine Development Plan (MTPDP), 1993–1998. The Plan's emphasis rests squarely on industrial development in selected regional industrial centres where incentives encourage the location of foreign direct investment in the export oriented electronics and garments sectors. The plan also calls for 'agri-industrialization', with linkages to be established between industry and local agricultural producers, but the mechanisms for creating these linkages are not spelled out. Indeed, the sectoral focus of the plan leaves little space for such linkages. Agri-industrialization, it seems, has come to mean industrial development located in agricultural areas rather than the formation of functional linkages between the two sectors.

Non-governmental organizations (NGOs) and some scholars have been outspoken in criticizing these development priorities.[19] The Philippine Peasant Institute, for example, argues that '… of all the gaps in the MTPDP, its most crucial oversight is still its insubstantive emphasis on agriculture and its failure to recognize the sector's role as the key to sustainable growth.'[20] Similarly, Greg Bankoff argues that there is an '… inherent inconsistency at the center of government policy' between a policy of rapid industrialization and a programme of agrarian reform and agricultural development.[21] The main thrust of such opposition focuses on the neglect of the agricultural sector when it still constitutes the livelihood of approximately 50 per cent of the country's workforce. In addition, many argue that experiences elsewhere in East Asia have shown that improving rural incomes through vigorous agrarian reform is the most effective means of stimulating aggregate demand and inducing industrial development. Such sentiments have not been limited to scholars and research institutes. Farmers regularly picket the DAR headquarters in Quezon City (Metro Manila) and, in May 1997, a group of farmers staged a demonstration at a shareholders' meeting of Fil-Estate, one of the country's largest real-estate developers, to protest against the unregulated conversion of irrigated farmland for residential sub-divisions.[22]

For reasons based on each of the issues described above, land conversion has been a contested issue at both local and national level in the Philippines. And yet the process has continued and accelerated in recent years. To understand why this is so, it is necessary to explore not only the political *issues* involved in land conversion but also the political *process* as it is constituted at multiple levels in the Philippines. This question will be addressed in the subsequent three sections, which focus on the national, local and 'everyday' politics of land conversion.

Laws of the land: The national politics of land conversion

Land use conversion in the Philippines is currently regulated through a bewildering variety of laws, administrative orders, memoranda and legal precedents. Most significantly, the Comprehensive Agrarian Reform Law (CARL) of 1988 (Republic Act 6657) protects from conversion those rice and corn lands eligible for redistribution (from landlord to tenant farmer). Such lands may only be converted after a lapse of five years from the time that a Certificate of Land Transfer is issued. Even then, the land must have ceased to be economically usable for cultivation or must be situated in a predominantly 'urbanized' locality. In addition, the CARL gave the DAR authority to regulate the conversion of any agricultural land, regardless of tenure arrangements and crop types. In these cases, the land use plans drawn up by local government units (usually municipalities or cities) and approved by regional planning bodies would form the basis for deciding the appropriate use for specific parcels of land.

The CARL, however, far from assuaging land conversion has, in many cases, actually accelerated the process. Landlords keen to avoid losing their land could convert it to other crops or to non-agricultural uses. In many cases, tenant farmers have been removed and the land has just been left idle. This might seem to be an irrational use of a productive asset but the institutional and legal framework established by the CARL makes it an attractive option for landowners. Leaving a farmer to cultivate rice would make it difficult to obtain a non-agricultural zoning from the local government. Moreover, the longer a tenant is allowed to farm while land prices increase, the higher the compensation packages. This extra compensation would likely far outweigh any rental payments the owner might receive from the tenant if cultivation continued for a few extra years. There are, therefore, both legal and economic rationales to explain why landowners are keen to remove their tenant farmers as soon as possible, and which explain the common sight of former rice land sitting idle, occupied only by grazing cattle.

The tension between agrarian reform and land conversion came to a head in 1990. In a widely publicized case, farmers in the village of Langkaan in Cavite came into conflict with the developers of an industrial estate over the fate of 232ha of rice land. The land was owned by a government agency, the National Development Corporation (NDC), which planned to develop the First Cavite Industrial Estate on the site in collaboration with the Marubeni Corporation of Japan. In October 1989, the partners applied to the DAR for permission to convert the land. By that time, however, the DAR had identified the property as eligible for redistribution under the CARL, with 180 potential farmer beneficiaries. The DAR denied permission for the conversion on the grounds that the land was irrigated and productive, that tenant farmers could be clearly identified, and because the process of acquisition for redistribution had started prior to the application for conversion.[23]

The dispute came down to a simple choice. Would the property be retained as productive agricultural land and redistributed to tenant farmers under the CARL or would the owners of the land be allowed to develop it as an industrial estate? The new Secretary of State for Agrarian Reform, Florencio 'Butch' Abad, then undergoing a confirmation hearing on his appointment before Congress, made abundantly clear his opinion that the land should be retained and redistributed under CARL. This position pitted him against the Department of Trade and Industry (DTI) which favoured the development of an industrial estate on the site. The result was a tense and public standoff between two branches of the government and a controversy that delayed congressional confirmation of Abad's appointment (and eventually led to his resignation).[24] The DTI finally prevailed by seeking and obtaining a legal opinion from the Department of Justice (Opinion Number 44, Series of 1990) that the authority of DAR to rule on conversions applied only to those conversions made after 15 June 1988 (when CARL or RA 6657 became effective). In other words, where a municipal or city development plan prior to that date zones land as non-agricultural, then it takes precedence even if the land is, in fact, still being cultivated.

The result was that the development of the industrial estate in Langkaan could proceed. More importantly, however, a decision had been made that undermined the authority of DAR to control land conversion and which, instead, allowed conversion to go ahead if a document could be produced, dated prior to June 1988, indicating that a piece of land was zoned for non-agricultural activities. The outcome of the Langkaan controversy was, therefore, less a technical legal decision and more a political decision to prioritize industrial development over the agricultural sector. The consequences of the decision are apparent in Table 13.1, which shows that conversions exempted under Opinion 44 far exceed those approved by DAR.

The following year, the scope of land use management by local governments was substantially enhanced through the Local Government Code (LGC) (Republic Act 7160). The LGC is a broad-ranging piece of legislation that devolves significant administrative and revenue-raising powers to local government units with the intention of enhancing service provision, accountability and local democracy.[25] Section 20 of the Code gives municipalities the power to reclassify up to 15 per cent of agricultural land not covered by CARL to non-agricultural uses if it is deemed by the local council (*sanggunian*) to be either: no longer 'sound' for agriculture or of substantially greater value if used for residential, commercial or industrial purposes. These remarkably loose conditions effectively gave power over land use conversion to local municipalities – an issue that will be examined further in the next section.

By the end of 1992, public concern over the extent to which agricultural lands were being converted prompted presidential involvement. In November, Malacañang Palace issued Administrative Order (AO) Number 20, directing that all irrigated and irrigable land covered by existing irrigation projects should be immune from conversion. The purpose of the Order was to protect prime agricultural lands from conversion but the one-page directive lacked any implementing regulations or punitive measures to deter transgressors.

While such legislative support for preserving agricultural land lacked mechanisms for enforcement, the political process of undermining protective regulations continued. In September 1993, Executive Order (EO) 124 outlined guidelines for prioritizing agricultural land conversion in areas designated as regional agri-industrial centres, regional industrial centres, tourism development areas and 'socialized' housing sites. The Order did not supersede the President's previous directive to protect irrigated lands but it did provide a mechanism for presidential approval if such lands were needed. Once again, however, no sanctions were stipulated for non-compliance.

On a national scale, the areas involved in the provisions of EO 124 are relatively small, although not insignificant. In 1993, regional agri-industrial centres across the country amounted to 5526ha, while tourism development areas totalled 12,873ha.[26] But, perhaps more than any other piece of legislation, EO 124 highlights the political decisions that were, and are, being made at a national level about the priority given to urban-industrial development over the agricultural sector. The legal setting for land conversion, therefore, is one in which various steps have been taken to protect agricultural land but with few provisions for punishing offenders. At the same time, various laws have undermined the control of the DAR. But, perhaps more importantly, the political climate created by these legislative moves has been one in which industrial development is aggressively promoted while agricultural land (and by extension, the agricultural sector) is seen as expendable where it conflicts with other priorities. Such flexibility has made the circumvention of land conversion regulations relatively easy for those with the means and the connections.

Several steps can be taken by landowners to enable land conversion (and avoid agrarian reform). First, national and regional officials in various government agencies are frequently found to be open to 'persuasion'. Reports circulate of officials in the National Irrigation Authority certifying land as unirrigated or the DAR failing to recognize legitimate tenants eligible for agrarian reform. One land developer in Cavite talked openly to me about using high-level government contacts in Manila to secure a land conversion clearance from the DAR. Second, landlords may simply pay disturbance compensation to tenants, removing them from land that will then sit idle. After a few years in such a state, the owner can claim that the land is 'non-productive' and therefore eligible for conversion.[27] Third, cases have been reported of irrigation canals being destroyed and filled so that regulations such as AO 20 do not apply. In July 1997, the Agrarian Reform Secretary, Ernesto Garilao, publicly condemned this practice and called on the National Irrigation Authority to stop certifying irrigated areas as unproductive lands.[28] Finally, local officials have the authority to redefine land as zoned for non-agricultural use even when it is still being cultivated. The result of these loopholes and avoidance strategies is that relatively few land conversions are technically illegal but many clearly contravene the spirit and intent of the laws regulating conversion. For several years, the Philippine government has acknowledged the need for a national land use plan that would rationalize the various land conversion laws into an integrated set of regulations with appropriate sanctions to punish non-compliance. In 1992, President Fidel Ramos declared such a plan to be a personal priority for his first 100 days in office. It took until June 1994, however, before a draft of the National Land Use Code was released by the National Economic and Development Authority. In October 1997, after two years of deliberation, the House of Representatives approved the Code as House Bill 9147, the National Land Use Act.[29]

The Act integrates various national policies on the allocation, utilization and development of land resources, and includes sections that consolidate existing legislation governing the conversion of agricultural land. In particular, it confirms the exclusive jurisdiction of the DAR over conversion decisions and limits the role of local governments to authorizing the conversion of non-agricultural land to other uses. The decision to convert agricultural land is, however, placed solely with the DAR. The Act also includes provisions for a land conversion tax which would both discourage speculative conversion and would generate revenue for agricultural development. The National Land Use Act is, however, now with the Senate where it has been shelved due to lack of time and probably will not receive attention before the May 1998 elections. This ongoing saga gives some indication of the political sensitivity of the issue, particularly among legislators with extensive business interests in farming and real estate.

At the national level, then, there exists a pattern of legislative action that has produced regulations which lack punitive sanctions and which provide numerous ways for circumvention. At the same time, industrial development has been aggressively promoted, creating a political environment in which urban-industrial land uses have taken priority over agriculture. Examining legislation, however, shows only the policy directions and frameworks that are provided. It is at a local level that key decisions are made and the practical politics of land conversion are activated.

The local politics of land conversion

National legislation on land conversion provides flexibility in implementation and, in many cases, opportunities for non-compliance with little threat of punishment. It is, however, largely in the murky world of Philippine local politics that regulations and procedures become open to interpretation and selective enforcement.

In a formal sense, this local level control is mandated by the LGC of 1991 described earlier. But the LGC assumes the existence of an independent and efficient bureaucratic system at a local level and a clear division between regulators and developers. In most instances neither of these conditions apply. Many towns do not even have precisely defined or publicly available zoning maps, leaving decisions over the re-classification of land to local officials, particularly mayors. Numerous reports and personal interviews suggest that such re-zoning decisions often involve bribery and kickbacks.[30] Moreover, as the process of DAR conversion clearance starts with the Municipal Agrarian Reform Officer, that process too can be open to abuse by local officials who may certify that the land has 'ceased to be economically feasible and sound for agricultural purposes' and that farmers on the land have been properly compensated, when the opposite is true. Farmers' rights as agrarian reform beneficiaries have also been compromised where redistribution has been prevented or withdrawn, often with pressure being applied to local agrarian reform officials. It should also be said, however, that many farmers have been only too happy to sell their tenancy rights given the marginal profitability of rice cultivation and the often generous compensation packages that are negotiated.

In addition to their regulatory roles, municipal mayors are also frequently powerful political 'bosses' in a more informal sense, with considerable coercive resources in the form of law enforcement officers (the LGC also placed local police detachments under the jurisdiction of municipal officials) and private retainers. Numerous documented examples exist of pressure being brought to bear on farmers in Cavite who have resisted the decision to convert farmland. As a result, municipal politicians have been able to exert considerable control over the land conversion process. When asked why irrigated land has been converted even though the law states that it is protected, one village official told me that '... with our current system [of government] it passes through.' Another Caviteno, this time a relatively wealthy banker, elaborated on this sentiment:

> In fact, they're the ones selling all the lands. No lands here move without the mayor
> knowing it. People will not buy agricultural lands and therefore they will only buy land
> if there is a chance of having it converted. And therefore you'd have to go to the mayor,
> because he's the only one empowered to certify that this land is part of a zone converted
> to industrial use (Cavite resident, 1995).

The result, according to John Sidel, is that '... Cavite's municipal mayors have evolved into the province's leading real estate agents and brokers.'[31]

The heavy involvement of local politicians in the land conversion process relates partly to a desire to foster residential and industrial growth within their jurisdictions – land uses which provide far greater revenue-raising potential than agricultural production. But mayors and councillors are also usually significant players in the local economy in their own right and, in many cases, have vested interests in the land conversion process. These interests might involve ownership of land which will increase in value as other parcels of land are urbanized, or simply kickbacks from developers wishing to smooth the process of obtaining permission for land conversion and development permits. During an interview in 1995, one farmer in Cavite commented:

> I don't know why [it happens], but I really don't like it. We cannot do anything about
> it. It's our leaders who let it happen. They [developers] pay them so that it will be built.
> There's nothing that can be done (1995, translated from Tagalog).

Another villager echoed that sense of powerlessness: '... even if you protest, the person to whom you take your grievance will have something to do with the project.' Moreover, the involvement of local politicians was evident in more than just the hearsay of villagers. Land developers too described encounters with mayors who demanded kickbacks in exchange for granting certification that the land could be converted. In one case, this demand, made behind closed doors, was for two lots in the planned sub-division and a substantial cash payment.

Provincial authorities technically have little power to influence land conversion decisions but in Cavite accusations were widespread in the early 1990s that Governor Juanito Remulla (1979–1995) was complicit in coercing conversion in several instances.[32] The principal ways in which this influence was exercised was through the persuasion or coercion of uncooperative municipal officials and tenant farmers. Such persuasion took the form of money to add a further incentive for compliance or the provision of man-power for forced evictions:[33]

> In numerous documented cases, he [Remulla] has dispatched armed goons, ordered the bulldozing of homes and engineered the destruction of irrigation canals so as to expedite the departure of 'squatters' and tenant farmers demanding compensation for their removal from lands designated for sale to Manila based or foreign companies for 'devel-opment' into industrial estates. Though Remulla typically tempers such hardball tactics with offers of a 'settlement', the 'carrot' is never as impressive as the 'stick'.[34]

In another study of land use change in Cavite in the 1980s, John McAndrew notes that:

> ... legal measures to impede the conversion of farmland into sub-divisions remained largely ineffective. While tenanted rice and corn lands were covered under the agrarian reform programme, resistance to relinquish family farms met with harassment and even threat to life. Tenants had really no option but to forfeit their rights of tenure and accept the cash payments offered to them in compensation. On their part, local government officials often acted as brokers or agents of landlords and corporate developers.[35]

The local politics of individual enrichment and bureaucratic corruption cannot, how-ever, be divorced from the wider politics of development that lie behind the changes occurring in Cavite. In broad terms, this refers to the political agenda described earlier that focuses on industrialization through globalized development. But, more practically, this strategy translates into the priorities set for government agencies. In the case of irrigation authorities, for example, some farmers in Cavite complain that the irrigation system, while constructed with substantial loans from the World Bank for the Second Laguna de Bay Irrigation Project, is in fact neglected on the ground with dyke mainte-nance and water supply inadequate for their needs: '... it's because of the interest of many government officials. That is a very big question for us.'

Two sets of forces, then, work against the proper regulation of the land conversion process. One is in the priorities set by the administration in terms of development strat-egies, and particularly the relative importance given to agricultural versus industrial development. Appeals against land conversion fall on deaf ears at both provincial and national levels. The other is the power given to local level political leaders and their susceptibility to influence through bribes or personal favours.

The 'everyday politics' of land conversion

The institutional politics of land conversion at national and local levels provide only a partial picture of the process of land conversion as it is actually experienced by individual tenant farmers. To complete the picture, a less formal set of 'everyday' power politics must be explored in the form of personal relationships between landlords and tenants.[36] Such relationships carry with them substantial weight in propelling the conversion process.

The start of the land conversion process from the farmer's point of view comes when the landowner approaches with the suggestion that he/she might wish to sell the land and tries to evaluate the tenant's likely demands for compensation:

> What they will do is they will approach us. Naturally, we first talk about farming. [Then they say] 'If perhaps I were to sell this land, would you be agreeable to my suggestion.' And the tenant says, 'If you can grant our rights, we could reach an agreement.' Two or three times they'll approach you. Of course, he is the one who is more eager to sell. In our case, since what we want is to avoid a dispute, then we agree. That is how the system works (Ex-farmer in Cavite, 1995, translated from Tagalog).

Negotiations inevitably vary according to the individuals involved but the social relationship between landlord and tenant, going beyond their economic arrangements, means that farmers often feel 'ashamed' or 'embarrassed' to negotiate as strongly as they might. Farmers feel unable to go beyond certain culturally prescribed bounds:

> It is inappropriate for you to act superior to the owner of the land (Cavite farmer, 1995, translated from Tagalog).

> For us, we just go along with the agreement, because it's theirs, and it's inappropriate for us to say we don't want to. It will appear that we are becoming greedy over it (Cavite farmer, 1995, translated from Tagalog).

A farmer's association with the owner is thus more than just a legalistic, landlord-tenant relationship. The bond between the two families may date back several generations and the landlord might, for example, be a godparent to the tenant's children. Consequently, tenants are reluctant to try forcing their legal rights and souring personal relationships:

> That's it, that's their proposal. Of course, you're ashamed because we've been together for a long time. We don't want them to say we were greedy when the law [agrarian reform] came, doing everything by the letter of the law. We don't want that, so I just accepted it. Even though what is happening is painful, there's nothing we can do about the situation (Ex-farmer, Cavite, 1995, translated from Tagalog).

The result is that landowners are able to persuade tenants to relinquish their tenancy rights even where farmers might have legal rights to the land or legal means to block a conversion. In any case, the system of verbal agreements and unwritten understandings on which agrarian life is based is inconsistent with a legal system of documentation and regulation. In such circumstances, it is invariably the educated landlord, with high social status, sufficient resources to bribe officials and access to legal counsel, whom the situation will favour. But, once again, it should also be added that there are farmers (and potential agrarian reform beneficiaries) who would rather enjoy a lucrative cash settlement than continue farming with marginal profits or take on the added burden of amortization payments under agrarian reform. Thus, all land is effectively negotiable if the two parties can reach an agreement. As one village official noted: '... with every law there is an exception, if two persons agree with each other.'

The settlement that is eventually reached between landlord and tenant will usually provide both a cash payment and a small parcel of land on which the tenants can build houses for themselves and for their children. Cash payments have escalated in recent years but individual settlements vary according to the location of the land involved and the negotiating skills of the tenant. In 1995, a typical compensation package amounted to approximately P 500,000 (UK£12,500 at 1995 rates) for each hectare of farmland (or 50 pesos per square metre) and a house lot of 1000–2000m². The selling price of land to a developer, meanwhile, might be many times greater. One price being quoted by a landowner in Tanza in 1995 was 350 pesos per square metre (3.5 million pesos per hectare).

Conclusion: The politics of the rural–urban interface

For at least a century, land has been the key source of power and conflict in the Philippines. In the past, the struggle has focused on the control of agricultural land as the basis for wealth, patronage and political dominance. This paper has shown that land continues to be a highly politicized asset but it is now the potential of agricultural land for urban-industrial uses that motivates the will to control it rather than the need to dominate the agricultural economy and workforce. Nowhere is this more apparent than in the struggle over land conversion in the hinterland of metropolitan Manila.

Land conversion has, however, been a contested process. For reasons of social dislocation and injustice, and environmental conflicts between urban and rural sectors, the conversion of land for urban-industrial uses has been resisted at a local level. At the same time, issues of food security and the relative merits of a globalized industrialization strategy for development have motivated political opposition on a wider scale. Such resistance has not, however, proven to be effective in curbing the accelerating process of conversion. This paper has described the political processes that have facilitated land conversion at three different levels of analysis. At the national level, a complex web of legislation has created numerous loopholes and opportunities for evasion without adequate deterrents. At the same time, the government's national development strategy has been based on the 'Philippines 2000 vision' which aims to bring the country into the ranks of the newly industrialized economies by the year 2000. Industrial development is thus aggressively promoted while the agricultural sector has been implicitly neglected. At the local level, power over land use decisions has been de-centralized into contexts where boundaries between public sector regulation and private economic interests are blurred. This has, in turn, created a political framework conducive to conversion. Finally, at the level of personal relationships between landlords and tenants, the 'everyday politics' of conversion is played out in a cultural context of patron-client ties that preclude farmers from asserting their legal rights.

Urban–rural relations, at least in the context of Manila's mega-urban region, cannot therefore be seen solely in terms of household strategies, flows of exchange (in the form of migration, capital etc) or new and distinctive forms of 'urbanization' in which the 'rural' and 'urban' coexist. Instead, the relationship between urban and rural sectors must be seen as existing in tension as different developmental priorities are played out. The tension over these priorities must, moreover, be recognized as a highly political struggle, in terms of both the consequences of land conversion from agricultural to urban uses and in terms of the processes through which this conversion is facilitated.

Notes

1   See, for example, Potter, R. and Unwin, T. (eds) (1989) *The Geography of Urban–Rural Interaction in Developing Countries*, Routledge, London.
2   See, for example, Trager, L. (1988) *The City Connection: Migration and Family Interdependence in the Philippines*, University of Michigan Press, Ann Arbor, MI.
3   Ginsburg, N., Koppel, B. and McGee, T. (eds) (1991) *The Extended Metropolis: Settlement Transition in Asia*, University of Hawai'i Press, Honolulu.
4   The Department of Agrarian Reform (DAR) was created in 1971 as part of the Marcos administration's agrarian reform programme. As clearance from the DAR is needed in any land conversion case to certify that the area is not covered by the Comprehensive Agrarian Reform Law (Republic Act 6657 of 1987), the department is the principal agency for regulating and monitoring conversions.
5   'Proposed national land use plan gets House okay', *Business World*, 14 October 1997.
6   'Land prices in Metro towns, Calabarzon rising', *Philippine Daily Inquirer*, 11 July 1995.
7   Bureau of Agricultural Statistics (n.d.) *Selected Statistics on Agriculture, 1989–1993*, Region IV, Manila.
8   'Cavite has a high rate of illegal land conversions, claim farmers groups', *Business World*, 10 June 1991.
9   Of the legal conversions, 254.2ha were for residential uses, 77.1ha for industrial, 13.1ha for institutional, 11.8ha for tourism resorts and 11.1ha were for unspecified uses (*Source:* unpublished data on land conversion, Municipal Agrarian Reform Office, Tanza, Cavite, 1995).
10 Unpublished data on farmers in Tanza, 1989 and 1995, Municipal Agricultural Officer, Tanza, Cavite.
11 Kelly, P. (forthcoming) 'Everyday urbanization: The social dynamics of development in Manila's extended metropolitan region', *International Journal of Urban and Regional Research*.
12 Canlas, C. (1991) *Calabarzon Project: The Peasants' Scourge*, Saliksik, Philippine Peasant Institute research papers, Manila.

13 Philippine Peasant Institute (1993) 'Philippine NIChood: Stunting agriculture for fast-track growth', *PPI Briefing Papers*, vol II, no 3, August.

14 Zoleta-Nantes, D. (1992) 'Changes in land use of irrigated paddies: A study of land conversions in Plaridel, Bulacan', *Philippine Social Sciences Review*, vol L, nos 1–4.

15 Ladlad, V. (1993) *Land Use Problems in Urbanizing Regions: The Case of Laguna Lake Basin*, Philippine Peasant Institute, Manila.

16 See Note 13.

17 'Rice imports of 0.5 million tons a year predicted', *Business World*, 28 January 1997.

18 'No more rice imports this year – NFA', *Business World*, 9 June 1997

19 A detailed account of one example of local resistance to land conversion and the broader politics that surrounded it is provided in Kelly, P. (1997b) 'Globalization, power and the politics of scale in the Philippines', *Geoforum*, vol 28, no 2.

20 See Note 13, p5.

21 Bankoff, G. (1996) 'Legacy of the past, promise of the future: Land reform, land grabbing and land conversion in the Calabarzon', *Bulletin of Concerned Asian Scholars*, vol 28, no 1, p41.

22 'Focus: Land conversion: Threat to productivity', *Business World*, 14 May 1997. Examples of popular protest against land conversion in Cavite have been numerous. They include resistance to a new dumpsite servicing Manila to be located in Carmona; the export processing zone in Rosario; and various residential and industrial developments in Dasmarinas. For an overview, see McAndrew, J. (1994) *Urban Usurpation: From Friar Estates to Industrial Estates in a Philippine Hinterland*, Ateneo de Manila University Press; also Sermeno, D. (1994) *Circumventing Agrarian Reform: Cases of Land Conversion*, PULSO Monograph no 14, Institute of Church Social Issues, Manila.

23 See Note 22, Sermeno (1994).

24 See Note 22, McAndrew (1994).

25 Tapales, P. (1992) 'Devotion and empowerment: LGC 1991 and local autonomy in the Philippines', *Philippine Journal of Public Administration*, vol XXXVI, no 2, April.

26 Joint NEDA and DAR memorandum, Circular No 1, 1993 series.

27 'Government wants replacement tax for land conversion plans', *Business World*, 25 August, 1997.

28 'Government strictly monitoring land conversion applicants', *Business World*, vol 3 July, 1997.

29 See Note 5.

30 'Gangster politics thrives in Cavite', *Philippine Daily Inquirer*, 2 May 1995; also Sidel, J. (1995) *Coercion, Capital and the Post-colonial State: Bossism in the Postwar Philippines*, unpublished PhD thesis, Cornell University.

31 See Note 30, Sidel (1995) p247.

32 See Note 30, Sidel (1995) p381.

33 Various instances of provincial law enforcement officers or hired 'goons' being involved in tenant evictions are recounted in McAndrew (1994) (see Note 22) and in Coronel, S. (1995) 'The killing fields of commerce' in *Boss: Five Case Studies of Local Politics in the Philippines*, Philippine Centre for Investigative Journalism, Manila.

34 See Note 30, Sidel (1995) p381.
35 See Note 22, McAndrew (1994) p175.
36 The notion of everyday politics is derived from the work of Benedict Kerkvliet, in particular, Kerkvliet, B. (1990) *Everyday Politics in the Philippines: Class and Status Relations in a Central Luzon Village*, University of California Press, Berkeley, CA.

Chapter 14

Ecological Footprints and Appropriated Carrying Capacity: What Urban Economics Leaves Out

William E. Rees

Introduction

This chapter uses the concepts of human carrying capacity and natural capital to argue that prevailing economic assumptions regarding urbanization and the sustainability of cities must be revised in light of global ecological change. While we are used to thinking of cities as geographically discrete places, most of the land 'occupied' by their residents lies far beyond their borders. The total area of land required to sustain an urban region (its 'ecological footprint') is typically at least an order of magnitude greater than that contained within municipal boundaries or the associated built-up area. In effect, through trade and natural flows of ecological goods and services, all urban regions appropriate the carrying capacity of distant 'elsewheres', creating dependencies that may not be ecologically or geopolitically stable or secure. Wealthy nations appropriate more than their fair share of the planet's carrying capacity. The global competition for remaining stocks of natural capital and their productive capacity therefore explains much of the environment-development related tension between North and South. Such macro-ecological realities are often invisible to conventional economic analyses yet have serious implications for world development and sustainability in an era of rapid urbanization and increasing ecological uncertainty.

The ecological perspective

This chapter is based on the premise that human bio-ecology may soon become more important to understanding the political and socio-economic implications of urban

Note: Reprinted from *Environment and Urbanization*, vol 4, no 2, Rees, W. E. 'Ecological footprints and appropriated carrying capacity: What urban economics leaves out', October, pp121–130, copyright © (1992) with permission from IIED, London.

development than economics. There are three simple reasons for this. First, despite our technological wizardry and assumed mastery over the natural environment, humankind remains a biological entity and creature of the ecosphere.[1] On the simplest level, our fundamental relationship to the rest of the ecosphere is indistinguishable from that of the millions of other species with which we share the planet. Like all other organisms, we survive and grow by extracting energy and materials from those ecosystems of which we are a part. Like all other organisms, we 'consume' these resources before returning them in altered form to the ecosphere. Second, the five-fold increase in the scale of human economic activity in the post-war period has begun to induce ecological change on a global scale which simply cannot be ignored in planning for human settlements. Finally, orthodox economic analysis is so abstracted from reality that its ability to detect let alone offer policy advice on socially critical macro-environmental dimensions of global urbanization is severely compromised.

Rationale: Urban economy as urban ecology

Ecology is the scientific study of the flows of energy and material resources through ecosystems and of the competitive and cooperative mechanisms that have evolved for the allocation of resources among different species. Similarly, economics is the scientific study of the efficient allocation of scarce resources (energy and material) among competing uses in human society. Thus, ecology and economics share not only the same semantic roots, but also much the same substantive focus. In fact, it could logically be argued that economics is really human ecology.

Or rather, it should be. The problem is that mainstream economics has deviated markedly from the theoretical foundations that support its sister discipline. Ecology has firm roots in the real world chemical and thermodynamics laws that are the universal regulators of all energy and material transformations in the organic world. Economics, by contrast, had abandoned its classical organic roots by the end of the 19th century. Neoclassical economics (currently enjoying a remarkably uncritical renaissance the world over) is firmly based on the methods and concepts of Newtonian analytic mechanics.

The result of this divergence is a dominant economic paradigm which 'lacks any representation of the materials, energy sources, physical structures, and time dependent processes basic to an ecological approach'. Prevailing theory therefore produces analytic models based on reductionist and deterministic assumptions about resources, people, firms, and technology that bear little relationship to their counterparts in the real world.[2] In short, mainstream economists have abandoned ecological theory entirely, having sought refuge in the more theoretically tractable but environmentally irrelevant realm of mechanical physics. Ironically, economists, the most influential of human ecologists, are also the most ecologically errant.[3]

Four important consequences of this theoretical dichotomy will serve to illustrate the dilemma:

1   Economic models often represent the economy as essentially separate from and independent of 'the environment'.[4] By contrast, the ecological perspective sees the

human economy as an inextricably integrated, completely contained, and wholly dependent sub-set of the ecosphere.

2   Economic theory treats capital and individual inputs to production as inherently productive, ignoring both their physical connectedness to the ecosphere and the functional properties of exploited ecosystems. By contrast, ecology is a science of connectivity, preoccupied with material and energy flows and their relationships to the functional integrity of ecosystems.

3   According to neoclassical theory, resource depletion is not a fundamental problem – rising prices for scarce resources automatically lead to conservation and the search for substitutes. Conventional wisdom holds that substitution through technological progress has been more than sufficient to overcome emerging resource scarcities.[5] This enables Nobel Prize-winning economist Robert Solow to argue that '... the world can, in effect, get along without natural resources.'[6] By contrast, ecology argues that humankind remains in a state of obligate dependency on numerous biophysical goods and services which have immeasurable positive economic value but for which there are no markets (e.g. the stratospheric ozone layer). In the absence of prices, the already questionable scarcity indicators of conventional economics fail absolutely.

4   Finally, the mechanical metaphor describes an economy which is self-regulating and self-sustaining in which complete reversibility is the general rule. From this perspective, the starting point for economic analysis is the circular flow of exchange value. By contrast, thermodynamic reality means that the economy is sustained entirely by low entropy energy and matter produced 'externally' by ecosystem and biophysical processes. Thus, all economic production is actually consumption – the ecologically relevant material and energy flows through the economy are unidirectional and irreversible.[7]

This last factor is crucial to any attempt to account for the ecological effects of any economic process, including urban development. Without reference to entropic throughput '... it is virtually impossible to relate the economy to the environment', yet the concept is '... virtually absent from economics today'.[8]

Why is any of this significant? There can be no doubt that sustainable urban development requires a sophisticated understanding of human ecology. In today's world, however, the primary values and criteria determining human material relationships with the rest of reality come from ecologically empty economic models. As we strive for sustainability, we would do well to reconsider these models in light of a key cybernetic theorem: 'We cannot regulate our interaction with any aspect of reality that our model of reality does not include because we cannot by definition be conscious of it'.[9]

Urban development and environment

Let's turn now to the task at hand – accounting for the environment in urban economic development. Traditional environmental economics is most likely to perceive the problem in industrial countries largely in terms of deteriorating local amenities – inadequate open space, air pollution and congestion from an expanding auto fleet, and landfills approaching capacity from the solid waste stream. The solution may be cast in terms of making more efficient trade-offs between economic growth and environmental quality, improved land use planning, and finding policy instruments that will internalize the costs of pollution to those firms causing the problems (or better still, getting rid of smokestack industries and attracting clean 'high-tech' industries). Public pressure is also mounting for policies that emphasize economic incentives to encourage more ecologically benign waste management, urban land use, and transportation patterns than are achieved at present.

In developing countries, the emphasis is more likely to be on breaking the debilitating cycle of poverty, environmental decay and deteriorating public health. Many cities in developing countries are unable to provide basic infrastructure and essential services. The human excreta and other wastes generated by burgeoning populations and unregulated industry overwhelm the capacity of inadequate and poorly maintained waste disposal systems. The poor are particularly hard hit. A quarter of urban residents live in absolute poverty. These millions have no access to sewers or clean water and their substandard housing is crowded, filthy and noisy. Little wonder that gastrointestinal and respiratory diseases and malnutrition are chronic on a massive scale and the economic losses incalculable. In cities in developing countries the solutions are naturally oriented to economic measures that will improve allocative efficiency (true-cost pricing) and increase equity (reduced subsidies to the rich); increase economic productivity by improving services and removing constraints; alleviate poverty; and generally generate the wealth needed to upgrade the urban environment.[10]

Clearly, cities both North and South suffer from ecological dysfunction albeit differing in kind and scale, and the prescribed policy measures seem appropriate in the circumstances. Nevertheless, current responses to urban ecological malaise reveal an incomplete perception of the problem. Failure to appreciate the systemic spatial and structural dimensions of the human ecosystem limits the substantive scope for policy responses, confines remedies to the local environment, and often results in the treatment of symptoms rather than causes.

We tend to think of cities as political or administrative entities or, more loosely, as geographic areas dominated by features of the built environment. Economists see them as the locus for intense socio-economic interaction among individuals and firms and the engines of production and national economic growth. By contrast, systems ecology focuses on the broader relationship between the human population, ecologically significant consumption and the sustainability of essential energy and material flows. This reveals dimensions of the urban system that are invisible to conventional policy models including the total dependency of cities on the productivity of distant landscapes and their negative impacts on the very land that feeds them.

The urban ecological footprint: Appropriated carrying capacity

We can illustrate the general idea by relating the novel concept of 'natural capital' to the more venerable concept of carrying capacity at the regional level. While arguably central to urban ecology/economy integration, the ideas explored here are ignored in the mainstream policy arena.

Living on the interest of natural capital

Some economists have accepted the ecological argument that sustainability depends on the conservation of certain biophysical entities and processes. These 'resources' maintain the life-support functions of the ecosphere, the risks associated with their depletion are unacceptable, and there are no technological substitutes. The emerging hybrid discipline of ecological economics therefore regards such assets as a special class of 'natural capital' and has advanced a 'constant capital stock' criterion as a necessary condition for sustainable development:[11] each generation should inherit an adequate stock of natural capital assets no less than the stock of such assets inherited by the previous generation.[12] In effect, ecological economics argues that, for the foreseeable future, humankind must learn to live on the annual production (the 'interest') generated by remaining stocks of natural capital.[13]

Carrying capacity revisited

The concept of natural capital can readily be linked to that of carrying capacity. Ecologists define 'carrying capacity' as the population of a given species that can be supported indefinitely in a given habitat without permanently damaging the ecosystem upon which it depends. For human beings, carrying capacity can be interpreted as the maximum rate of resource consumption and waste discharge that can be sustained indefinitely in a given region without progressively impairing the functional integrity and productivity of relevant ecosystems. The corresponding human population is a function of per capita rates of resource consumption and waste production (i.e. sustainable production divided by per capita demand).[14] This formulation is a simple restatement of Hardin's 'Third Law of Human Ecology': (Total human impact on the ecosphere) = (Population) x (Per capita impact).[15]

The inverse of carrying capacity provides an estimate of natural capital requirements in terms of productive landscape. Rather than asking what population a particular region can support sustainably, the question becomes: 'How much land in various categories is required to support the region's population indefinitely at a given material standard?'

Our preliminary data for industrial cities suggest that primary consumption of food, wood products, fuel, waste-processing capacity etc, co-opts on a continuous basis several hectares of productive ecosystem for each inhabitant, the exact amount depending on individual material standard of living. This average per capita index can be used to estimate the land area functionally required to support any given population. The resultant aggregate area can be called the relevant community's total 'ecological footprint' on the Earth.

This approach reveals that the land 'consumed' by urban regions is typically at least an order of magnitude greater than that contained within the usual political boundaries or the associated built-up area. However brilliant its economic star, every city is an ecological black hole drawing on the material resources and productivity of a vast and scattered hinterland many times the size of the city itself. Borrowing from Vitousek et al[16] we say that high density settlements 'appropriate' carrying capacity from distant elsewheres.[17]

The lower Fraser Valley of British Columbia, Canada (Vancouver to Hope) serves as an example. For simplicity's sake consider our ecological use of forested and arable land alone: assuming an average Canadian diet, the per capita land requirement for food production is 1.9ha, while forest products and fossil fuel consumption require an additional 3–4ha of forested land (2–3ha of this is required to absorb per capita carbon dioxide production and/or to produce the bioenergy equivalent of per capita fossil energy use). Thus, to support only the food and fossil fuel demands of their present consumer lifestyle, the region's 1.7 million people require, conservatively, 8.3 million hectares of land in continuous production. The valley, however, is only about 400,000ha. Thus, our regional population 'imports' at least 20 times as much land for these functions as it actually occupies. (At about 425 people per square kilometre, the population density of the valley is comparable to that of the Netherlands or less than twice that of the UK.)

Implications of inter-regional trade for global carrying capacity

If all human populations were able to live within their own regional carrying capacities (i.e. on the 'interest' generated by natural capital within their home regions) the net effect would be global sustainability. However, no region exists as an independent unit – the reality is that the populations of all urban regions and many whole nations already exceed their territorial carrying capacities and depend on trade for survival. Such regions are running an unaccounted ecological deficit – their populations are appropriating carrying capacity from elsewhere.[18]

Regional ecological deficits do not necessarily pose a problem if import dependent regions are drawing on true ecological surpluses in the exporting regions. A group of trading regions remains within net carrying capacity as long as total consumption does not exceed aggregate sustainable production. The problem is that prevailing economic logic and trade agreements ignore carrying capacity and sustainability considerations. In these circumstances, the terms of trade may actually accelerate the depletion of essential natural capital thereby undermining global carrying capacity.

Open urban economies: The 'distancing' effect of urbanization and trade

Several factors are involved. First, urbanization and trade have the effect of physically and psychologically distancing urban populations from the ecosystems that sustain them. Access to bioresources produced outside their home region both undermines peoples' sense of dependency on 'the land' and blinds them to the far-off social and ecological effects of imported consumption.

Importing carrying capacity: because the products of nature can so readily be imported, the population of any given region can exceed its local carrying capacity unknowingly and with apparent impunity. In the absence of negative feedback from the land on their economy or lifestyles, there is no direct incentive for such populations to maintain adequate local stocks of productive natural capital. For example, the ability to import food makes people less averse to the risks associated with urban growth spreading over locally limited agricultural land. Even without accelerated capital depletion, trade enables a region's population and material consumption to rise beyond levels to which it might otherwise be restricted by some locally limiting factor. Ironically then, the free exchange of ecological goods and services without constraints on population or consumption, ensures the absorption of global surpluses (the safety net) and encourages all regions to exceed local carrying capacity. The net effect is increased long-range risk to all.

This situation applies not only to commercial trade but also to the unmonitored flows of goods and services provided by nature. For example, northern urbanites, wherever they are, are now dependent on the carbon sink, global heat transfer, and climate stabilization functions of tropical forests. There are many variations on this theme touching on everything from drift-net fishing to ozone depletion, each involving open access to, or shared dependency on, some form of threatened natural capital.[19]

Exporting ecological degradation: the importing of sustainability by wealthy industrialized countries may equate to exporting ecological and social malaise to the developing world. Many impoverished countries have little other than agricultural, fisheries, and forest products to offer world markets and current development models encourage the 'modernization' and intensification of production of specialized commodities for export. Unfortunately, the consolidation of land and other scarce resources to produce luxury export crops often jeopardizes domestic staples production, contributing to local food shortages and malnutrition. The process also displaces thousands of small farmers, farm workers, and their families from the better agricultural lands. This concentrates wealth in relatively few hands while forcing the dislocated peasants either to eke out a subsistence existence on inferior land that should never go under the plough, or to migrate to already overcrowded cities.[20] Erosion, desertification, and deforestation in the countryside and debilitating social and environmental problems in burgeoning squatter settlements around many developing cities are the frequent result.

These trends are invisible to developed country consumers who otherwise might not feel so sanguine about their imported coffee, tea, bananas, cocoa, sugar etc. The distancing of consumers from the negative impacts ('externalities') of their consumption therefore only makes things easier for local élites, international capital and transnational corporations all of whom benefit from the expanding commodity trade. Meanwhile, the developing country itself becomes increasingly dependent on export earnings much of which must go to pay off the original 'development' loans.

Overall this pattern contributes to the net transfer of both wealth and sustainability from the poor to the rich within developing countries and from the poorest countries to the richest among the trading nations.[21] Ultimately, of course, debt servicing based on commodity exports in an increasingly competitive global market accelerates the erosion of the export regions' best lands and associated natural capital assets. Such capital liquidation both jeopardizes present levels of commodity production and reduces the future potential for more sustainable forms of development.

Conclusions: Cities and the ecosphere in an era of global change

The world's great cities are among the finest achievements of civilization. In every country, cities are the social, cultural, communication, economic and commercial centres of national life. However, typical urban development policies ignore the fact that the city's role in wealth creation invariably depends on the continuous production of ecological goods and services somewhere else. In ecological terms, the city is a node of pure consumption existing parasitically on an extensive external resource base.[22] While the latter may be spatially diffuse '... the relevant knowledge is that it must be somewhere, it must be adequate, it must be available, and it must grow if the city grows'.[23]

Consider this 'relevant knowledge' in light of current trends pertaining to the state of global natural capital: encroaching deserts (6 million hectares/year); deforestation (11 million hectares/year of tropical forests alone); acid precipitation and forest dieback (31 million hectares damaged in Europe alone); soil oxidation and erosion (26 billion tonnes/year in excess of formation); soil salination from failed irrigation projects (1.5 million hectares/year); draw-down and pollution of groundwater; fisheries exhaustion; declining per capita grain production since 1984; ozone depletion (5 per cent loss over the US [and probably globally] in the decade to 1990); atmospheric and potential climate change (25 per cent increase in atmospheric carbon dioxide alone). Far from growing with the expansion of the urban world, the resource base sustaining the human population is in steady decline.[24]

William Catton has detailed the ecological reality behind these disquieting trends: the expansion of the human enterprise, particularly since the industrial revolution, has been sustained first by the 'takeover' of other species' niches (energy and material flows) accompanied, more recently, by the 'draw-down' of accumulated stocks of resources as shown above.[25] Recent studies have revealed the remarkable extent of the 'takeover' component. Nearly 40 per cent of terrestrial net primary production (photosynthesis) is already being appropriated by humans, one species among millions, and this fraction is steadily increasing.[26] Catton argues that humankind has long since 'overshot' the permanent carrying capacity of the Earth. His bleak prognosis is that we must now do whatever we can '... to ensure that the inevitable crash consists as little as possible of outright die-off of *homo sapiens*.'

The ecological perspective also supports a disturbing interpretation of urban environmental problems, North and South. The pollution, congestion and land use problems of Northern industrial cities stem largely from wealth and associated high levels of material consumption. By contrast, the deplorable physical conditions and appalling public health standards of burgeoning Southern cities stem from debilitating poverty and material deprivation. However, there is a connection. Much of the industrial countries' wealth came from the exploitation (liquidation) of natural capital, not only within their own territories, but also in their former Southern colonies. As noted above, this appropriation of extra-territorial carrying capacity continues today in the form of commercial trade (as well as natural flows).

To the extent that the restructuring of rural economies in the South to supply the North displaces people from productive landscapes to the cities, it is a direct cause of impoverishment, urban overpopulation and local ecological decay. To the extent that current development models and terms of trade favour net transfers of wealth to the North and the continued depletion of natural capital in the South, both poverty and ecological decline in the South are permanent conditions. There simply isn't sufficient natural capital to support the present world population at Northern material standards. If the entire world population of 5.2 billion consumed productive land at the rate of our Fraser Valley example, the total requirement would be 25.5 billion hectares. In fact, the total land area of Earth is only just over 13 billion hectares of which only 8.8 billion hectares is productive cropland, pasture, or forest. The implication is that we would require an additional Earth or two with existing technology to provide for the present world population at Canadians' ecological standard of living.

Although never stated in quite these terms, the appropriation of most of the world's carrying capacity by the urban industrial North (and reluctance to give it up) and the insistence by the South of its right to a fair share (and the threat to seize it through sheer growth in numbers) was really the only issue at the Earth Summit in Rio in June 1992. There are other geopolitical dimensions to the increasing inter-regional dependencies created by trade. Populations that rely on imports have no direct control over the natural capital stocks that sustain them from afar. This raises a question as to the inherent stability of trading relationships in an era of global change. To the extent that excess inter-regional dependency threatens geopolitical security we have another argument for policies to enhance regional economic diversity, independence and self-reliance. In this context, bio-regionalism stands out as an appropriate ecopolitical philosophy. Needless to say, prevailing development rhetoric calls for precisely the opposite – economic specialization, concentration of capital, unrestricted access to resources, freer markets and expanded trade – as the route to future prosperity.

Rethinking urban development

Mainstream economists generally reject the concept of carrying capacity outright on grounds that technology will continuously improve productivity, that manufactured capital can substitute for natural capital and that inter-regional trade will relieve any local constraints on growth.[27] As Daly has observed, prevailing economic mythology assumes a world in which carrying capacity is infinitely expandable.[28]

By contrast, the ecological perspective advanced here shows carrying capacity as fundamental to demographic/resource analysis. It reveals relationships and dependencies that are invisible to conventional models – marginal prices and monetary analyses reveal nothing about the functional roles, remaining volumes, necessary quantities or absolute values of declining stocks of natural capital.

Global ecological change suggests that the productive capacity of some forms of natural capital has already been breached on the scale of the ecosphere. While economic analysis properly treats individual urban regions as open to exchange, it does not recognize that the ecosphere is materially closed and ultimately limiting. Clearly, not all countries or regions can run ecological deficits indefinitely – some must remain surplus producers if the net effect is to be global balance and stability. (We have yet to acquire the means to import carrying capacity from off-planet.) Inter-regional relationships (especially North–South) should be re-examined in light of this reality. For example, given the role of trade in the appropriation of carrying capacity, its use as an economic development tool requires careful scrutiny.

This analysis has made no allowance for potentially large efficiency gains or techno-logical advances. Even at carrying capacity, further economic growth is possible if resource consumption and waste production continue to decline per unit of gross domestic product (GDP). We would be mistaken, however, to rely on this conventional rationale. New technologies frequently require decades to achieve the degree of market penetration needed to influence significantly negative ecological trends. Moreover, there is nothing to ensure that savings will not simply be directed into alternative forms of consumption. Meanwhile, we are already at the limit in a world of rising material expec-tations in which the human population is increasing by 94,000,000 people per year. (The minimal food-land requirements alone each year for this number of new people [at 5.5 people/hectare] is about 17,100,000 hectares, nearly equivalent to all the cropland in France.)

Such basic human ecology has serious implications for urbanization and the mate-rial basis of urban life in the 21st century. At the centre is the disparity between North and South in terms of access to the productivity of natural capital revealed above. The appropriation of a vastly disproportionate share of 'net planetary product' by wealthy industrialized nations is likely to become an increasingly destabilizing geo-political fac-tor as evidence mounts that the global economy is pressing on biophysical limits. In any event, to the extent that limited access to resources is a cause of poverty, it remains a serious impediment to the sustainable development of developing countries.

These problems can only be addressed through structural adjustments to the econ-omy that will greatly affect urban form and function. In Northern industrial cities eco-nomic incentives and other planning measures to increase land use efficiency, to reduce consumption of material resources, and to enhance the viability of remaining local stocks of ecologically productive land should be implemented immediately. In the longer term, the quest for urban sustainability must address at least the following questions:

- What are the necessary ecological conditions for urban/regional sustainability? Are these conditions under active management and control or simply assumed to be available in perpetuity?
- Given the apparent deterioration of the global environment, can we reasonably talk about sustainable urban development without considering the implications of all urban regions simultaneously becoming reliant on ecological productivity 'else-where'?
- How should considerations of carrying capacity and natural capital affect urban form and the spatial scale?
- How can we correct for excessive abstraction, problems with discounting, and mar-ket failure in the economic valuation of land and ecosystems?
- Is the present pattern of developing country urbanization inevitable or is it a by-product of maladaptive development models? How can developing countries gain the most from their wealth-producing natural capital?
- Should dependent urban regions formalize their relationships with export regions to ensure adequate maintenance of essential natural capital stocks thereby enhancing their ecological security, or ...

- Should urban regions (provinces? nations?) develop policies explicitly to support and sustain local/regional agriculture, forestry, fisheries, etc, in order a) to reduce potentially unstable inter-regional dependencies, and b) create a hedge against global ecological change and declining productivity elsewhere?
- What is the appropriate level of government to deal with these matters? Should we move towards regional systems of governance incorporating more life-support landscapes (natural capital)? Does the bio-regional model offer useful guidance?

Notes

1 There are of course important differences of degree and kind. Unlike other species populations, the human population continues to expand imposing increasing demands on the ecosystems that sustain us. In addition, the ecosphere must cope not only with the natural metabolites of our bodies but also with thousands of industrial metabolites, the synthetic by-products of economic activity. While the former are readily assimilated and recycled, there is often no assimilative capacity for the latter which, in fact, may be toxic to biological functions.

2 Christensen, P. (1991), 'Driving forces, increasing returns and ecological sustainability', in Costanza, R. (ed), *Ecological Economics: The Science and Management of Sustainability*, Columbia University Press, New York, pp75–87.

3 There is a double irony here. Academic ecologists, who do have an appropriate body of theory, do not study humans.

4 The subject-object dualism of our Cartesian (scientific) paradigm turns 'environment' into its own pejorative. By definition, it alludes to whatever surrounds some other thing of greater interest or importance. (Rowe, S. (1989) 'Implications of the Brundtland Commission report for Canadian forest management', *The Forestry Chronicle*, vol 5–7, February).

5 Victor, P. (1991) 'Indicators of sustainable development: Some lessons from capital theory', *Ecological Economics*, vol 4, pp191–213.

6 Solow, R. M. (1974) 'The economics of resources or the resources of economics', *American Economics Review*, vol 64, pp1–14.

7 Georgescu-Roegen, N. (1975) 'Energy and economic myths', *Southern Economic Journal*, vol 41, no 3, pp347–381; Daly, H. (1989) 'Sustainable development: from concept and theory towards operational principles', presented to Hoover Institution Conference (Manuscript prepared for special issue of *Population and Development Review*); Rees, W. (1990) 'Sustainable development and the biosphere: Concepts and Principes', *Teilhard Studies*, no 23, American Teilhard Association.

8 See Note 7, Daly (1989).

9 Alternately, '... the regulation that the regulator can achieve is only as good as the model of reality that it contains.' (Beer, S. (1981) 'I said, you are gods', *Teilhard Review*, vol 15, no 3, pp1–33).

10 Bartone, C. (1991) 'Environmental challenge in Third World cities', *Journal of the American Planning Association*, vol 57, no 4, pp411–415; Hardoy, J. and Satterthwaite, D. (1991) 'Environmental problems of Third World cities: A global issue

ignored?' *Public Administration and Development*, vol 11, pp341–361; World Bank (1991) *Urban Policy and Economic Development: An Agenda for the 1990s*, World Bank, Washington, DC.

11 For various interpretations of this concept see: Rees, W. (1992) 'Understanding sustainable development: Natural capital and the new world order', MS under review, UBC School of Community and Regional Planning, Vancouver, BC; Costanza, R. and Daly, H. (1990) 'Natural capital and sustainable development', (Paper prepared for the CEARC Workshop on Natural Capital. Vancouver, BC, 15–16 March), Canadian Environmental Assessment Research Council, Ottawa; Pearce, D., Barbier, E. and Markandya, A. (1990) *Sustainable Development: Economics and Environment in the Third World*, Edward Elgar Publishing, Hants, England; Pearce, D., and Turner, R. (1990) *Economics of Natural Resources and the Environment*, Harvester Wheatsheaf, New York; Pearce, D., Markandya, A. and Barbier, E. (1989) *Blueprint for a Green Economy*, Earthscan Publications, London; Pezzey, J. (1989) *Economic Analysis of Sustainable Growth and Sustainable Development*, Environment Department Working Paper, no 15, World Bank, Washington, DC.

12 Note that if existing stocks are merely adequate (or less), then natural capital will have to be enhanced to accommodate added population and rising material consumption.

13 This is related to so-called Hicksian or 'sustainable' income, defined as the level of consumption that can be sustained from one period to the next without reducing productive wealth.

14 See Note 7, Rees (1990).

15 Hardin, G. (1991) 'Paramount positions in ecological economics', in Costanza, R., (ed), *Ecological Economics: The Science and Management of Sustainability*, Columbia University Press, New York.

16 Vitousek, P., Ehrlich, P. Ehrlichand, A. and Matson, P. (1986) 'Human appropriation of the products of photosynthesis', *Bioscience*, vol 36, pp368–374.

17 Wackemagel, M. (1991) 'Using "appropriated carrying capacity" as an indicator: Measuring the sustainability of a community', Report for the UBC Task Force on Healthy and Sustainable Communities, UBC School of Community and Regional Planning, Vancouver.

18 The relevant imports derive from both commercial trade and natural flows of ecological goods and services. That is, 'trade' is defined to include both international transactions in fisheries, forest, and agricultural products as well as the natural biogeochemical cycling of air, water, and essential nutrients.

19 We are now seeing pollution externalities and the so-called 'common property problem' extended to essential natural capital on a global scale.

20 In theory, the wealth generated by exporting local carrying capacity is supposed to 'trickle down' to ordinary people, enabling them to purchase staple foods imported from more efficient producers at a lower cost than they could grow it themselves. However, trickle-down development theory is largely discredited and the benefits of the so-called Green Revolution are increasingly called into question. See, for example, *The Ecologist*, vol 21, no 2 (March/April 1991) on the role of international development in 'promoting world hunger'.

21 The latter transfers amount to tens of billions of dollars annually in recent years.

22 In ecological and thermodynamic terms, all material economic 'production' is consumption.

23 Overby, R. (1985) 'The urban economic environmental challenge: Improvement of human welfare by building and managing urban ecosystems', Paper presented in Hong Kong to the POLMET 85 Urban Environment Conference, World Bank, Washington, DC.

24 We should note an important corollary to Liebig's law of the minimum in this context: carrying capacity is determined not by general conditions but by that single vital factor in least supply.

25 Catton, W. (1980) *Overshoot: The Ecological Basis of Revolutionary Change*, The University of Illinois Press, Urbana, IL.

26 See Note 16, Vitousek et al (1986).

27 National Research Council (Committee on Population) (1986) *Report of the Working Group on Population Growth and Economic Development*, National Academy Press, Washington, DC; Muscat, R. (1985) 'Carrying capacity and rapid population growth: Definition, cases and consequences', in Mahar, D. (ed) *Rapid Population Growth and Human Carrying Capacity: Two Perspectives*, Staff Working Paper, no 690 (Population and Development Series, no 15), World Bank, Washington, DC.

28 Daly, H. (1986) 'Comments on "population growth and economic development"', *Population and Development Review*, vol 12.

Chapter 15

An Overview of Urban Environmental Burdens at Three Scales: Intra-Urban, Urban-Regional and Global

Gordon McGranahan

There is a long history of environmentalists presenting urban settlements in purely negative terms. This article follows a more recent tradition that recognizes that urban settlements are unsustainable in and of themselves, but also that they may provide the key to moving towards a more environmentally sustainable world (Rees and Wackernagel, 1996; Satterthwaite, 1997). Urban residents and their activities undoubtedly create environmental burdens, but even from an ecocentric perspective there should be no presumption that these burdens would be less if the same people and their activities were dispersed across the rural landscape. Urban settlements concentrate environmentally harmful people and activities, but they also concentrate the people who must change their ways if environmental burdens are to be reduced, and they can be made to provide opportunities and incentives for them to do so.

Environmental burdens in an urbanizing and economically growing world

People are growing in number, producing and consuming more, increasingly likely to live in urban areas, and placing growing pressure on the global environment. Behind these widely accepted trends lie complex and uneven processes that are difficult to define and disentangle. There is not even agreement on the meaning and measurement of urbanization, or on the relationship between economic production and human well-being, let alone on the consequences of urbanization and economic growth for the environment or the well-being of future generations.

It is widely agreed that, compared to rural settlement, urban settlement is associated with higher population density, larger settlement size, more centralized administrative functions, and a less agricultural occupational profile. But different countries,

Note: Reprinted from *International Review for Environmental Strategies*, vol 5, no 2, McGranahan, G. 'An overview of urban environmental burdens at three scales: Intra-urban, urban-regional, and global', copyright © (2005) with permission from IGES, Kanagawa.

and in some cases even different agencies within countries, apply different definitions of urban, in terms of both the criteria applied and the cut-off points used (United Nations, 2002b; Cohen, 2004). In effect, international statistics are forced to rely on country-specific definitions that display numerous arbitrary differences (Montgomery et al, 2003).

The complex of demographic, social and economic characteristics that once maintained a multidimensional urban/rural distinction has been unraveling for some time (Pahl, 1965). Especially in affluent countries, agriculture has been becoming more industrial, and a great many rural dwellers have what would once have been considered urban occupations and lifestyles (Friedmann, 2002). Urban settlements, on the other hand, have become less industrial. Moreover, better transportation and communications have blurred the distinction between urban and rural living.

Urban regions and extended metropolises have grown in importance (McGee and Robinson, 1995), and in Asia the term *desakota*, combining the Indonesian words for village (*desa*) and city (*kota*), was coined to capture the emergence of new forms of economic interaction characterized by a concentrated mix of agricultural and non-agricultural activities that often stretches along corridors between large city cores (McGee, 1987, 1991; Sui and Zeng, 2001). Alternatively, the importance and special character of smaller urban centres is often neglected. Even in demographic terms the distinction between urban and rural fails to capture the changing densities and patterning of human settlements (Hugo et al, 2003).

The concept of economic growth is also contended, particularly when taken as a goal that governments should aspire to (Lawn, 2003). Few economists would claim that per capita gross national product (GNP) is a good measure of human well-being, let alone 'sustainable' well-being (Asheim and Buchholz, 2004; Hamilton and Dixon, 2003). Indeed it was not designed to measure well-being (Beckerman, 1988). Among other things, the importance of inequality has long been recognized, and recent decades have brought increasing attention on the importance of maintaining social and environmental capital. Even for identifying households and individuals living in poverty, income levels can be very misleading (Satterthwaite, 2004), and other dimensions of poverty such as social exclusion and environmental deprivation are receiving greater recognition (Rakodi, 1995; Wratten, 1995).

Yet even if concepts like urbanization and economic growth do not do justice to the complex shifts in human patterns of movement, settlement and well-being, by virtually any measure urbanization and economic growth have been two of the most striking trends of the past century. They have occurred very unevenly, but usually in tandem. Over the course of the 20th century, it is estimated that the world's urban population increased almost 15-fold, rising from less than 15 per cent to close to half of the total population. Over the same period, gross domestic product (GDP) at constant prices increased about 19-fold, or an almost 5-fold increase in GDP per capita – with, on average, faster growth in rich than in poor countries (International Monetary Fund, 2000). To a significant degree, rapid urbanization has taken place in the locations where there has been rapid economic growth (Satterthwaite, 2002). The relatively close relationship is hardly surprising: for much of the 20th century, modern economic growth was predicated on industrialization, commercialization, trade and the use of fossil fuels, all of which have helped to drive urbanization.

The expansion of urban land area is often presented as an environmental impact of urbanization, though urban settlements still cover less than 3 per cent of the Earth's total land area (McGranahan et al, forthcoming). Urban land area is a very poor indicator of the environmental burdens imposed by an urban settlement, however. On the one hand, many of the burdens of urban activities fall well outside urban boundaries, and depend upon the character and intensity of the activities. On the other hand, urban environmental burdens include hazards in the living and working environments in urban areas, which vary within and between urban areas.[1]

William Rees has compared urban settlements to anthills or cattle feedlots, characterized by extraordinarily high densities of their keystone species, and sustained primarily by biophysical processes that take place outside the high density areas themselves (Rees, 2003). A city's urban land area only represents a small share of the land whose services are required to sustain the city; what has come to be termed its 'ecological footprint' (Rees, 1992). Moreover, as an urban area develops it leaves its imprint on the surrounding countryside in numerous ways, only some of which are directly related to the demands of the urban residents themselves (Cronon, 1992).

Just as it is important to look to the extra-urban, it is also important to look at intra-urban scales, and in particular at urban environmental health profiles and how they vary within and between urban areas. Just as two cities of the same area can have very differently sized ecological footprints, so they can have very different environmental health profiles. Moreover, while more environmentally minded urban policies can reduce both environmental health risks and ecological footprints, they do not necessarily move together. Indeed, historically urban environmental burdens at different scales have often tended to move in opposite directions, as will be described in the following section.

The importance of scale

Urban environmental burdens vary enormously in scale. If faecal material from a latrine contaminates the water in a neighbour's well, the burden is, at least in the first instance, very localized. If, on the other hand, urban greenhouse gas emissions contribute to climate change, the burden is globalized. And to complicate matters, if an urban enterprise contaminates local wells and ships its products to distant cities, this is a local environmental burden from the perspective of urban production, but a global burden from the perspective of urban consumption.

There is also enormous variation in the severity of the environmental burdens cities impose, even among cities of similar populations and extents. Some urban and neighbourhood environments are extremely unhealthy to live in, while others are not. Some urban centres release large quantities of waste into the surrounding region, and deplete regional resources, while others of the same size are far less burdensome. And while the ecological footprint of virtually every urban settlement is larger than its urban area, ecological footprints also vary enormously.

The severity of urban environmental burdens at each scale depends upon the geographical setting; the social, economic and technical characteristics of the urban settlement(s); and the measures taken to reduce the burdens. The severity of the burdens at different scales are interrelated, but are not always positively correlated. Reducing local environmental burdens, for example, can increase or reduce large-scale burdens, depending in part on the specific measures taken to relieve the local burden. Introducing a piped water and sewerage system is likely to decrease the environmental health burdens within the city, at the cost of increasing the resource and waste burdens the city imposes on the region. On the other hand, increasing fuel efficiency or switching to cleaner fuels is quite likely to improve air quality within the city, and also to reduce greenhouse gas emissions and their contribution to global burdens.

The relationship between per capita income and the overall per capita environmental burden of an urban settlement is ambiguous, but there is a tendency for the environmental burdens of more affluent urban settlements to be more dispersed and delayed (McGranahan et al, 2001). In cities where average incomes are very low, local environmental health burdens relating to poor sanitation and indoor air pollution tend to be severe, while the global pressures resulting from resource use and waste generation tend to be low. On the other hand, in cities where average incomes are very high, environmental health burdens tend to be low, while consumption tends to be high, leading both directly and indirectly to high levels of resources use and waste generation. A number of studies have found that some intermediate-scale burdens, indicated, for example, by urban air pollution concentrations, first rise and then decline with income (the environmental Kuznet's curve), although these findings have been challenged and the relation to scale has not been generally accepted (Stern, 2004).

The relationship between income and the scale at which urban environmental burdens occur also involves the increasing separation of consumption from locally polluting production, with productive activities that cause pollution more likely to be displaced from affluent settlements. There are indications that 'dirty' industries are moving from more affluent to lower-income countries, although the evidence is not easy to interpret and other factors often seem to dominate (Cole, 2004). More specifically, for air pollution there is evidence that income starts to be associated with environmental improvements earlier in the case of pollutants for which spatial separation is relatively easy (Khanna and Plassmann, forthcoming).

The different scales at which urban environmental burdens occur are not only important because of the relation to economic growth. A recent book on assessing ecosystems and human well-being has a chapter outlining the importance of multi-scalar assessments (Millennium Ecosystem Assessment, 2003, Chapter 8, 'Dealing with scale'), which observes that:

- 'big' processes tend to be slower than 'small' processes;
- by focusing on one scale, assessments are likely to neglect critical processes at other scales;
- inter-scale effects are often critical;
- the choice of scale is not politically neutral;
- many environmental problems arise from a mismatch between the scale of the burden and the scale at which the response is taken.

All of these observations apply to urban environmental burdens, and are examined in turn below.

'Big' processes tend to be slower than 'small' processes

The burdens that urban consumption and pollution impose globally tend to be of longer term than the burdens that remain localized. Thus, global burdens, such as climate change and the global depletion of non-renewable resources, are long-term threats to future generations, while most of the local environmental health hazards in and around people's homes and workplaces affect the well-being of those exposed within a fairly short time.

By focusing on one scale, assessments are likely to neglect critical processes at other scales

Focusing on urban environmental burdens that are local in scale draws attention to intra-urban environmental health hazards, but can lead to the neglect of the larger-scale problems that result when, for example, local sanitation problems are resolved by conveying sewage to be carried away by rivers, or local air pollution problems are resolved by introducing taller stacks or forcing polluting industries to locate downwind of the town centre. On the other hand, focusing on urban environmental burdens at the global scale draws attention to the consumption of internationally traded resources and global pollutants (for example, greenhouse gas emissions), but can lead to the neglect of local environmental health hazards, particularly when these vary by location.

Inter-scale effects are often critical

It can be misleading to identify burdens exclusively with one scale. In many ways global warming is an archetypal global burden, since the mechanism is so clearly global in scale. The risks, however, are likely to be very location specific. Bad sanitation, on the other hand, is an archetypal local burden, since it involves local conditions allowing diseases to spread among local residents via faecal-oral routes. Yet when unsanitary conditions extend over large areas, there is a risk of epidemics or even pandemics, potentially threatening people on the other side of the globe from where the outbreak originated (Haggett, 2000). Furthermore, as noted above, international trade often links the local environmental burdens of production in one place to consumption in a different part of the globe, creating a global burden from a consumption perspective out of a local burden from a production perspective. For more on these contrasting perspectives, see the section on 'Urban consumption and global ecological footprints' below.

The choice of scale is not politically neutral

Environmental burdens usually have a public aspect, but fall unequally, some more unequally than others. The scale at which environmental burdens are being assessed not only influences the scale at which public responses are likely to be conceived, but the types of inequalities that are likely to be observed. Thus, for example, measures to improve environmental conditions in low-income neighbourhoods and cities are easier to justify when the focus is on localized environmental burdens, while measures to reduce burdens on future generations are better served by a global focus. Alternatively, a local focus is more favourable to the narrow pursuit of economic growth, while taking a global focus can support a stance more critical of high consumption patterns. It is no coincidence that anti-growth environmentalists (e.g. Daly, 1996) are primarily concerned with global environmental burdens, while pro-growth environmentalists (e.g. Lomborg, 2001) are more concerned with local environmental burdens – though it is often difficult to tell which came first, the focus or the attitude to growth. Moreover, environmental politics often centre on the shifting environmental burdens, which involves changing scales.

Despite all the substantial differences between environmental burdens at different scales, there are also important similarities. On the one hand, there are structurally similar institutional obstacles to reducing urban environmental burdens at every scale. On the other hand, urban settlements provide opportunities for reducing environmental burdens at every scale, and it cannot be presumed that a more rural population distribution would create less severe burdens, locally, regionally or globally.

At every scale, urban environmental burdens are difficult to address because they:

- involve complex and poorly understood processes;
- fail to conform to the boundaries of private property, circumventing market mechanisms and creating economic externalities (consequences of one party's action or decision on another party's well-being that occur without effective negotiation or agreement on compensation);
- fail to conform to the boundaries of administrative responsibilities, circumventing effective public-sector management, and creating what could be termed political externalities (consequences of actions undertaken within one administrative unit on the ability of another administrative unit's ability to meet its goals);
- fall most heavily on the politically or economically weak, although in the case of local burdens the most vulnerable are the urban and peri-urban poor, while in the case of global burdens, future generations are also extremely vulnerable.

While these obstacles are difficult to overcome, they are not specific to urban living. Indeed, while urban settlements can be very difficult to manage effectively and equitably, at every scale, they have a number of advantages over rural settlements when it comes to reducing environmental burdens. The following list has been adapted from McGranahan et al, 2004.

For *urban* and *peri-urban* environmental living conditions:

- returns to scale and proximity yield lower costs per capita of providing piped treated water, sewerage systems, waste collection, clean fuels, and many other environmental services;
- there are more possibilities for local governments to fund or manage other forms of infrastructure and services that reduce environmental health risks (for example, enforce pollution control and occupational health and safety).

For *regional* environmental burdens:

- high urban population densities can reduce the per capita demand for occupied land;
- the concentration of major polluters facilitates pollution control.

For *global* environmental burdens:

- compact urban settlement patterns reduce transport distances, increasing opportunities for more energy efficient public transport and thereby reducing carbon emissions;
- economies of scale and agglomeration make electrical co-generation possible and facilitate the use of waste process-heat from industry or power plants for local (neighbourhood) water and space heating, again reducing carbon emissions.

Urban areas as habitats for humans

In urban areas, humans are the defining species and built-over land is the defining land use. Yet most human evolution took place before sedentary living, let alone urban living, became the norm, and urban living has historically posed serious physical challenges for humans. Many non-human species, on the other hand, have adapted to urban living. Urban ecological landscapes are characterized by patchiness and variation (Collins et al, 2000) and by greater species richness than in the countryside (Rebele, 1994). With a wide range of contrasting habitats, there is more scope for biodiversity in urban areas than in, for example, agricultural mono-cultures. Even urban core areas usually contain a mix of land uses, though it is in peri-urban areas that variability and land use change is likely to be at its height.

The relationship between humans and the other species in their settlements has always been critical to human well-being, even if people have not generally been aware of the connection, and not all of the relationships have been positive. It has been proposed, for example, that one of the reasons why New World inhabitants came to be decimated by Old World diseases when the two populations came into contact, was that only in the Old World had people shared their settlements with domesticated animals. This led to the emergence of diseases that eventually began to spread from person to person: measles and smallpox from cattle, influenza from pigs or chickens, the common cold from horses, and most respiratory infections from one domestic animal species or another (Watts, 2003; Cohen, 1989). In the New World people had not been exposed to these diseases, which made them vulnerable when the two populations met. The risk of avian flu, a very contemporary concern, also derives from close relations between humans and other species in human settlements. Even when human settlements have not been the source of the initial outbreak, they affect disease transmission, as in the case of HIV/AIDS.

Many of the more serious infectious diseases can only have emerged as a serious threat to health when people began to congregate in large enough settlements to allow the infection to be maintained (Cohen, 1989; Mascie-Taylor, 1993). Research on measles, well before vaccinations altered transmission patterns, found that the time between epidemics was inversely proportional to the town's population, and implied that above a population of about 250,000, a continuous chain of infection would be maintained. For a number of infectious diseases, large cities can act as reservoirs of disease, and then spark an epidemic when the susceptible population builds up above a critical level (Haggett, 2000). Urban networks can then become conduits in the spread of infectious diseases regionally or even globally.

Disease transmission also depends on how urban environments are managed. Historically, the most serious urban environmental health hazards have involved unsanitary conditions, including inadequate access to clean water, which facilitate the spread of faecal-oral diseases (Cairncross and Feachem, 1993). Unsanitary conditions are believed to be a major factor in the urban health penalty – that is, the higher mortality and morbidity rates found in urban than in rural areas – that burdened so many urban areas well into the 19th century.

The sanitary revolution that began in some of the more affluent cities towards the end of the 19th century provides a revealing example of how better governance and urban environmental management can not only overcome but even reverse the disadvantages of urban living. In England, for example, there is evidence that despite their economic success urban areas were becoming increasingly unhealthy places to live for several decades of the 19th century (Szreter, 1997). The reforms initiated in the second half of the century, which eventually brought urban health up and above that of rural areas, were closely linked to changing urban politics and governance (Szreter, 2002).

From the perspective of environmental conditions in areas adjoining urban settlements, the reforms of the sanitary revolution added to the urban burden. Sewerage networks carried human waste out of the cities and released them untreated into nearby waterways. Piped water networks drove the search for more and more distant water sources. What we would now characterize as ecological concerns, such as over the disruption of natural cycles and the loss of soil nutrients, were voiced at the time. Edwin Chadwick, perhaps the most influential sanitary reformer, had hoped to recycle sewage onto the fields. As it transpired, however, sanitary reform led to major improvements in urban health, but at the cost of deteriorating environmental relations with the surrounding areas.

More important from the perspective of urban areas as habitats for humans, water and sanitation conditions remain extremely unhealthy in a great many low-income settlements in Africa, Asia, and Latin America (Hardoy et al, 2001; United Nations Human Settlements Programme, 2003). Official figures put the number of urban dwellers without improved water supplies at 173 million (WHO and UNICEF, 2000), though it has also been estimated that upward of 700 million are without adequate provision (United Nations Human Settlements Programme, 2003). Despite widespread agreement that improvements are necessary, the urgency evident in the 19th and early 20th centuries is missing, in both local and international policy arenas. True, one of the 18 international targets now associated with the Millennium Declaration adopted by the world's leaders at the Millennium Summit of the United Nations in 2000 was to 'halve by 2015 the proportion of people without sustainable access to safe drinking water and basic sanitation'.[2] But, most of the policy debate in the water sector still centres on issues of water resource management or private-sector participation, neither of which is critical to sanitary improvement in deprived areas (McGranahan and Satterthwaite, 2003). Even within the water sector, it is widely recognized that sanitation receives insufficient attention.

At least part of the reason why the urgency of sanitary reform has declined, despite so many evident deficiencies, is that faecal-oral diseases less often give rise to epidemics that threaten those who do not live in deprived settlements (Cairncross and Feachem, 1993). Endemic diseases that are rarely fatal except to infants and children in low-income neighbourhoods do not motivate international agencies, national governments, or even local governments in the way that epidemics did historically, as they spread from city to city. In September 1848 the *Times* of London described cholera as 'the best of all sanitary reformers' (Wohl, 1983), and to this day most governments can find extra resources for improving sanitation when a cholera epidemic threatens.

The crisis-driven sanitary reforms of the 19th century had their problems too. The epidemics helped to reinforce élite stereotyping of slum residents as dirty, morally suspect, and dangerous to deal with, just as contemporary epidemics reinforce prejudice and discrimination against deprived groups (Briggs and Mantini-Briggs, 2003). Equally important, fears of epidemics helped to justify a top-down approach still evident in most water and sanitation utilities. Even the technologies employed, such as piped water and sewerage networks, were attractive in part because they allowed the technical and managerial responsibilities for urban water and waste flows to be shifted from the residents to engineers.

Recent decades have seen considerable debate over the institutional forms appropriate for managing urban water and sanitation systems. Private-sector participation has been vigorously promoted from some quarters, especially in the World Bank (Finger and Allouche, 2002). However, while the choice between public and private utility operators is clearly of great importance to vested interests within the water sector, it not of obvious significance to those deprived of water and sanitation, who generally remain unserved whether the water and sanitation utilities are public or private (Budds and McGranahan, 2003). Moreover, while private-sector participation has generated the most heated debates, some of the most notable successes have come from initiatives directly supportive of community organization and action (Mitlin and Satterthwaite, 2004). Even the World Bank, in its recent World Development Report on *Making Services Work for Poor People*, argues that better services to low-income groups can only be achieved by 'by putting poor people at the center of service provision: by enabling them to monitor and discipline service providers, by amplifying their voice in policymaking, and by strengthening the incentives for providers to serve the poor' (World Bank, 2003).

While the history of infectious diseases has been closely bound up with the history of human settlements, for most people urbanization is more closely associated with the chemical pollution of air and water. Ever since people began to cook food and warm themselves around fires, rural dwellers have been exposed to health-threatening air pollution. Even today, rural exposure to indoor air pollution is probably more of a health burden than urban ambient air pollution (Ezzati et al, 2002). But industrialization and motorization brought new, more visible, and more public forms of pollution. While sanitary reformers of the 19th century did often try to introduce pollution controls, the politics were not favourable (Mosley, 2001). Even more than in industrializing and motorizing cities today, smoke and chemicals were associated in many people's minds with economic success. There was no equivalent to water pipes and sewers promising to address air pollution problems and to shift the intellectual and practical burdens of environmental management from individuals and enterprises to experts in a government agency or utility. It was not until the middle of the 20th century that a number of governments, spurred on by the evidence of high mortality rates resulting from severe air pollution episodes in a few major cities, were put under pressure to enact laws and introduce regulations capable of reducing the concentrations of the best-known pollutants (McGranahan and Murray, 2003). While exposure to chemical pollution remains a significant urban health issue, in countries that have taken strong measures to reduce emissions, reductions in concentrations of the targeted pollutants have been appreciable.

Even in affluent countries where ambient air and water pollution are increasingly regulated, chemical waste disposal can lead to serious and often inequitable urban environmental health burdens, and the urban developments can undermine public health. In the US, for example, the 'environmental justice' movement emerged in response to inequalities in exposure to environmental health hazards (Shrader-Frechette, 2002), and serious questions have been raised about the implications of urban sprawl for human health (Frumkin et al, 2004). Indeed, while local environmental health hazards may be far more severe in the urban settlements of low-income countries – and particularly their more deprived neighbourhoods – they remain an issue in virtually all urban areas.

Urban environmental relations with their adjoining regions

Urban settlements have always been dependent on their hinterlands, as a source of natural resources and rural products, as a sink for wastes, and as sites for expansion. While the distances involved have grown in recent centuries, and an increasing number of products and resources can be sourced globally, urban regions remain critical loci of urban–rural flows and environmental impacts.

The metabolism of an urban area, described by the flows of energy and materials in and out of a settlement, is revealing of the environmental burdens it is likely to impose on ecosystems beyond the urban boundaries (Douglas, 1981; White, 1994; Decker et al, 2000; Newman, 1999). The linear flows characteristic of urban external relations, as opposed to the circular flows characteristic of stable ecosystems, reflect the nature of the regional environmental challenges urban development poses: resources are susceptible to depletion and waste sinks to continued accumulation. The multifold increase in throughput per capita observed over the last few centuries is indicative of the size of the challenge.

A recent review examined the energy and material flows in and out of the world's 25 largest cities. Water was estimated to account for about 90 per cent of all material entering mega-cities, and it was found that these cities were usually more dependent on their proximate environments for water and waste processing than as a source of fuel, food or aggregates (Decker et al, 2000). Except for biofuels, fuels are now only rarely sourced locally, but urban air pollution from fuel combustion can contribute to direct exposure in the adjoining region, and to acid rain, often at a considerable distance from the polluting location. Food and other agricultural products are often imported from distant locations, but urban development does often lead to radical transformations in land use patterns in the surrounding region. The following sub-sections focus on water, fuel and land use in turn.

Water

Although urban water consumption is usually several times smaller than the amount of water consumed in irrigated agriculture (Gleick, 2003), getting sufficient water of adequate quality to meet growing demand has long been a challenge for urban settlements. The utilities that operate urban piped water networks have traditionally tried to meet this challenge by investing in water infrastructure so as to bring greater quantities of water from further away. Where water infrastructure is highly developed and urban centres are networked together, local variation in supply/demand balances are merged, and water shortage becomes a regional phenomenon. The tendency for urban settlements to tap more distant sources for their water supplies is not confined to affluent countries. Research on the changing urban water systems in Africa, where insufficient infrastructure is often cited as a major problem, indicates that while in the early 1970s many major cities still used groundwater supplies as their primary water sources, by the 1990s the primary water sources were more likely to be rivers, and increasingly these river sources were more than 25km away (Showers, 2002).

Although regional water scarcity is a very serious problem in many parts of the world, it does not explain the fact that so many urban residents do not have adequate water supplies. Indeed, for urban dwellers in countries subject to water stress – defined as less than 1700m^3 per capita per annum of renewable fresh water resources – the official figures indicate slightly higher coverage rates (McGranahan, 2002). For those without improved water supplies, water resource problems can be particularly severe. The amount of clean water households need to stay healthy is very small compared even to urban water demands, however, and the challenge for deprived households is to get access to the potable water supplies that do exist.

In any case, getting sufficient water to urban settlements is only one of the urban water challenges. Water enters and leaves urban areas in almost equal quantities, but while it is flowing through urban areas it is likely to be used, polluted and otherwise transformed. Urban areas usually have a high percentage of paved areas; they concentrate rainwater rather than dissipate it. This can intensify flooding and cause flash floods. Changes in the water flows can also affect downstream fish stocks, recreational opportunities, and biodiversity. Sewers convey human waste out of urban locations, often releasing it untreated into local waterways or coastal waters. Human waste not only poses a health risk for people who might come to ingest the contaminated water, but can also cause eutrophication and damage to aquatic ecosystems downstream. Chemical water pollution is also a major problem, particularly around large industrial centres. When cities and surrounding rural areas are competing for water resources, ecological water requirements (the water needed to maintain ecosystem function and local hydrological cycles) are often neglected.

Integrated water resource management has been advocated as a means of addressing these regional water issues. By getting different water stakeholders to negotiate acceptable solutions, and imposing regulations when necessary, basin-level authorities are in a good position to address urban-region water issues. In the Plan of Implementation of the World

Summit for Sustainable Development (United Nations, 2002a), countries are exhorted to develop integrated water resource management plans by 2005. The natural scales for water resource management are river basins and catchment areas, and the Plan of Implementation explicitly indicates that countries should 'adopt an integrated water basin approach' (United Nations, 2002a, p21). However, river basin and catchment management organizations are unlikely to have the political power to address issues of equitable access to urban water networks. In effect, while equity is often emphasized as a goal of integrated water resource management, organizations adapted to the scale most suitable to urban-region issues are unlikely to be able to address the most critical intra-urban issues.

Fuel consumption and air pollution

Fossil fuels have not only enabled radical changes to urban form, but have also broken urban dependence on local energy sources. The urban settlements where resource links remain strong are in those low-income countries where charcoal is an important fuel for urban households. Charcoal is sometimes blamed for 'rings' of deforestation around some African cities, although charcoal producers are often not as destructive as they are portrayed to be (Hosier, 1993). Electricity produced from hydropower also draws on regional resources, and dams can have major environmental consequences. Otherwise the strongest environmental links between urban energy use and environmental conditions in the surrounding region derives from air pollution, which results primarily from fuel combustion.

Certain types of air pollution involve transformations in the environment that take place away from the site of emission (Smith and Akbar, 2003). For example, it can take several hours for ozone to form, creating concentrations quite far from the site where the precursors were originally emitted. Some particulates are also formed through chemical reactions in the atmosphere. These particulates and ozone may be created outside of the urban centres where the emissions originated, imposing health risks in areas downwind, as well as damage to crops. Acid depositions (e.g. acid rain) are the result of emissions of oxides of sulfur and nitrogen, which can be carried hundreds of kilometres by the air. In addition to harming crops, acid depositions can disrupt natural ecosystems.

There is the potential to use cross-scale effects to exploit synergies and find the best means of reducing air pollution problems at all scales. Unfortunately, there is still a tendency to treat these air pollution issues separately, or to assume that reducing air pollution at one scale also reduces it at others. Historically this has not always been the case. Higher stacks, for example, were used for many years to reduce local concentrations, at the cost of allowing the pollution to disperse over longer distances. Even greater energy efficiency does not always reduce air pollution at every scale – a wood stove that transfers a greater share of the fuel energy to heating a pan, for example, may achieve this at the cost of greater emissions of the products of incomplete combustion because the combustion site is more confined.

Unlike watersheds, airsheds are not easy to identify, and they do not provide the spatial basis for air pollution management organizations. National governments have been more important, as sources of both local air pollution regulation and of global air pollution governance. On the other hand, global air pollution governance (including negotiation over greenhouse gas emissions) remains rudimentary, local air pollution regulation is still a challenge, and efforts to coordinate measures targeting different scales have barely begun. And as with water, there is little evidence that the higher-level institutions responsible for air pollution management will be in a position to address the indoor air pollution burdens that tend to be more severe in low-income settlements – and especially rural settlements.

Urban development and changing regional land use

Urban land areas have been expanding, historically because of population growth (which is still the main driver of urban expansion in many lower-income countries), and more recently as the result of increasing numbers of smaller households and urban sprawl (especially in some higher-income countries). A disproportionate share of urban area is located in coastal zones, and the loss of wetlands to urban expansion is of special concern.[3] In North America, where compared to other continents a large share of the urban population is located in agricultural zones, and urban sprawl is leading to the expansion of what are already some of the world's least densely settled urban areas, the loss of agricultural land to urban expansion is also of particular concern.

While urban land area is undoubtedly increasing, it is misleading to draw a sharp distinction between environmental impacts that involve rural land being converted to urban land, and those that involve rural (or for that matter urban) land whose usage is being influenced by urban development. First, urban boundaries are arbitrary. There is not even agreement on the criteria by which urban areas should be identified—whether, for example, boundaries should be based on population densities, land cover, the occupational profile of residents, administrative limits, or some combination. Official urban boundaries rarely match the extent of contiguous built-up area; they may be smaller (as urban development has spilled over boundaries set many years ago) or larger (as urban boundaries have been defined that encompass large areas of agriculture, forest and water). In addition, an aerial view of a major urban regions is unlikely to display a concentrated urban centre surrounded by countryside; more likely there will be a complex spatial pattern of urbanized and non-urbanized areas, with built-up areas stretching along major transport corridors for long distances, and green areas reflecting planning decisions as much as distance from an urban centre. In addition, it is common for residential communities and industrial and commercial concentrations to develop close to major cities, but separated from the main built-up area.

In any case, urban expansion transforms not only the land that becomes urbanized (however defined) but also the land whose use is determined by demand both for land-based products and for resources (such as water) whose appropriation changes land use patterns. Large demands are made on the regions around cities for building materials and landfill as a result of the construction of buildings, roads, industries and other components of the urban fabric. Many of the urban-generated solid wastes impact the surrounding region – for instance, urban solid wastes are often transported to parts of the surrounding region and disposed of at open-air sites with little or no provision for protecting nearby soil and water from contamination. Moreover, urban development changes agricultural land use patterns. As Cronon has illustrated for the case of Chicago, rural environments and ecologies reflect demands and innovations that occur in nearby urban centres (Cronon, 1992).

Urban consumption and global ecological footprints

Contemporary urbanization is based upon that quintessentially global resource, petroleum. Petroleum products have not only fuelled the transportation systems that enable modern urban systems to function, and are a dominant influence on urban form, but they fuel many of the productive activities undertaken to meet urban demands. However, petroleum consumption itself only accounts for a small share of the burden that urban consumption is placing on the world's resources and waste sinks.

In principle, it is possible to assign environmental burdens to an urban settlement either by considering the impact of the transformations that take place within the urban settlement's boundaries or by considering all of the transformations undertaken globally in supplying the goods and services consumed by the settlement's residents. The former provides a more suitable basis for examining urban technologies and production patterns, and the environmental pressures exerted on the surrounding region. The latter provides a more suitable basis for examining lifestyles and consumption patterns, and the environmental pressures exerted globally to sustain the settlement's residents. Perhaps equally important, the former will tend to assign higher burdens to settlements where resource- or waste-intensive industries are concentrated, while the latter will tend to assign higher burdens to more affluent urban settlements. For the cities that industrialized early, there was a significant overlap between the two, but affluent cities are now unlikely to be centres of heavy industry.

Some of the differences between taking either a consumption or a production perspective on global urban environmental burdens can be illustrated with CO_2 emissions. A recent study of urban energy use and greenhouse gas emissions in Asian mega-cities has estimated the CO_2 emissions of Beijing, Shanghai and Tokyo, distinguishing between the CO_2 emitted within the urban areas and the CO_2 emitted in supplying the demands of the people who live in these cities (Dhakal, forthcoming). Table 15.1 is based on estimates calculated for this study.

Tokyo does comparatively well in terms of CO_2 emissions per capita, and as the wealthiest city it fares even better in terms of CO_2 emissions per unit of economic output. A detailed analysis of the changing sources of emissions over time indicates that emissions per unit of economic output have been declining in Beijing and Shanghai, but still remain far higher than in the major Japanese cities (Dhakal, forthcoming).

On the other hand, as indicated in the second row of Table 15.1, things look very different from a consumption perspective, with the highest emissions per capita associ-

Table 15.1 *Carbon dioxide emissions per capita for Beijing, Shanghai and Tokyo*

	Beijing (1997)	Shanghai (1997)	Tokyo (1995)
CO_2 emitted in city (tons per capita)	6.4	7.8	4.9
CO_2 emitted in providing goods and services consumed in city (tons per capita)	8.3	11.6	12.1

Source: Data provided in Dhakal, forthcoming

ated with the far higher consumption levels of Tokyo. Indeed, while for Beijing the emissions associated with consumption are only 30 per cent above the direct emissions per capita, in Tokyo this figure rises by almost 150 per cent.

Measuring the burden of the CO_2 emissions brought about by an urban settlement's consumption is complicated by data problems, issues of imputation (that is, whether it is misleading to assign the CO_2 emitted in producing a good to the end consumer), and uncertainty about the effects (that is, climate change and its consequences). On the other hand, the impacts of CO_2 emissions are clearly externalities, since CO_2 is emitted without any negotiation or consent on the part of those who will be affected by climate change. This is not true for all consumption-driven environmental pressures, however, and in many contexts it is important to consider the economic institutions through which the pressures of consumption have their environmental consequences, even if these institutions are located elsewhere.

When demand increases, private property and markets can yield higher prices rather than higher consumption, and higher prices can stimulate the development and use of substitutes or alternatives. Similarly, governmental and common property arrangements can operate to prevent resource degradation and waste generation. There are limits to substitutability, especially at the global scale. Markets do not just stimulate resource-conserving innovation, they encourage competitive enterprises to reduce costs, even when this means seeking out poorly managed resources and locating waste-generating processes where wastes are poorly controlled. However, while resource use and waste production have physical consequences whatever the institutional form, it is important to recognize that the link between consumption and resource use is not as straightforward as physical accounting systems might seem to suggest. For example, physical accounting relates consumption in the present with resource use in the past, while an economic analysis of the consequences of the same consumption will link it to resource use in the future, and these two resource uses need not be the same. Nevertheless, physical accounting can provide very useful indicators of environmental burdens.

Various indicators have been developed in order to estimate the aggregate environmental burdens of urban settlement, often applying a variant of the Commoner-Ehrlich equation: $I = PAT$, where I is the environmental impact, P is population, A is affluence measured as consumption or production per capita and T an environmental impact coefficient.

The best-known indicator developed specifically with urban settlements in mind is the ecological footprint, although several other indicators have been adapted to urban applications (Nijkamp et al, 2004). The ecological footprint has been defined as: the area of land 'required, on a continuous basis, to produce the resources that the population consumes, and to assimilate the wastes that the population produces, wherever on Earth the relevant land/water is located'.[4]

Current accounting procedures for ecological footprints include built-up area and area under crops, under pasture, under forest and under fisheries, as well as estimates of the forest land that would be required to provide for energy consumption and sequester sufficient carbon to compensate for carbon emissions. The common unit into which other land areas are converted is a 'global hectare' with a productivity equal to the average productivity of the roughly 11.4 billion bioproductive hectares in the world (Monfreda et al, 2004).

One of the heuristic benefits of presenting the global burden of urban areas in terms of ecological footprints is that it serves to emphasize the fact that urban settlements are heavily dependent on biophysical processes taking place elsewhere, and provides a common 'currency' rooted in biophysical rather than economic productivity. They also help to illustrate how misleading it can be to view different urban settlements (or countries) as occupying different positions on a common development trajectory, given the limited ecological 'space' available. In short, imperfect though they may be, ecological footprints provide a useful counterpoint to conventional economic accounts.

Ecological footprints are meant to measure outcomes, in the sense that they provide an accounting of services appropriated. From the perspective of spatial externalities, they are better interpreted as pressure or stress indicators. Environmental and ecological externalities are extremely difficult to measure, but one would expect them to be more closely associated with ecological appropriation, as measured by the ecological footprint, than with the economic value of consumption/production as measured in national income accounts. To some degree, global markets also globalize the side effects of economic activity (Mol, 2001). Some researchers have even interpreted the ecological footprint as an attempt to measure these environmental externalities (Nijkamp et al, 2004). An ecological footprint does not, however, even attempt to measure the extent to which environmental burdens remain external to market transactions and are incurred without any private negotiation or public regulation. Thus, while a larger ecological footprint is likely to be associated with greater environmental externalities, the two are both empirically and conceptually distinct.

Ecological footprints are increasingly being calculated for nations rather than urban settlements. The availability of national data allows for more extensive statistical analysis. Ecological footprint estimates have, for example, been used as a measure of environmental impact in a framework that treats the IPAT equation (above) as the basis for examining statistical relationships rather than as an accounting identity (York et al, 2003). Not surprisingly, population and GDP were found to be highly significant in all of the models tested. Latitude was also found to be significant, a result interpreted as reflecting the important role climate can play in influencing consumption patterns and environmental impacts. Somewhat more surprising, the percentage of population that is urban was also found to be highly significant in models where it was included, suggesting that urbanization either directly (for example, through impacts associated with the physical features of urban settlements) or indirectly (for example, through impacts associated with lifestyles that urban residents are more inclined to adopt) increases the size of a country's ecological footprint.

Ecological footprint analysis is sometimes presented as a more comprehensive measure of environmental impact than local or regional measures because global impacts are included. This can be taken to imply that environmental impacts increase monotonically with economic growth, and that the different relationships associated with local environmental health hazards (which tend to be at their worst in low-income settings) or city-regional impacts (which tend to be at their worst in large, industrialized and often middle-income cities) reflect the partial nature of their indicators. Thus, for example, it has been argued that the rise and fall of the environmental Kuznet's curve reflects the omission of global impacts, whose inclusion would transform the curve into something more S-shaped (see York et al, 2003, figure 1). This is misleading, however, as the form of the relationship also depends on how environmental burdens are measured. It is perfectly conceivable that a measure based on human health impacts would still display the aggregate environmental burden declining with economic growth (see, for example, Holdren and Smith, 2000, Figure 3.10), while a measure based on economic value might rise and then fall, and a measure based on appropriated bio-physical productivity might rise monotonically.

It should be possible to combine insights from different scales, but this requires more than simply extending analysis from one scale to the others. Ecological footprint analysis is not a useful tool for examining local environmental burdens, just as burden-of-disease analysis is not a useful tool for examining global environmental burdens; yet both provide information relevant to any multi-scaled assessment of urban environmental burdens.

Scaling urban environmental policy agendas

An optimist looking at the environmental history of most affluent cities sees: a centuries-old and highly successful sanitary revolution (addressing environmental health burdens in and around people's homes); a more recent and partially successful pollution revolution (addressing pollution, waste and resource burdens in the urban-region sphere); and perhaps the beginnings of a sustainability revolution (addressing the global environmental burdens of urban consumption patterns). A pessimist, looking at the same history, sees the progressive displacement of environmental burdens from local to regional to global scales.

There is some truth to both of these views. On the one hand, past urban sanitary reforms, pollution management and efficiency improvements do illustrate the potential for quite radical and effective responses to severe environmental burdens. On the other hand, the tendency to shift towards larger-scale and more delayed burdens is a real concern, particularly if it is going to require a global crisis to invoke a meaningful response.

Looking across the wide range of urban settlements around the world, there are also other concerns. Economic success is very unequally distributed, and environmental burdens tend to accentuate these inequalities. The environmental burdens of poverty tend to be localized, while the environmental burdens of affluence affect a larger public. Some of the most deprived groups are also the most likely to face multiple burdens: they are more vulnerable to the global threats driven by affluence such as climate change, are more exposed to problems of regional pollution and resource abuse associated with urban industrialization, and live in neighbourhoods where sanitation is poor, water is difficult to access, and smoky fuels are used.

Also, while a great deal of attention is paid to the globalization of environmental burdens, for low-income groups the localization of environmental burdens is also a concern. Water and sanitation problems, for example, were once associated with epidemics that threatened all urban residents, and even the inhabitants of other cities and towns. This helped to inspire a social movement, and motivated municipalities and national governments to help drive sanitary reform. Endemic diseases, largely restricted to low-income neighbourhoods, do not provide the same public motivation. This may help to explain why the conventional top-down approaches to water and sanitation improvement no longer inspire, and why even relatively successful locally driven initiatives rarely receive much attention internationally.

More generally, the multi-scalar character of urban environmental burdens is itself a challenge for developing effective urban environmental agendas. International and inter-urban variation suggests that in different locations environmental burdens at different scales need to be prioritized. Ideally, priorities should be adapted to reflect the state of local environmental health conditions, the quality of environmental relations with the surrounding region, and the size of a settlement's ecological footprint. Generally, this would justify a greater focus on environmental health issues in low-income settlements, and a greater focus on ecological footprints in high-income settlements.

There is also a relationship between the scale of the environmental burdens and the appropriate roles of different levels of government. Some governance failures can be traced to a mismatch between the scale of the problem and the scale at which the response has been articulated. Local governance should not be expected to reduce carbon emissions voluntarily, although it can be a very appropriate level for driving local water and sanitation improvements. Global governance, on the other hand, is clearly needed to help develop institutional mechanisms to reduce contributions to global climate change, but is inappropriate to developing institutional mechanisms for managing local water and sanitation systems. It is, however, easy to exaggerate the extent to which the scale of the problem determines the appropriate level of governmental responsibility. Reducing local environmental burdens often requires support (or at least the absence of opposition) from global processes and institutions, while responses to global burdens often need to be rooted in local agency (Wilbanks and Kates, 1999).

Acknowledgements

This chapter benefited from work funded by the Danish Ministry of Foreign Affairs (Danida) and the Swedish Agency for Development and Cooperation (Sida), and draws on a draft chapter on urban systems prepared as part of the contribution of the Condition and Trends Working Group to the Millennium Ecosystem Assessment (published by the Island Press in 2005).

Notes

1   Urban environmental burdens can be defined as threats to present or future human well-being (or other things of value), arising from damage to the physical environment caused directly or indirectly by activities undertaken in urban areas (IIED, 2001).
2   The reference to sanitation was added after the World Summit for Sustainable Development in Johannesburg in 2002 – see the Millennium Development Goals, described at www.developmentgoals.org (accessed 24 November 2004).

3   The boundary limits used for mapping coastal zones in the Millennium Ecosystems Assessment area were between 50m below mean sea level and 50m above the high tide level or extending landwards to a distance of 100km from the shore (Millennium Ecosystem Assessment, 2003). Globally, an estimated 10 per cent of land in the coastal zone is urban, as compared with less than 3 per cent overall.

4   Levin, S. A. (ed) (2001) *Encyclopedia of Biodiversity*, Academic Press, San Diego, 'ecological footprint, concept of' (by W. E. Rees).

References

Asheim, G. B. and Buchholz, W. (2004) 'A general approach to welfare measurement through national income accounting', *Scandinavian Journal of Economics*, vol 106, no 2, pp361–384

Beckerman, W. (1988) 'National income', in Eatwell, J., Milgate, M. and Newman, P. (eds) *The New Palgrave: A Dictionary of Economics*, Macmillan, Basingstone

Briggs, C. L. and Mantini-Briggs, C. (2003) *Stories in the Time of Cholera: Racial Profiling During a Medical Nightmare*, University of California Press, Berkeley, CA

Budds, J. and McGranahan, G. (2003) 'Are the debates on water privatization missing the point? Experiences from Africa, Asia and Latin America', *Environment and Urbanization*, vol 15, no 2, pp87–113

Cairncross, S. and Feachem, R. G. (1993) *Environmental Health Engineering in the Tropics: An Introductory Text*, 2nd edition, John Wiley & Sons, Chichester

Cohen, B. (2004) 'Urban growth in developing countries: A review of current trends and a caution regarding existing forecasts', *World Development*, vol 32, no 1, pp23–51

Cohen, M. N. (1989) *Health and the Rise of Civilization*, Yale University Press, New Haven, Conn

Cole, M. A. (2004) 'Trade, the pollution haven hypothesis and the environmental kuznets curve: Examining the linkages', *Ecological Economics*, vol 48, no 1, pp71–81

Collins, J. P., Kinzig, A., Grimm, N. B., Fagan, W. F., Hope, D., Wu, J. G. and Borer, E. T. (2000) 'A new urban ecology', *American Scientist*, vol 88, no 5, pp416–425

Cronon, W. (1992) *Nature's Metropolis: Chicago and the Great West*, W.W. Norton, New York

Daly, H. E. (1996) *Beyond Growth: The Economics of Sustainable Development*, Beacon Press, Boston

Decker, E. H., Elliott, S., Smith, F. A., Blake, D. R. and Rowland, F. S. (2000) 'Energy and material flow through the urban ecosystem', *Annual Review of Energy and the Environment*, vol 25, pp685–740

Dhakal, S. (forthcoming) *Urban Energy Use and Greenhouse Gas Emissions in Asian Mega-cities*, Institute for Global Environmental Strategies, Kitakyushu

Douglas, I. (1981) 'The city as ecosystem', *Progress in Physical Geography*, vol 5, no 3, pp315–367

Ezzati, M., Lopez, A. D., Rodgers, A., Hoorn, S. V. and Murray C. J. L. (2002) 'Selected major risk factors and global and regional burden of disease', *Lancet*, vol 360, no 9343, pp1347–1360

Finger, M. and Allouche, J. (2002) *Water Privatisation: Trans-national Corporations and the Re-regulation of the Water Industry*, Spon Press, London

Friedmann, J. (2002) *The Prospect of Cities*, University of Minnesota Press, Minneapolis, Minn

Frumkin, H., Frank, L. and Jackson, R. (2004) *Urban Sprawl and Public Health: Designing, Planning and Building for Healthy Communities*, Island Press, Washington, DC

Gleick, P. H. (2003) 'Water use', *Annual Review of Environment and Resources*, vol 28, pp275–314

Haggett, P. (2000) *The Geographical Structure of Epidemics, Clarendon Lectures in Geography and Environmental Studies*, Oxford University Press, Oxford

Hamilton, K. and Dixon, J. A. (2003) 'Measuring the wealth of nations', *Environmental Monitoring and Assessment*, vol 86, no 1–2, pp75–89

Hardoy, J. E., Mitlin, D. and Satterthwaite, D. (2001) *Environmental Problems in an Urbanizing World*, Earthscan, London

Holdren, J. P. and Smith, K. R. (2000) 'Energy, the environment and health', in Goldemberg, J. (ed) *World Energy Assessment: Energy and the Challenge of Sustainability*, UNDP, New York, pp62–110

Hosier, R. H. (1993) 'Charcoal production and environmental degradation: Environmental history, selective harvesting, and post-harvest management', *Energy Policy*, vol 21, no 5, pp491–509

Hugo, G., Champion, A. and Lattes, A. (2003) 'Toward a new conceptualization of settlements for demography', *Population and Development Review*, vol 29, no 2, pp277–297

IIED (2001) *Urban Environmental Improvement and Poverty Reduction*, IIED for Danida, London

International Monetary Fund (IMF) (2000) 'The world economy in the twentieth century: Striking developments and policy lessons', in *World Economic Outlook, May 2000*, IMF, Washington, DC

Khanna, N. and Plassmann, F. (forthcoming) 'The demand for environmental quality and the environmental Kuznets Curve hypothesis', *Ecological Economics*

Lawn, P. A. (2003) 'A theoretical foundation to support the Index of Sustainable Economic Welfare (ISEW), Genuine Progress Indicator (GPI), and other related indexes', *Ecological Economics*, vol 44, no 1, pp105–118

Lomborg, B. (2001) *The Sceptical Environmentalist: Measuring the State of the World*, Cambridge University Press, Cambridge

Mascie-Taylor, C. G. N. (ed) (1993) *The Anthropology of Disease* (Biosocial Society Series 5), Oxford University Press, New York

McGee, T. G. (1987) 'Urbanisasi or Kotadesasi? The emergence of new regions of economic interaction in Asia', Working paper, Environment and Policy Institute, East-West Center, Honolulu, Hawai'i

McGee, T. G. (1991) 'The emergence of Desakota regions in Asia: Expanding a hypothesis', in Ginsburg Norton, S., McGee, T. G. and Koppel, B. (eds) *The Extended Metropolis: Settlement Transition in Asia*, University of Hawai'i Press, Honolulu

McGee, T. G. and Robinson, I. M. (eds) (1995) *The Mega-Urban Regions of Southeast Asia*, UBC Press, Vancouver, BC

McGranahan, G. (2002) *Demand-Side Water Strategies and the Urban Poor*, IIED, London

McGranahan, G., Jacobi, P., Songsore, J., Surjadi, C. and Kjellén, M. (2001) *The Citizens at Risk: From Urban Sanitation to Sustainable Cities*, Earthscan, London

McGranahan, G., Marcotullio, P. J., Bai, X., Balk, D., Braga, T., Douglas, I., Elmqvist, T., Rees, W., Satterthwaite, D., Songsore, J. and Zlotnik, H. (forthcoming) 'Urban systems', in 'Millennium ecosystem assessment, current state and trends: Findings of the Condition and Trends Working Group', *Ecosystems and Human Well-being*, vol 1, Island Press, Washington, DC

McGranahan, G. and Murray, F. (eds) (2003) *Air Pollution and Health in Rapidly Developing Countries*, Earthscan, London

McGranahan, G. and Satterthwaite, D. (2003) 'Improving access to water and sanitation: Rethinking the way forward in light of the Millennium Development Goals', in Bigg, T. (ed) *Survival for a Small Planet: The Sustainable Development Agenda*, Earthscan, London

McGranahan, G., Satterthwaite, D. and Tacoli, C. (2004) 'Rural-urban change, boundary problems and environmental burdens', in *Rural-Urban Series*, IIED, London

Millennium Ecosystem Assessment (2003) *Ecosystems and Human Well-being: A Framework for Assessment*, Island Press, Washington, DC

Mitlin, D. and Satterthwaite, D. (2004) *Empowering Squatter Citizen: Local Government, Civil Society and Urban Poverty Reduction*, Earthscan, London

Mol, A. P. J. (2001) *Globalization and Environmental Reform: The Ecological Modernization of the Global Economy*, MIT Press, Cambridge, Mass

Monfreda, C., Wackernagel, M. and Deumling, D. (2004) 'Establishing national natural capital accounts based on detailed ecological footprint and biological capacity accounts', *Land Use Policy*, vol 21, pp231–236

Montgomery, M. R., Stren, R., Cohen, B. and Reed, H. E. (eds) (2003) *Cities Transformed: Demographic Change and its Implication for the Developing World*, National Academy Press, Washington, DC

Mosley, S. (2001) *The Chimney of the World: A History of Smoke Pollution in Victorian and Edwardian Manchester*, White Horse, Cambridge

Newman, P. W. G. (1999) 'Sustainability and cities: Extending the metabolism model', *Landscape and Urban Planning*, vol 44, no 4, pp219–226

Nijkamp, P., Rossi, E. and Vindigni, G. (2004) 'Ecological footprints in plural: A meta-analytic comparison of empirical results', *Regional Studies*, vol 38, no 7, pp747–765

Pahl, R. (1965) *Urbs in Rure*, Weidenfeld and Nicolson, London

Rakodi, C. (1995) 'Poverty lines or household strategies? A review of conceptual issues in the study of urban poverty', *Habitat International*, vol 19, no 4, pp407–426

Rebele, F. (1994) 'Urban ecology and special features of urban ecosystems', *Global Ecology and Biogeography Letters*, vol 4, no 6, pp173–187

Rees, W. E. (1992) 'Ecological footprints and appropriated carrying capacity: What urban economics leaves out', *Environment and Urbanization*, vol 4, no 2, pp121–130

Rees, W. E. (2003) 'Understanding urban ecosystems: An ecological economics perspective', in Berkowitz, A. R., Nilon, C. H. and Hollweg, K. S. (eds) *Understanding Urban Ecosystems: A New Frontier for Science and Education*, Springer-Verlag, New York

Rees, W. and Wackernagel, M. (1996) 'Urban ecological footprints: Why cities cannot be sustainable – And why they are a key to sustainability', *Environmental Impact Assessment Review*, vol 16, no 4–6, pp223–248

Satterthwaite, D. (1997) 'Sustainable cities or cities that contribute to sustainable development?' *Urban Studies*, vol 34, no 10, pp1667–1691

Satterthwaite, D. (2002) *Coping with Rapid Urban Growth*, Royal Institution of Chartered Surveyors (RICS), London

Satterthwaite, D. (2004) 'The under-estimation of urban poverty in low and middle-income nations', Working paper on poverty reduction in urban areas 14, IIED, London

Showers, K. B. (2002) 'Water scarcity and urban Africa: An overview of urban–rural water linkages', *World Development*, vol 30, no 4, pp621–648

Shrader-Frechette, K. (2002) *Environmental Justice: Creating Equality, Reclaiming Democracy*, Oxford University Press, New York

Smith, K. and Akbar, S. (2003) 'Health-damaging air pollution: A matter of scale', in McGranahan, G. and Murray, F. (eds) *Health and Air Pollution in Rapidly Developing Countries*, Earthscan, London

Stern, D. I. (2004) 'The rise and fall of the environmental Kuznets curve', *World Development*, vol 32, no 8, pp1419–1439

Sui, D. Z. and Zeng, H. (2001) 'Modeling the dynamics of landscape structure in Asia's emerging desakota regions: A case study in Shenzen', *Landscape and Urban Planning*, vol 53, pp37–52

Szreter, S. (1997) 'Economic growth, disruption, deprivation, disease, and death: On the importance of the politics of public health for development', *Population and Development Review*, vol 23, no 4, pp693–728

Szreter, S. (2002) 'The state of social capital: Bringing back in power, politics, and history', *Theory and Society*, vol 31, no 5, pp573–621

United Nations (2002a) 'Report of the World Summit on Sustainable Development', Johannesburg, South Africa, 26 August–4 September, United Nations, New York

United Nations (2002b) *World Urbanization Prospects: The 2001 Revision*, United Nations, New York

United Nations Human Settlements Programme (2003) *Water and Sanitation in the World's Cities: Local Action for Global Goals*, Earthscan, London

Watts, S. J. (2003) *Disease and Medicine in World History*, Routledge, New York and London

White, R. R. (1994) *Urban Environmental Management: Environmental Change and Urban Design*, John Wiley & Sons, Chichester

WHO and UNICEF (2000) *Global Water Supply and Sanitation Assessment 2000 Report*, World Health Organization and United Nations Children's Fund, Geneva and New York

Wilbanks, T. J. and Kates, R. W. (1999) 'Global change in local places: How scale matters', *Climatic Change*, vol 43, no 3, pp601–628

Wohl, A. S. (1983) *Endangered Lives: Public Health in Victorian Britain*, Methuen, London

World Bank (2003) *World Development Report 2004: Making Services Work for Poor People*, World Bank and Oxford University Press, Washington, DC

Wratten, E. (1995) 'Conceptualizing urban poverty', *Environment and Urbanization*, vol 7, no 1 pp11–36

York, R., Rosa, E. A. and Dietz, T. (2003) 'Footprints on the earth: The environmental consequences of modernity', *American Sociological Review*, vol 68, no 2, pp279–300

Further Reading

There is a growing literature on many aspects of rural–urban linkages, and it would be impossible to capture it all. Below is a list of what my colleagues and I have found most useful throughout the years, but there are certainly many more references that are missed here. We welcome any additional references and links, which we will be happy to put up in our rural–urban web page at IIED. Please send them to cecilia.tacoli@iied.org.

Journals

The main journals that publish papers explicitly related to rural–urban linkages are *Environment and Urbanization*, and the *International Development Planning Review* (formerly *Third World Planning Review*). Most journals that are concerned with development issues (such as *World Development* and the *European Journal of Development Research*) also publish relevant articles, although less frequently.

Websites

Websites that publish research on rural–urban linkages:

Eldis (www.eldis.org) is a gateway to development information and well worth exploring.

The Development Planning Unit at University College London has a research programme on the peri-urban interface, and reports can be downloaded from: www.ucl.ac.uk/dpu/pui/research/previous/synthesis/index.html.

The International Food Policy Research Institute (IFPRI) has recently published a number of papers on rural–urban linkages in its Food Consumption and Nutrition Division. The papers and related briefs can be downloaded from IFPRI's website: www.ifpri.org/divs/fcnd/fcndp.asp.

Chowdhury, S., Negassa, A. and Torero, M. (2005) 'Market institutions: Enhancing the value of rural–urban links', October

Dercon, S. and Hoddinott, J. (2005) 'Livelihoods, growth, and links to market towns in 15 Ethiopian villages', July

Fan, S., Chan-Kang, C. and Mukherjee, A. (2005) 'Rural and urban dynamics and poverty: Evidence from China and India', August

Quisumbing, A. R. and McNiven, S. (2005) 'Migration and the rural-urban continuum: Evidence from the rural Philippines', October

Chapters from a very detailed paper on The Urban Transition in Vietnam by Mike Douglass and Mike DiGregorio can be downloaded from UNDP Vietnam Office's site www.undp.org.vn/projects/vie00021/.

The Institute for Development Studies in Sussex runs the *Livelihoods Connect website*, supported by the UK Department for International Development. The website has two 'hot topics' pages, one on urban–rural change: www.livelihoods.org/hot_topics/UrbanRural.html#5 and the other on migration: www.livelihoods.org/hot_topics/migration.html with useful information, downloadable papers and further links.

IIED's web page on rural–urban linkages includes reports of collaborative research projects, links to other websites of interest, links to the two special issues of the journal *Environment and Urbanization* on rural–urban linkages (and free downloads of articles), www.iied.org/HS/themes/ru.html.

The following rural–urban Working Papers can be downloaded from the site:

No 1 Diyamett, B., Diyamett, M., James, J. and Mabala, R. (2001) 'The case of Himo and its region, northern Tanzania'

No 2 Kibadu, A., Lerise, F., Mbutolwe, E. and Mushi, N. (2001) 'The case of Lindi and its region, southern Tanzania'

No 3 Diyamett, B., Diyamett, M., James, J., Kibadu, A., Lerise, F., Mabala, R., Mbutolwe, E. and Mushi, N. (2001) 'Exploring rural–urban interactions in Tanzania: A critical review of the methods and tools used'

No 4 Okali, D., Okpara, E. and Olawoye, J. (2001) 'The case of Aba and its region, southeastern Nigeria'

No 5 Groupe Recherche/Actions pour le Développement (2001) 'Potentialités et conflits dans les zones péri-urbaines: Le cas de Bamako au Mali' (in French)

No 6 Groupe Recherche/Actions pour le Développement (2001) 'Potentialités et conflits dans les zones péri-urbaines: Le cas de Mopti au Mali (in French)

No 7 Tacoli, C. (2002) 'Changing rural–urban interactions in sub-Saharan Africa and their impact on livelihoods: A summary

No 8 Rengasamy, S., Devavaram, J., Marirajan, T., Ramavel, N., Rajadurai, K, Karunanidhi, M. and Rajendra Prasad, N. (2002) 'Farmers' markets in Tamil Nadu: Increasing options for rural producers, improving access for urban consumers'

No 9 Tacoli, C. and Satterthwaite, D. (2003) 'The urban part of rural development: The role of small and intermediate urban centres in rural and regional development and poverty reduction'

No 10 McGranahan, G., Satterthwaite, D. and Tacoli, C. (2004) 'Rural–urban change, boundary problems and environmental burdens'

No 11 Xuan Thanh, H., Nguyen Anh, D. and Tacoli, C. (2005) 'Livelihood diversification and rural–urban linkages in Vietnam's Red River Delta'

No 12 McGranahan, G. and Tacoli, C. (2003) 'Rural–urban migration in China: Policy options for economic growth, environmental sustainability and equity'

No 13 Momen, S. F. (2006) 'Toward synergistic rural–urban development. The experience of the Rural Urban Partnership Programme (RUPP) in Nepal'

Shorter Briefing Papers are also available for each Working Paper.
Other materials available from the page include:

- The papers from the first (1998) special issue of *Environment and Urbanization* on rural–urban linkages, including a Guide to the Literature, and the papers in the second issue of the journal on this topic (2003).
- A summary of policy issues related to rural–urban linkages, published in IIED's Gatekeeper Series.
- A paper on 'Understanding the opportunities and constraints for low-income groups in the peri-urban interface: The contribution of livelihood frameworks' prepared by IIED staff for the Development Planning Unit's Peri-Urban Interface project.
- A policy brief on the impact of rural–urban interactions on urban food security was produced as part of IFPRI's 2020 Focus Series No 3 – 'Achieving urban food and nutrition security in the developing world'.
- A recent issue of Id21 Insights on 'Bridging the rural–urban divide'.
- A contribution submitted in November 2003 to help the UK International Development Committee's enquiry on 'Migration and Development'.

Websites of international agencies

The Rural–urban Partnership Programme (RUPP) is a programme supported by the Government of Nepal and UNDP. Its website is www.rupp.org.np/index.asp.

UN-Habitat has also a long-standing interest in rural–urban linkages and regional development planning. Its website is www.unhabitat.org.

The World Bank has launched a joint initiative on rural–urban linkages. Background documents and workshop reports are available at: http://wbln0018.worldbank.org/External/Urban/UrbanDev.nsf/0/D02D4131298EF6A68525688D0052B27B?OpenDocument.

The Asian Development Bank is interested in rural–urban linkages in the Mekong Region. More information can be searched at www.adb.org.

Books

In the 1990s, the Scandinavian Institute of African Studies (SIAS) established a research programme entitled *Urban Development in Rural Context in Africa*, coordinated by Jonathan Baker. A number of excellent edited books have resulted from the programme:

Baker, J. (ed) (1990) *Small Town Africa: Studies in Rural–Urban Interaction*
Baker, J. and Pedersen, P. O. (eds) (1992) *The Rural–Urban Interface in Africa: Expansion and Adaptation*
Baker, J. and Akin Aina, T. (1995) *The Migration Experience in Africa*
Baker, J. (ed) (1997) *Rural–Urban Dynamics in Francophone Africa*

The books can be purchased from SIAS at the following address:

PO Box 1703
SE-751 47 Uppsala
Kungsgatan 38
Sweden
Telephone: +46 18 56 22 00
Fax: +46 18 56 22 90
E-mail: nai@nai.uu.se
Website: www.nai.uu.se

Another book that presents findings from a long-term research programme on small towns is the edited collection by Milan Titus and Jan Hinderink (eds) (1998) *Town and Hinterland in Developing Countries*, Thela Thesis, Amsterdam. The case studies were conducted by the University of Utrecht in a number of countries in Africa, Asia and Latin America.

The edited collection by Paul van Lindert and Otto Verkoren (eds) (1997) *Small Towns and Beyond: Rural Transformation and Small Urban Centres in Latin America*, Thela Latin America Series, Amsterdam, has several good case studies with a more narrow geographical focus.

A good and up-to-date introduction to the main issues is the book by Kenneth Lynch (2005) *Rural–Urban Interaction in the Developing World*, Routledge Perspectives on Development Series, published by and available from Routledge, Park Square, Milton Park, Abingdon, Oxford OX14 4RN, United Kingdom.

On rural livelihoods diversification, Frank Ellis (2000) *Rural Livelihoods and Diversity in Developing Countries*, Oxford University Press, Oxford, is a good conceptual introduction. Frank Ellis has recently published articles drawn from case studies of rural diversification in Africa in *World Development*.

Also on rural livelihood diversification is the collection of papers in Deborah Fahy Bryceson and Vali Jamal (eds) (1997) *Farewell to Farms: De-agrarianisation and Employment in Africa*, Ashgate, Aldershot.

The recent report of the US National Academy of Sciences: National Research Council (2003) *Cities Transformed: Demographic Change and its Implications in the Developing World*, National Academies Press, Washington, DC, has several sections that include rural–urban issues. Copies of the book can be ordered from:

The National Academies Press
500 Fifth Street, N.W.
Lockbox 285
Washington, DC
US
Website: www.nap.edu

A detailed analysis is contained in the book by Vincent L. Rotge' with Ida Bagoes Mantra and Ryanto Rijanta (2000) *Rural–Urban Integration in Java: Consequences for Regional Development and Employment*, Ashgate, Aldershot.

The book by Poul Ove Pedersen (1997) *Small African Towns: Between Rural Networks and Urban Hierarchies*, Avebury, Aldershot, is based primarily on the study of two district service centres in Zimbabwe's communal areas, but also offers a detailed conceptual discussion with special attention to small enterprises and the environment in which they operate.

The edited collection by Mirjam de Bruijn, Rijk van Dijk and Dick Foeken (eds) (2001) *Mobile Africa: Changing Patterns of Movement in Africa and Beyond*, Brill, Leiden, The Netherlands, contains several papers with a rural–urban linkages perspective.

A very recent book on peri-urban issues: Duncan McGregor, David Simon and Donald Thompson (eds) (2005) *The Peri-Urban Interface: Approaches to Sustainable Natural and Human Resource Use*, Earthscan, London

Index

Join our
online community
and help us save paper and postage!

www.earthscan.co.uk

By joining the Earthscan website, our readers can benefit from a range of exciting new services and exclusive offers. You can also receive e-alerts and e-newsletters packed with information about our new books, forthcoming events, special offers, invitations to book launches, discussion forums and membership news. Help us to reduce our environmental impact by joining the Earthscan online community!

How? – Become a member in seconds!

>> Simply visit **www.earthscan.co.uk** and add your name and email address to the sign-up box in the top left of the screen – You're now a member!

>> With your new member's page, you can subscribe to our monthly **e-newsletter** and/or choose **e-alerts** in your chosen subjects of interest – you control the amount of mail you receive and can unsubscribe yourself

Why? – Membership benefits

✔   Membership is free!
✔   10% discount on all books online
✔   Receive invitations to high-profile book launch events at the BT Tower, London Review of Books Bookshop, the Africa Centre and other exciting venues
✔   Receive e-newsletters and e-alerts delivered directly to your inbox, keeping you informed but not costing the Earth – you can also forward to friends and colleagues
✔   Create your own discussion topics and get engaged in online debates taking place in our new online Forum
✔   Receive special offers on our books as well as on products and services from our partners such as *The Ecologist*, *The Civic Trust* and more
✔   Academics – request inspection copies
✔   Journalists – subscribe to advance information e-alerts on upcoming titles and reply to receive a press copy upon publication – write to info@earthscan.co.uk for more information about this service
✔   Authors – keep up to date with the latest publications in your field
✔   NGOs – open an NGO Account with us and qualify for special discounts

Join now?
Join Earthscan now!

name

surname

email address

Earthscan Member
[Your name]

Click to Change

My profile
My forum
My bookmarks
All my pages

www.earthscan.co.uk

The Natural Advantage of Nations
Business Opportunities, Innovation and Governance in the 21st Century

Edited by Karlson 'Charlie' Hargroves and Michael Harrison Smith

Forewords by Amory B. Lovins, L Hunter Lovins, William McDonough, Michael Fairbanks and Alan AtKisson

'I am particularly pleased with the new book, *The Natural Advantage of Nations*, which will, in effect, follow on from *Natural Capitalism*, and bring in newer evidence from around the world'
AMORY B. LOVINS, Rocky Mountain Institute

'This is world-leading work, the team deserves the loudest acclamation possible'
BARRY GREAR AO, World Federation of Engineering Organisations

'A seminal book, a truly world changing book... As part of the process of pulling together the people whose ideas they wanted in the book, [the editors] have pulled together a whole movement'
L. HUNTER LOVINS, Natural Capitalism, Inc

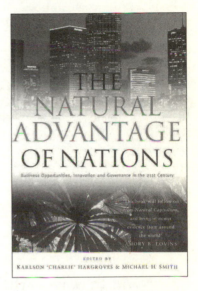

This collection of inspiring work, based on solid academic and practical rigour, is an overview of the 21st century business case for sustainable development. It incorporates innovative technical, structural and social advances, and explores the role governance can play in both leading and underpinning business and communities in the shift towards a sustainable future.

The team from The Natural Edge Project have studied and incorporated key works from over 30 of the world's leaders in sustainability. The book is also supported by an extensive companion website. This work takes the lessons of competitive advantage theory and practice and combines them with the sustainability paradigm, in light of important developments in economics, innovation, business and governance over the last 30–50 years.

Far from being in conflict with economics and business practices, this book demonstrates how we can improve the well-being of society and the environment while driving innovation in an increasingly competitive world.

Hardback 1-84407-121-9 Published January 2005

HOW TO ORDER:

ONLINE www.earthscan.co.uk
CUSTOMER HOTLINE +44 (0)1256 302699
EMAIL book.orders@earthscan.co.uk

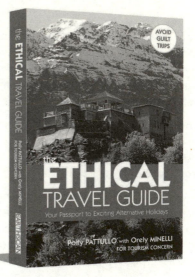